THE
WISDEN
GUIDE TO
CRICKET GROUNDS

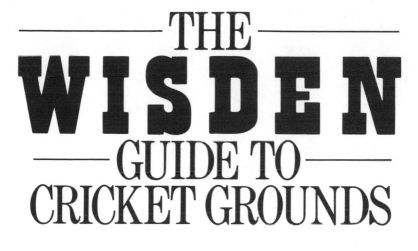

THE WISDEN GUIDE TO CRICKET GROUNDS

William Powell

with Peter Powell and Alex Bannister

Stanley Paul

London · Sydney · Auckland · Johannesburg

To Jamila, Jessima, Sophia and Wendy

Stanley Paul & Co. Ltd

An imprint of Century Hutchinson Ltd

62–65 Chandos Place, London WC2N 4NW

Century Hutchinson Australia (Pty) Ltd
89–91 Albion Street, Surrey Hills, NSW 2010

Century Hutchinson New Zealand Limited
PO Box 40-086, Glenfield, Auckland 10

Century Hutchinson South Africa (Pty) Ltd
PO Box 337, Bergvlei 2012, South Africa

First published 1989

© William Powell, Peter Powell, Alex Bannister 1989

Set in Trump Medieval (Linotron)

Printed and bound in Great Britain by Mackays, Letchworth

British Library Cataloguing in Publication Data
Powell, William A.
  Wisden guide to cricket grounds
  1. England. Cricket grounds
  I. Title II. Powell, Peter W.G. III.
  Bannister, Alex
  796.35′8′06842

ISBN 0 09 173830 X (paper) 0 09 174209 9 (cased)

Contents

Foreword

With all the cricketing blood flowing through the Powell family, it is hardly surprising that William – with suitable domestic encouragement – has produced such an excellent guide to our cricket grounds.

This work could have been achieved only by meticulous attention to detail and the support of so many dedicated county officials, without whom our game could not survive.

I congratulate the Powells, as well as my long-standing friend and critic Alex Bannister, and I hope that the book receives the acclaim it deserves. It is another important part of our cricketing history which both present and future lovers of the game will enjoy.

RAMAN SUBBA ROW
Chairman, Test and
County Cricket Board
March 1989

Acknowledgements

The publishers would like to thank Barry Doe for providing rail and bus information; also Laetitia Stapleton and *Kent Messenger* for additional photographs.

William and Peter Powell would like to thank the following who have assisted in a variety of ways in the preparation of this guide book:

M. Aaronson, P.A.B. Abbott, C.T. Adamson, D.J.M. Armstrong, M. Atkinson, P.G.M. August, S.P. Austin, A.G. Avery, A.D.P. Baird, R.W. Barclay, R.S. Barker, M. Beaty, L. Beaumont, W. Bell, T. Billson, A.J. Birch, N.H. Birch, C. Bracey, J.M. Brearley, D.J.W. Bridge, R.W. Brooke, A. Brown, G.C. Capper, P.G. Carling, D.G. Collier, S.P. Coverdale, D. Cracknell, J. Davies, S. Davies, B.T. Denning, C.F. Driver, Miss D. Edgeley, Miss T. Edwards, P.J. Edwards, H.S. Evans, Miss C. Fardell, F.J. Farmer, D.G. Fleetwood, W.R. Ford, J. Fox, A. Francis, R.A.N. Gillett, P.W. Gooden, G. Gorski, S. Green, P. Griffiths, D. Guest, L.W. Hancock, R. Harrison, C.D. Hassell, L.W. Hatton, P.W. Haynes, A.K. Hignell, M.F. Hill, C.E. Holland, E. Howard, J.W.G. Howells, B.H. Hurst, J. Iley, R.V. Isaacs, V.H. Isaacs, C. James, Col. L.R. James, W.D. Jones, Hon. T.M. Lamb, E.I. Lester, J. Lister, D. Littlewood, Miss V. Lloyd, Rev. M. Lorimer, A. Lowe, J.D. Mace, S. Malik, T.J. Maple, C.F.V. Martin, M.F. Martin, W.O. Matthews, B. Maylen, T.D. Meneer, H.R. Milton, K. Montgomery, L.T. Newell, L.F. Newnham, C.F. Niker, H.A. Osborne, D. Paul, F.G. Peach, A.J. Pearce, D. Pearce, R. Pearman, B. Perkins, J.B. Pickup, P. Piggott, I.W. Plant, M. Pope, Dr. S.R. Porter, M. Powell, R.N. Prentice, D.P. Price, M. Pritchard, D. Pyne, D.E. Radcliffe, A. Rees, R.H. Renold, P. Robinson, P.J. Robinson, B. Robson, D. Scott, I. Scott-Browne, C.R. Sheppard, K. Slaney, A.C. Smith, A.T. Smith, J.E.O. Smith, E.E. Snow, E. Solomon, E.J.H. Stephens, J.A. Stephens, Col. J.R. Stephenson, M. Stones, J. Stroud, R. Subba-Row, S.W. Tacey, C.H. Taylor, J.J. Taylor, R. Thomas, S.J. Tomlin, K.S.C. Trushell, K.C. Turner, Rev. M.D. Vockins, S.J. Wade, J. Warham, Rev. K.J. Warren, R. Whitworth, D.K. Wild, R.D. Wilkinson, G. Williams, W. Williams, C.F. Woodhouse, D.H. Wright, G. Wright, L. Wynne, P. Wynne-Thomas.

The plans of grounds have in part been derived from Ordnance Survey material with the sanction of the Controller of Her Majesty's Stationery Office (Crown copyright reserved).

The Ground Plans

All ground plans are diagrammatic and are to an approximate scale of
1:2000. Every attempt has been made to include as much information
as possible bearing in mind the size of the plans.

When defining seating areas, covered seating has taken preference
over open seating in those areas where open seating is banked above
covered seating (as is found at the major grounds). Executive boxes
and similar restricted covered areas have also been defined as covered
seating.

Toilets situated in separate buildings have been defined on the
plans, but additional toilets are to be found below most of the areas
of tiered seating and in other permanent buildings. Similarly, the
refreshment facilities are usually to be found in the existing
permanent buildings or in temporary accommodation specially
provided on match days.

The areas available to the general public and to club members are
clearly defined at all the county grounds, but at local club grounds
only used on a single or a few days each year arrangements may vary
from match to match, and from year to year. Special arrangements
apply at the six Test Match grounds and at any other grounds where
reserved seat tickets and car park tickets are sold in advance.

Key

ENTRANCE		PITCH	
PAVILION		EXTENT OF PLAYING AREA	
COVERED SEATING		MARQUEES AND TENTS	
OPEN SEATING		WALL OR FENCE	
SB	SCOREBOARD	HEDGE	
T	TOILETS	TREES	
OTHER BUILDINGS		BANKING	

1 Chesterfield	**21** Gloucester	**41** Worksop
2 Heanor	**22** Moreton-in-Marsh	**42** Bath
3 Cheadle	**23** Swindon	**43** Weston-super-Mare
4 Ilkeston	**24** Basingstoke	**44** Guildford
5 Knypersley	**25** Bournemouth	**45** Eastbourne
6 Leek	**26** Portsmouth	**46** Hastings
7 Repton	**27** Dartford	**47** Horsham
8 Colchester	**28** Folkestone	**48** Nuneaton
9 Ilford	**29** Maidstone	**49** Kidderminster
10 Southend-on-Sea	**30** Tunbridge Wells	**50** Hereford
11 Abergavenny	**31** Liverpool	**51** Harrogate
12 Neath	**32** Lytham	**52** Middlesborough
13 Pontypridd	**33** Southport	**53** Scarborough
14 Swansea	**34** Blackpool	**54** Sheffield
15 Aberystwyth	**35** Hinckley	**55** Hull
16 Ebbw Vale	**36** Uxbridge	**56** Cambridge
17 Llanelli	**37** Wellingborough	**57** Oxford
18 Merthyr Tydfil	**38** Luton	**58** Arundel
19 Newport	**39** Finedon	
20 Cheltenham	**40** Tring	

Introduction

The grounds used regularly for county cricket now number about 75 in all and vary from Lord's to the simplest of small club grounds, and from the established stadia that can accommodate some 25,000 spectators with facilities of every type including covered seating and executive boxes to simple local recreation grounds used for cricket (and other sports) with a modest clubhouse, a scoreboard and with space for no more than 2,000 spectators on temporary seats.

Despite the contrasting nature of these grounds, all now provide the opportunity for the playing and watching of county cricket. This arises in part from the willingness of the county clubs to travel from their home base – the county ground – and, in the case of Northamptonshire, Derbyshire and Gloucestershire, to travel into adjoining counties which have no first-class cricket. All this requires dedicated work not only from the county officials but also from the officials and members of the local clubs concerned. This work involves the provision of many hundreds of temporary seats, the construction of temporary tiered seating, the erection of tents for refreshments and entertaining, accommodation for officials, temporary toilets and first-aid facilities and the designation of suitable car parking areas. In this manner, therefore, nearly sixty grounds which otherwise attract only a few local club spectators and have only a single permanent building – a pavilion – and a carefully nurtured cricket square are transformed into venues for first-class county cricket attracting perhaps 5,000 or more spectators on a single day.

In addition to the familiar county grounds (which include as a result of television coverage the even more familiar six Test Match Grounds), first-class cricket is played at a variety of venues including private clubs, public recreation grounds, public schools and even grounds which form a part of a factory premises.

During recent years we have communicated with all club secretaries and other representatives, and each ground has been visited personally in order to record in detail its features and to check on the information supplied. Facts have been assembled on the establishment of the clubs and their general history and the cricket that has taken place since the inception of each ground. We are particularly grateful to all those clubs who have provided detailed plans of their grounds and the layout during a county match. However, improvements and changes are constantly being made at most grounds. At the smaller grounds, which only provide county cricket on a single day per year, layouts may vary as their facilities are set out differently from year to year. This particularly applies to areas restricted to members and sponsors.

Some of the grounds included will be unfamiliar to many regular cricket followers and it is hoped that this volume will become an indispensable guide for all those interested in cricket, whether they are intending to visit one of the grounds or simply watching on the television or listening to the radio. Our visits to the grounds and our discussions and correspondence with those involved have been extensive in an attempt to be as accurate as possible, but there will still be omissions and no doubt errors. We trust that readers will keep the authors informed of discrepancies and changes so that a future edition may be as thorough and up-to-date as possible.

All the team photographs in the book date from 1935, except the Oxford and Cambridge teams, which are dated 1895.

This introduction cannot be concluded without thanking the many people who have assisted us with this work. We have tried to record all those who have made some contribution in the acknowledgements.

William A. Powell
Peter W.G. Powell

Key to Ground Records and Scores

(PC)   Prudential Cup

(PT)   Prudential Trophy

(TT)   Texaco Trophy

(GC)   Gillette Cup

(NWBT)   National Westminster Bank Trophy

(BHC)   Benson & Hedges Cup

(JPL)   John Player League/John Player Special League

(RAL)   Refuge Assurance League

(RAC)   Refuge Assurance Cup

(FT)   Fenner Trophy

(Asda)   Asda Challenge Trophy

Notes on Where to Stay and How to Get There

If you are planning a longer stay or require further details on where to eat en route, special bargain stays and local facilities/places of interest, contact local Tourist Information Centre for City/Town which you are visiting. Telephone numbers and address of Centre from Directory Enquiries.

If you plan to use public transport or your own – whether by bus, car, rail or air – refer to your local Bus Station, AA, RAC, British Rail Travel Centre/Station or travel agent for specific details.

MCC

LONDON – LORD'S

MCC

The Marylebone Cricket Club was founded in 1787 and its early history relates directly to the development of Lord's cricket ground itself. Thomas Lord, a Yorkshireman born in Thirsk in 1755, had by 1780 found his way to London where he took employment at the recreation ground at White Conduit Fields, Islington. Here he met members of the White Conduit Cricket Club (founded in 1782) who were not satisfied with the cricket ground in Islington and suggested to Lord that he should find them a more exclusive ground for their use. This he found at Dorset Fields (Dorset Square now forms part of this area) and leased the ground from the Portman Estates. In 1787 the first match was played on this ground between Middlesex and Essex and the MCC was founded by Thomas Lord's patrons from the White Conduit Club headed by Lord Winchelsea.

Thomas Lord and the cricket ground prospered as the ground became the principal cricket venue in London, which then had a population of little more than 750,000. MCC inherited from the Hambledon CC the responsibility for the government of the game throughout the country and two hundred years later still retain the power to make the Laws of Cricket. It was, however, not too long before the expansion of the built-up area of London forced Lord and the MCC to move in 1810 to another ground in the area south of the present Lodge Road. This did not prove a popular ground and in 1812 the decision to construct the Regents Canal forced Lord to make a second move, taking with him on each occasion, it is said, the turf from the original pitch.

The first match on this third ground at St John's Wood was played between MCC and Hertfordshire on 22 June 1814 and it was here that the MCC found its permanent home. In 1825 Lord had visions of developing much of the ground area for housing as the district of St John's Wood was being developed at this time. This was probably prevented by the action of William Ward, a member of the Club who bought out Lord. Later in 1835 Ward handed over to James Dark, under whose control the ground remained until 1864 when he sold the lease of the ground to the Club. (To this day the sweet shop below the Mound Stand still retains the name Dark's Shop.) In 1860 the Club had missed the opportunity to purchase the freehold but finally six years later paid Mr Moses £18,000 for the freehold of the ground as it then existed. This precipitated the improvement and extension of the pavilion and a new grandstand for the public. The first full-time groundsman was also employed. It was about this time that the then Secretary, R.A. Fitzgerald, introduced the now familiar red and yellow colours of the Club in place of the original blue and white.

In 1877 the Club came to an agreement with Middlesex CCC to provide a home for the County and this arrangement has continued ever since. While the Australians were to meet MCC in a one-day match on their first tour of England in 1878, it was not until 1884

THE KING AT A TEST MATCH. LORDS

M.C.C.

that England met Australia in a Test Match at Lord's, the Oval having led the way in staging Test cricket.

In 1887 the centenary of MCC was celebrated with a dinner in the pavilion and during this period the membership, then just over 5,000, was constantly increasing. While the then grandstand had two stories of covered seating, it was realized that the pavilion would have to be replaced. A new pavilion was built in 1889/90 (designed by architect, Frank T. Verity, who had worked on details of the Albert Hall), which stands to this day with little alteration to its external appearance; the only extensions being the professionals' changing rooms and the press box adjoining the north end which have since been converted to a members' bar and Club offices. Shortly afterwards the Club purchased the 'nursery' at the eastern end of the ground, but no sooner had this been done than the Manchester and Sheffield Railway Company attempted to purchase the area for the development of the railway line from Marylebone Station. After due consideration the Club relinquished the freehold of the strip of land bordering Wellington Road (currently the car park area) and received in exchange the site of the Clergy Orphan School to the south, where the indoor school and shop are now sited.

It has been said that certain of the excavations from the tunnels below the Wellington Road side of the ground were used as banking for the original Mound Stand built in 1898/99 on the area which was previously the old tennis and racket courts, and which were rebuilt at the rear of the pavilion. Already critics were likening the ground to an amphitheatre and suggesting that Thomas Lord would 'turn in his grave' at the transformation.

Expansion continued apace with the advent of the 20th century and the Club was to acquire new responsibilities. In 1898 the Board of Control was set up under the chairmanship of the President of MCC to organize Test cricket in England. In 1904 the Advisory County Cricket Committee was founded and in 1909 England, Australia and South Africa founded the Imperial Cricket Conference. In 1903 the MCC also took over from various sponsors the responsibility of arranging and financing official England tours overseas. All these bodies had their headquarters at Lord's and still do to this day, although now re-formed and completely separated administratively from the MCC in the form of the Test & County Cricket Board and the International Cricket Conference.

The new grandstand was built on the north side of the ground to the designs of Sir Herbert Baker, who had been responsible for many public buildings including the Bank of England and India House. He also presented to the Club the now famous 'Father Time' weather vane which was to become an internationally known Lord's landmark.

In 1923 the Grace Gates were erected at the entrance on St John's Wood Road and in 1934 the Garden was developed in memory of Lord Harris. It has since become traditional for team photographs to be taken in this garden. The 'Q' Stand was also built at the same time and all were the work of Sir Herbert Baker. The Stands at the nursery end were also erected and the car park developed beyond the nursery ground, and care was taken to retain the tree screen dividing the main ground from the nursery. 1937 saw the celebration of the Club's 150th anniversary. The Second World War gave the 66-year-old Sir Pelham Warner the opportunity to take charge at Lord's as acting Secretary while Col. R.S. Rait-Kerr was on war service. While the nursery ground became a barrage balloon site and Father Time was pulled down by a balloon cable, Lord's stayed open and 13,000 spectators watched a match on 10 August 1940. Lord's escaped serious damage and in 1945 international cricket recommenced, with matches against the Australians, in the 'Victory' Test and later against the Dominions.

In 1945 the MCC appointed its first curator and this led to the establishment of the Memorial Gallery which was opened in 1953. Further development took place in 1958 with the building of the Warner Stand with its two levels, snack bars and press box on the site of the single storey 'A' enclosure between the pavilion and the grandstand. In 1968 the tavern and the adjoining buildings were swept away to be replaced by the New Tavern Stand and the tavern itself re-sited adjoining the Grace Gates and the new banqueting suite. By 1969 the Club's direct control of first-class professional cricket in the UK had been relinquished to the Test & County Cricket Board – in 1968 the National Cricket Association had taken over the responsibilities for amateur cricket, and in the same year all professional cricket in the UK became the responsibility of the TCCB (Test & County Cricket Board), leaving the MCC with the responsibility only for the Laws of Cricket. The Cricket Council was also established in 1968, composed of representatives of all cricketing authorities in the UK.

While so much of the Club's public duty has been transferred to other bodies, the MCC remains a large private club of some 19,000 members (and a substantial waiting list) with a magnificent ground, and is to most cricket lovers worldwide still the spiritual home of the game. In 1987 the Club celebrated its bicentenary and marked this by the complete redevelopment of the Mound Stand and the erection of the Bicentenary Gates. The ground is now truly closer to the amphitheatre which had first been a criticism in 1903.

It is impossible to do justice to more than 200 years' development in these few paragraphs, we recommend that you consult the several books written on the MCC and Lord's and particularly *Double Century* by Tony Lewis (Hodder & Stoughton, 1987).

The reverse side of the scorecard for the bicentenary match between MCC and Rest of the World in 1987.

Founded 1787
Colours Red and yellow
Crest The letters 'MCC'
Secretary Lt. Col. J.R. Stephenson OBE
Assistant secretary administration Lt. Col. L.G. James
Assistant secretary cricket J.A. Jameson
Assistant secretary finance M.R. Blow
Assistant secretary marketing and personnel Wg. Cdr. V.J.W.M. Lawrence
Head Coach D. Wilson
Groundsman M.J. Hunt **Scorer** E. Solomon
Address Lord's Cricket Ground, St John's Wood Road, London NW8 8QN
Telephone: 01-289 1611 (pavilion reception)
01-286 3577 (indoor school)
01-286 1757 (shop)
01-286 8011 (prospects of play)
01-289 1288 (tennis courts)

Grounds:

London (Lord's Cricket Ground)

Lord's

DESCRIPTION OF GROUND AND FACILITIES

The main entrance to the ground is from St John's Wood Road through the Grace Gates, and is used by members and their guests. The public gain entrance through the North Entrance and the North Gate (which is also the entrance to the members' car park) from Wellington Road, and through the East Gate and adjoining turnstiles in St John's Wood Road.

All the buildings in the ground are permanent. The pavilion is the centre-piece and includes the famous 'Long Room'. The members and their guests also have exclusive use of the Warner Stand, the Tavern Stand and the lower 'Q' stand (upper section members only). The New Mound Stand, constructed in 1986–87, has a floor level of executive boxes, an upper level of debenture holders' seats and covered and open seating at the lower level for public spectators. The Nursery End is comprised of an upper and lower tier and is accessible to members of the public. The grandstand, balcony and lower tier are also available to members of the public; this building also includes a number of private boxes at each end and adjoining the main scoreboard. Under the grandstand there are a number of refreshment areas and the scorecard printers' office. The Warner Stand includes a refreshment area at first floor level and above it is the press box. The computerized scoreboard installed in 1988 is situated between the Tavern Stand and the New Mound Stand and is operated from the main scoreboard. At the rear of the pavilion are the Memorial Gallery and Musem together with the MCC library, squash and real tennis courts. At the rear of this building is the Test & County Cricket Board headquarters and National Cricket Association office. To the south the Lord Harris Memorial Garden and the Middlesex CCC offices. To the rear of the Warner Stand is the Coronation Garden, where members picnic during lunch intervals of popular matches.

The Lord's Tavern is now situated next to the Grace Gates and adjoining the Banqueting Suite. There are two souvenir shops on the ground, a temporary one close to the Grace Gates and the main shop adjoining the East Gate. At the Nursery End in addition to the car park and Nursery practice area where players take nets (and the Cross Arrows CC play during September) there is the MCC Indoor Cricket School and the MCC cricket shop where cricket equipment can be obtained throughtout the year. All toilets are permanent and all stands include appropriate facilities for spectators. All the stands have covered accommodation and refreshments can be obtained at a number of points around the ground. Lunches can be taken in the Banqueting Suite and the Tavern itself. The playing area is 152 metres by 133 metres, within which the actual playing area is defined by a rope stretching to the appropriate dimensions depending on the position of the playing strip being used. There are facilities for disabled persons both adjoining the pavilion, and in the public areas a special section is situated near the 'Q' Stand and the Tavern concourse. The TV camera position is sited on the first floor balcony of the pavilion and the radio commentary from high above the players' dining area and visitors' dressing rooms at the top of the pavilion.

The current ground capacity is 26,000 and this is regularly achieved on most Test match days as well as one-day internationals, the Benson & Hedges Cup and National Westminster Bank Trophy Finals. The stands are numbered A to Q from the Warner Stand round to the 'Q' Stand, and for the above matches spectators are advised to book seats in advance as all seats are reserved and numbered. Middlesex matches rarely attract a full house except when the county progress in one of the limited-over knockout competitions. For Middlesex matches spectators can choose to sit wherever they like in the public areas. From 1989 the lower part of the 'Q' Stand will include an enclosed Middlesex members' room.

Lord's is the mecca of cricket and has surely the best facilities of all the grounds included within this guide book.

GROUND RECORDS AND SCORES

TEST MATCHES
Highest innings total for England 629 *v.* India, 1974
Highest innings total against England 729 for 6 dec. by Australia, 1930

Lowest innings total for England   53 *v.* Australia, 1888
Lowest innings total against England   42 by India, 1974
Highest individual innings for England   240 W.R. Hammond *v.*
Australia, 1938
Highest individual innings against England   254 D.G. Bradman for
Australia, 1930
Best bowling performance in an innings for England   8 for 34
I.T. Botham *v.* Pakistan, 1978
Best bowling performance in an innings against England   8 for 53
R.A.L. Massie for Australia, 1972
Best bowling performance in a match for England   15 for 104
H. Verity *v.* Australia, 1934
Best bowling performance in a match against England   16 for 137
R.A.L. Massie for Australia, 1972

LIMITED-OVERS INTERNATIONALS
Highest innings total   334 for 4 by England *v.* India (PC), 1975
Lowest innings total   132 for 3 by India *v.* England (PC), 1975
Highest individual innings   138 I.V.A. Richards for West Indies *v.*
England (PC), 1979
Best bowling performance   5 for 38 J. Garner for West Indies *v.*
England (PC), 1979

LIMITED-OVERS FINALS (COUNTIES)
Highest innings total   317 for 4 by Yorkshire *v.* Surrey, (GC/
NWBT), 1969/290 for 6 by Essex *v.* Surrey (BHC), 1979
Lowest innings total   118 by Lancashire *v.* Kent (GC/NWBT),
1974/117 by Derbyshire *v.* Hampshire (BHC), 1988
Highest individual innings   146 G. Boycott for Yorkshire *v.* Surrey
(GC/NWBT), 1965/132 n.o. I.V.A. Richards for Somerset *v.* Surrey
(BHC), 1981
Best bowling performance   6 for 29 J. Garner for Somerset *v.*
Northamptonshire (GC/NWBT), 1979/5 for 13 S.J. Jefferies for
Hampshire *v.* Derbyshire (BHC), 1988

FIRST-CLASS MATCHES
Highest innings total for MCC   607 *v.* Cambridge University, 1902
Highest innings total against MCC   609 for 8 dec. by Cambridge
University, 1902
Lowest innings total for MCC   15 *v.* Surrey, 1839
Lowest innings total against MCC   20 by Middlesex, 1864
Highest individual innings for MCC   214 E.H. Hendren *v.*
Yorkshire, 1919
Highest individual innings against MCC   281 n.o. W.H. Ponsford
for Australia, 1934
Best bowling performance in an innings for MCC   10 for 73
A. Shaw *v.* North, 1874
Best bowling performance in an innings against MCC   9 for 29
J. Lillywhite for Sussex, 1862
Best bowling performance in a match for County   16 for 60
W.G. Grace *v.* Nottinghamshire, 1885

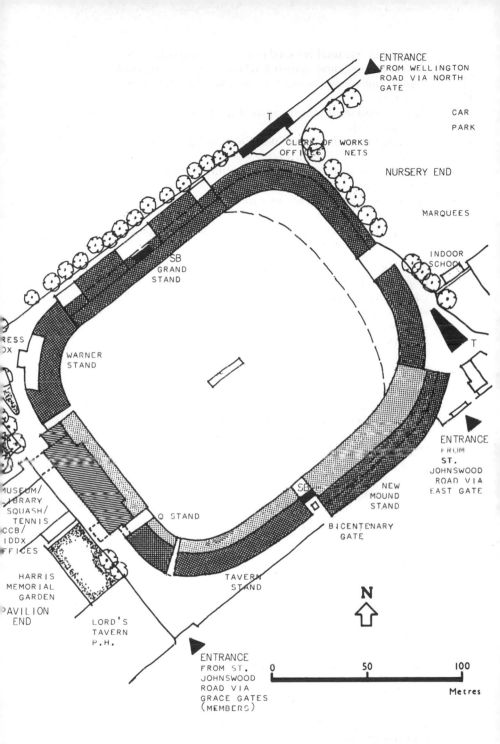

Best bowling performance in a match against County 15 for 97
J.C. Laker for Surrey, 1954

For Middlesex ground records and scores at Lord's, see Middlesex section.

HOW TO GET THERE

Rail   St John's Wood Underground (Jubilee line), ½ mile
Bus   LRT 6, 8, 13, 16, 16A, 46, 74, 82, 113, 159. (Tel: 01-222 1234); coaches 719, 757, 768 and 797
Car   From north: M1 to motorway terminal roundabout at Brent Cross, then follow North Circular Road, East A406, then branch left and follow signs West End, take A41 signposted Swiss Cottage and follow Finchley Road to St John's Wood, follow signs Lord's Cricket Ground and A5205 for St John's Wood Road and main Grace Gates entrance. The ground is situated opposite St John's Wood Church and bounded by Wellington Road, Wellington Place, St John's Wood Road and Grove End Road, or follow A1 via Hendon and A41 (signposted West End) then as above. From east: From Holloway district follow signs West End A503, then at Camden Town follow signs Regent's Park A4201, enter Regent's Park at Gloucester Gate and use Outer Circle signposted London Zoo. After passing London Mosque, take immediate right into Hanover Gate and at T-junction take right into Park Road A41 for St John's Wood, keep left for St John's Wood Road A5205 at roundabout for Lord's Cricket Ground. From west: A40(M)/M41 follow signs Central London, then follow signs Paddington and A4026 in Bishop's Bridge Road, follow one-way system signposted Euston and follow A5 Edgware Road, then take right into St John's Road A5202 for Lord's Cricket Ground. From south: From Hyde Park Corner follow signs Ring road, Oxford into Park Lane A4202, then at Marble Arch follow signs Oxford Circus into Oxford Street A40, then at second traffic lights take A41 Portman Street, follow through Portman Square and Gloucester Place, follow signs A41 Aylesbury and the North, at St John's Wood roundabout take left into St John's Wood Road A5205 for Lord's Cricket Ground.

No street parking, though limited areas available on meters and on Sundays. Car park access for members from Cavendish Road

WHERE TO STAY AND OTHER INFORMATION

The Hilton International Regents Park Hotel, London NW8 (01-722 7722) is adjoining, but stay anywhere in central or NW London

Disabled Areas   Between 'Q' Stand and Pavilion
Local Radio Station(s)   Greater London Radio (94.9 MHz FM/1488 KHz MW), Capital Radio (95.8 MHz FM/1548 KHz MW), LBC (97.3 MHz FM/1152 KHz MW)
Local Newspaper   Evening Standard

DERBYSHIRE

DERBY

CHESTEFIELD

HEANOR

CHEADLE

ILKESTON

KNYPERSLEY

LEEK

REPTON

Derbyshire

Derbyshire's reputation as a bowling force took root in their first first-class match at Manchester in 1871 when Lancashire, the only opponents deigning to meet them on equal terms, were routed for 25. To this day it is their lowest total in county cricket. Two years on Nottinghamshire, apparently succumbing to the lavish hospitality of a wine merchant at Wirksworth, staggered to 14 all out, an ignominy redressed in the course of time at Trent Bridge with Derbyshire dismissed for 16.

In 1874 Derbyshire, having won three and drawn one, were hailed as champions as the title at the time went to the side with the fewest defeats. A second opinion prevailed, however, that with only four matches played by Derbyshire it was an unfair situation and Gloucestershire were declared winners.

Inevitably the early years were an uphill climb and results were so bad that Derbyshire lost their first-class status for seven years. Money was tight, and the fraudulent enterprises of an assistant secretary were unmasked by none other than the legendary Australian fast bowler, F.R. ('Demon') Spofforth, who briefly played for the county after marrying a local girl. The miscreant bolted and was next heard of in Madrid where he became tailor to the King of Spain.

While he was qualifying Yorkshire, with generous imprudence, allowed Spofforth to play against them and he responded with a 15-wicket demonstration of his genius.

There was a bleak period up to and after the First World War culminating in the disaster of 1920 when 17 defeats were suffered in 18 matches. The other was washed out without a ball bowled, which suggests in a more typical summer they might have got off a little lighter! Drastic remedies were sought, and included the appointment of a 40-year-old captain in G.M. Buckston, and the re-engagement of the 45-year-old fast bowler, Bestwick, who had been sacked for intemperance. Bestwick must have dryly pondered how many glasses were raised to him to salute his 147-wicket haul, including all ten for 40 at Cardiff.

Derbyshire moved up four places and gradually the foundation was laid for the summit achievement of 1936. It took an exceptional side to wrest the honours from Yorkshire in the 'thirties. Derbyshire had proved their strength with successive positions of 3rd and 2nd, and, true to tradition, their strength rested much on bowling. Only Worthington, Townsend and Denis Smith reached the comparatively modest batting average of between 30 and 35, while Copson, Alf Pope, Townsend and the leg spinner, Mitchell, took wickets at a cost from 12 to 20. They also carried the burden of the absence of George Pope, who completed only five overs before retiring for the season with cartilage problems.

The county's pride has been in its strain of pace bowlers, and a remarkable line of long-serving wicket-keepers: W. Storer, Hum-

OUNTY CRICKETERS.

MR. C. A. OLLIVIERRE,
DERBYSHIRE.

DERBYSHIRE C.C.C

phries, H. Elliott, Dawkes and Taylor, whose 1,648 victims is a record. The boast was that a shout down a pit shaft produced a hostile bowler. But times change. Now it is more likely to be a phone call to the Caribbean to recruit a Holding. Who would have thought a West Indian and a Dane, Ole Mortensen, would be the new-ball successors to the Pope brothers, Rhodes, Jackson, Gladwin, Bestwick, Hendrick and Co.

In the 'fifties the shortage of runs provoked the captain, Guy Willatt, to compare Derbyshire batsmen to sailors in the Spanish Armada – subordinate and consigned to a secondary role. Not much was expected of them, and not much was forthcoming, but his successor, Donald Carr, later a top administrator at Lord's, lifted standards with graceful efficiency. He had few batting peers in the country.

Other shining examples include Worthington, the first Derbyshire player to score a Test century, Denis Smith, Hamer, Bolus and Barnett. Overseas blood, Wright and Kirsten, considerably enriched the stream, and the importation of Barlow, the combative South African all-rounder, was as wise an investment as the county ever made. As captain he left his mark with his infectious zeal and high fitness levels.

Derbyshire's contrasting fortunes were mirrored by the events of 1981. During the season the chairman, chief executive, the captain Miller, and the scorer resigned. Wood, formerly of Lancashire, took over the captaincy hours before a county match on 25 July, and on 5 September, accepted the NatWest Trophy after the closest of all finals at Lord's. With the scores level, Derbyshire beat Northamptonshire by virtue of losing fewer wickets. Derbyshire reached their second Benson and Hedges final in 1988 and were again beaten by a southern county in this competition. A decade before they had gone down to Kent. By now they were splendidly led by Barnett, who gained Test recognition. [A.B.]

T. S. WORTHINGTON

G. H. POPE

MR. L. G. WRIGHT. DERBYSHIRE.

Founded   1870
Colours   Chocolate, Cambridge blue and amber
Crest   Rose and imperial crown
Secretary   I. Edwards
Coach   P.E. Russell
Groundsman   B. Marsh
Scorer   S.W. Tacey
Address   County Cricket Ground, Nottingham Road, Derby, DE2 6DA
Telephone: 0332 383211
Cricketcall   0898 121466

Achievements:

County Championship   Champions (1) 1936
Gillette Cup   Finalists 1969
National Westminster Bank Trophy   Winners 1981
Benson & Hedges Cup   Finalists 1978 and 1988
John Player Sunday League   Champions (0) 3rd 1970
Refuge Assurance Sunday League   Champions (0) 5th 1987
Asda Trophy   Winners 1982 and 1985
Tilcon Trophy   Finalists 1977

Grounds:

Derby (County Cricket Ground, Nottingham Road)   Chesterfield (Queen's Park, Boythorpe Road)   Heanor (Town Ground, Mayfield Avenue)   Knypersley (Victoria and Knypersley Social Welfare Centre, Tunstall Road)   Leek (Highfield, Macclesfield Road)   Ilkeston (Rutland Recreation Ground, West End

Drive)   Cheadle (Tean Road Sports Ground, Tean Road)   Repton (Repton School Ground, Repton).

Other grounds that have been used since 1969 are: Burton-on-Trent (Ind-Coop Brewery Ground, Belevedere Road), (Allied Brewery Sports Ground), Long Eaton (Trent College, Derby Road) Darley Dale (Station Road) and Buxton (The Park, Park Road).

Derby

The ground occupies part of the former Derby racecourse and was known as the Racecourse Ground until officials became anxious that it be termed the County Cricket Ground. For racing Derby boasted a straight mile and a grandstand complete with a copper-domed viewing cupola and stables. All these still exist today (except the straight mile) as the ground is now enclosed from the rest of the former racecourse, which now provides recreational facilities for people of the city. The grandstand was built in 1911 as is defined on a stone tablet below the county crest.

The cricket pitch used to be located in the centre of the racecourse, but in 1939 when racing ceased due to poor crowds and lack of finance, the ground moved to its present position. In 1970, the year of the club's centenary, there was talk of closing the ground altogether due to its poor facilities and wicket. Not until 1982 when the Lund Pavilion was built, was there truly a cricket pavilion on the ground; the players used to change in the old jockeys' quarters.

The ground now occupies an area of 17 acres and in 1982 a lease of 125 years was purchased from the owners, Derby City Council, thanks to a generous loan from the local authority. Since 1982 much building has taken place: in addition to the pavilion, a new scoreboard, the Butterley and Streetley stands and the Supporters' Club have been erected.

The ground was for many years called the Charter Land as it was a portion of land given to the city by Queen Mary Tudor in her Charter of 1554. Once considered one of the least attractive of county grounds, it has been much improved in recent years. New roadworks have considerably altered the approach to the ground.

County matches were played on the racecourse from 1884 to 1954. In 1955 the wicket was moved to its present position. Derby County F C played some of their first matches at the Racecourse Ground before moving to the Baseball Ground in 1891; the ground even staged one F A Cup Final replay and five semi-finals. The ground was first used in 1863, fifteen years after the establishment of the racecourse by South Derbyshire C C. It was on this ground that South Derbyshire played and defeated the Australian Aborigines, the first touring side, in 1868. Following the formation of the county club in November 1870 at the Guildhall, the first county match was staged in 1871.

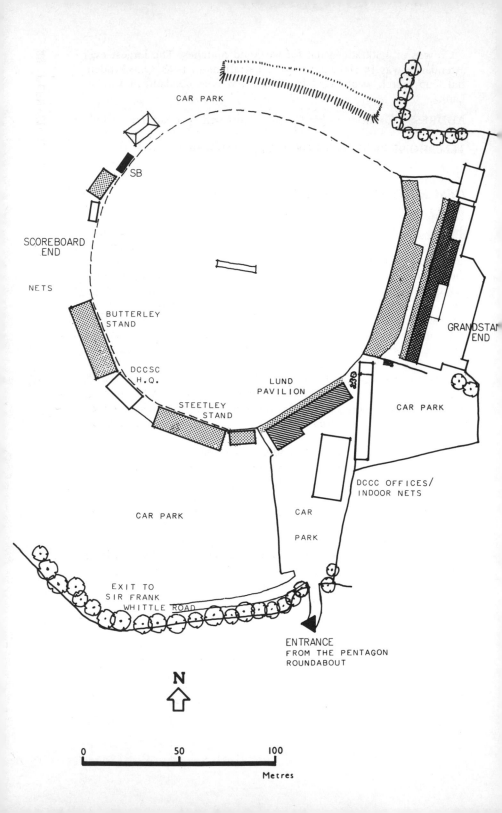

Crowds of 4,500 are usual for weekend matches. The largest ever attendance was 14,500 against the Australians in 1948. One Prudential Cup match was staged in 1983 when New Zealand played Sri Lanka.

ADDRESS   County Cricket Ground, Nottingham Road, Derby DE2 6DA
TELEPHONE PROSPECTS OF PLAY   0332 383211

DESCRIPTION OF GROUND AND FACILITIES

The main entrance to the ground is from the Pentagon roundabout at the junction with Nottingham Road. The main permanent buildings on the ground are the remains of the racecourse grandstand and the new Lund Pavilion which are both on the east side of the ground; on the south side there are new tiered seating stands, the new South Stand and an area for disabled persons' vehicles. A new scoreboard has been erected on the west side opposite the grandstand. The old scoreboard building now houses radio commentators. The north side of the ground consists of a grassy bank which is the remains of an old stand. On and in the front of this area it is possible to park and view the cricket from your car. There is a good number of seats for members at the front of the old grandstand area. This together with the Lund Pavilion are restricted to use by members and visiting members. The public seats are on the south side; while the number of these has been increased in recent years, you are still advised to bring your own to popular matches.

The playing area is large, extending to 152 metres by 167 metres; although the playing area is restricted on the north and west sides by a boundary rope inside the pale fencing which encloses the ground, the boundary can still be as much as 78 metres from the square.

All refreshment facilities, including the Grandstand public house, are available to the public, with the exception of the members' bar. Toilets are provided in the grandstand and on the ground floor of the old scorebox. Sponsors' tents are usually sited in the north-west corner between the new scoreboard and the grassy bank. The club shop is at the rear of the Lund Pavilion and the indoor school adjoins the entrance and the club offices.

This is a large spacious ground with a capacity of some 9,500 and the facility to shelter in the grandstand in the event of rain. There are good tree backcloths to the north and recent planting following new road alignments has much improved the west and south sides.

GROUND RECORDS AND SCORES

FIRST-CLASS MATCHES

Highest innings total for County   645 *v.* Hampshire, 1898
Highest innings total against County   661 by Nottinghamshire, 1901
Lowest innings total for County   26 *v.* Yorkshire, 1880
Lowest innings total against County   28 by Warwickshire, 1937
Highest individual innings for County   230 n.o. T.S. Worthington
v. Sussex, 1937
Highest individual innings against County   273 n.o. E.G. Hayes for
Surrey, 1904
Best bowling performance in an innings for County   9 for 39
G. Davidson *v.* Warwickshire, 1895
Best bowling performance in an innings against County   9 for 29
J. Briggs for Lancashire, 1885
Best bowling performance in a match for County   14 for 100
G. Porter *v.* Hampshire, 1895
Best bowling performance in a match against County   16 for 101
G. Giffen for Australians, 1886

LIMITED-OVERS MATCHES

Highest innings total for County   365 for 3 *v.* Cornwall (NWBT),
1986
Highest innings total against County   300 by Northamptonshire
(BHC), 1987
Lowest innings total for County   70 *v.* Surrey (JPL), 1972
Lowest innings total against County   61 by Sussex (JPL), 1978
Highest individual innings for County   153 A. Hill *v.* Cornwall
(NWBT), 1986
Highest individual innings against County   125 n.o. by R.J. Bailey
for Northamptonshire (RAL), 1987
Best bowling performance for County   5 for 11 A. Ward *v.* Sussex
(JPL), 1970
Best bowling performance against County   6 for 34 R.D. Jackman
for Surrey (JPL), 1972

HOW TO GET THERE

Rail   Derby Midland, 1¼ miles.
Bus   Trent Buses 29 from BR Station to ground. Derby City 42–7
from BR Station to Bus Station, thence numerous services to
ground (Tel: 0332 754433)
Car   From north: M1 junction 28 follow signs Derby A38 or A6 to
Pentagon Island, ground adjoining Sir Frank Whittle Road and
Nottingham Road, ground on north side of roundabout. From east:
M1 junction 25 follow signs Derby A52 and A61 to Pentagon
Island, then as north. From south: M1 junction 24 follow signs
Derby A6 then A52 ring road to Spondon then A61 to Pentagon
Island, then as north. From west: A52, A38 and A5111 to ring road
then A61 to Pentagon Island, then as north.

Midland Hotel (0332 45894), Clarenden Hotel (0332 365235), Post House Hotel, Sandiacre (0602 397800)

Disabled Areas   Next to boundary fence, near the South Stand, with space for 6 cars
Local Radio Station   BBC Radio Derby (104.5 MHz FM/1116 KHz MW), Radio Trent (96.2 MHz FM/999 KHz MW)
Local Newspaper(s)   Derby Evening Telegraph, Derbyshire Times, Derby Trader

Chesterfield

Queen's Park was laid out in 1897 to celebrate Queen Victoria's Diamond Jubilee and has remained a recreational area for the people of Chesterfield ever since. Derbyshire first used the ground in 1898 when Yorkshire were the visitors, and have staged fixtures annually, including cricket weeks. Limited-overs matches and even matches with touring sides have come to Chesterfield.

Queen's Park is probably one of the most picturesque grounds in the country and is owned and maintained by Chesterfield Borough Council. It is also the home of Chesterfield C C who play in the Derbyshire County and Bassetlaw cricket leagues. The ground is circular and was once surrounded by a cycle track and banking. The pavilion, which is half timbered, was built in 1897 and with the scoreboard is the only permanent feature on the ground. There is a marked slope from south (the pavilion end) to north (the Lake End, as it is known to locals). The famous twisted spire of All Saints' Church, some 238 feet high, looks down upon Queen's Park where so much cricket history has been made. For a public park there are ample facilities and crowds have been known to be large. Probably 14,000 attendance at the match against Yorkshire in 1948 was the greatest. Nowadays crowds of 5,000 are to be expected. The capacity is 7,500.

The ground has one unusual feature, a boating lake which is situated behind the sightscreen at the end opposite the pavilion. The lake is well populated by ducks and it has been known for the birds to find their way onto the square. This has provided the press with plenty of stories over the years.

Queen's Park was the ground where C.A. Ollivierre, the first West Indian to play county cricket, scored 229 against Essex in 1904. P.A. Perrin replied with 343 not out for the visitors, and this match still stands out as possibly the most famous ever staged on the ground.

Ken Graveney of Gloucestershire took 10 for 66 in Derbyshire's second innings here in 1949 to set up victory by 184 runs. Queen's Park is one of the few grounds to have been used by the county club in the north of the county, the others being Buxton and Darley Dale.

ADDRESS Chesterfield C C, Queen's Park, Boythorpe Avenue, Chesterfield, Derbyshire

TELEPHONE PROSPECTS OF PLAY 0246 73090

DESCRIPTION OF GROUND AND FACILITIES

The ground is entered from Boythorpe Avenue or Park Road, where there are a number of entrances including one over a bridge from the town centre. The only permanent buildings are the pavilion and press box at the southern end and a scorebox on the east side under the trees. To the east and west of the pavilion are permanent terraces for members, with bench seats. Elsewhere permanent timber seating areas are provided, as well as benches on the tarmac track surrounding the playing area. Seating is provided for about 55 per cent of the normal attendance and for limited-overs matches spectators are advised to bring their own seats. Refreshments are to be found in the pavilion and in the kiosk to the west of the playing area.

Chesterfield is possibly the most scenic ground played on by Derbyshire. The ground is on a marked slope towards the boating lake end and very pleasantly situated within the trees and shrubs of the beautiful Queen's Park. Limited car parking is available within the ground but street parking and multistorey car parks in the town are within walking distance.

The playing area is 127 metres by 117 metres, defined by a rope and advertising boards. The position for T V cameras is on the pavilion balcony. A Derbyshire C C S C caravan can be found on the west side of the ground near the bank.

GROUND RECORDS AND SCORES

FIRST-CLASS MATCHES
Highest innings total for County 552 v. Essex, 1928
Highest innings total against County 662 by Yorkshire, 1898
Lowest innings total for County 30 v. Nottinghamshire, 1913
Lowest innings total against County 29 by Middlesex, 1957
Highest individual innings for County 229 C.A. Ollivierre v. Essex, 1904
Highest individual innings against County 343 n.o. P.A. Perrin for Essex, 1904
Best bowling performance in an innings for County 8 for 21 E. Smith v. Worcestershire, 1951
Best bowling performance in an innings against County 10 for 66 J.K.R. Graveney for Gloucestershire, 1949
Best bowling performance in a match for County 14 for 48 A.G. Slater v. Somerset, 1930
Best bowling performance in a match against County 13 for 108 T.W. Cartwright for Somerset, 1972

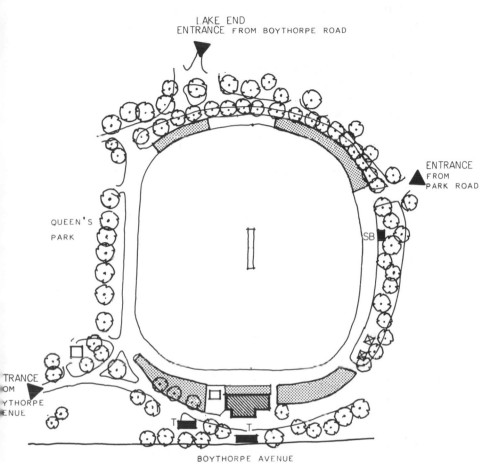

LAKE END
ENTRANCE FROM BOYTHORPE ROAD

ENTRANCE
FROM
PARK ROAD

QUEEN'S
PARK

SB

TRANCE
OM
YTHORPE
ENUE

T   T

BOYTHORPE AVENUE

PAVILION END

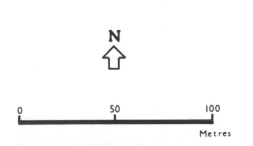

N

| 0 | 50 | 100 |

Metres

LIMITED-OVERS MATCHES

Highest innings total for County   236 for 8 *v.* Leicestershire (BHC), 1986

Highest innings total against County   249 for 3 by Lancashire (BHC), 1980

Lowest innings total for County   92 *v.* Sussex (GC), 1973/92 *v.* Kent (JPL), 1979

Lowest innings total against County   49 by Sussex (GC), 1969

Highest individual innings for County   111 n.o. P.J. Sharpe *v.* Glamorgan (BHC), 1976

Highest individual innings against County   109 B.W. Reidy for Lancashire (BHC), 1980

Best bowling performance for County   6 for 18 T.J.P. Eyre *v.* Sussex (GC), 1969

Best bowling performance against County   6 for 9 R.A. Woolmer for Kent (JPL), 1979

HOW TO GET THERE

Rail   Chesterfield, ¾ mile

Bus   Chesterfield Transport 1 from BR Station to within ¼ mile of ground (Tel: 0246 76666); Trent Buses and South Yorkshire Traction; also services from surrounding areas to Bus Station (200m from ground)

Car   From north: M1 junction 30 then follow signs Chesterfield A619, then signs to Buxton A619 and A632 for Queen's Park. From east: A632 or A617 to Chesterfield, then as north for Queen's Park. From south: M1 junction 29 then A617 to Chesterfield, then as north for Queen's Park or A61 to Chesterfield then as north for Queen's Park. From west: A619 or A632 to Chesterfield then as north for Queen's Park.

WHERE TO STAY AND OTHER INFORMATION

Chesterfield Hotel (0246 71141), Portland Hotel (0246 34504)

Disabled Areas   Next to boundary fence at Pavilion End, with space for approximately 6 cars.

Local Radio Station(s)   BBC Radio Sheffield (104.1 MHz FM/1035 KHz MW), BBC Radio Derby (104.5 MHz FM/1116 KHz MW), Radio Hallam (103.4 MHz FM/1548 KHz MW), Radio Trent (96.2 MHz FM/999 KHz MW)

Local Newspaper(s)   Derby Evening Telegraph, Derbyshire Times, Chesterfield Gazette, Chesterfield Star, Sheffield Star

Heanor

Situated off Mayfield Avenue this ground has been the home of Heanor Town Cricket Club since 1864. It is shared with the town football club and the floodlights can be seen as soon as you enter the east Derbyshire mining town. The ground is owned by Amber Valley District Council. The club is a member of the Derbyshire County Cricket League, formerly the Notts and Derbyshire Border Cricket League. It was founder member of the original league in 1920.

The ground slopes from the football stand end of the ground towards the cricket pavilion and tennis courts. It has fairly short boundaries, 50 metres compared with 75 metres at the County Cricket Ground, Derby. With such a small playing area high scoring totals are frequent. In the recent championship match Malcolm Marshall of Hampshire was asked to stop bowling fast; when the wicketkeeper missed the ball it was dangerous for spectators, so short are the boundaries.

Derbyshire have played Sunday League matches at Heanor since 1976 when Somerset visited for a John Player League fixture. The county play one Sunday League match each season and have in recent years staged benefit matches under the floodlights for players from Derbyshire, Leicestershire and Nottinghamshire. The ground is well maintained and has a fast outfield and reasonably good facilities for an out ground. Advantage of this was taken in 1987 when Derbyshire staged a championship match with Hampshire for the first time at the Town Ground. The pavilion houses the Heanor Town Sports Social Club and events are staged there throughout the year.

Matches tend to attract crowds of 4,000–5,000 for limited-overs matches. The capacity is 5,000 and the best crowd was 4,000 for the 1986 John Player League game with Hampshire.

ADDRESS Heanor Town C C, Town Ground, Mayfield Avenue, Commonside, Heanor DE7 7EN
TELEPHONE PROSPECTS OF PLAY 0773 766703

DESCRIPTION OF GROUND AND FACILITIES

The ground is entered from Mayfield Avenue to the west. There are two entrances, one for members and players/officials close to the Heanor Town Football and Social Club, and another for the public at the football ground end. In addition to the social club the only permanent cricket buildings on the ground are at the southern end, the pavilion and press room along with the members' enclosure. To the east is the scoreboard and to the north the covered football stand, toilets and tea bar. Terracing and banking can be found at the football end. From this end there is a marked slope towards the tennis courts and bowling green. The sponsors' area is in the south-eastern corner. The rest of the ground is used by the public.

A refreshment tent is located on the football field and there are a number of mobile refreshment positions. A Derbyshire C C S C table

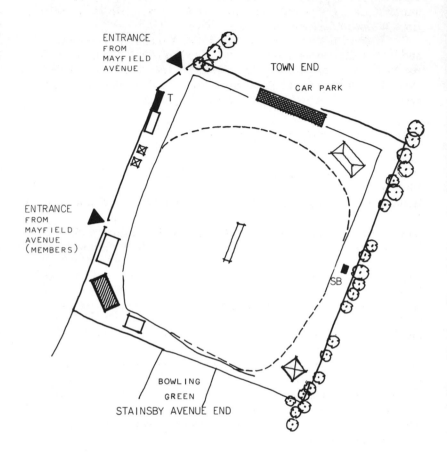

ENTRANCE
FROM
MAYFIELD
AVENUE

T

ENTRANCE
FROM
MAYFIELD
AVENUE
(MEMBERS)

TOWN END

CAR PARK

SB

BOWLING
GREEN
STAINSBY AVENUE END

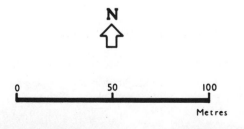

N

0   50   100

Metres

and caravan can be found on the Mayfield Road side of the ground close to the radio point. No car parking is available in the ground but ample space exists on the recreation ground to the north, with access from Wilmot Street and the Market Place.

The ground is owned by Amber Valley Council which provides about 1,000 seats. Spectators are advised to bring their own collapsible seats. The playing area is 118 metres by 106 metres, one of the smallest playing areas on the county circuit. All the seating is open except that in the football stand and social club.

GROUND RECORDS AND SCORES

FIRST-CLASS MATCHES

Highest innings total for County   314 for 7 dec. v. Hampshire, 1987
Highest innings total against County   349 for 2 dec. by Hampshire, 1987
Lowest innings total for County   298 for 6 v. Hampshire, 1987
Lowest innings total against County   261 for 6 dec. by Hampshire, 1987
Highest individual innings for County   106 B. Roberts v. Hampshire, 1987
Highest individual innings against County   104 n.o. D.R. Turner for Hampshire, 1987
Best bowling performance in an innings for County   3 for 92 P.G. Newman v. Hampshire, 1987
Best bowling performance in an innings against County   4 for 123 R.J. Maru for Hampshire, 1987
Best bowling performance in a match for County   4 for 171 P.G. Newman v. Hampshire, 1987
Best bowling performance in a match against County   7 for 213 R.J. Maru for Hampshire, 1987

LIMITED-OVERS MATCHES

Highest innings total for County   242 for 8 v. Somerset (JPL), 1976
Highest innings total against County   258 for 8 by Gloucestershire (RAL), 1988
Lowest innings total for County   184 v. Hampshire (JPL), 1986
Lowest innings total against County   219 for 8 by Somerset (JPL), 1983
Highest individual innings for County   100 n.o. K.J. Barnett v. Somerset (JPL), 1983
Highest individual innings against County   95 by R.A. Smith for Hampshire (JPL), 1986
Best bowling performance for County   3 for 29 M.A. Holding v. Hampshire (JPL), 1986
Best bowling performance against County   4 for 25 C.A. Connor for Hampshire (JPL), 1986

HOW TO GET THERE

Rail   Langley Mill, 1 mile
Bus   Trent 120/3/4/5 from Derby (passing BR Langley Mill Station),
132, 220, 231 and 330 from Nottingham (Tel: 0332 292200)
Car   From north: M1 junction 27 then A608 to Heanor, ground
situated in town centre. From east: A610 or A608 then as north.
From south: M1 junction 26 then A610 and A608 to Heanor, then
as north. From west: A608 then as north.

WHERE TO STAY AND OTHER INFORMATION

Sun Inn, Eastwood (0773 712940)

Disabled Areas   No specific area, request position
Local Radio Station(s)   BBC Radio Derby (104.5 MHz FM/116 KHz
MW), BBC Radio Nottingham (95.5 MHz FM/1548 KHz MW), Radio
Trent 96.2 MHz FM/999 KHz MW)
Local Newspaper(s)   Derby Evening Telegraph, Ripley and Heanor
News, Derby Trader, Ilkeston and Heanor Shopper

Cheadle

The ground of Cheadle Cricket Club has been the home headquarters
of the town club since 1922. The club plays in the North Staffordshire
and South Cheshire Cricket League and has 3 elevens.

The club was founded sometime in the nineteenth century and has
hosted limited-overs county matches since the first in 1973 when
Derbyshire visited Tean Road to play Minor Counties (North) in a
Benson and Hedges Cup zonal fixture. Derbyshire won the match by
5 wickets thanks to the bowling of Fred Rumsey (4 for 19) and Indian
Test spinner Venkataraghavan (2 for 32). Fifteen years later county
cricket returned to Tean Road when Derbyshire staged a home Refuge
Assurance Sunday League match with Glamorgan.

The county club have an agreement with Staffordshire County
Council to stage three Sunday matches at different venues in
Staffordshire on a basis of one in each district. The other grounds are
Knypersley and Leek. The grounds are visited in alternate seasons:
Cheadle the year after Leek and before Knypersley.

The ground has also been used for Minor County cricket by
Staffordshire.

The current ground capacity is 4,000. Probably the largest crowd
was between 1,500 and 2,000 for the Talbot Cup Final between
Cheadle and Stone in 1981. A crowd of similar number watched the
previous two county cricket matches. The ground is not to be
confused with Cheadle in Cheshire, a mistake made by cricketers in
the past!

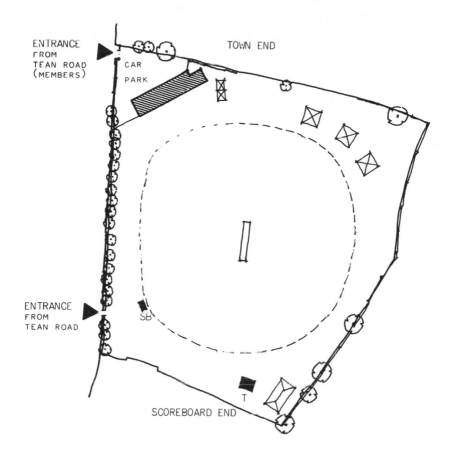

ENTRANCE
FROM
TEAN ROAD
(MEMBERS)

TOWN END

CAR
PARK

ENTRANCE
FROM
TEAN ROAD

SB

T

SCOREBOARD END

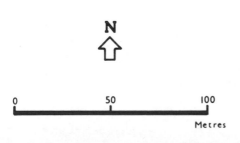

N

| 0 | 50 | 100 |

Metres

ADDRESS   Cheadle C C, Tean Road, Cheadle, Staffordshire
TELEPHONE PROSPECTS OF PLAY   0538 752728

DESCRIPTION OF GROUND AND FACILITIES

The only access to the ground is from Tean Road where there are two entrances, one for members/officials and disabled persons (at the rear of the pavilion) and the second for the public (at the south-western corner close to the scorebox). The pavilion is in the north-west corner with the members' enclosure in front. Sponsors' tents are at the north end of the ground. The Derbyshire C C S C caravan and office is situated close to the pavilion and at the southern perimeter of the playing area there are ample refreshment facilities, the toilets and groundsman's store. The playing area is 118 metres by 113 metres and is approximately circular. There is no car parking within the ground but ample facilities are available 200 yards away at a nearby public car park or at the Master Potter public house in Tean Road. The only covered accommodation is in the pavilion and spectators are advised to take their own collapsible seats as only 300 are provided.

GROUND RECORDS AND SCORES

LIMITED-OVERS MATCHES
Highest innings total for County   176 for 9 v. Glamorgan (RAL), 1987
Highest innings total against County   173 for 9 by Glamorgan (RAL), 1987
Highest individual innings for County   49 J.E. Morris v. Glamorgan (RAL), 1987
Highest individual innings against County   41 R.J. Shastri for Glamorgan (RAL), 1987
Best bowling performance for County   3 for 38 M. Jean-Jacques v. Glamorgan (RAL), 1987
Best bowling performance against County   3 for 25 S.R. Barwick for Glamorgan (RAL), 1987

HOW TO GET THERE

Rail   Blyth Bridge, 4 miles; Stoke-on-Trent, 9 miles
Bus   Potteries Motor Traction PMT X43, 247 Hanley–Cheadle (passing BR Blyth Bridge Station) (Tel: 0782 747000). Nos. 236, 232 Cheadle–Hanley
Car   8 miles east of Stoke-on-Trent M6 junctions 14 or 15. From north: A521 or A522 from A52, ground situated off A522. From east: A52 then A521 or A52 then B5032, then as north. From south: A522 from A50 then as north. From west: A521 from A50 then as north.

WHERE TO STAY AND OTHER INFORMATION

The Manor, High Street, The Wheatsheaf, High Street (or in Stoke-on-Trent)

Disabled Areas   Use members and officials' entrance for access, then request suitable position
Local Radio Station(s)   BBC Radio Stoke-on-Trent (94.6 MHz FM/ 1503 KHz MW), Radio Signal 102.6 MHz FM/1170 KHz MW), Radio Trent (96.2 MHz FM/999 KHz MW)
Local Newspaper(s)   Derby Evening Telegraph, Cheadle and Tean Times, Cheadle Post and Times, Evening Sentinel

Ilkeston

Derbyshire visit the Rutland Recreation Ground, Ilkeston once a season and made their first visit in 1925 two months after the ground was re-opened. Nearby visitors Nottinghamshire were the opponents. The ground is the home of Ilkeston Rutland C C which was founded in 1829 and played at Market Street behind St Mary's Church and Lawn Cottage until the Duke of Rutland allowed the club the use of a field in the Pimlico district of the town. Eight years later the ground was leased to the corporation on the understanding that it would be developed for recreational purposes. When King George V visited the town in 1914 the ground was given to the corporation to commemorate his visit. Six years later the ground was extended. The County have also staged limited-overs matches on the ground, the most recent being against Gloucestershire in the 1987 Refuge Assurance Sunday League. A number of club players have represented the county including the Attenborough brothers, Tilson and Paxton. More recently there were Cliff Gladwin, Jackson, Dawkes and Lee. The ground is now owned by Erewash District Council which maintains the whole area. The ground is saucer-shaped and provides a natural banking around the arena extending to 20 acres. The only permanent buildings on the ground are the pavilion built after the 1914–18 War and the scoreboard/groundsman accommodation. There are also facilities for tennis, football, bowling and golf (putting) and during the winter months the Ilkeston Ladies Vaders and Derby Ladies hockey clubs use the cricket club's facilities. In 1979 a 150th anniversary match was staged between Frank Nicklin's XI and Ilkeston Rutland C C. Crowds have been quite good over the years. Possibly the largest were 8,000 against Somerset in 1977 and 10,000 against Nottinghamshire in 1948. A jubilee match was staged in 1977 between the Mayor's XI and Derbyshire C C C.

Ilkestonians refer to the ground, which forms part of the 2,000 acres former estate of the Duke of Rutland, as the 'Queen of the Erewash Valley', certainly a picturesque title for this excellent cricket ground.

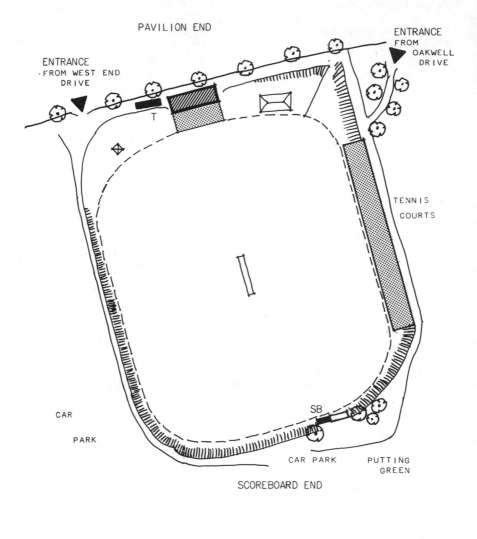

PAVILION END

ENTRANCE FROM WEST END DRIVE

ENTRANCE FROM OAKWELL DRIVE

T

TENNIS COURTS

CAR PARK

SB

CAR PARK

PUTTING GREEN

SCOREBOARD END

N

0   50   100

Metres

ADDRESS Ilkeston Rutland C C, Recreation Ground, Oakwell Drive, Ilkeston, Derbyshire
TELEPHONE PROSPECTS OF PLAY 0602 303036

DESCRIPTION OF GROUND AND FACILITIES

The Ilkeston ground is entered off West End Drive for members and cars and from Oakwell Drive for the public and members on foot. Car parking is available for some 85 cars in a position to view the cricket and there is plenty of street parking close by and in the town centre car parks. Some cars can be parked to the west of the ground on the football field.

The only permanent buildings are the pavilion and the scoreboard/groundsman's building which are situated at opposite ends of the playing area. To the west are the public enclosures and to the east a terrace with permanent seating. The north or West End Drive end of the ground includes a store/equipment area, Derbyshire C C S C tent and a refreshment tent which is situated within the members' area and adjoining the pavilion. The south side includes a scoreboard and T V camera positions. Both the press box and radio commentary positions are situated in the scorebox building. Ample toilets can be found close to the bowling green on the Oakwell Drive side of the ground and at the rear of the pavilion.

The ground is situated in a bowl with ample banking from which to view the field. The playing area is 163 metres by 133 metres and is defined by a rope and boards. Seating for only about 2,500 is provided so spectators are advised to bring their own for attractive matches. Part of the terracing area is fitted with benches. Ample refreshment stalls exist but alcohol is sold only to members. The surrounding trees and buildings are fairly close to the ground, as are some busy traffic routes.

GROUND RECORDS AND SCORES

FIRST-CLASS MATCHES
Highest innings total for County 529 for 7 dec. v. Nottinghamshire, 1952
Highest innings total against County 443 by South Africans, 1935
Lowest innings total for County 62 v. Somerset, 1936
Lowest innings total against County 72 by Nottinghamshire, 1958
Highest individual innings for County 217 E.J. Barlow v. Surrey, 1976
Highest individual innings against County 234 n.o. John Langridge for Sussex, 1949
Best bowling performance in an innings for County 8 for 8/ A.G. Slater v. Essex, 1931
Best bowling performance in an innings against County 9 for 50 A.P. Freeman for Kent, 1930

Best bowling performance in a match for County 12 for 101
G.H. Pope *v.* Nottinghamshire, 1947
Best bowling performance in a match against County 14 for 113
R. Harman for Surrey, 1968

LIMITED-OVERS MATCHES
Highest innings total for County 222 for 5 *v.* Warwickshire (BHC),
1978
Highest innings total against County 248 for 4 by Somerset (GC),
1977
Lowest innings total for County 119 *v.* Essex (JPL), 1976
Lowest innings total against County 105 for 8 by Glamorgan (JPL),
1972
Highest individual innings for County 102 n.o. A. Hill *v.*
Warwickshire (BHC), 1978
Highest individual innings against County 128 B.C. Rose for
Somerset (GC), 1977
Best bowling performance for County 6 for 24 A. Ward *v.* Essex
(JPL), 1976
Best bowling performance against County 5 for 30 J. Garner for
Somerset (GC), 1977

HOW TO GET THERE

Rail Langley Mill, 4 miles; Nottingham Midland, 9 miles
Bus Barton 4, 18, 51 from Nottingham, Broad Marsh – close BR
Nottingham Station (Tel: 0602 254881)
Car From north: M1 junction 26 then A610 and A6096 to
Ilkeston, ground situated in town centre off A6007. From east:
A609 then as north. From south: M1 junction 25 then A52 to
Stapleford then A609, then as north. From west: A609 or A6096
then as north.

WHERE TO STAY AND OTHER INFORMATION

Rutland Arms Hotel, Bath Street (0602 323259). Post House Hotel,
Sandiacre (0602 397800)

Disabled Areas No specific area although easy access is possible to
all parts of the ground for disabled, with the possible exception of
the main Pavilion Terrace
Local Radio Station(s) BBC Radio Derby (104.5 MHz FM/1116 KHz
MW), BBC Radio Nottingham (95.5 MHz FM/1584 KHz MW), Radio
Trent (96.2 MHz FM/999 KHz MW)
Local Newspaper(s) Derby Evening Telegraph, Nottingham
Evening Post, Ilkeston Advertiser

Knypersley

The ground is located off the A527 trunk road between Congleton and Stoke-on-Trent at Knypersley and forms part of the Victoria and Knypersley Social Welfare Centre. The Knypersley club was founded in 1870 and cricket has been played on the ground ever since, despite its geographical location in a basin.

The pavilion is of black and white timber and stands on a bank high above the square at right angles to the wicket. The Latin words *Floriat Knyperslium* are displayed on the pavilion above the entrance doors. Knypersley Cricket Club plays in the North Staffordshire and South Cheshire Cricket League and has 2 elevens throughout the season. The ground is shared with the Social Welfare football team and there are fine facilities for bowling and tennis. The scoreboard and the Old Pavilion Clubhouse are the only other permanent buildings on the ground. The Hall includes the bar and games room of the Social Welfare Centre.

The first match played here by Derbyshire was in 1985 when a John Player Sunday League fixture was staged with Worcestershire. The county returned with the same opponents in 1988 for a Refuge Assurance Sunday League match. In 1985 Derbyshire hit 18 sixes here in the innings against Worcestershire. This still stands as a record in the Sunday League. The ground is also used by Staffordshire for home Minor County matches.

The two matches Derbyshire staged here have attracted crowds of 3,500–4,000. The current ground capacity is set at 5,000.

ADDRESS Knypersley C C, Victoria & Knypersley Social Welfare Centre, Tunstall Road, Knypersley, Staffordshire
TELEPHONE PROSPECTS OF PLAY 0782 513304

DESCRIPTION OF GROUND AND FACILITIES

Access to the ground is from Tunstall Road only for pedestrians and cars. The football ground area is used for car parking (about 100 spaces) as is the next field, if dry, and the local council car park a short walk from the ground. The only permanent building is the pavilion which houses changing rooms, refreshments for members, and the toilets and showers. The press are located in a tent near to the scorers adjoining the scoreboard. The pavilion and seating within the fenced area is for members only; from where there is a fine view of the playing area down the slope at right angles to the wicket. On the south side of the ground are refreshment facilities, toilets and the Derbyshire C C S C tent. The other buildings close to the entrance are the Old Pavilion and the social club, which houses the bar and toilets.

The playing area is 142 metres by 120 metres and oval. Around 500 seats are provided around the pavilion. This is a very pleasant ground and despite being close to a main road appears rural compared with other grounds used by the county.

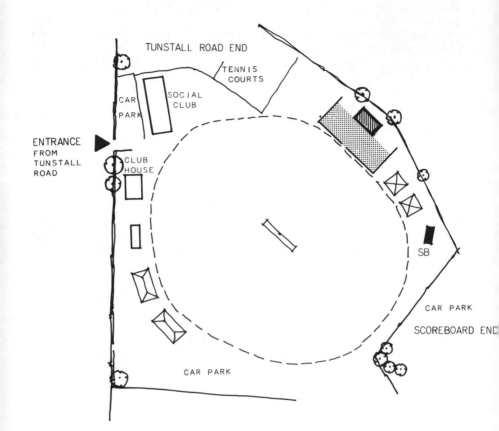

TUNSTALL ROAD END

TENNIS COURTS

SOCIAL CLUB

CAR PARK

ENTRANCE
FROM
TUNSTALL
ROAD

CLUB HOUSE

SB

CAR PARK

SCOREBOARD END

CAR PARK

N

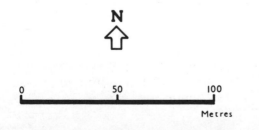

0   50   100

Metres

GROUND RECORDS AND SCORES

LIMITED-OVERS MATCHES

Highest innings total for County   292 for 9 v. Worcestershire (JPL), 1985
Highest innings total against County   280 for 9 by Worcestershire (RAL), 1988
Lowest innings total for County   211 v. Worcestershire (RAL), 1988
Lowest innings total against County   259 for 8 by Worcestershire (JPL), 1985
Highest individual innings for County   70 B. Roberts v. Worcestershire (JPL), 1985
Highest individual innings against County   91 P.A. Neale for Worcestershire (RAL), 1988
Best bowling performance for County   5 for 39 A.E. Warner v. Worcestershire (JPL), 1985
Best bowling performance for County   4 for 37 S.M. McEwan for Worcestershire (RAL), 1988

HOW TO GET THERE

Rail   Congleton or Kidsgrove, both 4 miles
Bus   Crosville K87/8 from BR Congleton Station (Tel: 0270 505350); PMT 6A/B from Hanley or 98, 96 from BR Longport Station (Tel: 0782 747000)
Car   10 miles north of Stoke-on-Trent, M6 junctions 15 or 18. From north: M6 junction 18 then A54, A527 to Biddulph, ground situated off A527 at Knypersley. From east: A54 and A527 then as north. From south: M6 junction 15 then A500 and A527 then as north. From west: A53 to Stoke-on-Trent then A527 then as north.

WHERE TO STAY AND OTHER INFORMATION

Lion & Swan Hotel, Congleton (0260 273115)

Disabled Areas   No special area, request position
Local Radio Station(s)   BBC Radio Stoke-on-Trent (94.6 MHz FM/ 1503 KHz MW), Radio Signal (102.6 MHz FM/1170 KHz MW), Radio Trent (96.2 MHz FM/999 KHz MW)
Local Newspaper(s)   Derby Evening Telegraph, Evening Sentinel, Biddulph and Congleton Chronicle

Leek

The ground is the home of Leek Town Cricket Club, which was founded in 1844. It has been the club's ground since 1919, when Leek and Leek Highfield amalgamated, mainly because so many members

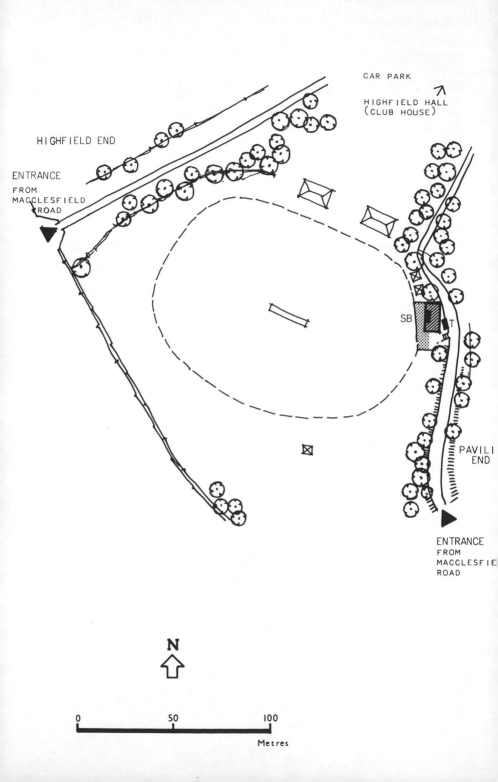

CAR PARK

HIGHFIELD HALL
(CLUB HOUSE)

HIGHFIELD END

ENTRANCE
FROM
MACCLESFIELD
ROAD

SB

T

PAVILI
END

ENTRANCE
FROM
MACCLESFIE
ROAD

N

0   50   100

Metres

had lost their lives in the Great War. The ground is situated off the main A523 Leek to Macclesfield road and is on the edge of the town as you enter from the north. The cricket field occupies part of the grounds of Highfield Hall (now the main clubhouse). The club has its own cricket pavilion located closer to the field of play.

The club has staged a number of significant matches, including a match with All India in 1931 when Syd Barnes and C.J. Taylor, whose combined ages were 110 years, between them dismissed the All India team. Taylor took 7 for 51 and 3 for 50 and Barnes 2 for 56 and 3 for 29. The ground is used rent-free, thanks to the generosity of Mr John Tatton who first allowed this in 1944.

The club plays in the North Staffordshire and South Cheshire Cricket League and has 3 elevens. The first Derbyshire visit was in 1986 for a John Player League match with Warwickshire which proved a success. Derbyshire are to return in 1989 as part of the round-robin matches staged in Staffordshire.

It is necessary to bring your own seats as only 400 are provided. The capacity is 3,000; 2,500 people attended the Warwickshire match in 1986 and a similar crowd came when the racehorse Red Rum appeared at a donkey derby!

A benefit match was staged by the club in 1961 for John MacMahon when Keith Miller guested and some 3,500 people attended. It was the best crowd ever seen on the ground. The most recent Test star to play for the club was Athula Samarasekera, the Sri Lankan all-rounder, in 1985.

ADDRESS Leek Town C C, The Club House, Highfield Hall, Macclesfield Road, Leek, Staffordshire
TELEPHONE PROSPECTS OF PLAY 0583 383693

DESCRIPTION OF GROUND AND FACILITIES

Entry to the ground is from Macclesfield Road (A523) for pedestrians and cars. Car parking is available on the grass in front of Highfield Hall, the clubhouse. The pavilion includes a scoreboard facility and limited seating for members; there is an adjacent fenced enclosure.

This is a very pleasant tree-enclosed ground with views of the surrounding fine countryside southwards. The north side of the ground is slightly sloping from the Hall down towards the cricket field where refreshment tents and toilets are situated. Also on this side of the ground is the radio/press point. On the Macclesfield Road side of the ground is the Derbyshire C C S C caravan and some permanent timber seating.

Additional car parking is available at Leek Town F C and the hockey pitches within walking distance from the ground. The playing area is 140 metres by 103 metres and is defined by a rope.

There is no covered accommodation except inside the pavilion or Highfield Hall which is some distance from the playing area.

GROUND RECORDS AND SCORES

LIMITED-OVERS MATCHES

Highest innings total for County   132 v. Warwickshire (JPL), 1986
Highest innings total against County   133 for 5 by Warwickshire (JPL), 1986
Highest individual innings for County   43 A. Hill v. Warwickshire (JPL), 1986
Highest individual innings against County   37 n.o. B.M. McMillan for Warwickshire (JPL), 1986
Best bowling performance for County   2 for 32 O.H. Mortensen v. Warwickshire (JPL), 1986
Best bowling performance against County   3 for 22 B.M. McMillan for Warwickshire (JPL), 1986

HOW TO GET THERE

Rail   Congleton, 8 miles
Bus   PMT 218 BR Stoke-on-Trent Station–Leek, thence 1 mile walk to ground (Tel: 0782 747000)
Car   10 miles north-east of Stoke-on-Trent M6 junctions 15 or 16. From north: A523 or A53 to Leek, ground situated off A523 on northern town outskirts. From east: A523 and A52 then as north. From south: A523 or A520 then as north. From west: A53 then as north.

WHERE TO STAY AND OTHER INFORMATION

The Jester, Mill Street (0538 383997). Peak Weaver, King Street. Red Lion Hotel, Market Square

---

Disabled Areas   Area roped off for special matches
Local Radio Station(s)   Radio Stoke-on-Trent (94.6 MHz FM/1503 KHz MW), Radio Signal (102.6 MHz FM/1170 KHz MW), Radio Trent (96.2 MHz FM/999 KHz MW)
Local Newspaper(s)   Derby Evening Telegraph, Leek Post and Times, Evening Sentinel

---

Repton

The ground is located within the remains of the twelfth century Augustinian Priory on the middle reaches of the River Trent, which today forms part of Repton School. The pitch is located close to the school buildings where First Eleven matches are staged, and bounded by Brook End (known as the Boot End because of the public house of that name) and Willington Road. The priory was destroyed at the

Reformation of the monasteries. The executors of Sir John Port paid £37 10s. for those buildings which survived; these now form the buildings of Repton School, which was founded in 1557. The former kitchen garden of the priory was converted in the nineteenth century to a splendid cricket ground.

It is a beautiful setting for cricket and, only the second school ground to be used by the county club (the first was Trent College, Long Eaton in the late 1970s). Derbyshire first staged a Refuge Assurance Sunday League fixture at the ground in 1988 when Middlesex with John D. Carr, a former pupil, were the visitors. The match was witnessed by a 2,500 crowd.

Repton School has plenty of cricket history. Three previous Derbyshire captains attended the school: D.B. Carr, D.J. Green and G.L. Willatt. Repton can justifiably claim to having produced one of the greatest schoolboy cricketers of all time, J.N. Crawford (1902–05) who subsequently played for Surrey and England. An earlier Golden Age of Repton was represented by the play of C.B. Fry, often described as one of the most talented of all English athletes. Before World War One, Miles and John Howell maintained the line of outstanding Repton cricketers playing county cricket. John was killed in 1915, and the John Howell Room in the cricket pavilion commemorates him.

Other famous cricketers who played for the school are: R.A. Young, H.S. Altham (the cricket author), A.T. Sharp, E.A. and W.T. Greswell, R. Sale, L.C.H. and R.C.N. Palairet, B.H. Valentine, R.H.C. Human, and R.A. Hutton not forgetting the brothers Ford (A.F.J., F.G.J. and W.J.) The current master in charge of cricket is Mike Stones. Tours have been arranged to Barbados with the old Boys' team, the Repton Pilgrims.

ADDRESS   Repton School, Willington Road, Repton DE6 6FH
TELEPHONE PROSPECTS OF PLAY   0283 701921

DESCRIPTION OF GROUND AND FACILITIES

The only entrance to the Repton ground is from Willington Road through the main gates near to St Wystan's Church. Limited car parking is available within the ground but only for players and officials. A large car park is available at the rear of the chapel and main school buildings, a short walk from the cricket pitch. In the ground itself, the only permanent buildings are the pavilion with its thatched roof and the scoreboard on the east side of the ground. The members' area and refreshment tents are located on the steep bank close to the school buildings as is the Derbyshire C C C S C caravan. The remainder of the ground is open for the public.

All spectators should bring their own collapsible seats as no seats are provided whatsoever, except adjoining the front of the pavilion for the press. There is no space for seating at the Brook End as the playing area is tight against the perimeter wall.

The north and east sides of the ground are lined with trees which, with the school buildings, provide a fine scene for cricket. The playing

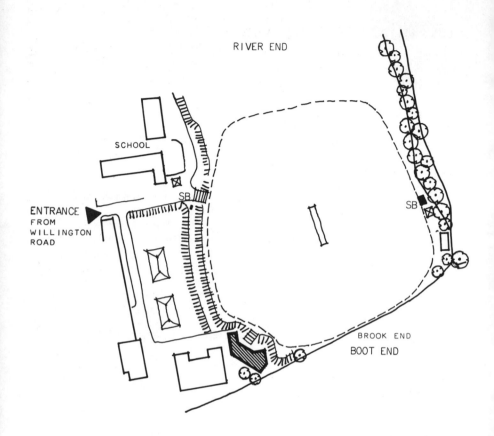

RIVER END

SCHOOL

SB

ENTRANCE
FROM
WILLINGTON
ROAD

SB

BROOK END

BOOT END

N

0   50   100

Metres

area is 115 metres by 120 metres and is defined only by advertisement boards.

GROUND RECORDS AND SCORES

LIMITED-OVERS MATCHES
Highest innings total for County   130 *v.* Middlesex (RAL), 1988
Highest innings total against County   32 for 0 by Middlesex (RAL), 1988
Highest individual innings for County   61 S.C. Goldsmith *v.* Middlesex (RAL), 1988
Highest individual innings against County   15 n.o. J.D. Carr for Middlesex (RAL), 1988
Best bowling performance for County   0 for 9 A.E. Warner *v.* Middlesex (RAL), 1988
Best bowling performance against County   3 for 8 A.R.C. Fraser for Middlesex (RAL), 1988

HOW TO GET THERE

Rail   Burton-upon-Trent, 5 miles
Bus   Trent 103/4 Derby Bus Station–Burton-upon-Trent (passing ½ mile from BR Burton-upon-Trent Station, also Derby City 42–7 link BR Derby Station with Bus Station) (Tel: 0332 292200)
Car   5 miles north-east of Burton-upon-Trent. From north: A38 and A5008 to Repton, ground situated off Willington Road adjoining school buildings. From east: A50 and A5132 then B5008 then as north. From south: A38, A50 and B5008 then as north. From west: A50 or A5132 then B5008 then as north.

WHERE TO STAY AND OTHER INFORMATION

Bulls Head, High Street (0283 703297)

Disabled Areas   No special area, request position
Local Radio Station(s)   BBC Radio Derby (104.5 MHz FM/1116 KHz MW), Radio Trent (96.2 MHz FM/999 KHz MW)
Local Newspaper(s)   Derby Evening Telegraph, Burton Mail

ESSEX

CHELMSFORD

COLCHESTER

ILFORD

SOUTHEND-ON-SEA

Essex

It took Essex 103 years to land their first championship, and less than a decade to confirm their status as arguably the best team, and the best led in the land. From the breakthrough season of 1979 until 1986 homely Essex, who had never won a first-class competition and were rarely in a challenging position, won the championship four times, the Benson and Hedges Cup, the NatWest Trophy and the John Player Sunday League three times. Twice they were beaten Benson and Hedges finalists by margins of 6 and 4 runs.

Fletcher, the wily campaigner, rightly acclaimed for his rare tactical insight, became the first captain to carry off all four major competitions. Three of the championships were under him, the other under Gooch, and it is generally considered a folly that his captaincy of England was confined to the tour of India and Sri Lanka in 1981–2. A dozen or so years of far-seeing preparation produced the Fletcher team of class and adaptability, and he owed a lot to wise stewardship, a new and firm financial base, a permanent focal-point home at Chelmsford, a devoted following, and the enthusiasm of his predecessor, Taylor, who handed on playing quality and confidence.

Essex have always played with spirit and enterprise, and the modern attitude was born in the watershed 'sixties when the club was in such low financial water that the playing staff was reduced to twelve without the Test all-rounder Knight, who had moved to Leicestershire.

Historic events need a starting point, and the acquisition of the Chelmsford ground began the rise to glory. But for a chance remark by Trevor Bailey, a man of many parts in his 21-year association, at a dinner to celebrate Worcestershire's 1965 championship the opportunity to buy the land might have passed by. The happy sequel was an interest-free loan by the Warwickshire CCC Supporters' Association. Seldom has the chivalry between one club and another been better illustrated or more opportune.

Brentwood was the club's first home from 1876–85. The batting heroes were Perrin, whose record run aggregate for Essex was passed by Fletcher, and it is still said that Kortright was the fastest bowler ever known. Oddly Perrin and Kortright, who clean bowled 226 of his 319 wickets between 1885 and 1888, never played for England. Just after the second war Kortright declared he would have been afraid to have bowled to the batsmen of the day. 'I'd have cut 'em in half', he said.

Spinner Head, who played against Australia in 1899, was the first to take 100 wickets in a season for the county. J.W.H.T. ('Johnny Won't Hit Today') Douglas was one of the dominant personalities. A fine swing bowler and obdurate batsman he captained England in Australia and South Africa, and Essex from 1911 to 1928 – his highest place was 6th – and as a diversion from cricket won the middle-weight boxing title at the 1908 Olympics. He was drowned trying to rescue his father as their ship sank after a collision in thick fog.

ESSEX COUNTY C.C.

Russell was the first England batsman to score a century in each innings in a Test match, against South Africa in 1922–3 at Durban – where Insole, another of the club's mainstays on and off the field, also hit a century for England 34 years later.

When Leyton was vacated in 1933 the team took to the road, and the circus trundled around nine different club grounds. There was no show like it on the county circuit. The equipment accompanying the team included hundreds of yards of seven-foot high screening with poles, marquees, tents, temporary stands, sundry seating, a press to print score cards, a heavy roller, a mobile office and two pensioned off double decker buses serving as a score board and a ladies toilet.

Perhaps the constant change of wickets was a handicap, but Essex's reputation for inconsistency was long established. Perrin had the experience of scoring 343 not out, containing a record 68 fours, out of a total of 597 at Chesterfield in 1904 and finishing on the losing side by 9 wickets. On the same ground Peter Smith, who was considerably better than his allotted No. 11 position, and Vigar scored 218 in 140 minutes for the 10th wicket. Smith's contribution was 163.

A famous performance saw Yorkshire beaten by an innings before one o'clock on the second morning at Huddersfield in 1935. Nichols (4 for 17, Read 6 for 11) tumbled Yorkshire out for 31. In Essex's 334 Nichols hit 146 and proceeded to take 7 for 37 when Yorkshire were dismissed for 99 in their second innings. Nichols did the double in five successive seasons and was one of five pace bowlers of the time, including Farnes, England's choice in fifteen Tests. He lost his life in a flying accident in the war.

One of Essex's most impressive runs came in the late 'thirties, and but for Hitler's intervention they might have not had to wait so long to strike gold.

Essex played it hard but never so hard as not to have room for a laugh. 'I played frequently against them in those days of their progress to the unknown' wrote former Glamorgan captain Tony Lewis in *Wisden.* 'They had a quality which shone through even their worst performance – humour. They planned their one-day cricket like a war but played it like a party game.'

Pearce, an interested fielder during one of Compton's notorious running misadventures, observed Denis had three calls 'Yes', 'No', and 'Sorry', the first merely serving as a basis for negotiations. Canon F.H. Gillingham, a muscular batsman of the cloth, described his feeling after hitting a boundary off Yorkshire. 'I thought I was in Heaven,' he said and, after a pause, added, 'I just hope Heaven will last longer next time.'

At the burial of Walter Mead, the 'Essex treasure,' who took almost 2,000 wickets with spin, the Minister intoned the hope that he would find perfect pitches to bowl on in the Elysium Field. There was a horrified silence from his old team-mates and a whispered, 'That's the *last* thing he wants.'

Even Douglas did not escape a leg pull. A flying ball on a dodgy pitch at Colchester brushed his gloves and went on to strike his head. He collapsed on to the ground and when he got to his feet was given out. He strode off without a word, but let vent his wrath in the dressing room. 'I've got a bump as big as a pigeon's head. How could I have been out?' he stormed. Perrin turned from watching the play and with a straight face said: 'Leg before.'

Pearce was a splendid influence in the re-building, and Fletcher, Gooch, Lever and Foster were among those who added to the long list of Essex players who served both their country and their county. [A.B.]

Founded   1876
Colours   Blue, gold and red
Crest   Three seaxes with word 'Essex' underneath
Secretary/General Manager   P. J. Edwards
Deputy Secretary/Manager   B. A. Chatterley
Groundsman   A. Atkinson
Scorer   C. F. Driver
Address   County Cricket Ground, New Writtle Street, Chelmsford CM2 0PG
Telephone 0245 354533
Cricketcall   0898 121416

Achievements:

County Championship   Champions (4) 1979, 1983, 1984 and 1986
Gillette Cup   Semi-Finalists 1978
National Westminster Bank Trophy   Winners 1985
Benson & Hedges Cup   Winners 1979
John Player Sunday League   Champions (3) 1981, 1984 and 1985

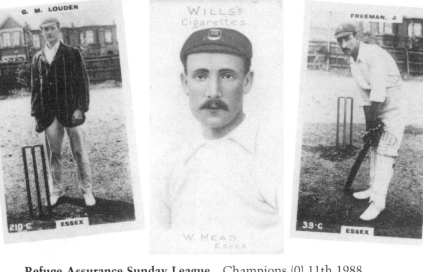

Refuge Assurance Sunday League Champions (0) 11th 1988
Fenner Trophy Finalists 1977 and 1981
Asda Trophy Finalists 1986
Ward Knockout Cup Winners 1988

Grounds:

Chelmsford (County Cricket Ground, New Writtle Street) Ilford (Valentine's Park, Cranbrook Road) Southend-on-Sea (Southchurch Park, Northumberland Road) Colchester (Castle Park, Sportsway off Catchpool Road)

   Other grounds that have been used since 1969 are: Colchester (Garrison 'A' Ground, Napier Road), Brentwood (Old County Ground, Shenfield Road), Harlow (Sportscentre, Hammarskjold Road), Leyton (Leyton High Road Youth Sports Ground, High Road), Westcliff-on-Sea (Chalkwell Park) and Purfleet (Thames Board Mills Sports Ground).

Chelmsford

The County Ground, New Writtle Street has been the headquarters of Essex cricket since 1967 and the majority of the county club's matches are staged there. The ground had been used previously by Essex in 1926–39, 1946–48 and 1950–56 as Chelmsford C C rented the ground annually from the Wenley Trust. In those days the county headquarters was at Leyton.

   Other matches in Chelmsford have been staged at Hoffman's Athletic Ground in 1959 and 1961.

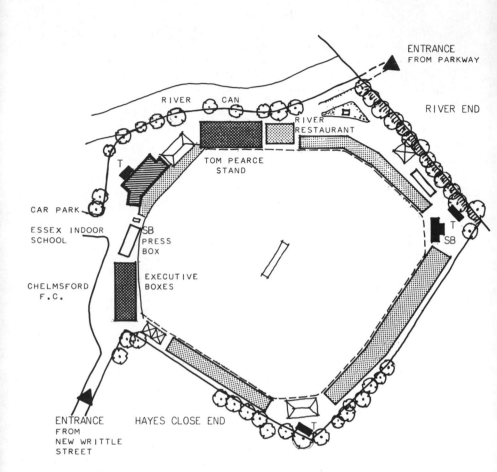

ENTRANCE
FROM PARKWAY

RIVER END

RIVER CAN

RIVER
RESTAURANT

TOM PEARCE
STAND

T

CAR PARK

ESSEX INDOOR
SCHOOL

SB
PRESS
BOX

T
SB

CHELMSFORD
F.C.

EXECUTIVE
BOXES

ENTRANCE
FROM
NEW WRITTLE
STREET

HAYES CLOSE END

T

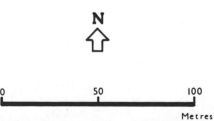

N

0   50   100
Metres

The ground is situated barely half a mile from where the rivers Can and Chelmer meet and the River Can passes alongside the ground at the Town End. In February 1964, assisted by a loan from the Warwickshire C C S C, Essex were able to purchase the ground for £15,000. Much development has taken place since then; about £750,000 has been spent to build a pavilion (which was completed in 1970) and other stands. Much of the facilities are now permanent. The ground was without a permanent scoreboard until 1981 when an attractive building was erected by Wimpey Construction.

Essex first staged a county championship match here in 1926 against Somerset, at a time when most matches were still staged at Leyton. It is a compact ground for a county headquarters, but much has been made of the space available. The ground slopes from south-east to south-west and since the installation of a drainage system in 1982 is known as one of the best-drained grounds on the county circuit. Previously the ground was liable to flood because of the close proximity of the River Can and the high water table. The cricket field was for some time used as an emergency helicopter pad for the nearby hospital, until the casualty department was moved elsewhere in the town.

Many memorable performances have taken place here, including Ken McEwan's 218 against Sussex in 1977 and Surrey's lowest innings of 14 in 1983. This is the lowest total ever recorded by opponents on an Essex ground. Graham Gooch has hit two scores of 138 in limited-overs matches against Warwickshire and Somerset in the Benson and Hedges Cup.

The Chelmsford City Football Club is located close to the ground and provides car parking for matches. Crowds of 6,500 are usual and the ground capacity is set at 9,500. This is regularly attained for popular games. The ground hosted international cricket in 1983 when a Prudential Cup match was staged between Australia and India.

ADDRESS County Cricket Ground, New Writtle Street, Chelmsford CM2 0PG
TELEPHONE PROSPECTS OF PLAY 0245 287921

DESCRIPTION OF GROUND AND FACILITIES

Entry to the ground for both pedestrians and members' cars is from New Writtle Street. There is another entrance for pedestrians off Parkway and under the bridge over the River Can. Main car parking is in the multistorey car park on the north side of the River Can.

All the permanent buildings have been built over the past twelve years and occupy the west and north sides of the ground, the areas of the ground allocated to members. The pavilion contains the players' accommodation on the first floor with a members' bar and lounge below. The Tom Pearce Stand and the adjoining River Restaurant Stand provide open seating at first-floor level and probably provide the best view of the cricket. The scoreboard is on the east side, whilst the west side has an executive suite and executive boxes for entertaining. All other seating is open, with some areas of raised seating. Some 6,500 seats are provided. There are two club shops and ample bars and facilities for refreshments. There is little cover in the event of bad weather. Toilets are situated in various parts of the ground; facilities for disabled persons are in the pavilion.

The playing area, which is defined by advertisement boards, is about 132 metres by 128 metres but is reduced on the north side in front of the Tom Pearce Stand due to the proximity of the nearby river. Chelmsford is a pleasant tree-surrounded ground on which much work has been done in recent years.

GROUND RECORDS AND SCORES

FIRST-CLASS MATCHES

Highest innings total for County 592 for 9 dec. v. Leicestershire, 1988

Highest innings total against County 634 for 7 by Middlesex, 1983

Lowest innings total for County 65 v. Worcestershire, 1947 and 1973

Lowest innings total against County 14 by Surrey, 1983

Highest individual innings for County 218 K.S. McEwan v. Sussex, 1977

Highest individual innings against County 244 W.R. Hammond for Gloucestershire, 1928

Best bowling performance in an innings for County 9 for 59 M.S. Nichols v. Hampshire, 1927

Best bowling performance in an innings against County 8 for 155 C.W.L. Parker for Gloucestershire, 1928

Best bowling performance in a match for County 13 for 117 J.K. Lever v. Leicestershire, 1979

Best bowling performance in a match against County 11 for 235 C.W.L. Parker for Gloucestershire, 1928

LIMITED-OVERS MATCHES

Highest innings total for County 350 for 3 v. Combined Universities (BHC), 1979

Highest innings total against County 274 for 8 by Kent (NWBT), 1983

Lowest innings total for County 99 v. Worcestershire (JPL), 1973

Lowest innings total against County 58 by Somerset (JPL), 1971

Highest individual innings for County 138 G.A. Gooch v. Warwickshire (BHC), 1979 and v. Somerset (BHC), 1981

Highest individual innings against County 124 B.W. Luckhurst for Kent (JPL), 1973

Best bowling performance for County 5 for 12 D.R. Pringle v. Oxfordshire (NWBT), 1985

Best bowling performance against County 6 for 16 P.J. Hacker for Nottinghamshire (JPL), 1980

HOW TO GET THERE

Rail Chelmsford, ½ mile
Bus From surrounding areas to Bus Station, thence ½ mile
Car From north: M1 junction 8 then A120 and A130 to
Chelmsford, ground situated close to town centre, on the southern
bank of the River Cam, in New Writtle Street off Parkway (A130).
From east: A414 or A12 or A130 then as north. From south: M25
junction 28 then A12 to Chelmsford then as north. From west:
A414 or as from south, then as north.

WHERE TO STAY AND OTHER INFORMATION

County Hotel (0245 266911), Beechcroft Hotel (0245 352462), South
Lodge Hotel (0245 264564) – all within walking distance

Disabled Areas No restrictions – wheelchairs may be a problem
Local Radio Station(s) Greater London Radio (94.9 MHz FM/1458
KHz MW), BBC Essex (103.5 MHz FM/765 KHz MW), Essex Radio
(96.3 MHz FM/1431 KHz MW)
Local Newspaper(s) Essex Chronicle, Chelmsford Weekly News,
Yellow Advertiser

Colchester

The Castle Park ground is the home of the Colchester and East Essex
C C, which was founded in 1862 and fields 2 elevens throughout the
season. The ground is located off Cathpool Road very close to the
River Colne, which flows around the ground at the southern end.

Castle Park is the second ground used by the County in Colchester.
The Military Garrison 'A' ground was used from 1920 to 31 and in
1958 due to flooding at Castle Park. A move to the Garrison was also
made during a championship match with Derbyshire in 1966. This
was to have been played at Castle Park, but after the first two days
had been washed out, the final day's play was transferred to the
Garrison ground. Castle Park is susceptible to flooding due to the high
water table. The ground is near the Castle Mound from which
parkland slopes away to the rich meadows of the valley and the
cricket field. Castle Park also suffers from poor weather and this is
well recorded in the club's history. In 1958 on the third day of a match
with Leicestershire the ground was totally submerged in water; chairs
and boundary boards floated across the ground and the Colchester
Secretary had to use waders to get about.

Essex first staged a championship match at Castle Park in 1914
when Worcestershire were the visitors. After a break of some years
Essex returned in 1934–9 and then after World War Two, in 1946.
Essex today take one limited-overs and two championship matches
to the ground, usually in August.

Colchester has one unique cricket record: it is the only ground on which a player has scored a double century in each innings of a match (Arthur Fagg for Kent in 1938). Castle Park was also a favourite ground of Doug Insole, who scored his only double century against Yorkshire in 1949. More recently Ken McEwan in four consecutive seasons scored over 500 runs on the ground including 181 and 189 in one week. Ground records have included centuries before lunch by Gordon Barker and Arthur Fagg, a career-best bowling performance by Peter Smith (9 for 77 against Middlesex in 1947) and an aggregate of 600 runs in a Sunday League match with Warwickshire in 1982. The pavilion was built in 1909.

Crowds of 5,000 are usual for most matches.

ADDRESS Colchester & East Essex C C, Castle Park (Lower), Sportsway, off Cathpool Road, Colchester, Essex
TELEPHONE PROSPECTS OF PLAY temporary line – refer to British Telecom (B T) Directory Enquiries

DESCRIPTION OF GROUND AND FACILITIES

The main entry to the Castle Park Ground is in the north-west corner off Catchpool Road. Car parking is in Kings Meadow to the west and along Sportsway to the east, where there are further entrances. There are also members' entrances near the pavilion.

The River Colne forms the southern boundary of the ground. Adjoining the river in the south-west corner is the pavilion, the only permanent building, which is some 50 metres from the playing area. All other facilities are temporary and include tiered seating for both members and the public. Generally the west side of the ground is allocated to sponsors' tents and entertainment areas while the public are allocated much of the east and north sides of the ground.

The playing area is approximately circular, being 132 metres by 128 metres, and is defined by advertisement boards. The scoreboard is the temporary travelling scoreboard used by the county club. The capacity of the ground is 6,000 and sufficient seats are provided. This is a pleasant park ground at which to watch cricket in good weather. There are no arrangements for disabled persons.

GROUND RECORDS AND SCORES

FIRST-CLASS MATCHES
Highest innings total for County   588 for 9 dec. v. Northamptonshire, 1937
Highest innings total against County   487 by Kent, 1946
Lowest innings total for County   44 v. Nottinghamshire, 1986
Lowest innings total against County   56 by Sussex, 1957
Highest individual innings for County   219 n.o. D.J. Insole v. Yorkshire, 1949

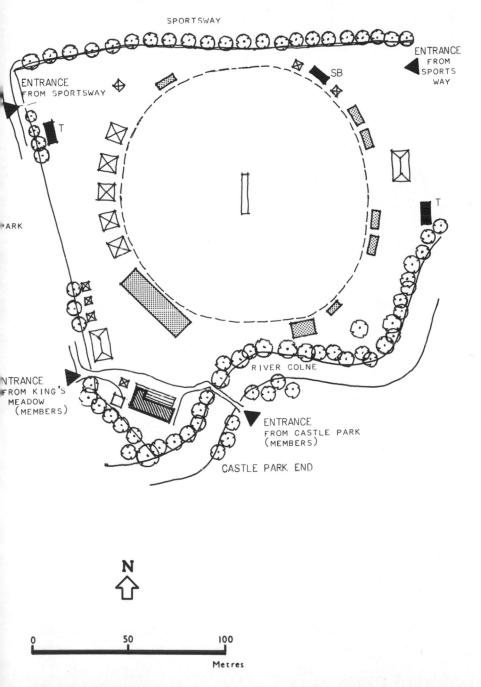

SPORTSWAY END

SPORTSWAY

ENTRANCE
FROM
SPORTS
WAY

ENTRANCE
FROM SPORTSWAY

SB

T

ARK

T

RIVER COLNE

NTRANCE
FROM KING'S
MEADOW
(MEMBERS)

ENTRANCE
FROM CASTLE PARK
(MEMBERS)

CASTLE PARK END

N

0   50   100

Metres

Highest individual innings against County   244 A. Fagg for Kent, 1938
Best bowling performance in an innings for County   9 for 77
T.P.B. Smith *v.* Middlesex, 1947
Best bowling performance in an innings against County   8 for 57
C.W.L. Parker for Gloucestershire, 1920
Best bowling performance in a match for County   16 for 215
T.P.B. Smith *v.* Middlesex, 1947
Best bowling performance in a match against County   12 for 59
C.I.J. Smith for Middlesex, 1936

LIMITED-OVERS MATCHES
Highest innings total for County   299 for 4 *v.* Warwickshire (JPL), 1982
Highest innings total against County   301 for 6 by Warwickshire (JPL), 1982
Lowest innings total for County   133 *v.* Yorkshire (JPL), 1979
Lowest innings total against County   123 by Derbyshire (JPL), 1985
Highest individual innings for County   156 n.o. K.S. McEwan *v.* Warwickshire (JPL), 1982
Highest individual innings against County   114 D.R. Turner for Hampshire (JPL), 1984
Best bowling performance for County   5 for 20 R.E. East *v.* Yorkshire (JPL), 1979
Best bowling performance against County   4 for 22 D.P. Hughes for Lancashire (JPL), 1975

HOW TO GET THERE

Rail   Colchester, ¾ mile
Bus   Eastern National and Colchester Corporation from surrounding areas to Bus Station, thence ¾m, though those from the north pass closer
Car   From north: A12 or A134 follow signs Colchester, then Castle Park off A12. From east: A120, A137 or A133 follow signs Colchester, then as north. From south: A12 to Colchester then as north or B1025 or B1026 then as north. From west: A120 or A604 to Colchester then as north, or follow A12 then as north.

WHERE TO STAY AND OTHER INFORMATION

George Hotel (0206 578494), Marks Tey Hotel (0206 210001)

Disabled Areas   No restrictions, but park is not concrete and wheelchairs may be a problem
Local Radio Station(s)   Essex Radio (96.3 MHz FM/1431 KHz MW), Radio Orwell (97.1 MHz FM/1170 KHz MW)
Local Newspaper(s)   Colchester Leader, Essex County Standard, Evening Gazette, Yellow Advertiser

Ilford

Valentine's Park is a public park and caters for many games; tennis courts and bowling greens are adjacent to the cricket field. It is one of the largest and most attractive parks in the east of Greater London. The park, which extends to 136 acres, used to surround the home of a Mrs Ingleby and it was from her that the Ilford C C obtained a lease in 1897 on roughly 8 acres to make the present ground. The only condition she demanded was that the pavilion should be built under the trees. Several years later she also insisted that the sightscreens be lowered so that they could not be seen from the windows of her home. In 1899 Ilford Council purchased a large part of the parkland and lake. In 1906, when Mrs Ingleby died, they purchased the remainder of the park including her house.

The ground is the home of Ilford C C (founded in 1879) and is also used by Ilford and Woodford R A F A formerly R A F A (Ilford) (established in 1951). Essex first played a match at Valentine's in 1923 when the West Indian touring team were the visitors. This first match against West Indies was also made conspicuous by the fact that the great Leary Constantine then only twenty-one, collected a pair! The ground lies on the west side of the park and today is the property of Redbridge Borough Council who maintain the grounds. The cricket week is eagerly looked forward to by the local cricket fraternity. A good relationship exists between Ilford C C and Essex County Club in the organization of the festival week. As the ground is such a pleasant venue for top-level cricket, it is not surprising that every first-class county and all the overseas touring countries except Pakistan and Sri Lanka have played on the ground. Essex have played on a number of club grounds and the Ilford ground in Valentine's Park will always rank as one of the most picturesque in the county.

Terracing along the Cranbrook Road side of the ground was built in 1949 in time for the visit of Glamorgan, the 1948 champions. A crowd of 13,000 including members was present on the Saturday; this was probably the largest crowd ever to watch a day's play at Valentine's Park. Crowds in recent years have been 5,000–6,000.

Since World War Two the groundsman has kept the middle of the square entirely free from use until the county cricket week, so that the Ilford week is usually held in the early part of the season. Today the County play two championship and one limited-overs match each season in mid-June. Valentine's Park was the first ground to stage a championship match on a Sunday – against Somerset in 1981. The first Sunday League match was against Middlesex in 1970; 8,000 people attended.

Players who have represented Ilford and Essex include G.M. Louden, J.K. Lever and G.A. Gooch.

ADDRESS Ilford C C, Valentine's Park, Cranbrook Road, Ilford, Essex
TELEPHONE PROSPECTS OF PLAY   01-554 8381

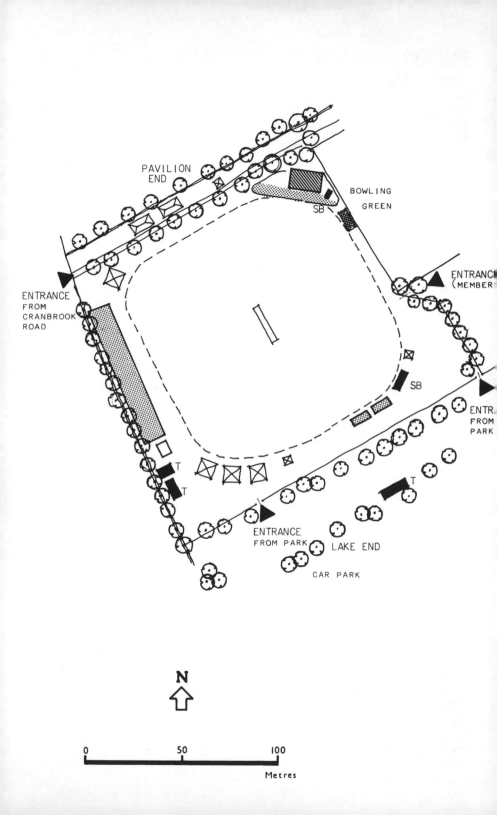

PAVILION
END

BOWLING
GREEN

SB

ENTRANCE
(MEMBERS)

ENTRANCE
FROM
CRANBROOK
ROAD

SB

ENTR.
FROM
PARK

T

T

T

ENTRANCE
FROM PARK

LAKE END

CAR PARK

N

0   50   100

Metres

DESCRIPTION OF GROUND AND FACILITIES

Members enter the ground from Cranbrook Road while the public go in through the two entrances in Valentine's Park to the south. Main car parking is in the adjoining streets. The only permanent structures are the pavilion and some grassed terracing on the Cranbrook Road side. All other facilities are temporary. Members' areas are to the north of the ground while the public areas are generally to the south. The playing area is approximately circular and comparatively small, being only 124 metres by 122 metres. Sponsors' tents are sited in the south-west corner of the ground, as is the Essex C C S C tent.

GROUND RECORDS AND SCORES

FIRST-CLASS MATCHES

Highest innings total for County 457 for 5 dec. v. Northamptonshire, 1978
Highest innings total against County 491 for 8 dec. by Lancashire, 1938
Lowest innings total for County 69 v. Somerset, 1924
Lowest innings total against County 64 by Worcestershire, 1982
Highest individual innings for County 186 K.S. McEwan v. Northamptonshire, 1978
Highest individual innings against County 181 G.S. Chappell for Australians, 1972
Best bowling performance in an innings for County 8 for 30 R.E. East v. Nottinghamshire, 1977
Best bowling performance in an innings against County 8 for 58 D.St.E. Atkinson for West Indians, 1957
Best bowling performance in a match for County 13 for 145 J.K. Lever v. Northamptonshire, 1978
Best bowling performance in a match against County 13 for 61 J.C. White for Somerset, 1924

LIMITED-OVERS MATCHES

Highest innings total for County 256 for 5 v. Hampshire (JPL), 1986
Highest innings total against County 257 for 4 by Hampshire (JPL), 1986
Lowest innings total for County 127 for 9 v. Lancashire (JPL), 1979
Lowest innings total against County 45 by Northamptonshire (JPL), 1971
Highest individual innings for County 123 K.S. McEwan v. Warwickshire (JPL), 1976
Highest individual innings against County 112 n.o. B.C. Rose for Somerset (JPL), 1980
Best bowling performance for County 5 for 22 B.E.A. Edmeades v. Leicestershire (BHC), 1973
Best bowling performance against County 5 for 32 W. Larkins for Northamptonshire (JPL), 1978

HOW TO GET THERE

Rail Ilford or Gants Hill (Central Line Underground), both ¾ mile
Bus LRT 123/9, 144, 150, 167, 179, 247, 296 (all passing BR Ilford
Station and Gants Hill Underground Station) (Tel: 01-222 1234)
Car 10 miles north-east of central London in the district of
Redbridge. From north: M25 junction 27, then M11 and A12 to
Gants Hill, then at roundabout follow Cranbrook Road, ground
situated off this road. From east: M25 junctions 28 or 29 then A12
or A126 to Ilford, ground situated close to A118, A1083 and A124,
then as north. From south: A13 then A117 and A124 to Ilford, then
as north. From west: A13 then A117 and A124 to Ilford, then as
north.

WHERE TO STAY AND OTHER INFORMATION

Cranbrook Hotel (01-554 6544). Park Hotel (01-554 9616)

Disabled Areas No restrictions, preferably by site screen or in
front of pavilion
Local Radio Station(s)s Greater London Radio (94.9 MHz FM/1458
KHz MW), Essex Radio (96.3 MHz FM/1431 KHz MW), Capital
Radio (95.8 MHz FM/1548 KHz MW), LBC (97.3 MHz FM/1152
KHz MW)
Local Newspaper(s) Ilford Independent, Ilford Recorder,
Walthamstow Guardian Group, Yellow Advertiser

Southend-on-Sea

Southend has two cricket grounds which have been used for first-class
cricket by the county club, Southchurch Park and Chalkwell Park at
Westcliff-on-Sea. Southchurch Park has recently regained favour at
the expense of Westcliff because it can accommodate larger crowds
and has plenty of space surrounding the cricket pitch.

Essex made their first visit to Southchurch Park in 1906 when the
visitors were Leicestershire; a copy of the scorecard of this first match
hangs in the pavilion today. Essex played off and on there until 1977,
since when all matches at Southend have been staged on the ground.
There are two pavilions at Southchurch Park. One is for players and
officials and the other belongs to the hockey club, who play on the
ground during winter. The ground is the home of the Southend-on-
Sea C C which was established in 1874. They have played here since
1895. The cricket pavilion was built in 1929 and the club plays in the
Essex League and fields 4 elevens on a Saturday and two on a Sunday.
It won the Essex Cricket League in 1981. Southchurch Park is now
owned and maintained by the local council. Incidentally, it was in the
ownership of the monks of Christ Church Canterbury from AD 823;

and it was on the Southchurch foreshore that the cultivation of oysters is said to have begun.

The ground is sufficiently large to allow two club games to be played simultaneously. There are three separate squares, of which the central one is used exclusively by the County. Essex now play two championship and one limited-overs match at Southend as a festival week, because Southchurch Park nearly always attracts a good crowd. It is a quiet park barely half a mile from the seafront, the crowded beach and a large boating lake. The largest crowd was 16,000 for the visit of the Australians in 1948, when the visitors scored 721 in a single day. Bradman's 187 was scored in 125 minutes. Crowds today are around 5,000.

The most recent piece of history made on the ground was in 1983 when Essex managed 310 for 5 against Glamorgan, (a Sunday League record innings total) and Graham Gooch scored 176 (a Sunday League individual innings record).

ADDRESS Southend-on-Sea C C, Southchurch Park, Northumberland Crescent, Southend-on-Sea, Essex
TELEPHONE PROSPECTS OF PLAY 0702 67876

DESCRIPTION OF GROUND AND FACILITIES

Entry to Southchurch Park can be gained from Northumberland Avenue to the north and from Kensington Road to the west. The ground is situated north of the boating lake and the two pavilions are on the north side of the lake. The pavilion to the south-west is used by the players and that on the south-east by the members. These, together with the terracing to the north and south of the ground, are the only permanent structures. Seating is provided for some 75 per cent of the capacity of 8,000. You are not encouraged to bring your own seats not least because there is no car parking available at the ground and it is necessary to find parking in the town. No provisions exist for disabled persons. The east side of the ground is allocated to sponsors' tents and the main refreshment areas for members. The north side is available to the public. There are temporary toilet facilities.

The playing area is usually about 170 metres by 123 metres and defined by advertisement boards. This is a well-maintained, tree-enclosed recreation ground and a good view of the cricket may be obtained from all parts of the ground.

GROUND RECORDS AND SCORES

FIRST-CLASS MATCHES
Highest innings total for County 503 v. Hampshire, 1936
Highest innings total against County 721 by Australians, 1948
Lowest innings total for County 56 v. West Indians, 1963
Lowest innings total against County 43 by Kent, 1925

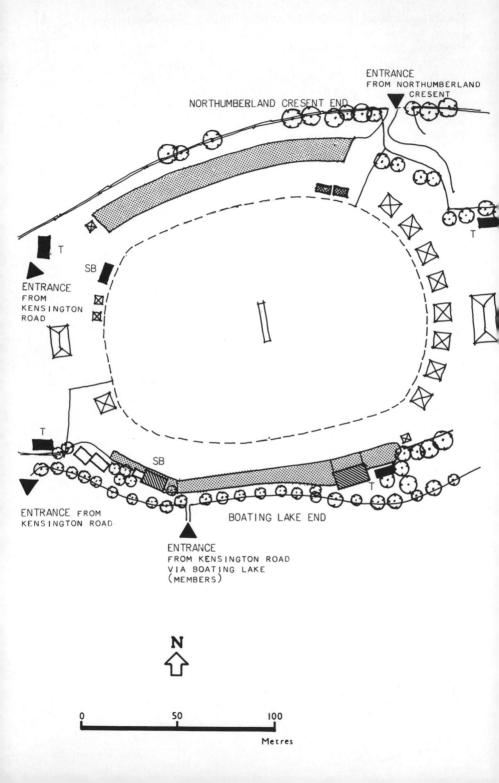

ENTRANCE
FROM NORTHUMBERLAND
CRESENT

NORTHUMBERLAND CRESENT END

ENTRANCE
FROM
KENSINGTON
ROAD

T

SB

T

T

SB

T

ENTRANCE FROM
KENSINGTON ROAD

BOATING LAKE END

ENTRANCE
FROM KENSINGTON ROAD
VIA BOATING LAKE
(MEMBERS)

N

0   50   100

Metres

Highest individual innings for County   205 M.S. Nichols *v.* Hampshire, 1936
Highest individual innings against County   255 n.o. H. Sutcliffe for Yorkshire, 1924
Best bowling performance in an innings for County   9 for 117 T.P.B. Smith *v.* Nottinghamshire, 1948
Best bowling performance in an innings against County   10 for 53 A.P. Freeman for Kent, 1930
Best bowling performance in a match for County   12 for 131 G.M. Louden *v.* Derbyshire, 1920
Best bowling performance in a match against County   16 for 94 A.P. Freeman for Kent, 1930

LIMITED-OVERS MATCHES
Highest innings total for County   310 for 5 *v.* Glamorgan (JPL), 1983
Highest innings total against County   254 for 4 by Glamorgan (JPL), 1983
Lowest innings total for County   138 *v.* Leicestershire (GC), 1977
Lowest innings total against County   153 for 6 by Lancashire (JPL), 1981
Highest individual innings for County   176 G.A. Gooch *v.* Glamorgan (JPL), 1983
Highest individual innings against County   99 B.F. Davison for Leicestershire (GC), 1977
Best bowling performance for County   5 for 41 D.R. Pringle *v.* Gloucestershire (JPL), 1985
Best bowling performance against County   5 for 19 J.F. Steele for Leicestershire (GC), 1977

HOW TO GET THERE

Rail   Southend East, ½ mile
Bus   Eastern National 20 Shoeburyness–Hullbridge (passing BR Southend Central and Victoria Stations) (Tel: 0702 430534); also 67, 68, 7 and 8
Car   From north and west: A127 or A130 follow signs Southend then A13 to Southchurch, 1½m east of town centre.

WHERE TO STAY AND OTHER INFORMATION

Airport Moat House (0702 546344), Argyle Hotel (0702 339483), and many seaside hotels. Also Balmoral Hotel at Westcliff-on-Sea (0702 342947)

Disabled Areas   No restrictions, but request position on ground
Local Radio Station   Essex Radio (96.3 MHz FM/1431 KHz MW)
Local Newspaper(s)   Evening Echo, Yellow Advertiser, Southend Standard, Southend District News, London Advertiser

GLAMORGAN

CARDIFF

ABERGAVENNY

NEATH

PONTYPRIDD

SWANSEA

ABERYSTWYTH

EBBW VALE

LLANELLI

MERTHYR TYDFIL

NEWPORT

Glamorgan

In 1921 Glamorgan, having met MCC's condition of finding eight clubs willing to guarantee home and away fixtures, became the 17th member of the first-class county community and began, in the words of John Clay, the 'rag time days'. Clay, a brilliant off spinner who bowled for England, was thought to be the author of an annual report which candidly admitted: 'In the first few seasons Glamorgan were like no other side; some will say it was not a side at all.' The same Clay at the age of 50 was to be a member of Wilfred Wooller's side of champions in 1948.

Glamorgan started with a financial burden carried over from their Minor Counties days, and too many of the players were past their prime. In the first season the bowling mainstays were Nash, aged 48, and Creber, 47, and often there were no specialist slip catchers and the elderly needed to be hidden in the field. The selection committee was thirty-two members strong including players.

According to Dai Davies, Glamorgan's first Welsh-born pro, the occasional amateur pressed into service didn't score a run, took nought for plenty, the only thing he caught in the field was sunstroke, he fell down the hotel stairs, left his luggage on the train and arrived home to find his wife had run away with his closest friend.

Reinforcements of the quality of Mercer from Sussex and the Irish-American spinner, Ryan, added potency to the attack, and, in due course, genuine Welsh talent was as welcome as spring daffodils.

The most significant arrival was Maurice Turnbull, a schoolboy from Downside. In 1930, having captained Cambridge, he took over the leadership, and a year later was appointed secretary. Glamorgan's second phase of development centred around his influence. At once he tackled the financial problems, and took Glamorgan to their highest position of 7th. In sixteen previous seasons only once, 8th in 1926, had Glamorgan escaped the lower half of the county table. Turnbull, the first from the county to score a century for England, also played rugby and hockey for Wales, and, alas, at the age of 33 fell to a sniper's bullet in Normandy.

Wooller, another Cambridge man and rugby international, succeeded Turnbull as the strong man captain-secretary, and, in 1948, shrewdly planned the fulfilment of an impossible dream. By the standards of other champions Glamorgan batted and bowled moderately, but the fielding and catching close to the wicket to support a leg stump attack was superb, at times miraculous. Wooller, Allan Watkins, whose all-round ability was appreciated by England, Clift and Dyson took 120 catches between them. Muncer, ex-Middlesex off-spinner, had 139 victims, but, fittingly, in the climax of victory at Bournemouth, Clay took six for 48, and Emrys Davies, another survivor of the difficult days, scored 74.

For weeks afterwards Clay said he felt as if he was floating in fairyland, and Cardiff station was packed to greet the homecoming

J. C. CLAY

GLAMORGANSHIRE

GLAMORGAN C.C.C

heroes and rang to the sounds of a huge choir. Nothing like it had been seen since Cardiff City FC brought the English FA Cup back to Wales.

Twenty-one years later Tony Lewis, yet another Cambridge-trained leader, and soon to captain England, expertly guided Glamorgan to their second county title. Lewis had the further distinction of remaining unbeaten, a record no champions in the previous thirty-one seasons had managed. A decisive factor was a record bag of batting points which served to emphasise an excellent team's attitude. Again the crowds congregated in front of the pavilion, as they had done at Bournemouth, now at the new ground of Sophia Gardens.

Lewis was magnificently supported by Alan Jones, a worthy successor to the old batting favourites, Willie Jones and Parkhouse, Majid Khan, the exciting Pakistani, Nash's clever bowling, all-rounder Walker, as fine a close-in fielder as the game has known, and his first lieutenant Shepherd.

Like Clay and McConnon – considered good enough to be picked before Laker for Australia in 1954–5 – Shepherd was converted from pace to off spin. Born in a hamlet in the Gower peninsular Shepherd became the first bowler of other than English birth to pass 2,000 wickets, and ended with 2,218, a record which will be hard to equal. An all-Welsh side may be an unrealistic dream, but Shepherd is one of many to demonstrate genuine cricket talent exists in Wales.

Glamorgan have shown prudent reality with the recruitment of overseas stars, the latest of which, no less than Vivian Richards, showed the club's initiative. Matthew Maynard also emerged as one of England's most exciting batting prospects. [A.B.]

Founded 1888
Colours Blue and gold
Crest Gold daffodil
Chief Executive P.G. Carling

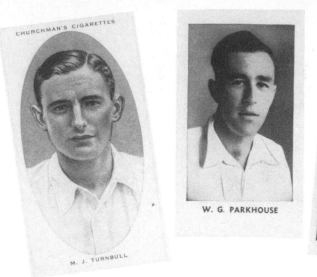

W. G. PARKHOUSE

M. J. TURNBULL

E. DAVIES

Secretary T. Dilloway
Senior Coach A. Jones MBE
Scorer B. T. Denning
Groundsman L. Smith/A. Francis
Address Sophia Gardens, Cardiff CF1 9XR. Telephone 0222 43478
Cricketcall 0898 121430

Achievements:

County Championship Champions (2) 1948 and 1969
Gillette Cup Finalists 1977
National Westminster Bank Trophy Quarter-finalists 1985 and 1988
Benson & Hedges Cup Semi-finalists 1988
John Player Sunday League Champions (0) 8th 1977
Refuge Assurance Sunday League Champions (0) 6th 1988
Tilcon Trophy Winners 1980

Grounds:

Cardiff (Sophia Gardens, Cathedral Road) Swansea (St. Helen's
Ground, Bryn Road) Neath (The Gnoll, Dyfed Road) Ebbw Vale
(Eugene Cross Park, Newchurch Road) Abergavenny (Pen-y-Pound,
Avenue Road) Merthyr Tydfil (Hoover Sports Ground, Merthyr
Road) Llanelli (Stradey Park, Denham Avenue) Pontypridd
(Ynysangharad Park, Ynysybwl Road) Newport (Athletic Club
Sports Ground, Rodney Parade) Aberystwyth (University College
of Wales Sports Ground, Llanbadarn Road).

Other grounds that have been used since 1969 are: Colwyn Bay
(Penrhyn Avenue, Rhos-on-Sea), Llandudno (The Oval, Gloddaeth
Avenue) and BP Llandarcy (BP Oil Llandarcy Refinery Ltd Sports
Ground, Crymlyn Bog).

Cardiff

The first matches staged by Glamorgan at Sophia Gardens, in 1967, were against the Indians and Northamptonshire (the first championship match). This was after the club's removal from Cardiff Arms Park adjoining the National Stadium. The current ground is located close to the River Taff and takes its name from Sophia, the second wife of the second Marquess of Bute. The ground was originally part of the Bute Estate which stretched from the city north along both banks of the Taff and close to Cardiff Castle. The Sophia Gardens were previously gardens where people of the city could promenade and listen to bands during the summer. There were ample outbuildings including the Sophia Gardens Pavilion, which was built in 1951 and which has held many events, including competitions in 1958 for the Commonwealth Games. The pavilion collapsed in 1982 and was demolished to make way for a car parking area.

Glamorgan C C C had requested use of the gardens during the 1950s but were turned down. In 1963 a scheme was put forward and agreed for the 23 acres of land at Gala Field to be developed to accommodate the Cardiff Athletic Club and the various sports sections which could no longer be housed at the Arms Park due to the redevelopment of the National Stadium. Cricket was included and Glamorgan moved to its present home in 1966–67 ready for the new season. 10½ acres was used for cricket. The rest was taken in 1970–71 when Cardiff Corporation offered land to the Sports Council so that the National Sportscentre for Wales could be constructed. The ground is also used by Cardiff C C, who first played in 1966 at Sophia Gardens.

With a 99-year lease on the ground the Cardiff Athletic Club built a new pavilion and offices and a scoreboard in 1966–67, the latter thanks to a donation from a London Welsh sportsman Sir Edward Lewis. In 1967 Cardiff C C held a cricket week to celebrate the centenary of the club and the opening of the new ground. Matches were played with a number of sides including M C C, the Glamorgan Nomads and the Forty Club. The latter side including: Wilf Wooller, Harold Gimblett, Dick Spooner, Bob Broadbent and Bob Appleyard. After the M C C game a civic reception was held at Cardiff Castle.

A pavilion built by E. Taylor and Company of Treforest houses all the facilities on the ground. At the River Taff End there is a covered stand and press/scorers' facilities and to the Cathedral Road End are ample open terraces and behind them hockey pitches and nets. The ground is also used by Cardiff R F C's second team and facilities also exist for tennis, this being the home of Cardiff Tennis Club. In 1987 the club's offices moved from the High Street to the ground and these are now housed in the south-western corner of the ground.

Some notable matches have been staged on the ground including that in 1969 when Glamorgan won the championship, beating Worcestershire. Some 16,000 people attended this match, still a record attendance for the ground. In 1976 Glamorgan deprived Somerset of the John Player Sunday League before 11,000 spectators;

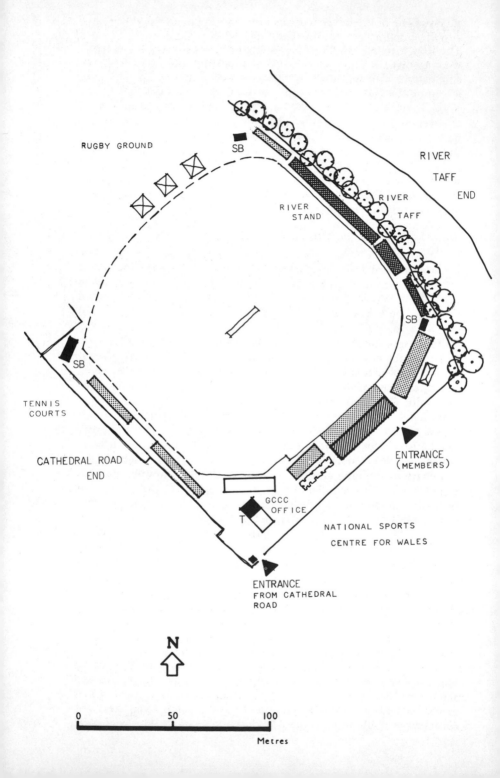

RUGBY GROUND

SB

RIVER STAND

RIVER TAFF

RIVER TAFF END

SB

SB

TENNIS COURTS

CATHEDRAL ROAD END

ENTRANCE (MEMBERS)

GCCC OFFICE

T

NATIONAL SPORTS CENTRE FOR WALES

ENTRANCE FROM CATHEDRAL ROAD

N

0   50   100

Metres

this was one of the largest crowds for a one-day match at the ground.

Wilf Wooller has commented that Sophia Gardens is 'a quite delightful rural setting, spacious and well-treed but somehow it has never reproduced the cosy atmosphere of Cardiff Arms Park'. In 1985 Glamorgan lost so many days to poor weather that members suggested the ground's name should be changed to Sophia Lakes due to the number of lakes forming on the outfield. Ground records have only including one double century of 252 scored by Wayne Larkins for Northamptonshire in 1983. Records change nearly every season and in 1988 Glamorgan achieved their highest innings total in first-class matches on the ground when they declared at 543 for 8 against Somerset. There is a proposal that the club should move to a new ground in Cardiff Docks where they will at last have sole responsibility for their own ground and future.

ADDRESS Cardiff Athletic Club, Sophia Gardens, Cathedral Road, Cardiff CF1 9XR
TELEPHONE PROSPECTS OF PLAY 0222 43478/29956

DESCRIPTION OF GROUND AND FACILITIES

Sophia Gardens is situated just off the Cathedral Road, adjacent to the National Sports Centre for Wales and within a short distance of the River Taff. The ground is surrounded by trees and attractively landscaped areas. The pavilion which houses a museum and library for use by members and the public by appointment, club offices, press/scorers box, river stand and scoreboard are the only permanent, covered buildings on the ground. The pavilion is to the south of the playing area, at right angles to the wicket and provides ample facilities for members. To the north side, opposite the pavilion, is a rugby field which is used by sponsors and during much of the season tents and large marquees can be found here. At the Cathedral Road End is the main computerised scoreboard; this is similar to the one at Abergavenny but larger. There are also two temporary, raised seating areas made of steel and timber. Behind the scoreboard are the hockey pitches which are both artificial and floodlit. The T V camera position is also at this end of the ground.

There are two entrances to the ground, one for members which is directly behind the pavilion and another for the public which is at the rear of the club offices. The toilets and refreshments, the Glamorgan C C C souvenir caravan and areas of open seating, can be found near the public entrance to the ground, at the rear of the Sports Centre.

The playing area is 142 metres by 146 metres and is defined by a rope and, on two sides, by a white pale fence with advertisement boards. The seating capacity of the ground is 10,000 of which 50 per cent is provided permanently with additions made for popular matches as required. Spectators are advised not to bring their own seats to matches. Car parking within the ground is only for players/ officials and committee members. Outside the ground car parking is available at the National Sports Centre, sometimes during festival weeks on the rugby pitch at the rear of the marquees, and in Sophia Gardens Car Park south of the Sports Centre facilities.

GROUND RECORDS AND SCORES

FIRST-CLASS MATCHES

Highest innings total for County   543 for 8 dec. v. Somerset, 1988
Highest innings total against County   529 for 8 dec. by Northamptonshire, 1983
Lowest innings total for County   43 v. Leicestershire, 1971
Lowest innings total against County   52 by Hampshire, 1968
Highest individual innings for County   177 Younis Ahmed v. Middlesex, 1985
Highest individual innings against County   252 W. Larkins for Northamptonshire, 1983
Best bowling performance in an innings for County   8 for 63 A.W. Allin v. Sussex, 1976
Best bowling performance in an innings against County   9 for 57 P.I. Pocock for Surrey, 1979
Best bowling performance in a match for County   13 for 127 R.C. Ontong v. Nottinghamshire, 1986
Best bowling performance in a match against County   13 for 102 D.L. Underwood for Kent, 1979

LIMITED-OVERS MATCHES

Highest innings total for County   302 for 6 v. Combined Universities (BHC), 1988
Highest innings total against County   330 for 4 by Somerset (GC), 1978
Lowest innings total for County   76 v. Middlesex (JPL), 1975
Lowest innings total against County   85 by Lancashire (BHC), 1976
Highest individual innings for County   115 H. Morris v. Kent (BHC), 1987/115 M.P. Maynard v. Combined Universities (BHC), 1988
Highest individual innings against County   145 P.W. Denning for Somerset (GC), 1978
Best bowling performance for County   5 for 17 J.G. Thomas v. Sussex (NWBT), 1985
Best bowling performance against County   6 for 20 T.E. Jesty for Hampshire (JPL), 1975

HOW TO GET THERE

Rail Cardiff Central, 1 mile
Bus Cardiff Bus 32, 62 from BR Cardiff Central Station (Tel: 0222 396521); also 25, 33 and 21
Car From north: A470 follow signs to Cardiff until Junction with Cardiff bypass, then A48 Port Talbot and city centre. Cathedral Road is situated off (A48) for Sophia Gardens. From east: M4 junction 29 then A48, then as north. From west: A4160 follow signs Cardiff, then A48, then as north.

WHERE TO STAY AND OTHER INFORMATION

Crest Hotel (0222 388681), Post House (0222 731212), Park Hotel (0222 383471), Inn on the Avenue (0222 732520)

Disabled Areas No special area, request position
Local Radio Station(s) BBC Radio Wales (882 KHz MW), Red Dragon Radio (97.4 MHz FM/1359 KHz MW)
Local Newspaper(s) South Wales Evening Post, South Wales Echo, Western Mail, Cardiff Independent, Cardiff Post Series

Abergavenny

Avenue Road is the home of Abergavenny C C, which was established in 1834, and is known to locals as Pen-y-Pound. It is situated on the northern outskirts of the Gwent town, off Avenue Road and adjoining Avenue Crescent.

The 4½ acre ground was opened in 1896 when a match was staged between a South Wales XI and an Abergavenny XI. There are ample facilities for hockey, bowls and tennis at the ground and the pavilion which was rebuilt in 1977 after a fire has ample amenities. The clock over the entrance door survived the fire; its plaque notes that it was presented to the club by Mr and Mrs Lyons in 1921. The club during its early years moved from one ground to another until in 1895 an approach was made to the Marquess of Abergavenny a keen follower of cricket (and a one time President of Kent C C C), who leased the ground to the club. The ground took its name from the nearby lane Pen-y-Pound. The Marquess provided the original pavilion in 1915 after generously giving further land in 1910 and again in 1912.

As with Ebbw Vale, the ground was also used by Monmouthshire for Minor County matches. Glamorgan first played Second Eleven matches on the ground in 1948. The club has always shown an interest in staging benefit matches; these have included games for Dennis Brookes and George Tribe of Northamptonshire and Warwickshire players David Brown, Rohan Kanhai, Denis Amiss and Neal

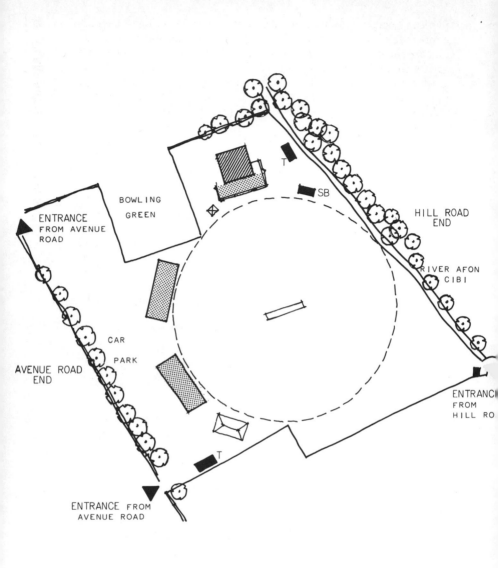

BOWLING
GREEN

ENTRANCE
FROM AVENUE
ROAD

T

SB

HILL ROAD
END

RIVER AFON
CIBI

CAR
PARK

AVENUE ROAD
END

ENTRANCE
FROM
HILL RO

T

ENTRANCE FROM
AVENUE ROAD

N

0   50   100

Metres

Abberley. Abergavenny plays in the Seven Counties Cricket League; the most well known player to have represented club and county was Malcolm Nash. Glamorgan were so impressed with the wicket and facilities that following several Second Eleven, club and ground, and benefit matches, they decided to play more cricket in Gwent. The initial first-class match was with Worcestershire in the John Player Sunday League in 1981. Thanks to the work of the local groundstaff, the match went ahead despite torrential rain during the morning. As a result of this successful visit another Sunday match was staged in 1982. In 1983 the first championship match was staged when Worcestershire were again the visitors. Championship cricket returned in 1985 when Worcestershire made their third visit. Subsequent visits have brought Derbyshire, Leicestershire and in 1988 Worcestershire, when Graeme Hick scored 159 setting up victory for the future champions.

The ground has two scoreboards, one manual near the pavilion, and another electronic scoreboard which has been in use since 1985. The new scoreboard is in memory of Bill McPherson who had been groundsman for many years. The ground is certainly one of the most beautiful in Wales and thanks to the organization from the local club visits are made very pleasant for players and spectators. Crowds at Abergavenny have been good when the weather has been kind and in 1988 5,000 attended the Worcestershire match. Crowds are usually around 3,500–4,000.

The ground is set at the foot of the Sugar Loaf Mountain, which is within the Brecon Beacons National Park, and known as the gateway to Wales. The club celebrated 150 years in 1984 and issued a book titled *Looking Back*, which no doubt will provide fond memories to all who have played or visited the ground. Glamorgan today play one championship match at the ground, usually in mid-June.

ADDRESS Abergavenny C C, The Pavilion, Pen-y-Pound Cricket Ground, Avenue Road, Abergavenny, Gwent
TELEPHONE PROSPECTS OF PLAY 0873 2350

DESCRIPTION OF GROUND AND FACILITIES

The ground is surrounded by residential housing and has two entrances, one in Hill Road via Pen-y-Pound across the River Afron Cibi and a second in Avenue Road. The pavilion is situated to the north of the playing area, close to the bowling green and at right angles to the wicket. The members' enclosure is situated in front of the pavilion and the new electronic scoreboard. At the Avenue Road, western end of the ground there is a large, temporary, tiered area of seating. Behind this car parking and temporary facilities including toilets, bars and refreshment tents are available. Car parking is also available at the football ground, off Hill Road and in the surrounding roads. To the south of the playing area is a further area of temporary seating and some practise nets. A secretary's office (in a caravan), the

Glamorgan C C C souvenir caravan and press tent are situated close to the bowling green near the pavilion. The playing area is 117 metres by 118 metres and is circular in shape. It is defined by a rope and some advertising boards. The radio point and T V camera position is at the Avenue Road End at a high level situated directly behind the sightscreen. The capacity is 5,000 and 60 per cent are provided with seating by the council for matches. Spectators are advised only to take their own seating to popular matches.

GROUND RECORDS AND SCORES

FIRST-CLASS MATCHES

Highest innings total for County   386 v. Leicestershire, 1987
Highest innings total against County   394 for 6 dec. by Worcestershire, 1983
Lowest innings total for County   168 v. Derbyshire, 1986
Lowest innings total against County   143 for 7 dec. by Derbyshire, 1986
Highest individual innings for County   135 A.R. Butcher v. Leicestershire, 1987
Highest individual innings against County   159 G.A. Hick for Worcestershire, 1988
Best bowling performance in an innings for County   3 for 36 G.C. Holmes v. Worcestershire, 1985
Best bowling performance in an innings against County   3 for 31 D.E. Malcolm for Derbyshire, 1986
Best bowling performance in a match for County   5 for 152 R.J. Shastri v. Leicestershire, 1987
Best bowling performance in a match against County   3 for 31 D.E. Malcolm for Derbyshire, 1986

LIMITED-OVERS MATCHES

Highest innings total for County   229 for 7 v. Northamptonshire (JPL), 1982
Highest innings total against County   170 for 7 by Worcestershire (JPL), 1981
Lowest innings total for County   152 v. Worcestershire (JPL), 1981
Lowest innings total against County   153 for 7 by Northamptonshire (JPL), 1982
Highest individual innings for County   100 R.C. Ontong v. Northamptonshire (JPL), 1982
Highest individual innings against County   43 E.J.O Hemsley for Worcestershire (JPL), 1981
Best bowling performance for County   2 for 21 M.A. Nash v. Northamptonshire (JPL), 1982
Best bowling performance against County   3 for 17 J. Birkenshaw for Worcestershire (JPL), 1981

HOW TO GET THERE

Rail Abergavenny, 2 miles
Bus National Welsh 20 Newport–Hereford; 21 Newport–Brecon.
Alight Bus Station, thence 1½ miles (Tel: 0222 371331)
Car From north: A465 or A40 follow signs Abergavenny, ground
situated in Avenue Road off (A40) Brecon Road. From east: A40 or
A465 then as north. From west: A465 or A40 then as north. From
south: M4 junction 26 then A4042 follow signs Abergavenny then
as north or A40 then as east.

WHERE TO STAY AND OTHER INFORMATION

Angel Hotel (0873 7121), Kings Arms, Nevill Street

Disabled Areas No special area, request position
Local Radio Station(s) BBC Radio Wales (882 KHz MW), BBC
Radio Cymru (93.1 MHz FM/882 KHz MW)
Local Newspaper(s) South Wales Evening Post, Western Mail,
Abergavenny Chronicle, Abergavenny Gazette, South Wales Argus

Neath

The Gnoll Cricket Ground at Neath is the home of the Neath C.C.
(founded in 1848) and situated close to the better-known home of
Neath Rugby Football Club. It is also the home of Glamorgan Indoor
Cricket School. Behind the pavilion, which is set at the foot of the
Gnoll, is the high slope which rises behind like a timber curtain
where on the top was once to be found Gnoll House, the former home
of Sir Humphrey Mackworth who owned much of the land.

The Neath club has been renowned for having fine cricketers.
Those who have represented the club include: Tom Box, W.G. Grace,
Tony Lewis, C.F. Walters, T.A. Whittington and A. Rees. Bill
Bestwick, after leaving Glamorgan for Derbyshire, returned to the
Gnoll to bowl out his old county. Bestwick's ball is mounted in the
pavilion as is the bat with which W.G. failed to score, and many other
cricket photographs and items are to be found in the pavilion.

The first recorded mention of cricket in the town was in 1844 and
the first games at the Gnoll were played in 1864. These included a
match between Carmarthenshire and Glamorganshire. Neath R F C
was formed in 1871 and rugby has been played on the ground since.
Other sports played on the ground around that time were six-a-side
football and bicycle races. In 1908 Glamorgan played Carmarthenshire but not until 1934 did Glamorgan stage their first championship
match on the ground, when Essex were the visitors. In 1923 the Gnoll
House and estate was acquired by Neath Corporation from the Evan
Thomas Family as a war memorial and to provide recreational and

sporting facilities in the town. During World War Two the Gnoll sustained some damage and in 1947 the county club gave Neath Council £300 towards repairing the cricket arena. In 1948 cricket returned and in 1950 the county club decided to establish an indoor cricket school. The school was opened by R.E.S Wyatt in 1954. More recently after modernisation and refurbishment it was reopened by C.F. Walters in 1984.

Crowds at the Gnoll have been quite substantial; 12,000 watched the Warwickshire match in 1948 and 9,000 watched Somerset in 1963. Today crowds are usually 4,500–5,000. During the 1960s and 1970s the ground staged limited-overs matches in the John Player Sunday League and Benson and Hedges Cup series. In 1985 after an absence of eleven years Glamorgan returned to the Gnoll thanks to sponsorship from Neath Borough Council to stage the tour match with the Australians. This venture was so successful that championship matches have continued to be staged on the ground. The Australians are due to return in 1989 for a tour match in July. There are ample amenities and close by in the adjoining sports centre are facilities for squash and swimming.

Ground records at Neath have included: 200 not out from Javed Miandad and 219 not out from Graeme Hick both during the 1980s. Len Muncer has the best bowling performance on the ground and in limited-overs matches two B B C commentators hold individual records on the ground – Tony Lewis (once himself a Neath player) and Tom Graveney.

ADDRESS Neath C C, The Pavilion, The Gnoll Cricket Ground, Dyfed Road, Gnoll, Neath, West Glamorgan
TELEPHONE PROSPECTS OF PLAY 0639 3719

DESCRIPTION OF GROUND AND FACILITIES

The main entrance to the Gnoll is from Dyfed Road, through the entrance to the swimming baths and tennis club. This is for spectators and cars. However there are two further entrances, for pedestrians, from Gnoll Park Road via the Neath Rugby Club, and from Llantwit Road to the north-east of the ground. The pavilion and terracing and the Glamorgan C C C Indoor Cricket School are situated south of the playing area and at right angles to the wicket. A scoreboard and outdoor nets are situated close to the indoor school along with sponsors' marquees. At the north-east end of the ground are two tiered, temporary, open-seating areas and refreshment facilities, close to the football floodlight pylon. Terracing, which is used by spectators for both rugby to the north and cricket to the south, is situated opposite the pavilion and also a press tent/box which also includes a radio point. The pavilion houses a number of cricket photographs and even a plaque commemorating W G Grace's 'pair' at the ground in 1868. At the south west, Dyfed Road End there are two areas of temporary seating and a T V camera position situated directly behind

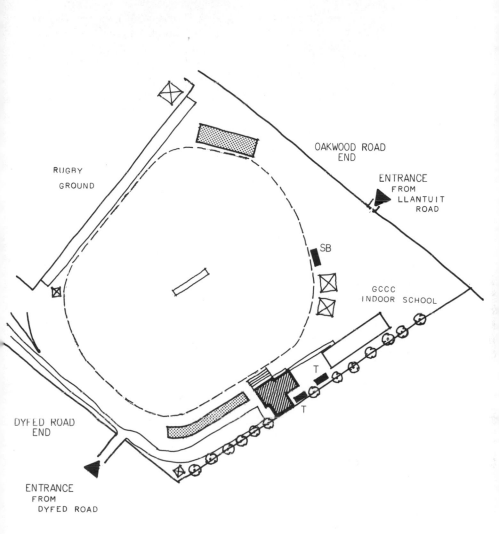

RUGBY
GROUND

OAKWOOD ROAD
END

ENTRANCE
FROM
LLANTUIT
ROAD

SB

GCCC
INDOOR SCHOOL

T

T

DYFED ROAD
END

ENTRANCE
FROM
DYFED ROAD

N

0   50   100

Metres

the sightscreen. Members' facilities can be found in the pavilion where there is a bar and refreshment area. There is also a temporary bar/refreshment tent near the tennis courts, toilets and a C C C souvenir caravan. Toilets can also be found in the pavilion and near the groundsman's stores.

The playing area is 133 metres by 115 metres and is defined by a rope and advertisement boards. The ground capacity is 6,000 and with the exception of the pavilion terrace where seats are permanent, the council provide temporary seating but the number of seats depends on the particular game.

Car parking within the ground is for players and officials only but the car parks in town are within 5 minutes walk of the ground and are recommended to spectators.

GROUND RECORDS AND SCORES

FIRST-CLASS MATCHES
Highest innings total for County   409 for 3 dec. v. Australians, 1985
Highest innings total against County   347 for 4 dec. by Warwickshire, 1959
Lowest innings total for County   43 v. Essex, 1935
Lowest innings total against County   57 by Surrey, 1937
Highest individual innings for County   200 n.o. Javed Miandad v. Australians, 1985
Highest individual innings against County   219 n.o. G.A. Hick for Worcestershire, 1986
Best bowling performance in an innings for County   8 for 48 B.L. Muncer v. Somerset, 1949
Best bowling performance in an innings against County   9 for 39 D.J. Halfyard for Kent, 1957
Best bowling performance in a match for County   12 for 94 B.L. Muncer v. Somerset, 1949
Best bowling performance in a match against County   13 for 51 A.E. Moss for Middlesex, 1960

LIMITED-OVERS MATCHES
Highest innings total for County   208 for 9 v. Essex (GC), 1964
Highest innings total against County   238 for 8 by Worcestershire (GC), 1963
Lowest innings total for County   90 v. Yorkshire (JPL), 1969
Lowest innings total against County   97 by Leicestershire (JPL), 1971
Highest individual innings for County   78 A.R. Lewis v. Worcestershire (GC), 1963
Highest individual innings against County   93 T.W. Graveney for Worcestershire (GC), 1963
Best bowling performance for County   4 for 20 D.J. Shepherd v. Leicestershire (JPL), 1971
Best bowling performance against County   5 for 43 J.A. Flavell for Worcestershire (GC), 1963

HOW TO GET THERE

Rail   Neath, ½ mile
Bus   South Wales Transport from surrounding areas to Bus Station, thence ¼ mile
Car   From north: A465 or A474 follow signs Neath, ground is situated north-west of town centre between River Neath and B4434 adjoining sports complex and rugby ground. From east and south: M4 junction 41 then follow A48 and A474 Neath, then as north. From west: M4 junction 44 then follow A48 and A465 Neath, then as north.

WHERE TO STAY AND OTHER INFORMATION

Cimla Court Hotel (0639 3771), Castle Hotel (where WRU was founded)

Disabled Areas   No special area, request position
Local Radio Station(s)   BBC Radio Wales (882 KHz MW), BBC Radio Cymru (93.1 MHz FM/882 KHz MW), Swansea Sound (96.4 MHz FM/1170 KHz MW)
Local Newspaper(s)   South Wales Evening Post, South Wales Echo, Western Mail, Neath Guardian Series

Pontypridd

The Ynysangharad Park ground is the home of Pontypridd C C which was formed in 1870 and plays in the Glamorgan Cricket League. The ground is also the town's war memorial and is located on a flat area of land on the eastern side of the River Taff between the river and the main A470 trunk road. The parkland in which the ground now stands was originally given to the town by the Lenox family as a memorial to the soldiers and servicemen from the town who died in World War One. The Park was opened in 1923 by Marshall Lord Allenby and during the period 1924–30 facilities were built there for bowling, swimming and tennis. The ground was also used by Pontypridd R F C until they moved to another ground in the town, at Sardis Road, during the late 1970s.

The first visit by Glamorgan to the ground was in 1926 when Derbyshire were the visitors and during the late Twenties matches were staged annually; these included a tour match with the South Africans in 1929. Over the years the ground has had problems with rain, and the majority of county matches so affected appear to be at Pontypridd. This was commented upon by Webber and Arnott in the 1947 *Glamorgan C C C* Review: 'Pontypridd appears to be Glamorgan's most unlucky ground as rain interferes with the majority of matches played there.'

The County continued to play championship matches at Pontyp-

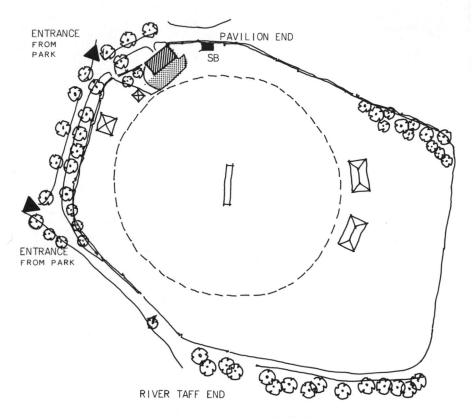

ENTRANCE
FROM
PARK

PAVILION END

SB

ENTRANCE
FROM PARK

RIVER TAFF END

RIVER TAFF

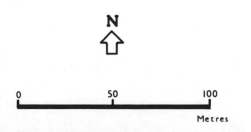

N

0   50   100

Metres

ridd until in 1969 when these were discontinued due to falling attendances and poor weather. The last limited-overs matches were a Benson and Hedges Cup and a John Player Sunday League fixture against Somerset and Essex in 1972. Not until 1988, as part of the county club's centenary celebrations, did Glamorgan return to Ynysangharad Park. They played Lancashire in a Refuge Assurance Sunday League fixture only for the match to be ruined by rain – not for the first time! In 1989 the County have four days set aside in September for the visit in the championship by Worcestershire when hopefully weather will be kind. Previously matches have been staged in May.

Crowds at Pontypridd average around 3,000–3,500. The largest was in 1933 when 6,000 were attracted by the visit from neighbours Gloucestershire.

A photograph of George Geary can be found in the pavilion showing just the stumps standing on the wicket, a worn strip known as Geary's Wicket, after he took 16 for 96 for Leicestershire in 1929. Jack Mercer holds bowling records for Glamorgan and high scores have come from both James Pressdee and Charlie Barnett for Gloucestershire.

ADDRESS Pontypridd C C, The Pavilion, Ynysangharad Park, Pontypridd, Mid Glamorgan
TELEPHONE PROSPECTS OF PLAY 0443 400785

DESCRIPTION OF GROUND AND FACILITIES

The ground is located within the Ynysangharad Park, and is enclosed by a fence and well matured grounds from the rest of the park and the only permanent buildings are the pavilion, terrace and scoreboard. The members' enclosure is in front of the pavilion and on the adjoining terracing area. A radio point and press tent is also found close to the pavilion as is the T V camera position. The playing area is 120 metres by 114 metres and is defined by a line and advertising boards. The playing area is flat and there is ample space surrounding it for temporary facilities including seating, refreshment tents, temporary toilets and a Glamorgan C C C souvenir caravan. The east side of the ground is used mainly by sponsors. The ground capacity is 6,000 and seating is provided for 50 per cent. Spectators are advised to take their own seating to popular matches.

There is no car parking available within the ground for spectators but ample car parks are available in the town centre, only a short distance away.

GROUND RECORDS AND SCORES

FIRST-CLASS MATCHES
Highest innings total for County 421 v. Warwickshire, 1937
Highest innings total against County 398 by Nottinghamshire, 1929
Lowest innings total for County 68 v. Leicestershire, 1929

Lowest innings total against County   53 by Somerset, 1946
Highest individual innings for County   150 n.o. J.S. Pressdee *v.*
Cambridge University, 1965
Highest individual innings against County   154 C.J. Barnett for
Gloucestershire, 1933
Best bowling performance in an innings for County   8 for 60
J. Mercer *v.* South Africa, 1929
Best bowling performance in an innings against County   10 for 18
G. Geary for Leicestershire, 1929
Best bowling performance in a match for County   14 for 119
J. Mercer *v.* South Africa, 1929
Best bowling performance in a match against County   16 for 96
G. Geary for Leicestershire, 1929

LIMITED-OVERS MATCHES
Highest innings total for County   163 for 9 *v.* Lancashire (RAL),
1988
Highest innings total against County   193 for 7 by Essex (JPL),
1970
Lowest innings total for County   129 *v.* Essex (JPL), 1970
Lowest innings total against County   121 by Somerset (BHC), 1972
Highest individual innings for County   40 K.J. Lyons *v.* Somerset
(BHC), 1972
Highest individual innings against County   58 n.o. K.D. Boyce for
Essex (JPL), 1970
Best bowling performance for County   3 for 8 S.R. Barwick *v.*
Lancashire (RAL), 1988
Best bowling performance against County   4 for 12 G.I. Burgess for
Somerset (BHC), 1972

HOW TO GET THERE

Rail   Pontypridd, ¼ mile
Bus   Bus to Ynysangharad Park, Yinysybwl Road, from surrounding
areas to Bus Station, thence ½ mile
Car   From north: A470 follow signs Pontypridd, ground is situated
off B4273 Ynysybwl in Ynysangharad Park. From east and south:
M4 junction 32 then A470 follow signs Pontypridd, then as north.
From west: A4058 or A473 follow signs Pontypridd, then as north.

WHERE TO STAY AND OTHER INFORMATION

The Graig Hotel (0443 402844)

Disabled Areas   no special area, request position
Local Radio Station(s)   BBC Radio Wales (882 KHz MW), Red
Dragon Radio (97.4 MHz FM/1359 KHz MW)
Local Newspaper(s)   South Wales Evening Post, South Wales Echo,
Western Mail, Pontypridd Observer

Swansea

The second major ground at which Glamorgan play is St Helen's, Swansea, the home of the Swansea Cricket and Football Club. The ground is located to the west of the city centre off the Mumbles Road and enclosed by Bryn Road, Gorse Lane and Mumbles Road. The ground is shared, and the majority of the terracing facilities are available for viewing both games. The pavilion was built in 1927 and has had extensions and additions since, the most recent in 1980 when a new eastern wing was constructed.

Glamorgan first played at the ground in 1921 when Leicestershire were the visitors. Today four championship matches are staged during a season plus several limited-overs matches. The ground was originally owned by an order of Augustinian nuns who built a convent dedicated to St Helen. Following the Dissolution of the Monasteries the ground and St Helen's estate passed to Baron Herbert of Cardiff and Earl of Pembroke. They subsequently passed to Colonel Llewellyn Morgan and his family, who were major landowners in the city. Cricket has been played in Swansea since 1780, but the first formal games were in 1848 and 1850. In 1850 a Swansea C C was established and the first match was with Llanelli. In 1868 a match was staged with the Australian Aboriginal Team. Before their move to St Helen's in 1873 after £2,000 had been spent in levelling the ground, the club played at Brunswick timber yard and Bryn-y-Mor. The new ground was known as New Cricket Field, St Helen's, and was used for athletics and cricket. In 1874 Swansea R F C. and Swansea C C amalgamated to form the Swansea Cricket and Football Club and today still retain the same name.

International rugby matches have been staged on the ground from 1882, when Wales played England, and until shortly after World War Two. The ground has hosted many famous rugby matches and rugby and cricket memorabilia can be found in the pavilion and St Helen's Lounge. Other events staged on the ground have included hockey, rugby league, jazz concerts and a programme in the 'It's a Knockout' B B C T V series. Swansea can thank Sir John T.D. Llewellyn not only for donations but for being the County's first Treasurer when the county club was founded at the Angel Hotel, Cardiff in 1888. In 1939 the ground was sold to the Swansea Town Corporation, now the City Corporation, which has remained the sole owner ever since. During World War Two the ground was used as a military training camp. Afterwards much building took place, including a new rugby grandstand, new terracing and pavilion facilities.

From the pavilion there used to be 67 steps down to the field. This could be a very long walk back for a batsman who had been dismissed first ball. Since building developments have taken place during the 1980s the distance has been reduced to 45 steps! In 1959 the Memorial Gates were installed opposite the the Cricketers Inn in memory of past players who have represented Swansea cricket and football clubs. The gates were donated by the Swansea and District R S C.

In 1964 140-feet high floodlight pylons were installed and they dominate the ground in each corner as do similar installations at Northampton. Much of the ground's facilities are used for both rugby and cricket; scoreboards for both can be found on the ground. Tourists usually play Glamorgan at Swansea and the County have defeated all Test nations here except West Indies and Sri Lanka. Two international matches have been staged at St Helen's: in 1973 a Prudential Trophy match between England and New Zealand and in 1983 a Prudential Cup match between Pakistan and Sri Lanka.

Many of Glamorgan's finest hours have come at Swansea including in 1927 a victory over Nottinghamshire by an innings and 81 runs which deprived Nottinghamshire of the championship and in 1948 a victory over the Australians by 36 runs. The attendance at the latter match was 50,000, which remains a record today. Crowds for recent matches are usually around 5,000–6,000. However 10,000 were attracted by the England Prudential Trophy match in 1973.

Two of the most significant cricket records took place here. In 1968, while batting for Nottinghamshire, Gary Sobers hit Malcolm Nash for 36 runs in a single six-ball over. (Frank Hayes of Lancashire hit 34 off one over from the same bowler in 1977.) Clive Lloyd hit 201 for the West Indians in two hours in 1976 and equalled Gilbert Jessop's record for the fastest ever double century in first-class cricket. Glamorgan have staged matches in all competitions on this ground including floodlit cricket.

ADDRESS   Swansea Cricket and Football Club, The Pavilion, St Helen's Cricket Ground, Bryn Road, Swansea, West Glamorgan
TELEPHONE PROSPECTS OF PLAY   0792 466321

DESCRIPTION OF GROUND AND FACILITIES

St. Helen's is the largest of Glamorgan's grounds with a capacity of 25,000. Members' seating is permanent and spectators are advised only to bring their own collapsible seats to popular matches. Members' entry to the ground is from Bryn Road, to the rear of the pavilion. There are two public entrances in Gorse Lane and also one in Mumbles Road. Refreshments for members are in the pavilion and for the public, mobile facilities are provided around the ground. Toilets can be found at various points around the playing area and there is a permanent scoreboard used for both cricket and rugby. The scorer's box and press box are high above the terracing, close to the pavilion and near the St. Helen's lounge. The T V camera position is directly above the sightscreen at the Mumbles Road End. Also at this end of the ground, close to the bar, is a supporters caravan selling Glamorgan souvenirs. The rugby pitch is used for sponsors' marquees and during festival week is heavily tented. The playing area is 130 metres by 118 metres and is defined by a rope and advertising boards.

The ground is dominated by the large floodlight pylons and huge areas of terracing. The members enclosure is in front of the pavilion

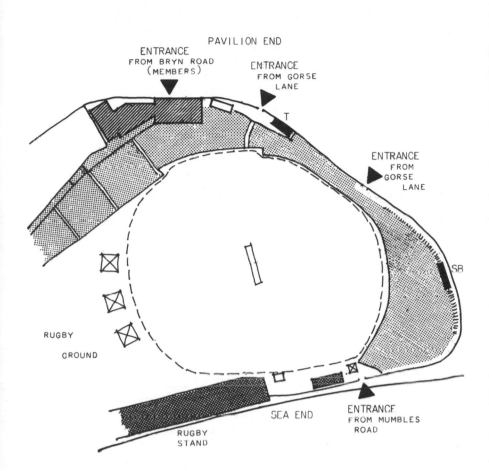

PAVILION END

ENTRANCE
FROM BRYN ROAD
(MEMBERS)

ENTRANCE
FROM GORSE
LANE

T

ENTRANCE
FROM
GORSE
LANE

SB

RUGBY
GROUND

SEA END

ENTRANCE
FROM MUMBLES
ROAD

RUGBY
STAND

N

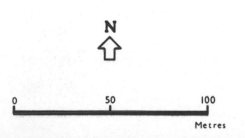

0   50   100

Metres

and due to its steepness is not recommended for disabled persons. No car parking is available in the ground except for players and officials but space is easily found in Bryn Road, King Edward Road (close to the Cricketers Hotel), St Helen's Avenue and in Mumbles car park, the former railway station near the seafront. Should play be interrupted by rain or bad light then a visit to the Cricketers Hotel opposite the ground may be of value. There are plenty of cricket items of interest here and meals are even served on placemats of old scorecards! Some photographs and historic items can also be viewed in the St. Helen's Lounge.

GROUND RECORDS AND SCORES

FIRST-CLASS MATCHES

Highest innings total for County   547 for 6 dec. v. Northamptonshire, 1933

Highest innings total against County   554 for 4 dec. by West Indians, 1976

Lowest innings total for County   36 v. Hampshire, 1922

Lowest innings total against County   40 by Somerset, 1968

Highest individual innings for County   233 M.J.A. Turnbull v. Worcestershire, 1937

Highest individual innings against County   257 n.o. A.H. Bakewell for Northamptonshire, 1933

Best bowling performance in an innings for County   9 for 43 J.S. Pressdee v. Yorkshire, 1965

Best bowling performance in an innings against County   9 for 60 H. Verity for Yorkshire, 1930

Best bowling performance in a match for County   17 and 212 J.C. Clay v. Worcestershire, 1937

Best bowling performance in a match against County   15 for 52 V.W.C. Jupp for Northamptonshire, 1925

LIMITED-OVERS MATCHES

Highest innings total for County   262 v. Leicestershire (JPL), 1984

Highest innings total against County   294 for 5 by Hampshire (NWBT), 1983

Lowest innings total for County   42 v. Derbyshire (JPL), 1979

Lowest innings total against County   76 by Minor Counties (BHC), 1985

Highest individual innings for County   103 n.o. M.A. Nash v. Hampshire (BHC), 1976/J.A. Hopkins v. Minor Counties (BHC), 1980

Highest individual innings against County   132 J.J. Whitaker for Leicestershire (JPL), 1984

Best bowling performance for County   5 for 16 G.C. Holmes v. Yorkshire (JPL), 1985

Best bowling performance against County   5 for 18 D.J. Brown for Warwickshire (GC), 1966

HOW TO GET THERE

Rail Swansea 1½ miles; Swansea High Street, ½ mile
Bus South Wales 1–3, 14 from Bus Station (¾ mile from BR
Swansea Station – numerous services link BR Station with Bus
Station) (Tel: 0792 475511); South Wales Transport to Mumbles,
Sketty, Oystermouth and Brynmill
Car From north: A465, A4067 or A48 follow signs city centre,
ground situated 1½ miles west of city centre off Mumbles Road
(A4067) close to Gorse Lane and Bryn Road. Ground shared with
rugby ground on seafront. From west: M4 junction 47 then A483
and A4216 to Mumbles Road, then as north or A4070. From east:
M4 junction 44 then follow signs Swansea on A4217 and A4067 to
Mumbles Road.

WHERE TO STAY AND OTHER INFORMATION

Dragon Hotel (0792 51074), Beaumont Hotel (0792 43044), Dolphin
Hotel (0792 50011)

Disabled Areas No special area, request position. Pavilion
enclosure not recommended due to steep steps
Local Radio Station(s) BBC Radio Wales (882 KHz MW), BBC
Radio Cymru (93.1 MHz FM/882 KHz MW), Swansea Sound (96.4
MHz FM/1170 KHz MW)
Local Newspaper(s) South Wales Evening Post, Western Mail,
South Wales Echo

Aberystwyth

The Aberystwyth ground is one of the two in Dyfed at which
Glamorgan play; the other is at Llanelli. The ground is the sports
arena of the University College of Wales in the town and is located
around half a mile from the town centre on the Llanbadarn Road and
close to the main railway line east to Shrewsbury. The ground lies at
the foot of the Penglais Hill and was previously known as Vicarage
Field. This name arose because the land was formerly part of the vicarage and Llanbadarn Church prior to its destruction by the Vikings.

In 1906 the field was leased to the university for sports by David
Davies, who was the treasurer of the college at the time. It is used for
all sports including athletics, soccer, and rugby. Permanent buildings
on the ground include a gymnasium built in 1908, a grandstand and
changing facilities built between 1922 and 1927 and a cricket pavilion
which is also used by tennis players. Cricket has only been played
regularly since 1939. There has been much development since
including the building of a swimming pool and athletics track.

Glamorgan Second XI have staged matches on the ground since
1967 when a match was staged with the Welsh Universities. In 1977

as part of the town's 900th centenary celebrations a John Player Sunday League match was staged with Essex. This attracted television coverage and a large crowd. Essex won by 15 runs thanks to 80 runs and 2 wickets for 28 from Graham Gooch. The West Indian Collis King scored 66 for Glamorgan but victory in their inaugural visit to the ground was not to be. Glamorgan have not played there since but after a lapse of twelve years cricket is to return to the Vic, as it is known to locals, for a Refuge Assurance Sunday League match with Warwickshire in 1989.

Cricket has been traced back to 1830 in Aberystwyth when the first matches were played at Gogerddan, home of the local M P Pryse Pryse.

ADDRESS   The University College of Wales Sports Ground, The Pavilion, Llanbadarn Road, Aberystwyth, Dyfed
TELEPHONE PROSPECTS OF PLAY   temporary line – refer to B T Directory Enquiries

DESCRIPTION OF GROUND AND FACILITIES

The only entrance to the University College of Wales Sports Ground is from Llanbadarn Road which is on the outskirts of town and some way from the main campus of the university. The permanent buildings are a pavilion which is used by players and officials, and in front, a members' enclosure; also a gymnasium and a covered grandstand which provides seating for members and adjoins the cricket pavilion at the northern end of the ground. There are also facilities for other sports including permanent pavilions for bowling and tennis. At the rear of the pavilion is St. Padarn's Convent School and it is to this side of the ground that the majority of facilities are located. Toilet facilities can be found in the pavilion and gymnasium area. In addition there are also a couple of temporary toilets to the south of the playing area near the tennis courts. Temporary seating, marquees with refreshment/bar areas are situated around the ground and the majority of seating is temporary and uncovered. The ground capacity is 5,000 with seating provided for only 10 per cent. Spectators are well advised to bring their own collapsible seating to matches. The playing area is 112 metres by 145 metres and is defined by a rope and several advertising boards. The radio point and T V camera position is at the Llanbadarn End and the trees of the Plascrug Avenue to the west of the ground provide a beautiful situation for this Welsh ground.

GROUND RECORDS AND SCORES

LIMITED-OVERS MATCHES
Highest innings total for County   219 for 7 v. Essex (JPL), 1977
Highest innings total against County   234 for 7 by Essex (JPL), 1977
Highest individual innings for County   66 C.L. King v. Essex (JPL), 1977

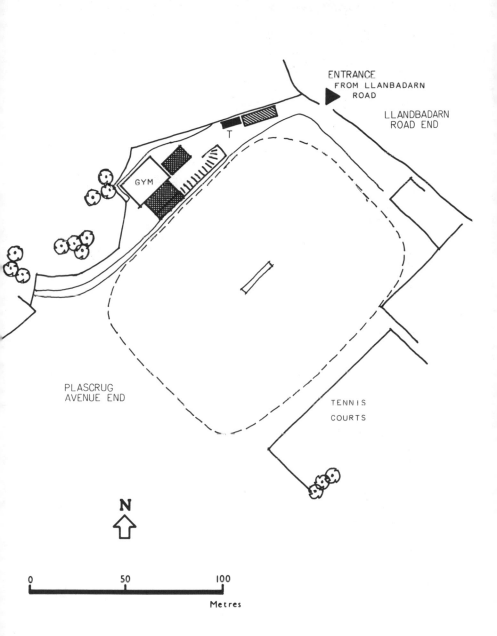

ENTRANCE
FROM LLANBADARN
ROAD

LLANDBADARN
ROAD END

T

GYM

PLASCRUG
AVENUE END

TENNIS
COURTS

N

0   50   100

Metres

Highest individual innings against County   80 G.A. Gooch for
Essex (JPL), 1977
Best bowling performance for County   3 for 42 G. Richards *v.*
Essex (JPL), 1977
Best bowling performance against County   2 for 28 G.A. Gooch for
Essex (JPL), 1977

HOW TO GET THERE

Rail   Aberystwyth, ½ mile
Bus   From surrounding areas to adjacent BR Station; bus from Station to university campus and Llanbadarn Farm
Car   From north: A487 follow signs Aberystwyth, ground situated at Llanbadarn off (A44) east of town centre. From east: A44 follow signs Aberystwyth, then as north. From south: A487 or A4120 follow signs Aberystwyth, then as north.

WHERE TO STAY AND OTHER INFORMATION

Bay Hotel (0970 617356), Belle Vue Royal Hotel (0970 617558)

Disabled Areas   No special area, request position
Local Radio Station(s)   BBC Radio Wales (882 KHz MW), BBC Radio Cymru (93.1 MHz FM/882 KHz MW)
Local Newspaper(s)   South Wales Echo, Western Mail, South Wales Evening Post

Ebbw Vale

The first game of cricket in Ebbw Vale dates back to 1852 when a match was staged with Blaenau. The ground is located in the hollow-like valley of the Ebbw river between Beaufort Road and New Church Road. With an altitude of around 288 metres, the ground is amongst the highest cricket grounds in the country. It is known today as Eugene Cross Park and is the home of the Ebbw Vale C C and shared with the Ebbw Vale Rugby Football Club. The ground originally belonged to the Ebbw Vale Steel, Iron and Coal Company but in 1919 changed name to the Ebbw Vale Welfare Association. At this time recreational facilities were available for football, rugby and cricket. The ground was known as the Welfare Association Sports Ground until in 1973 its name was changed to its present title, in honour of Sir Eugene Cross who had been the chairman of the welfare trustees. In 1981 a public trust was formed to take over the running and ownership of the ground.

Monmouthshire have used the ground for matches since 1901 and with the later affiliation with Glamorgan, Second XI matches were staged on the ground. The initial first-class game with Worcestershire was staged in 1946 when some 5,000 people watched the first day's play. With the exception of 1955 matches were played each season until in 1967 when the wicket was reported by the umpires to Lord's as being unfit for first-class cricket. Not until 1969 did cricket return and then only a John Player Sunday League match. Since then limited-overs matches have been staged annually and in 1983 the County played one first-class match to gain experience of the quality of the wicket.

The pavilion and the majority of the facilities are to be found at the northern end of the ground and the rugby field to the south. There are ample facilities for bowls and tennis within the sports complex, and badminton is also played in the Indoor Cricket School. Ebbw Vale C C was established in 1880 and plays in the Welsh Club Cricket Conference. The current secretary is the present Glamorgan C C C official scorer. Several famous cricketers have played for Ebbw Vale, including Percy Holmes, Harold Gimblett, George Macauley and Ted Whitfield. The most recent connection with Glamorgan was Kim Norket who played for both club and county.

Some strange events have taken place on this ground including in 1948 against Gloucestershire when *Wisden* commented 'A mountain of mist enshrouded the ground for most of the day, but the strangest diversion of all was the appearance of a flock of sheep on the field.' While batting, Peter Walker commented that after pushing a ball straight down the wicket, he could hear tapping noises from beneath the wicket, which he guessed came from a coalminer just below ground! In 1948 a civic event was staged on the playing area when Field Marshall Montgomery of El Alamein visited the Welsh valleys. The ground is also used by Cardiff Blue Dragons who play Rugby League. No tour matches have been staged on the ground but rugby tourists have visited for matches with Ebbw Vale R F C.

Crowds these days are around 2,500–3,500. Ground records have included fine spells of bowling from both Ossie Wheatley and Ken Preston in the 1960s. The limited-overs performances include only a single century from Younis Ahmed of 103 not out against Derbyshire in 1984 in front of 5,500 people. The largest crowd to attend a match here was in 1947 when 12,000 saw the match with Worcestershire.

ADDRESS Ebbw Vale C C, Eugene Cross Park, Newchurch Road, Ebbw Vale, Gwent
TELEPHONE PROSPECTS OF PLAY 0495 305368/212157

DESCRIPTION OF GROUND AND FACILITIES

Eugene Cross Park can be entered from both Newchurch Road and Beaufort Road and to the south from a footbridge via the Ebbw Vale Rugby Football Ground. The permanent buildings are located to the north of the playing area and are the pavilion, which includes a bar, together with an indoor school building which provides refreshments and toilet facilities. To the north of the playing area is the scoreboard and scorer's/press area. The members' area is in front of the pavilion and includes the adjacent terrace areas of seating. The west side of the ground is bounded by the Ebbw River and to the south are two raised seating areas. The radio point/T V camera position is located directly above the sightscreen at the rugby ground end. To the east is a shallow terrace and plenty of trees. The playing area is 126 metres

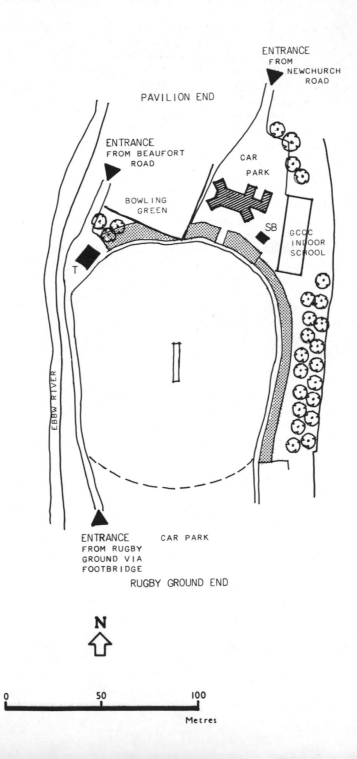

ENTRANCE
FROM
NEWCHURCH
ROAD

PAVILION END

ENTRANCE
FROM BEAUFORT
ROAD

CAR
PARK

BOWLING
GREEN

SB

GCCC
INDOOR
SCHOOL

T

EBBW RIVER

ENTRANCE
FROM RUGBY
GROUND VIA
FOOTBRIDGE

CAR PARK

RUGBY GROUND END

N

0   50   100

Metres

by 102 metres and defined by a rope and a white railing except to the south perimeter adjoining the rugby ground. Temporary facilities and a souvenir caravan are provided by the county club. The ground capacity is 5,000 and seating for about 50 per cent is provided. Spectators will therefore only be required to provide seating for popular matches.

Car parking is available for players/officials at the rear of the pavilion and there is limited space on the rugby ground for members' cars. A large car park can be found at the leisure centre only a short walk from the ground and also in the town centre car parks.

GROUND RECORDS AND SCORES

FIRST-CLASS MATCHES

Highest innings total for County   322 v. Essex, 1949
Highest innings total against County   354 for 9 dec. by Essex, 1954
Lowest innings total for County   64 v. Essex, 1962
Lowest innings total against County   33 by Leicestershire, 1965
Highest individual innings for County   118 n.o. J.S. Pressdee v. Essex, 1949
Highest individual innings against County   132 H. Horton for Hampshire, 1959
Best bowling performance in an innings for County   9 for 60 O.S. Wheatley v. Sussex, 1968
Best bowling performance in an innings against County   6 for 29 K.C. Preston for Essex, 1962
Best bowling performance in a match for County   11 for 115 O.S. Wheatley v. Sussex, 1968
Best bowling performance in a match against County   10 for 97 K.C. Preston for Essex, 1962

LIMITED-OVERS MATCHES

Highest innings total for County   277 for 6 v. Derbyshire (JPL), 1984
Highest innings total against County   241 for 7 by Sussex (JPL), 1981
Lowest innings total for County   92 v. Derbyshire (JPL), 1974
Lowest innings total against County   96 by Derbyshire (JPL), 1969
Highest individual innings for County   103 n.o. Younis Ahmed v. Derbyshire (JPL), 1984
Highest individual innings against County   80 A.R. Butcher for Surrey (JPL), 1977/N.E. Briers for Leicestershire (JPL), 1980
Best bowling performance for County   6 for 36 G.C. Kingston v. Derbyshire (JPL), 1969
Best bowling performance against County   5 for 13 J.K. Lever for Essex (JPL), 1975

HOW TO GET THERE

Rail Rhymney, 6 miles
Bus Inter Valley Link 49 from close to BR Rhymney Station (Tel: 0222 851506); National Welsh X4, 444 from Abergavenny (½ mile from BR Abergavenny Station); also from surrounding areas (Tel: 0222 371331). National Welsh 151 from Newport
Car From north and east: A465 and A4046 follow signs Ebbw Vale, ground situated close to town centre adjoining rugby ground off (A4046). From west: A465 and A4046 follow signs Ebbw Vale, then as north. From south: M4 junction 28 then A467 and A4046 follow signs Ebbw Vale, then as north.

WHERE TO STAY AND OTHER INFORMATION

County Hotel (0495 302418)

Disabled Areas No special area, request position
Local Radio Station(s) BBC Radio Wales (882 KHz FM), Radio Gwent (95.9 MHz FM), Red Dragon Radio (97.4 MHz FM/1359 KHz MW)
Local Newspaper(s) South Wales Echo, Western Mail, South Wales Evening Post, Newport Argus, Gwent Gazette

Llanelli

The Stradey Park cricket ground is located on the northern side of the famous Llanelli Rugby Club and the more famous Sospan Fach. Stradey Park, home of Llanelli C C, which was founded in 1837, has staged twenty-three first-class matches between the 1930s and 1960s. The club has played at Stradey Park since 1874. Llanelli play in the South Wales C A Cricket League. *Wisden* commented on the first match: 'The match against Worcestershire at Llanelli proved a very successful venture, for apart from the win by an innings, Carmarthenshire showed so much appreciation of being given the chance to see first-class cricket that on the first day the attendance exceeded 4,000.'

The ground used by Llanelli until their move to Stradey Park was situated where the Llanelli Market is now situated, hence the Cricketers public house in Murray Street. The name of the present ground is believed to have been derived from the Welsh *ystrad* meaning broad level area. The ground is part of the Stradey Recreational Complex which once formed the grounds of Stradey Castle, the home of Mansel Lewis in the seventeenth century. The ground has been used for matches by Carmarthenshire. In the early 1950s the ground was acquired from the Stradey Estate at a cost of £4,000 by the Llanelli Athletic Association in order to preserve for all time the playing area and to foster and encourage sport and athletics in the town.

The ground once staged an international rugby fixture in 1887 between Wales and England when the adjoining rugby field was semi-frozen. The match was watched by a crowd of 8,000. Crowds for cricket have not been as good, the best being 7,500 for the visit of Surrey the county champions in 1952. Today, matches attract crowds of 3,500–4,000 for limited-overs fixtures in the Sunday League. County cricket ceased in 1965 (the last first-class match was with Essex) due mainly to costs, limited seating and poor catering facilities on the ground. In 1981 the club took out a lease of sixty years on the ground and built a new pavilion costing £92,000 on the opposite side of the playing area to the old pavilion.

With the improvement in facilities Glamorgan returned for a one-day friendly with Somerset in 1986 for the Buckley's Brewery Challenge which Glamorgan won by 81 runs. With the success of this match further visits have included a Refuge Assurance League match with Leicestershire in 1988, which was restricted due to poor weather to 13 overs a side. Several professionals have appeared for the club and also represented Glamorgan. These include Roger Davis, Eifion Jones and Winston Davis.

The ground has seen some records including 161 by Gilbert Parkhouse and fine bowling from J.C. Clay and Robin Hobbs who achieved 12 for 94 and later captained Glamorgan. Peter Parfitt scored 118 for Middlesex in 1961 but Stradey Park will no doubt mean more to spectators of rugby rather than cricket!

ADDRESS Llanelli C C, The Pavilion, Stradey Park, Denham Avenue, Sandy, Llanelli, Dyfed
TELEPHONE PROSPECTS OF PLAY 0554 773721

DESCRIPTION OF GROUND AND FACILITIES

The only entrance to Stradey Park for spectators and vehicles is from Denham Avenue, to the west of the ground. There are two pavilions on the ground one for cricket and one for tennis. The only other permanent buildings for cricket are the two scoreboards. The majority of the facilities are temporary; there are marquees at the northern end, close to the pavilion and a members' enclosure, and to the south, backing onto the Llanelli Rugby Ground, a temporary stand of raised seats. Bar and refreshment facilities can be found in the pavilion and in the mobile outlets around the ground. The toilets are to be found in the pavilion, the temporary areas and the rugby clubhouse. The radio point and Glamorgan C C C souvenir caravan are at the rugby ground end. The cricket ground is bounded by a fence and wall to the west, north and east and by the rugby terracing to the south. There is also a rugby museum should rain or bad light stop play, and many an hour could be spent examining the history of Stradey Park's 4½ acre sports complex. The playing area is 117 metres by 125 metres

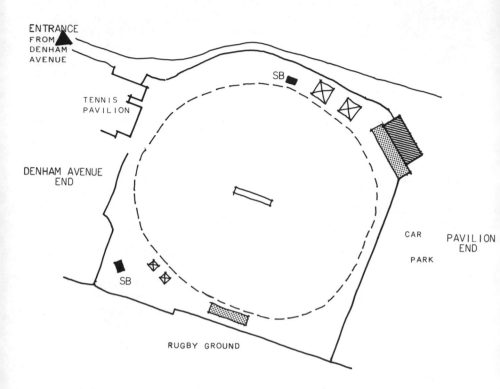

ENTRANCE FROM DENHAM AVENUE

TENNIS PAVILION

DENHAM AVENUE END

SB

SB

CAR PARK

PAVILION END

RUGBY GROUND

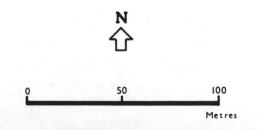

N

0   50   100

Metres

and is defined by a rope and advertisement boards. The ground capacity is approximately 5,000 and 75 per cent are provided with seating, both permanent and temporary. Spectators are advised to bring seats to all popular matches. Car parking is available at the rear of the pavilion for players and officials and in the Rugby car park for members.

GROUND RECORDS AND SCORES

FIRST-CLASS MATCHES

Highest innings total for County   434 for 6 dec. *v.* Worcestershire, 1933

Highest innings total against County   298 by Sussex, 1951

Lowest innings total for County   96 *v.* Lancashire, 1949

Lowest innings total against County   71 by Worcestershire, 1938

Highest individual innings for County   161 W.G.A. Parkhouse *v.* Gloucestershire, 1950

Highest individual innings against County   118 P.H. Parfitt for Middlesex, 1961

Best bowling performance in an innings for County   9 for 54 J.C. Clay *v.* Northamptonshire, 1935

Best bowling performance in an innings against County   8 for 43 V.E. Jackson for Leicestershire, 1956

Best bowling performance in a match for County   15 for 86 J.C. Clay *v.* Northamptonshire, 1935

Best bowling performance in a match against County   12 for 94 R.N.S. Hobbs for Essex, 1965

LIMITED-OVERS MATCHES

Highest innings total for County   221 for 5 *v.* Somerset (Buckleys Brewery Challenge), 1987

Highest innings total against County   140 by Somerset (Buckleys Brewery Challenge), 1987

Lowest innings total for County   77 for 7 *v.* Leicestershire (RAL), 1988

Lowest innings total against County   78 for 2 by Leicestershire (RAL), 1988

Highest individual innings for County   91 A.R. Butcher *v.* Somerset (Buckleys Brewery Challenge), 1987

Highest individual innings against County   43 B.C. Rose for Somerset (Buckleys Brewery Challenge), 1987

Best bowling performance for County   4 for 25 I. Smith *v.* Somerset (Buckleys Brewery Challenge), 1987

Best bowling performance against County   3 for 9 G.J.F. Ferris for Leicestershire (RAL), 1988

HOW TO GET THERE

Rail   Llanelli, 1½ miles
Bus   South Wales 111/2/3, 130 from Llanelli Bus Station (181/2 link BR Station and Bus Station) (Tel: 0792 475511)
Car   From north: A476 follow signs Llanelli and town centre, ground sited off Dyfed Road adjoining rugby ground at Stradey Park. From east: M4 junction 48 then A4138 Llanelli, then as north. From west: A484 and B4309 to Llanelli, then as north. From south: A484 or as east.

WHERE TO STAY AND OTHER INFORMATION

Stradey Park (0554 758171), Diplomat Hotel (0554 756156)

Disabled Areas   No special area, request position
Local Radio Station(s)   BBC Radio Wales (882 MHz FM), Swansea Sound (96.4 MHz FM/1170 KHz MW)
Local Newspaper(s)   South Wales Echo, Western Mail, South Wales Evening Post, Llanelli Star

Merthyr Tydfil

The cricket ground is part of the Hoover PLC sports ground complex and is situated in Merthyr Road (A470) adjoining the factory.

The county club visited for the first time in 1988 as part of their centenary celebrations to play a Refuge Assurance Sunday League match with Kent. The match was won by Kent by 5 wickets thanks to Chris Cowdrey the Kent skipper, who took 4 for 20 and a positive 62 from Neil Taylor. The event proved a great success – some 4,750 attended – and another Sunday League match is to be staged with Middlesex in 1989.

The record crowd before 1988 was for a visit from the Lord's Taverners XI in 1985, when 2,000 attended.

The ground is used by the Hoover Sports C C, which is affiliated to the Welsh Cricket Association. There are facilities for bowling and tennis, and plenty of space surrounding the playing area. The Hoover factory in Merthyr opened on St David's Day, 1 March, 1948 – the year Glamorgan first won the county championship. The factory covers some three-quarters of a million square feet and employs almost 2,000 people. To help test their washing machines, Hoover wash the kits of local rugby and football clubs.

Merthyr Tydfil is the only British ground currently in use which is adjoining a factory. Former factory grounds include Coventry (Courtaulds), Burton-on-Trent (Ind-Coop) and Yeovil (Westland's).

ADDRESS   Hoover Sports C C, Hoover PLC Sports Ground, Merthyr Road, Merthyr Tydfil, Mid Glamorgan
TELEPHONE PROSPECTS OF PLAY   0685 721222

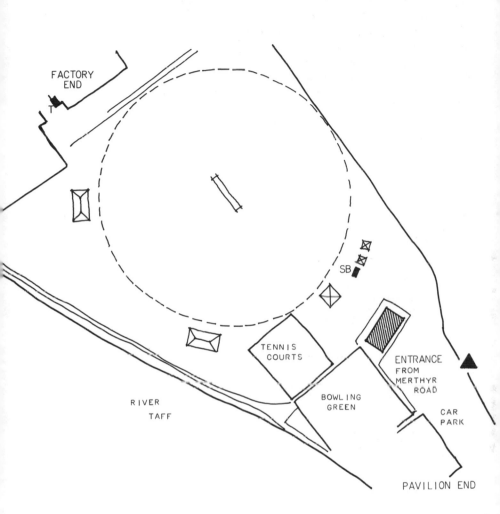

FACTORY
END

T

SB

TENNIS
COURTS

BOWLING
GREEN

ENTRANCE
FROM
MERTHYR
ROAD

CAR
PARK

RIVER
TAFF

PAVILION END

N

0   50   100

Metres

DESCRIPTION OF GROUND AND FACILITIES

The ground is situated next to the Hoover factory and the entry adjoins the roundabout at the junction of the A470 and Merthyr Road. Car parking for 50 cars is available in the ground and there are several car parks within 5 minutes walk.

The playing area is 136 metres by 131 metres and is defined by a rope and advertisement boards. The pavilion is the only permanent building for cricket and is also used by bowling and tennis players. Limited seating is provided for matches so spectators are well advised to bring their own collapsible seating to all matches. At the factory end of the ground there are refreshment facilities and mobile catering points. The ground capacity is 5,000 and seating is provided for about 10 per cent of this figure.

The radio point and Glamorgan C C C souvenir caravan are to be found close to the pavilion; sponsors' tents are located on the north-west side of the ground. The toilets are either temporary, in the pavilion, or adjoining the factory canteen.

GROUND RECORDS AND SCORES

LIMITED-OVERS MATCHES

Highest innings total for County   134 v. Kent (RAL), 1988
Highest innings total against County   135 for 5 by Kent (RAL), 1988
Highest individual innings for County   34 A.R. Butcher v. Kent (RAL), 1988
Highest individual innings against County   62 N.R. Taylor for Kent (RAL), 1988
Best bowling performance for County   1 for 10 S.R. Barwick v. Kent (RAL), 1988
Best bowling performance against County   4 for 20 C.S. Cowdrey for Kent (RAL), 1988

HOW TO GET THERE

Rail   Pentre-bach, 300m; Troed-y-rhiw, 1¼m
Bus   Merthyr Tydfil Transport local services (Tel: 0685 6161)
Car   26 miles north-west of Newport. From north: A470 or A465 follow signs Merthyr Tydfil, ground situated off (A470) near Pentrebach adjoining roundabout at Head of the Valley Road. From east: M4 junction 32 then follow A470 Head of the Valley Road to Pentrebach south of Merthyr Tydfil, for Hoover Sports ground. From west: A465 or A470 then as north. From south: A470 or A4054 to Merthyr Tydfil then as east.

WHERE TO STAY AND OTHER INFORMATION

Tregenna Hotel (0685 82055). Castle Hotel, Baverstocks (0685 2327)

Disabled Areas   No special area, request position
Local Radio Station(s)   BBC Radio Wales (882 KHz MW), BBC
Radio Gwent (95.9 MHz FM), Red Dragon Radio (97.4 MHz FM/
1359 KHz MW)
Local Newspaper(s)   South Wales Echo, Western Mail, South Wales
Evening Post, Merthyr Express

Newport

The cricket ground at Rodney Place is part of the sports complex in
the centre of the town owned by the Newport Athletic Club. The
ground lies to the east of the River Usk and to the south of Newport
Bridge and Clarence Park. It is also close to Newport Rugby Football
Ground to the north.

Cricket was first played on the ground in 1850 but ended in 1875
when the Victoria Club was formed and later the Newport Cricket
Athletic and Football Club. In 1877, 6 acres of the ground was leased
to the club by Lord Tredegar and in 1881 a Newport and District XXII
met an England XI at the ground. The England side included Dr W.G.
Grace, the captain, and his brother E.M. Grace. W.G. fared better with
the ball than the bat in this match for he only scored 17 and 7 but his
bowling figures were 12 for 28 and 10 for 46. In 1892 the
Monmouthshire C C Association was formed and that season,
matches were played with the M C C and Worcestershire

During the early years the Newport club engaged a number of fine
professionals including Beresfield of Sheffield, Killick of Tunbridge
Wells, Emmett of Nottinghamshire and Mee of Nottinghamshire and
Staffordshire. In 1895 a new pavilion was built costing £1,200
designed by Newport architects Swash and Bain. The pavilion was
opened on 1 June, 1901 by Lord Tredegar followed by a match with
the Cardiff C C.

Glamorgan played their first match here in 1935 against Leicestershire, and some 28 first-class and limited-overs matches have been
staged at Rodney Place, the last match being against Warwickshire in
1967. Not until 1988 as part of the county club's centenary
celebrations did county cricket return to Newport when Derbyshire
were the visitors in a Refuge Assurance Sunday League match. One
of the greatest matches staged on the ground was in 1939 when after
being dismissed for 196 by Gloucestershire the Welshmen then
succumbed to Hammond who hit 302 out of a Gloucestershire total
of 505 for 5 declared, which is still a ground record. Scores of 200 and
over have also come from Glamorgan's E. Davies, and Bob Gale for
Middlesex against a Glamorgan captained by Wilf Wooller who came
out of retirement because both Lewis and Wheatley were playing at
Lord's in a Gentlemen v. Players match.

The ground is also used for tennis and hockey and the club has

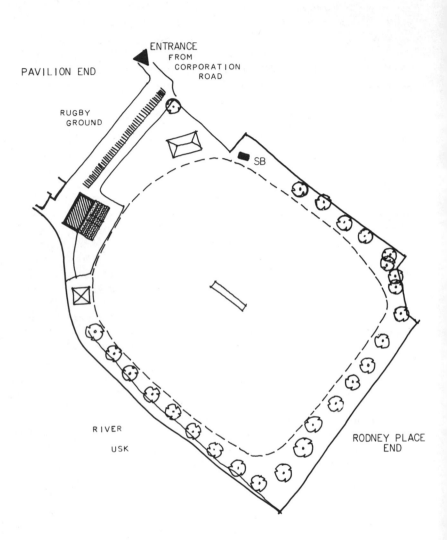

PAVILION END

ENTRANCE
FROM
CORPORATION
ROAD

RUGBY
GROUND

SB

RIVER

USK

RODNEY PLACE
END

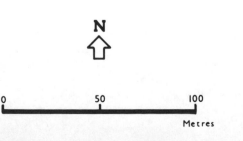

N

0   50   100

Metres

sections for bowls, badminton, table tennis, bridge and netball. The record crowd was 5,000 for the Gloucestershire game in 1939 and last year's Refuge match attracted 3,000–3,500.

ADDRESS Newport C C, Newport Athletic Sports Club, The Pavilion, Rodney Parade, Newport, Gwent
TELEPHONE PROSPECTS OF PLAY Temporary line – refer to British Telecom (BT) Directory Enquiries.

DESCRIPTION OF GROUND AND FACILITIES

Rodney Place is entered from Corporation Road which adjoins the Newport Rugby Football Ground. It is bounded by the River Usk to the south-west and also a number of buildings including the electricity control station, bus depot, post office depot and a large builder's yard. The pavilion is situated at the northern end of the ground close to the main rugby stands. The playing area is reasonably flat and is defined by a rope and advertising boards. The playing area is 143 metres by 121 metres and has a number of trees on three sides; the fourth provides a view of the rugby stadium which lies at the rear of the pavilion, and the embankment. Seating for members is in front of the pavilion in which refreshments and toilet facilities can be found. Temporary facilities, toilets and a Glamorgan souvenir caravan are also situated in the ground along with sponsors' marquees. Temporary seating is provided for spectators for only 25 per cent of the ground's capacity of 5,000. Spectators are therefore advised to take their own seating with them.

Quite a typical Welsh ground where rugby and cricket are played close to each other.

GROUND RECORDS AND SCORES

FIRST-CLASS MATCHES
Highest innings total for County   577 for 4 v. Gloucestershire, 1939
Highest innings total against County   505 for 5 dec. by Gloucestershire, 1939
Lowest innings total for County   69 v. Yorkshire, 1949
Lowest innings total against County   69 by Sir Julian Cahn's XI, 1938
Highest individual innings for County   287 n.o. D.E. Davies v. Gloucestershire, 1939
Highest individual innings against County   302 W.R. Hammond for Gloucestershire, 1939
Best bowling performance in an innings for County   7 for 74 J.E. McConnon v. Essex, 1960
Best bowling performance in an innings against County   9 for 77 D. Shackleton for Hampshire, 1953
Best bowling performance in a match for County   12 for 180 J.C. Clay v. Somerset, 1937

Best bowling performance in a match against County   13 for 99
T.W. Goddard for Gloucestershire, 1937

LIMITED-OVERS MATCHES
Highest innings total for County   199 for 8 *v.* Derbyshire (RAL),
1988
Highest innings total against County   174 by Derbyshire (RAL),
1988
Lowest innings total for County   120 for 9 *v.* Worcestershire (GC),
1964
Lowest innings total against County   119 by Worcestershire (GC),
1964
Highest individual innings for County   60 J.A. Hopkins *v.*
Derbyshire (RAL), 1988
Highest individual innings against County   90 n.o. K.J. Barnett for
Derbyshire (RAL), 1988
Best bowling performance for County   3 for 12 D.J. Shepherd *v.*
Worcestershire (GC), 1964
Best bowling performance against County   4 for 25 J.A. Flavell for
Worcestershire (GC), 1964

HOW TO GET THERE

Rail   Newport, ½ mile
Bus   South Wales Transport from surrounding areas to Bus Station,
thence ¾ mile
Car   From north: A4042 or A449 follow signs Newport, ground
situated in town centre at Rodney Place adjoining rugby ground.
From east: M4 junction 24 then A48 follow signs Newport, then as
north. From west: M4 junction 28 then follow signs Newport, then
as north.

WHERE TO STAY AND OTHER INFORMATION

Celtic Manor Hotel (0633 413000), Queen's Hotel (0633 62992)

Disabled Areas   No special area, request position
Local Radio Station(s)   BBC Radio Wales (882 KHz MW), BBC
Radio Cymru (96.8 MHz FM/882 KHz MW), BBC Radio Gwent
(95.9 MHz FM), Red Dragon Radio (97.4 MHz FM/1359 KHz MW)
Local Newspaper(s)   Western Daily Mail, South Wales Echo, South
Wales Evening Post, The News and Weekly Argus Series

GLOUCESTERSHIRE

BRISTOL

CHELTENHAM

GLOUCESTER

MORETON-IN-MARSH

SWINDON

Gloucestershire

Gloucestershire is the county of cricket's immortals, Dr W.G. Grace and Walter Hammond, of Jessop, Barnett and Graveney, and, from the overseas treasure chest, Procter and Zaheer Abbas.

Grace was the sporting idol of Victorian England, whose genius and personality revolutionized and popularized the game. On pitches which today's players would dismiss as impossibly bad – even at Lord's there were small pebbles on the surface – he scored 54,896 runs and 126 first-class centuries, took 2,876 wickets and held 877 catches. Yet his true greatness was, in the words of Prince Ranjitsinjhi, to turn batting from an accomplishment into a science. He was the first to recognize forward and back play are of equal importance.

At the age of 47 he completed 1,000 runs between 9 and 30 May, and in August 1876 he had successive innings of 344 for MCC and 177 out of 262 for Gloucestershire against Nottinghamshire at Clifton College, where there is talk of them returning for a one-day match in 1990. On their way to Cheltenham for the next match Yorkshire's players met the departing visitors. 'What did the black bearded blighter do?' they asked. When told they were pleased, thinking Grace might have exhausted his run form.

The next day he made 318, which prompted one of the Yorkshiremen Tom Emmett to complain: 'We have grace before meat, grace after meat, and Grace all bloomin' day!'

There were five Grace brothers, and they played a major part in the club's formation and early successes of 3 titles, another bracketed first with Nottinghamshire, and 3 runner-up places in the 9 seasons between 1873 and 1881.

Three of the Graces, E.M., W.G. and G.F. were in the England side for the first home Test in 1880, with W.G. scoring 152 and sharing an opening stand of 91 with E.M., who suffered only by comparison with his brother. Sadly 6 weeks later Fred, only 29, caught a chill after sleeping between damp sheets and died. With his death Gloucestershire's fortunes declined, and the Doctor, amid some acrimony, left to concentrate on managing London County.

Jessop's captaincy years, which relied heavily on his prowess as batsman, fast bowler and cover point, might have been better if Charles Townsend, founder of Gloucestershire's dynasty of spin bowlers, had been available regularly. Jessop was not the slogger of popular imagination, but leaning low on his bat – hence 'The Croucher' – he accumulated runs at an extraordinary pace. His longest innings at Brighton in 1903 lasted 3 hours and produced 286 – an impossible rate facing today's defensive bowling, field placings and slow, by comparison, over rates. Jessop gained eternal fame, winning the Oval Test in 1902 with a memorable innings.

Hammond was born in Dover, spent his childhood in Malta, and, luckily for Gloucestershire, his family returned to Cirencester. Magnificently and athletically built, Hammond excelled at any game

DR. W. G. GRACE.

GLOUCESTERSHIRE C.C.C.

he took up, and he had a majestic style on the cricket field whether cover driving, bowling or at slip, where he took the majority of his 819 catches. Nine of his 22 Test centuries were against Australia, and in his prime in the 1928–9 series he hit 905 runs and averaged 113. Australia's captain, Jack Ryder, said: 'My, how that man could hit a cricket ball. You'd need twenty fielders to stop him.'

For eight successive years Hammond headed the national batting averages, and, until Hutton broke it, he held the record individual Test score of 336 not out against New Zealand at Auckland in 1933. In all he scored 50,551 runs and 167 centuries.

To follow Grace as England and Gloucestershire captain Hammond was obliged by the conventions of the time to change his status from pro to amateur. The county were 3rd under him in 1939, but it is perhaps surprising that Hammond's brilliance could not bring the title south, short though they were of genuine speed. The irreverent Charlie Parker, quoted by David Foot in *Cricket's Unholy Trinity* had his own theory! 'There are only two weaknesses in our team – brewer's asthma and financial cramp, and, apart from the fact we ain't good enough.'

Parker's left arm spin brought 3,278 wickets. Dennett, before him, had 2,147 which meant a combined total of 5,425 with the one cap going to Parker between them. They were outstanding bowlers. Goddard, Allen, Mortimore and Cook were worthy successors.

The attack-minded Barnett, Graveney, with a touch as smooth as silk, and Emmett were extremely attractive, but Graveney left for Worcestershire in 1960 after the decision to depose him from the captaincy in favour of the amateur Tom Pugh. He not only enjoyed but flourished in his second career.

Milton, a double cricket and soccer international, the left-handed Crapp, were rightly called up by England, and under Tony Brown there was a consistency not achieved since the Graces. Though the title remained elusive – in four seasons since 1946 Gloucestershire were runners-up in tight finishes – the Gillette Cup was won in 1973, the first competitive victory for 96 years with the final a personal triumph for Brown.

The brilliant South African all-rounder Procter, a diamond ever sparkling, was also a decisive leader when the Benson and Hedges Cup was won and 3rd place was taken in the championship in 1977.

Pakistan's brilliant Zaheer Abbas achieved the unique distinction of scoring a double and a century in the same match on no less than four occasions, the victims being Surrey, Kent, Sussex and Somerset. Even more remarkably he was not dismissed once. He also scored two separate centuries in a match eight times. The next best was Hammond with seven, and Zaheer completed a career, comparable with the best in history, with 108 centuries. [A.B.]

Founded 1871
Colours Blue, green, gold, brown, sky-blue and red
Crest Coat of arms of the City and County of Bristol
Secretary P.G.M. August
Senior Coach J.N. Shepherd
Groundsman D. Brindle
Scorer A.G. Avery/B. Jenkins
Address Phoenix County Cricket Ground, Nevil Road, Bishopston, Bristol BS7 9EJ
Telephone 0272 45216/46743
Cricketcall 0898 121434

Achievements:

County Championship Champions (3) 1874, 1876 and 1877; Joint Champions (1) 1873
Gillette Cup Winners 1973
National Westminster Bank Trophy Semi-finalists 1987
Benson & Hedges Cup Winners 1977
John Player Sunday League Champions (0) 6th 1969, 1973 and 1977
Refuge Assurance Sunday League Champions (0) 2nd 1988
Refuge Assurance Cup Semi-finalists 1988
Tilcon Trophy Winners 1987
Ward Knockout Cup Semi-finalists 1988
Seven Trophy Winners 1987

Grounds:

Bristol (Phoenix County Cricket Ground, Nevil Road) Gloucester (Winget Sports Ground, Tuffley Avenue) Cheltenham (College Ground, Thirlestaine Road) Swindon (County Ground, County

OGDEN'S CIGARETTES

T. W. GODDARD

PARKER

GLOUCESTERSHIRE

WILLS'S CIGARETTES.

G. DENNETT (GLOUCESTERSHIRE).

Road) Moreton-in-Marsh (Moreton Cricket Ground, Batsford Road).

Other grounds that have been used since 1969 are: Cheltenham (Victoria Ground, Prince's Street), Lydney (Recreational Trust Ground, Swan Road), Stroud (Eriniod Ground) and Tewkesbury (The Swilgate).

Bristol

The Phoenix County Ground at Bristol, as it has been known since it was purchased by the Phoenix Assurance Company in 1976, is situated in Ashley Down, on the northern outskirts of the city. The observant visitor will notice that the surrounding roads bear the names of other first-class and minor counties. The County's previous home was Clifton College.

The present ground, which was first used by Gloucestershire in 1889 against Lancashire, was laid out to W.G. Grace's specification. Later, in 1916, it was sold to Fry's chocolate company to get the county club out of debt, and became known as the Fry's Ground. The county club repurchased the ground in 1932 after forming Gloucestershire C C C Ltd.

Since W.G. first contemplated the development of the ground a century ago, many changes have taken place, but there still remains a sense of spaciousness about the area. The ground now houses facilities for indoor nets, squash, tennis and even an outdoor golf driving range, as well as football and hockey pitches during the winter

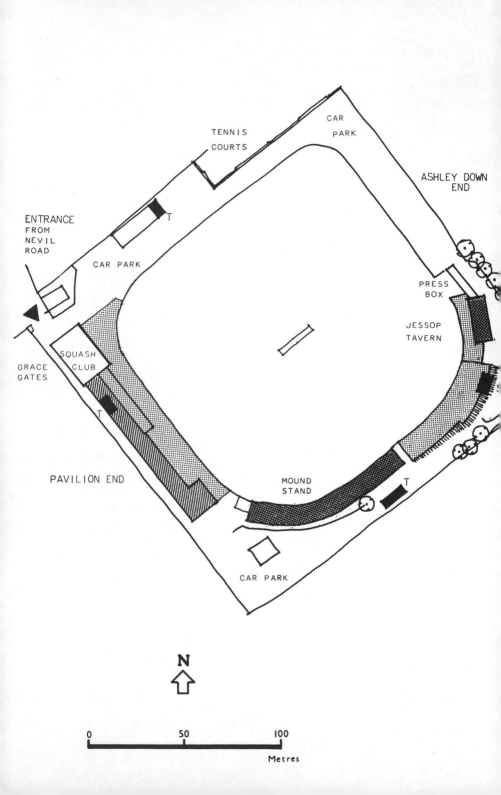

TENNIS
COURTS

CAR
PARK

ASHLEY DOWN
END

ENTRANCE
FROM
NEVIL
ROAD

CAR PARK

T

PRESS
BOX

JESSOP
TAVERN

GRACE
GATES

SQUASH
CLUB

T

PAVILION END

MOUND
STAND

T

CAR PARK

N

0   50   100

Metres

months. The County have played on three other grounds in the city, at Clifton College, Durdham Down and Greenbank, of which Clifton was the last to stage a match, in 1932.

From 1840 until the 1870s the ground was used by Muller's Orphanage. The orphanage building still exists today and now forms part of the Bristol Polytechnic campus. The entrance to the ground from Nevil Road is through the Grace Gates and the tablet was erected on the centenary of his birth, 18 July 1948. John Arlott wrote 'in the public mind W.G. was Gloucestershire'; he scored many of his hundreds at Bristol.

Ground improvements proposed for the future include a new indoor school and the replacement of wooden seating around the ground with the plastic tip-up variety. The pavilion was built during the 1880s, other additions have been made in recent years. The Jessop Tavern, which also houses the press box, was built in 1958 and the nearby scoreboard in 1971. The mound stand was built during the 1960s. The Grace Room and Hammond Room now form the restaurant at the Pavilion End.

Crowds at Bristol are usually around 5,000–6,000 for popular games. The best crowds were around 15,000 for the visits of the Australians in 1930 and 1948. In August 1930 Gloucestershire tied with the tourists and the city erupted with excitement. Gloucestershire were dismissed for 72 in their first innings and in their second Hammond scored 89 before Goddard and Parker tied up the match including Bradman and all.

All five limited-overs records on the ground have fallen to overseas players, two South Africans, two Pakistanis and one West Indian. Two overseas nations played on the ground in 1983 when a Prudential Cup game was staged between New Zealand and Sri Lanka.

With Grace and Jessop, Dipper and Hammond, Sinfield and Barnett, Crapp and Emmett, Goddard and Parker, Graveney and Allen, Zaheer and Proctor . . . few grounds can have a record to compare with Bristol's for nurturing some of the best players in the game.

ADDRESS Phoenix County Cricket Ground, Nevil Road, Bishopston, Bristol, Avon BS7 9EJ
TELEPHONE PROSPECTS OF PLAY 0272 48461

DESCRIPTION OF GROUND AND FACILITIES

There are two entrances to the Phoenix County Ground, the main entrance from Nevill Road through the 'Grace Gates' and a further access point from the Ashley Down Road, behind the Jessop Tavern. Most of the permanent buildings are sited at the south and south-east side of the ground including the pavilion which includes the county office, changing facilities, scorer's box and dining areas, plus the squash courts, indoor school, Hammond and Grace rooms, where refreshment/bar facilities are sited along with clubroom and bar.

There is some raised seating above the Hammond Room and ample ground level seating near to the playing area for members. The south-east side includes the Mound Stand, which is covered, and a terrace of yellow, plastic seats situated in front of the main scoreboard. Public refreshments are available in the Jessop Tavern, in front of which further seats can be found. The press box is sited at this end, above the store.

The north side of the ground includes car parking, a groundsman's store, toilets and tennis courts. Also, during festival week, a number of sponsors' tents are sited on this side. There is the facility to bring in further seating of the raised, temporary variety for popular matches and these are usually sited at the Ashley Down End and in front of the squash court building. The members' enclosure spans the pavilion end completely. The playing area is 154 metres by 156 metres and is defined by a rope and advertising boards completely surrounding the perimeter. The ground capacity is 8,000 and around 3,500 seats are provided but further seating is installed for popular matches. Spectators would however, be advised to bring their own. The T V camera position is sited on top of the pavilion and the radio point is sited next to the press box, above the Jessop Tavern.

The ground is surrounded by housing and to the south the Bristol Polytechnic buildings, built of similar stone to that of the pavilion. Many photographs of the history of the Club are to be found in the pavilion and bars.

GROUND RECORDS AND SCORES

FIRST-CLASS MATCHES

Highest innings total for County   653 for 6 dec. v. Glamorgan, 1928
Highest innings total against County   774 for 7 dec. by Australians, 1948
Lowest innings total for County   22 v. Somerset, 1920
Lowest innings total against County   25 by Somerset, 1947
Highest individual innings for County   302 n.o. W.R. Hammond v. Glamorgan, 1934
Highest individual innings against County   290 A.R. Morris for Australians, 1948
Best bowling performance in an innings for County   10 for 40 E.G. Dennett v. Essex, 1906
Best bowling performance in an innings against County   9 for 41 F.A. Tarrant for Middlesex, 1907
Best bowling performance in a match for County   17 for 106 T.W. Goddard v. Kent, 1938
Best bowling performance in a match against County   15 for 98 F.H. Parris for Sussex, 1894

LIMITED-OVERS MATCHES

Highest innings total for County   297 for 8 v. Scotland (NWBT), 1983

Highest innings total against County 349 for 6 by Lancashire (NWBT), 1984

Lowest innings total for County 49 v. Middlesex (JPL), 1978

Lowest innings total against County 77 by Hampshire (JPL), 1970

Highest individual innings for County 128 Sadiq Mohammad v. Minor Counties South (BHC), 1974 Zaheer Abbas v. Worcestershire (GC), 1976

Highest individual innings against County 129 B.A. Richards for Hampshire (BHC), 1974

Best bowling performance for County 6 for 52 J.N. Shepherd v. Kent (JPL), 1983

Best bowling performance against County 6 for 33 E.J. Barlow for Derbyshire (BHC), 1978

HOW TO GET THERE

Rail Montpelier, ¾ mile; Bristol Temple Meads, 2½ miles; Bristol Parkway, 5 miles

Bus City Line 78 from BR Temple Meads Approach Road; 72/3 from BR Parkway Station; 71–8 from City Centre (Tel: 0272 553231)

Car From north: M5 junction 17 follow signs Bristol A38 and city centre, then follow signs for County Cricket and Nevil Road. From east: M4 junction 19, then M32 to junction 2, then follow signs to Bristol A38 and city centre, then as north. From west: as north or A370, A369 or A38 to City Centre then A38 to Gloucester, follow signs County Cricket and Nevil Road. From south: A37 or A4 to city centre, then as west.

WHERE TO STAY AND OTHER INFORMATION

Grand Hotel (0272 291645), Holiday Inn (0272 294281), Clifton Hotel (0272 736882), Unicorn Hotel (0272 230333)

Disabled Areas No special area, request position

Local Radio Station(s) BBC Radio Bristol (95.5 MHz FM/1548 KHz MW), Great Western Radio (96.3 MHz FM/1260 KHz MW)

Local Newspaper(s) Bristol Evening Post, Western Daily Press, Bristol Journal, Bristol Observer, Sunday Independent

Cheltenham

Gloucestershire have staged a cricket festival at the College Ground since 1872. This usually takes place in August after the college term has ended. The initial match was with Surrey in July 1872 and the County have visited two other grounds in the town since, the East Gloucestershire Ground from 1888 until 1903 and then the Victoria

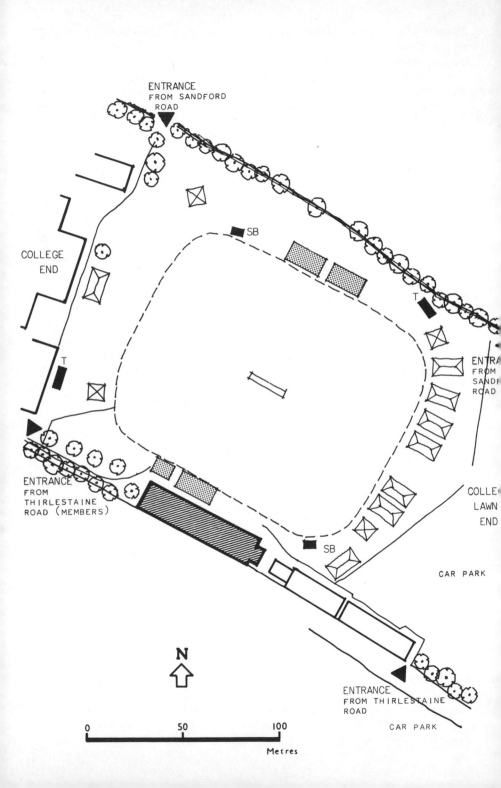

ENTRANCE
FROM SANDFORD
ROAD

SB

COLLEGE
END

T

T

ENTRANCE
FROM
THIRLESTAINE
ROAD (MEMBERS)

SB

ENTRA
FROM
SANDF
ROAD

COLLE
LAWN
END

CAR PARK

N

ENTRANCE
FROM THIRLESTAINE
ROAD

CAR PARK

0   50   100

Metres

Ground from 1923 to 1937. One match was played with the Indian touring team in May 1986 at Cheltenham C C (Victoria Ground) because the College Ground was being used, but otherwise all recent matches have been at the College Ground. Gloucestershire today take three championship and two limited-over matches to the ground. These are always well supported; crowds tend to be about 6,000 and the largest was 15,000 against Middlesex in 1947.

The first visits to Cheltenham College were organised by James Lillywhite, the former Sussex player. He died in 1882 and never knew the full success of the venture he had initiated. The festival is the longest on the County circuit and spans at least eleven consecutive cricket days, weather permitting!

The main permanent building on the ground used by the county is the gymnasium with its twin steeples of yellow brick and its trellised balcony. This is used as a pavilion and stands on the Thirlestaine Road side of the ground. Other buildings on this side of the ground are pavilions for schoolboy cricket, used during term time. The college chapel which overlooks the ground was built in 1893. It is possibly the most significant feature of the College Ground and appears in many photographs.

In 1969 the first limited-over match was staged and after good attendances a second was added in 1975. The ground has seen many achievements over the years including a 318 not out from Dr W.G. Grace and 17 for 89 in a match. The County collapsed to 17 all out against the Australians in 1896 thanks to fine bowling from the visitors – Trumble 6 for 8 and M'Kibbin 4 for 7. Others noteworthies include Jessop (born in Cheltenham) who hit 51 in 18 minutes against Yorkshire in 1895 and Hammond who in 1928, in his first match on the famous ground, scored 139 and 143 and took ten catches against Surrey. Tom Goddard and Charlie Parker, two great County bowlers, have both enjoyed matches here after rain and before wickets were covered. Three overseas players have fond memories of Cheltenham: Mike Proctor who in 1979 against Yorkshire repeated his own record of three l.b.w.'s in a hat trick (the previous against Essex in 1972), Zaheer Abbas of Pakistan who scored 205 and 108 (both not out) against Sussex in 1977 and finally Glenn Turner who scored 181 for Worcestershire in 1974 during their championship season. Matches have been staged with touring teams here rather than at Bristol.

ADDRESS Cheltenham College, College Sports Ground, Thirlestaine Road, Cheltenham, Gloucestershire
TELEPHONE PROSPECTS OF PLAY 0242 522000

DESCRIPTION OF GROUND AND FACILITIES

There are three entrances to the College Ground, two in Thirlestaine Road and one in Sandford Road. Car parking is available within the ground at the College Lawn End, through the entrance to the south of the ground, which is also used by spectators, and in the adjacent college fields. The permanent buildings, sited to the south of the playing area, are the gymnasium which is used as a pavilion by players and members for refreshments and the pavilion and stores which are used for catering requirements. Much of the south side is used as a members' enclosure and sponsors' marquees surround the College Lawn End. The Sandford Road side has two large, temporary, open tiered seating areas as well as a temporary scoreboard, press/scorer's tent and Gloucestershire C C S C souvenir marquee. At the College End is the Gloucestershire C C C secretary's temporary office (in a bus), telephones, several refreshment marquees and further sponsors' tents. In front of the pavilion (gymnasium) are two large, raised plastic seating stands, a further permanent green scorebox and more refreshment facilities. Most of the seating is temporary and of the bench, plastic or raised seating variety. The capacity is 8,000 and seating for about 65 per cent is provided. Spectators would be advised to bring their own seating to popular matches. The playing area is 120 metres by 150 metres and is defined by advertising boards and a rope around part of the playing area.

The School buildings provide a beautiful backcloth to the cricket festival.

GROUND RECORDS AND SCORES

FIRST-CLASS MATCHES
Highest innings total for County   608 for 7 dec. v. Sussex, 1934
Highest innings total against County   607 for 6 dec. by Kent, 1910
Lowest innings total for County   17 v. Australians, 1896
Lowest innings total against County   27 by Surrey, 1874
Highest individual innings for County   318 n.o. W.G. Grace v. Yorkshire, 1876
Highest individual innings against County   181 G.M. Turner for Worcestershire, 1974
Best bowling performance in an innings for County   10 for 113 T.W. Goddard v. Worcestershire, 1937
Best bowling performance in an innings against County   10 for 66 A.A. Mailey for Australians, 1921
Best bowling performance in a match for County   17 for 89 W.G. Grace v. Nottinghamshire, 1877
Best bowling performance in a match against County   15 for 184 W.H. Lockwood for Surrey, 1899

LIMITED-OVERS MATCHES
Highest innings total for County   233 for 5 v. Yorkshire (JPL), 1983
Highest innings total against County   283 for 6 by Essex (JPL), 1975
Lowest innings total for County   122 v. Hampshire (JPL), 1978
Lowest innings total against County   85 by Warwickshire (JPL), 1973
Highest individual innings for County   109 n.o. M.J. Procter v. Warwickshire (JPL), 1972

Highest individual innings against County   100 n.o. R.J. Hadlee for Nottinghamshire (JPL), 1982
Best bowling performance for County   5 for 20 J.H. Shackleton v. Surrey (JPL), 1977
Best bowling performance against County   4 for 18 D. Underwood for Kent (JPL), 1975

HOW TO GET THERE

Rail   Cheltenham Spa, 1 mile
Bus   Cheltenham and District L from City Centre (F/G link BR Station with City Centre) (Tel: 0242 522021)
Car   From north: M5 junction 10 then A4019 follow signs Cheltenham and town centre, ground situated in Thirlestaine Road adjoining Cheltenham College, or A435 to town centre. From east: A436 or A40 then follow signs Charlton Kings and Cheltenham, to town centre, then as north. From west: M5 junction 11, then follow A40 Cheltenham and town centre, then as north or A46 or A435 to town centre. From south: M4 junction 15 then A419, A417 and B4070 or A435 to Cheltenham and town centre, then as north.

WHERE TO STAY AND OTHER INFORMATION

Queen's Hotel (0242 514724), George Hotel (0242 35751), Carlton Hotel (0242 514453), Park Place Hotel (0242 525353)

Disabled Areas   No special area, request position
Local Radio Station(s)   BBC Radio Gloucestershire (104.7 MHz FM), Severn Sound (102.4 MHz FM/774 KHz MW)
Local Newspaper(s)   Gloucestershire Echo, Cheltenham News, Gloucestershire County Gazette, The Source

Gloucester

The first ground in the city used by Gloucestershire was the Spa Ground, between 1883 and 1921. The move to Tuffley Avenue came in 1923 when Lancashire were the visitors. Since that initial visit the ground has had various names, first it was known as the Gloucestershire Railway Carriage and Wagon Company Ground until in 1962 it was taken over after 102 years by the Gloucester Engineering Sports Club and then shortly afterwards the Babcocks and Wilcox Sports Club. The ground today is called Winget Sports Ground and used by the Winget C C. The ground was originally 33 acres or so and was bought by the railway carriage company from the executors of a Colonel Collett in 1917 under the provisions of the 1916 Finance Act for £4,005. 20 acres were sold off for £525,000 in 1973; the remainder forms the ground, which is situated in residential Gloucester south of the city centre. There used to be twelve plane trees in front of the pavilion but upon the death of a prominent club member and cricketer one tree was felled.

The connection of railways with the ground is still prominent: the pavilion serving the nearby bowling green adjacent to the main cricket pavilion is an old railway carriage. It was built for the Central Argentine Railway – Ferro Carril Central Argentina El Pacifico – in 1914 and was shipped early in 1915. The ship was torpedoed, but two carriages were salvaged and brought back to Gloucester and placed on the ground. One is still used by bowls players and cricketers but the second was burnt down some years ago. The scoreboard today is sponsored by Gloucester City Council.

In recent years the ground has again changed hands and is now owned by the city council which acquired it for £75,000 – a nominal price for the 13 remaining acres – and so saved the ground from being developed into a housing estate. The council's hope was that Gloucestershire C C C might make Gloucester, the county town its permanent home. This was not to be and the County today take two championship and one limited-over match to the ground in July as a festival week.

The ground has had many famous visitors including A.J. Paish, Dr W.G. Grace and G.L. Jessop who laid the ground out in 1917–18. The present groundsman is John Taylor who also prepares the wicket for first-class matches at Cheltenham College. Crowds have been good at Tuffley Avenue. The best was 9,000 in August 1959 against Surrey, but matches in recent years have only attracted 5,000–5,500.

The ground has seen its fair share of records including 317 from Walter Hammond in 1936 and fine bowling from Charlie Parker. McCorkell, Dollery and Hardinge scored double hundreds for the visitors the latter the highest.

Fast hundreds have included one from Tom Graveney against Combined Services. Limited-over records have included hundreds from players representing Leicestershire and Gloucestershire, Davison the Rhodesian and Dudleston (now a first-class umpire). Mike Proctor's 5 for 8 against Middlesex is also a significant limited-overs record.

ADDRESS   Winget Sports C C, Winget Sports Ground, Tuffley Avenue, Gloucester GL1 5NS
TELEPHONE PROSPECTS OF PLAY   0452 423011

DESCRIPTION OF GROUND AND FACILITIES

The ground is entered from Tuffley Avenue where there are two entrances, one for players and officials and another for spectators and vehicles. The pavilion, clubhouse and all permanent buildings are sited to the east of the playing area with the press, scorer's and

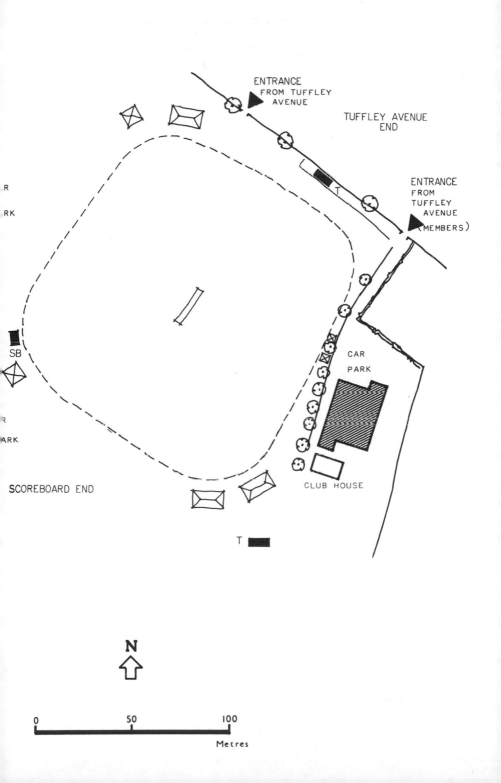

ENTRANCE
FROM TUFFLEY
AVENUE

TUFFLEY AVENUE
END

T

ENTRANCE
FROM
TUFFLEY
AVENUE
(MEMBERS)

R

RK

SB

R

ARK

CAR
PARK

CLUB HOUSE

SCOREBOARD END

T

N

0   50   100

Metres

groundsman's tents under the trees. A number of sponsors' marquees and a bus are sited to the south near the tennis courts and bowling green. At this end is the T V camera and radio point together with the main scoreboard. To the west is the large car parking area and, close to the main entrance, two large refreshment tents and a large marquee for public and members' bars. There is also a first aid caravan and Gloucestershire C C S C caravan where souvenirs are sold. A number of smaller refreshment and temporary toilets and a second, smaller scoreboard are sited near the Tuffley Avenue boundary. There is no covered seating and all seating is temporary, either made up of plastic seats or benches, 2-3 deep around the playing area. The playing area is defined by a rope and advertising boards and is 146 metres by 154 metres. It is roughly circular in shape. The ground capacity is 6,000 and 70 per cent are provided with seating. Spectators are only advised to bring seats to attractive fixtures. The members enclosure covers an area from the Tuffley Road End sightscreen eastwards to the sightscreen at the opposite end. The south and west side of the ground is slightly banked and hence a good view of cricket can be gained from this area towards the flat playing area.

GROUND RECORDS AND SCORES

FIRST-CLASS MATCHES
Highest innings total for County   529 *v.* Glamorgan, 1933
Highest innings total against County   553 by Essex, 1938
Lowest innings total for County   42 *v.* Yorkshire, 1924
Lowest innings total against County   34 by Cambridge University, 1946
Highest individual innings for County   317 W.R. Hammond *v.* Nottinghamshire, 1936
Highest individual innings against County   263 n.o. H.T.W. Hardinge for Kent, 1928
Best bowling performance in an innings for County   9 for 44 C.W.L. Parker *v.* Essex, 1925
Best bowling performance in an innings against County   9 for 37 M.S. Nichols for Essex, 1938
Best bowling performance in a match for County   17 for 56 C.W.L. Parker *v.* Essex, 1925
Best bowling performance in a match against County   15 for 165 M.S. Nichols for Essex, 1938

LIMITED-OVERS MATCHES
Highest innings total for County   216 for 6 *v.* Yorkshire (JPL), 1985
Highest innings total against County   272 for 4 by Derbyshire (JPL), 1984
Lowest innings total for County   107 *v.* Kent (JPL), 1979
Lowest innings total against County   86 by Middlesex (JPL), 1977
Highest individual innings for County   103 B.F. Davison *v.* Yorkshire (JPL), 1985

Highest individual innings against County   109 n.o. B. Dudleston
for Leicestershire (JPL), 1974
Best bowling performance for County   5 for 8 M.J. Procter *v.*
Middlesex (JPL), 1977
Best bowling performance against County   4 for 17 V.A. Holder for
Worcestershire (JPL), 1971

HOW TO GET THERE

Rail   Gloucester Central, 1 mile
Bus   City of Gloucester Bus Co. 8, 20/A, 50 from City Centre
(passing within 300m of BR Station) (Tel: 0452 27516)
Car   From north: M5 junction 11 then follow signs Gloucester A40
and A38 to Tuffley 1½ miles south of city centre, ground situated
in Tuffley Avenue off (A38). From east: A436, A417 to Gloucester
ring road then follow A38 to Tuffley, then as north. From west:
A417, A48 and B4215 follow signs Gloucester, then ring road and
A38 Tuffley, then as north. From south: M5 junction 12 then A38
to Tuffley, then as north, or A4173.

WHERE TO STAY AND OTHER INFORMATION

New County Hotel (0452 24977), Fleece Hotel (0452 22762),
Bowden Hall (0452 64121), Crest Hotel (0452 63311)

Disabled Areas   No special area, request position
Local Radio Station(s)   BBC Radio Gloucestershire (104.7 MHz
FM), Severn Sound (102.4 MHz FM/774 KHz MW), BBC Radio
Hereford and Worcester (94.7 MHz FM)
Local Newspaper(s)   Gloucester Citizen, Gloucestershire Echo,
Gloucester Express, Gloucester News, The Source

Moreton-in-Marsh

Gloucestershire travel once a season to the Cotswold village of
Moreton-in-Marsh to play a limited-over match. The first visit was
made in 1884 when a first class match was staged with Yorkshire.
The County also played at Batsford Road in 1886–8 and again in 1914
but not until the introduction of one-day cricket did the County
return. The first limited-overs at Moreton-in-Marsh was a Benson and
Hedges Cup match with Hampshire in 1972. Since then one match
has been staged each season, usually in late August.

The ground is the home of the Moreton-in-Marsh C C which was
founded in 1856: in that year, having no pavilion, members decided
to purchase a tent to serve the purpose. The decision is recorded in
the club's minute book which is still kept in the pavilion today.

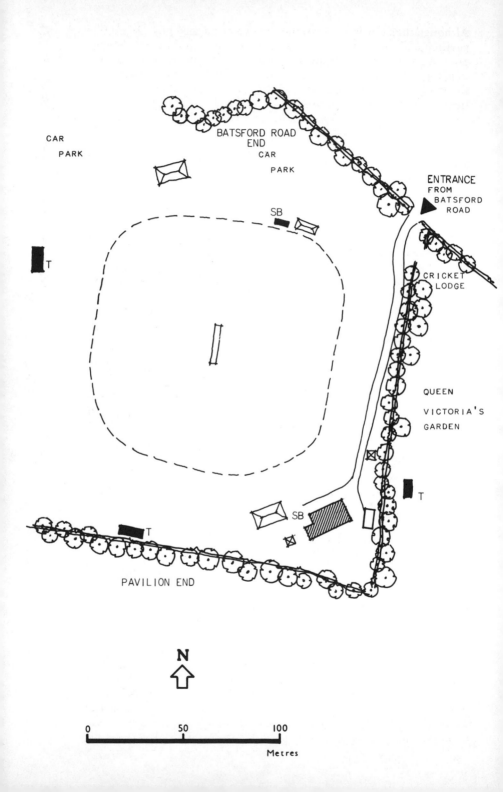

CAR PARK

BATSFORD ROAD END
CAR PARK

ENTRANCE
FROM
BATSFORD
ROAD

SB

T

CRICKET
LODGE

QUEEN
VICTORIA'S
GARDEN

T

SB

T

PAVILION END

N

0   50   100

Metres

Although the club do not own their own ground they now have a fine pavilion and the 15 acres of land on which the cricket pitch, hockey pitches and tennis courts are situated still costs the same annual fee that they have paid for as long as anyone can remember. Originally the land was owned by Baron Redesdale, a farmer (a local hostelry in the High Street still bears his coat of arms) and at one time the ground was the property of the Freeman-Mitford family. Whoever owned the land, however, cricket still continued.

The club has spent money on improving the drainage system but after heavy rain the field tends to be waterlogged and boggy in places. At the rear of the pavilion is Queen Victoria's Garden. The only entrance to the ground is from Batsford Road past the Cricket Lodge house which overlooks the field of play. Crowds have been good at Moreton, for the locals tend to support matches well, and 4,000–5,000 can be expected on a fine day. Moreton draws many visitors as Gloucestershire usually select opponents from the north of the country to visit the ground and this attracts a greater attendance from these areas than would be expected at Bristol. Moreton is closer to Edgbaston, Worcester and Northampton than the County's headquarters.

In the early years of Gloucestershire's visits to Moreton there were some outstanding performances, including a 227 not out by Arthur Shrewsbury for Nottinghamshire and 116 by H.V. Page against Somerset. Not until a hundred years later in 1985 did a Gloucestershire player score a century on the ground. This was in a limited-over match, when Bill Athey hit 121 not out against Worcestershire. In 1888 Lord Harris took his Kent side to Moreton and suffered the mortification of seeing them dismissed for 28 in a hour and a half when Woof and Roberts dismissed them with 5 for 18 and 5 for 8 respectively. In their second innings Kent only managed 52. With Gloucestershire scoring 124 the home team had enough to win.

ADDRESS Moreton-in-Marsh C C, The Pavilion, Batsford Road, Moreton-in-Marsh, Gloucestershire GL56 0JD
TELEPHONE PROSPECTS OF PLAY 0608 50190/50178

DESCRIPTION OF GROUND AND FACILITIES

The only entrance to the ground, for all pedestrians and vehicles, is from Batsford Road. The only permanent building on the ground is the pavilion which comprises changing facilities for players, and a dining area and bar refreshments for members. There is also a groundsman's store to the rear, and a scoreboard built within the pavilion structure. The members' enclosure is in front of the pavilion and, as with all the seating around the ground, is at ground level. All the facilities are temporary including the toilets, an additional scoreboard and Gloucestershire C C S C souvenir tent. Refreshments for members and the public are in two large marquees near the pavilion. The T V camera position and radio point is located at the pavilion end directly behind the sightscreen. Both sightscreens are temporary as the club sightscreens are not sufficient for county matches. This is due to the number of trees surrounding the enclosed ground. A press/scorers' tent is situated close to the temporary scoreboard, near the entrance. Car parking is available within the ground and also surrounding the seats which are usually 2-3 deep around the playing area. Cricket can therefore be viewed from the car. Space is available for approximately 2,000 cars and the ground capacity is 6,000 but seating is provided for only 10 per cent. Spectators are advised to bring their own seats with them to all matches. Car parking is also available in the adjacent show field or Queen Victoria's Garden over the bridge, behind the pavilion. The playing area is circular in shape and defined by a rope and several advertising boards. It is 126 metres by 132 metres.

GROUND RECORDS AND SCORES

FIRST-CLASS MATCHES

Highest innings total for County   448 v. Somerset, 1885
Highest innings total against County   430 by Nottinghamshire, 1886
Lowest innings total for County   96 v. Worcestershire, 1914
Lowest innings total against County   28 by Kent, 1888
Highest individual innings for County   116 H.V. Page v. Somerset, 1885
Highest individual innings against County   227 n.o. A. Shrewsbury for Nottinghamshire, 1887
Best bowling performance in an innings for County   7 for 28 W.A. Woof v. Somerset, 1885
Best bowling performance in an innings against County   9 for 38 A.J. Conway for Worcestershire, 1914
Best bowling performance in a match for County   12 for 50 W.A. Woof v. Somerset, 1885
Best bowling performance in a match against County   15 for 87 A.J. Conway for Worcestershire, 1914

LIMITED-OVERS MATCHES

Highest innings total for County   221 for 1 v. Worcestershire (JPL), 1985
Highest innings total against County   258 for 6 by Warwickshire (JPL), 1979
Lowest innings total for County   70 v. Hampshire (BHC), 1972
Lowest innings total against County   109 for 7 by Nottinghamshire (RAL), 1987
Highest individual innings for County   121 n.o. C.W.J. Athey v. Worcestershire (JPL), 1985
Highest individual innings against County   101 A.I. Kallicharran for Warwickshire (JPL), 1979
Best bowling performance for County   4 for 23 D.A. Graveney v. Worcestershire (JPL), 1976
Best bowling performance against County   4 for 17 P.J. Sainsbury for Hampshire (BHC), 1972

HOW TO GET THERE

Rail Moreton-in-Marsh, 1¼ miles
Bus Pullhams buses from surrounding areas to Terminal in town
Car From north: A429 follow signs Moreton-in-Marsh, ground situated north of main High Street off Batsford Road on village outskirts. From east and west: A44 follow signs Moreton-in-Marsh, then as north. From south: A429 follow signs Moreton-in-Marsh, then as north.

WHERE TO STAY AND OTHER INFORMATION

Manor House Hotel (0608 50501), Redesdale Arms (0608 50308), White Hart Royal Hotel (0608 50731)

Disabled Areas No special area, request position
Local Radio Station(s) BBC Radio Gloucestershire (104.7 MHz FM), Severn Sound (102.4 MHz FM/774 KHz MW), BBC Radio Oxford (95.2 MHz FM/1485 KHz MW)
Local Newspaper(s) The Citizen, Gloucestershire County Gazette, Gloucestershire Echo, Evesham Journal, Cotswold Standard

Swindon

Proud tenants of a ground they fairly claim to be one of the best in the west of England, Swindon C C was formed in 1844 when home and away fixtures were played with Malmesbury. In 1985 the club celebrated 90 seasons at their present ground, the County Ground.

In 1844 the club's home ground was in the area where Upham Road now is. It was in this era that one of the most famous cricketers ever to represent Swindon, E.H. Budd, played; in 1848 at the age of 63 he took 10 wickets in a match against Stroud. In the prime of his career Budd played for the Gentlemen against the Players each year from 1806 to 1830. In 1849 the club moved to a ground in the Greywethers Avenue area of the town; records indicate that during this period the club had no pavilion and instead used tents. 1860 saw the club merge with the Swindon Rangers Football Club; they played at a ground called the Sands in the Goddard Avenue area. In the early 1890s a small group of businessmen formed a company with a capital of £700 to acquire and develop the club's 5½ acre present headquarters at the County Ground. It was at this time that the Great Western Railway C C and Swindon C C combined to form the Swindon C C as we know it today. The new club moved to the ground in 1895. In the first year Bobby Reynolds scored 192 against Chippenham, still to this day the highest individual innings on the ground.

Another feat was that of Billy Overton who played regularly for Wiltshire and in 1903 was the first bowler to take 100 wickets in a

Minor Counties season. He helped Wiltshire to the Championship in 1907 and 1909, the last time they won it. Playing for the M C C against the club in 1903 he took 6 for 3 as Swindon were dismissed for 10. Other Swindon players to have made significant contribution to Minor Counties cricket were Ted Nash and Bert Lloyd. Nash kept wicket for the County and made almost 200 appearances, Lloyd is best remembered for his 196 against a Surrey second eleven at the Oval when he is alleged to have tamed the Bedser twins.

In 1940 the County Ground was requisitioned by the War Department and became a temporary prisoner-of-war camp. The ground is located at the rear of Swindon Town Football Ground and was first used by Gloucestershire in 1970 when a John Player Sunday League match was staged with Sussex. Not until fifteen years later did Gloucestershire return, this time again for a Sunday match when the opponents were once again Sussex. A year later Essex were the visitors and on this occasion Alan Border the Australian captain, who was playing for Essex, opened the new scorebox. In 1987 Sussex made their third visit, this time for a Refuge Assurance League match.

In 1988 Warwickshire were due to come and a Benson and Hedges zonal fixture was also planned between Minor Counties C A and Worcestershire but the two matches had to be rearranged at Bristol and Old Hill C C because the pitch had been damaged by weedkiller. The ground is also used by Wiltshire for Minor County matches; in recent years National Westminster Bank Trophy matches have been staged with Northamptonshire and Leicestershire. In 1967 the Minor Counties staged a match with the Pakistani tourists.

Crowds at the County Ground have usually been 2,500–3,000. In 1984 3,500 people attended the Wiltshire versus Leicestershire NatWest match and were rewarded by 155 from James Whittaker.

ADDRESS   Swindon C C, County Ground, County Road, Swindon, Wiltshire
TELEPHONE PROSPECTS OF PLAY   0793 23088

DESCRIPTION OF GROUND AND FACILITIES

The county ground is entered from County Road where there are two entrances. The pavilion, which includes first floor seating for members as well as two large groundsman's stores, is situated at the northern end of the ground, close to the bowling club. The ground is over-shadowed by the back of the large Swindon Town Football Stand and tall floodlight pylons to the south of the playing area. The members' enclosure is in front of the players pavilion and close to the sponsors' marquees and members'/public beer tent and refreshment area. There are a number of temporary toilets and at least two or three deep seats and benches surrounding the playing area which are transported for the day from Bristol. There is a new scoreboard at the south-east corner, and the T V camera position is sited directly behind the bowler's arm at the football ground end. A press tent and scorers'

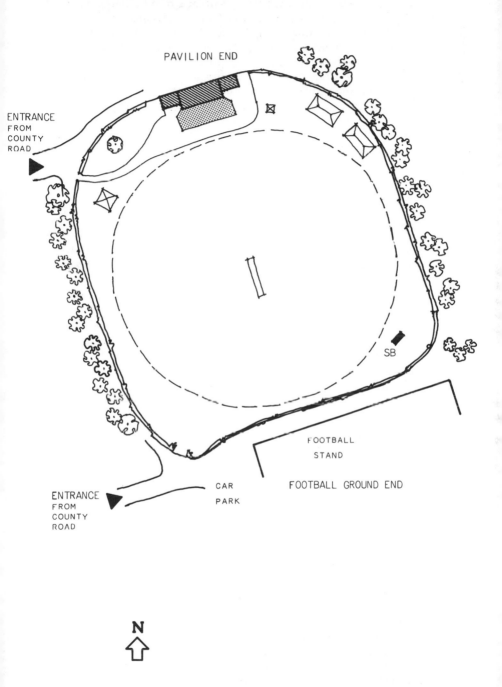

PAVILION END

ENTRANCE
FROM
COUNTY
ROAD

SB

FOOTBALL
STAND

FOOTBALL GROUND END

ENTRANCE
FROM
COUNTY
ROAD

CAR
PARK

N

0   50   100

Metres

area is situated close to the pavilion area near the Gloucestershire C C C secretary's caravan. A secondary scoreboard is sited in the pavilion for county matches. Car parking is available close to the pavilion for players/officials and to the west side of the football ground about 200 yards from the ground for members and the public.

The ground is sited close to the recreation ground and athletics track but is enclosed by trees and a hedge to the east, and housing and hedges to the west and north. The playing area is 148 metres by 142 metres and is defined by a rope and some advertising boards.

GROUND RECORDS AND SCORES

LIMITED-OVERS MATCHES

Highest innings total for County   224 for 6 v. Sussex (RAL), 1987
Highest innings total against County   221 for 5 by Sussex (RAL), 1987
Lowest innings total for County   115 for 5 v. Sussex (JPL), 1985
Lowest innings total against County   128 for 1 by Sussex (JPL), 1985
Highest individual innings for County   80 A.J. Wright v. Sussex (RAL), 1987
Highest individual innings against County   71 n.o. B.R. Hardie for Essex (JPL), 1986
Best bowling performance for County   3 for 25 M.J. Procter v. Sussex (JPL), 1970
Best bowling performance against County   3 for 11 Imran Khan for Sussex (JPL), 1985

HOW TO GET THERE

Rail   Swindon, ¾ mile
Bus   Thamesdown 7, 16–18 from BR Swindon Station (Tel: 0793 23700); Swindon TPT also from surrounding areas to Bus Station, thence ½ mile
Car   From north: A419, A361 or A420 to town centre, ground situated off County Road adjoining Swindon Town FC. From east: A420 to town centre, then as north or M4 junction 15 then A419 and A4253 to town centre then as north. From west: M4 junction 16 then follow signs Swindon and town centre, then as north. From south: A361 or A345 to town centre then as north.

WHERE TO STAY AND OTHER INFORMATION

Goddard Arms (0793 692313), Wiltshire Hotel (0793 28282),

Disabled Areas   No special area, request position
Local Radio Station(s)   BBC Radio Gloucestershire (104.7 MHz FM), Great Western Radio (96.3 MHz FM/1260 KHz MW)
Local Newspaper(s)   Swindon Evening Advertiser, Swindon Messenger, Wiltshire Star, Wiltshire Gazette and Herald, The Citizen, Gloucestershire Echo

HAMPSHIRE

SOUTHAMPTON

BASINGSTOKE

BOURNEMOUTH

PORTSMOUTH

Hampshire

Contrary to widely-held beliefs cricket's beginnings were in the Weald of Kent and Sussex, and not on Broadhalfpenny Down, but in the mid-1700s Hambledon's fame was unsurpassed. From John Nyren's writings, it would seem, the men of Hampshire enjoyed their cricket. 'The punch', records Nyren, 'would make a cat speak. Sixpence a bottle. Ale that would flare like turpentine. Twopence per pint.'

By 1793 Hambledon had given way to a Hampshire County Club, and by 1895 Hampshire had first-class status. No serious impact was made until the arrival from The Oval of Philip Mead, all-rounder Newman, bowler Kennedy and the character and man of all parts George Brown, in turn batsman, opening bowler and wicket-keeper. All gave yeomen and brilliant service until the 'thirties. Another pre-first war acquisition was C.B. Fry, who had taken charge of the training ship *Mercury* in the Hamble.

Mead scored 48,892 of his career's 55,061 runs for Hampshire, and, as he was the very devil to get out, his emergence from the pavilion is said to have provoked more unseemly language from fielders than any other batsman in history. For a batsman who scored 153 centuries, including four for England, in twenty-six innings, oddly he never overcame his nervousness in the 'nineties. But having completed a hundred he would turn to the wicket-keeper and say: 'That's another bag of coal for the winter.'

Life under the captaincy of the 3rd Baron Tennyson, captain from 1919 to 1933, was recalled by H.L.V. Day, rugby international and amateur batsman. He would cajole, harangue, curse or applaud as the fancy took him, and had a habit of sending telegrams to batsmen at the wicket couched in language less flowery than his grandfather's poetry. After being felled by a fast ball at Trent Bridge Day recovered to read: 'What do you think your — bat's for – Lionel.' A young amateur had the message: 'For God's sake get out and let someone else take a hundred off this jam.'

An occasional amateur, having an unhappy experience fielding on the boundary of Portsmouth, painfully exposed his inexperience by calling to his captain at the end of an over: 'And where do you want me now, Lionel?' The answer arrived loud and clear – but he remained on the field!

Day was invited in 1922 to travel with his captain from Southampton to Birmingham, a journey interrupted by visits to several country houses and ending as dawn was breaking. The next morning Hampshire were bowled out for 15 (Mead 6 not out) and following on 208 behind, made 521 at the second attempt, and won by 155 runs.

Tennyson was undaunted by adversity or speed merchants, and he is best remembered for the way he stood up to Gregory and McDonald during Australia's triumphant 1921 tour. After a brave 74 not out in the second Test Tennyson was appointed captain. A year before odds

HAMPSHIRE C C C

G. C. B. LLEWELLYN,
HAMPSHIRE.

of 1,000 to one against such a happening had been offered and taken!

With the passing of the grand old guard Hampshire suffered lean seasons leading up to Hitler's war. Arnold was the most consistent batsman, and joined the elite of double cricket and soccer internationals. Rogers was another fine opener, always on the edge of honours.

The path to the glory of Hampshire's first championship in 1961 – the first after sixty-six seasons – was laid by Desmond Eagar, a captain secretary of utter devotion to his club's cause. During his years Shackleton from Todmorden was changed from a moderate spinner-batsman into one of the most dangerous bowlers in the country at medium pace. His career ended with 2,857 wickets at only 18.65 apiece, and his new ball partnership with Cannings was consistently successful.

The gods were kind to Colin Ingleby-Mackenzie, Eagar's successor. He inherited mustard-keen fielders, and, though Cannings had left, Shackleton bowled with as much guile as ever and his new partner, White, was genuinely fast. Batting was powerful, and headed by Marshall, who exhibited all the exciting freshness of a player bred on Barbadian pitches. Horton, Gray, Livingstone, the captain himself, and all-rounder Sainsbury were just right for an apostle of brighter cricket, who thrived on declarations. At the time there was an experiment disallowing the follow on, and the engaging Ingleby-Mackenzie was a past master at judging situations. He also hit the right note in his attitude to the players and, if his declared discipline – nothing more than to have the players assembled at breakfast – was a leg pull, he had the knack of leadership. He was not to taste the fruits of victory again, but at least left his mark on Yorkshire when Shackleton, White and Cottam between them dismissed Yorkshire on a lively pitch at Middlesbrough for 23, their lowest total ever.

Twelve years later Richard Gilliat, no less enterprising, led a side, originally rated as no better than a fifty to one prospect, to

Hampshire's second county title. By then Barry Richards, the world's leading batsman from South Africa, and Gordon Greenidge, born in Barbados but a product of a Reading school, had been taken aboard. Later Andy Roberts, one of the breed of West Indies fast bowlers, spearheaded the attack, and, in due course, he was replaced by Malcolm Marshall.

As captain from 1971 to 1978 Gilliat had a championship, a second snatched from him by rain, and two victories in the Sunday League, to underscore Hampshire's strength. A third in the 40-over competition came to Mark Nicholas, who also broke the ice of Hampshire's failures in knock-out competitions by winning the Benson and Hedges Cup in 1988 – without the formidable assets of Greenidge and Marshall, who were otherwise engaged to the discomforture of England.

Not all Gilliat's triumphs were due to the presence of star quality. The championship was won with a supposedly weak attack. Taylor, Herman, Mottram and all-rounder Jesty made that prediction look silly. There was the evergreen Sainsbury, batsman Turner, and wicket-keeper Stephenson to emphasize the team spirit. Stephenson went on to the captaincy, and preserved the wicket-keeping tradition of McCorkell and Harrison, as did Parks, the latest in the line from the noted Sussex family of cricketers. [A.B.]

Founded 1863
Colours Blue, gold and white
Crest Tudor rose and crown
Chief Executive A.F. Baker FCA
Coach P.J. Sainsbury
Groundsman T. Flintoft
Scorer V.H. Isaacs
Address County Cricket Ground, Northlands Road, Southampton SO9 2TY
Telephone 0703 333788/333789
Cricketcall 0898 121444

Achievements:

County Championship Champions (2) 1961 and 1973
Gillette Cup Semi-finalists 1966 and 1976
National Westminster Bank Trophy Semi-finalists 1983, 1985, 1987 and 1988
Benson & Hedges Cup Winners 1988
John Player Sunday League Champions (3) 1975, 1978 and 1986
Refuge Assurance Sunday League Champions (0) 7th 1987
Fenner Trophy Winners 1975, 1976 and 1977
Asda Trophy Winners 1984 and 1986
Tilcon Trophy Winners 1976

BROWN. G. HAMPSHIRE

KENNEDY, A. HAMPSHIRE

C. P. MEAD, HAMPSHIRE

Grounds:

Southampton (County Cricket Ground, Northlands Road) Bournemouth (Dean Park, Cavendish Road) Portsmouth (US Officer's Ground, St Michael's Road) Basingstoke (Mays Bounty, Bounty Road).

Southampton

The county Ground at Northlands Road, which was opened on 9 May 1885 by the Countess of Northesk, wife of the then president of the club, was the third ground to be played on in the city. The ground was leased for an annual payment of £160 with the condition that a pavilion be built. This was done and £2,000 was raised before the grand opening and a match between North and South Hampshire took place afterwards. The first county match was with Derbyshire in 1885, and the initial first-class match with the M C C in the same year. In 1893 the Hampshire County Ground Company was founded and purchased the freehold of the ground from Sir Edward Hulse for £5,400. A football stand used to be sited close to where the main pavilion and offices are located and in 1896–97 Southampton Football Club used the ground. With crowds of over 12,000 the facilities were inadequate and after a couple of seasons the club moved to the Dell. 1896 saw the present pavilion frontage built, as well as a ladies pavilion adjacent. 1900 and 1911 saw more building: the football stand was redeveloped and a scoreboard built opposite the pavilion.

The ground has also been used for hockey and at the now Top Rank End of the ground (formerly the Bannister Park End) was Bannister Park Speedway Stadium. This has now been replaced by housing. Facilities for tennis and bowling are still available behind the indoor school which was built in 1958.

After World War Two donations were invited for ground improvements but the £10,927 raised was insufficient to carry out all the works envisaged. The 1960s saw the link between the two pavilions built and the present bell installed from the old Cunard liner *Athlone Castle*. There were no further major developments until in 1982 the Hampshire Squash and Sports Club was built comprising squash courts with sauna, jacuzzi and solarium (opened in April 1983) and the first-floor Desmond Eagar Room. The most recent addition in 1986 was the Phil Mead Stand which provides hospitality boxes close to the offices and next to the cricket nets.

Hampshire have played over 500 matches on the ground and over 100 limited-over matches since 1885. In 1985 they celebrated 100 years of county cricket at Southampton. It is said the ground is worth several million pounds and in 1990 the county club will move from Northlands Road to a new greenfield site to the east of the city.

Ground records at Northlands Road have included double hundreds from Phil Mead and L.C.H. Palairet. In limited-overs matches, a total of 371 for 4 against Glamorgan in the Gillette Cup (including 177 by Gordon Greenidge) in 1975 will be long remembered, as will Mike Proctor's spell of 6 for 13 to gain a Benson and Hedges Final place at Hampshire's expense in 1977. Other celebrations at Southampton were Hampshire's championship in 1973 and the Prudential Cup match in 1983 between Australia and Zimbabwe, the only international ever staged on the ground.

Crowds at the County Ground have been good; 5,000–6,000 is not unusual and limited-overs matches seem to attract the most (some 7,500 were present for the Gillette Cup semi-final with Northamptonshire in 1977). The largest crowd recorded was 15,000 for the visit of the 1934 Australians. The present ground capacity is set at about 7,000.

ADDRESS   County Cricket Ground, Northlands Road, Southampton SO9 2TY
TELEPHONE PROSPECTS OF PLAY   0703 333788/333789

DESCRIPTION OF GROUND AND FACILITIES

The main access to the Southampton ground is on Northlands Road. There is a pedestrian entrance from Hulse Road. Car parking is available within the ground for members but in the main it is necessary to park in adjoining roads. The main permanent buildings are the pavilion, the club offices and the new executive suite boxes. There is tiered seating on the north-east and south of the ground, while the west side is used for entertainment and other tents. The

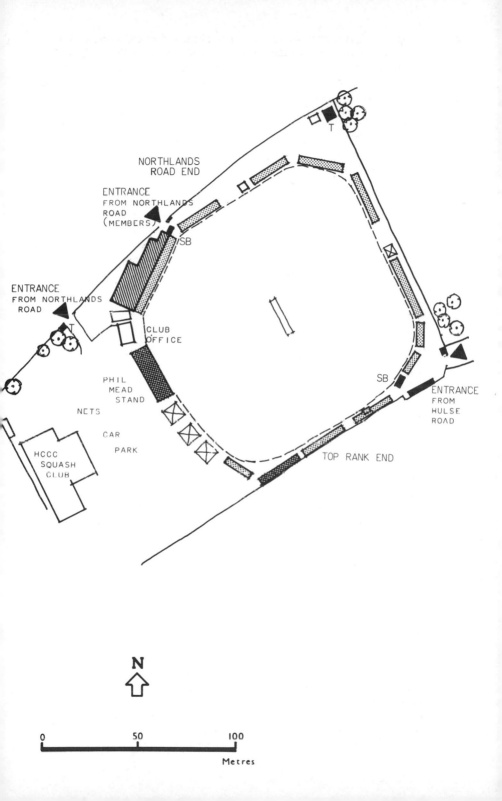

NORTHLANDS
ROAD END

ENTRANCE
FROM NORTHLANDS
ROAD
(MEMBERS)

SB

ENTRANCE
FROM NORTHLANDS
ROAD

T

CLUB
OFFICE

PHIL
MEAD
STAND

NETS

CAR
PARK

HCCC
SQUASH
CLUB

SB

ENTRANCE
FROM
HULSE
ROAD

TOP RANK END

N

0   50   100

Metres

members' areas are those directly in front of the club offices and the pavilion. The main scoreboard is in the south-east corner of the ground, with another adjoining the pavilion. The Hampshire C C C provide a caravan shop which is also taken to the out grounds. While both the pavilion and the new canvas-roofed executive suite are attractive buildings, this is a small ground of about 130 metres by 128 metres demarcated by advertisement boards. The players' accommodation is modest and housed in a small two-storey building wedged between the pavilion and club offices. The ground is now much overshadowed by housing, and the flats on the east side appear at first sight to be part of the ground, so close are they to the boundary. You are advised to bring your own seats to important matches. Only one small public stand on the south side is roofed.

Ask club officials if you wish to see the items of historic interest that are displayed on the staircase of the club offices. This building also houses, on the first floor, the scorers and the press.

GROUND RECORDS AND SCORES

FIRST-CLASS MATCHES
Highest innings total for County   559 v. Kent, 1912
Highest innings total against County   708 for 7 dec. by Australians, 1921
Lowest innings total for County   30 v. Nottinghamshire, 1932
Lowest innings total against County   32 by Kent, 1952
Highest individual innings for County   280 n.o. C.P. Mead v. Nottinghamshire, 1921
Highest individual innings against County   292 L.C.H. Palairet for Somerset, 1896
Best bowling performance in an innings for County   8 for 24 A.S. Kennedy v. Gloucestershire, 1924
Best bowling performance in an innings against County   9 for 40 W. Mead for Essex, 1900
Best bowling performance in a match for County   14 for 171 C.B. Llewellyn v. Worcestershire, 1901
Best bowling performance in a match against County   17 for 119 W. Mead for Essex, 1895

LIMITED-OVERS MATCHES
Highest innings total for County   371 for 4 v. Glamorgan (GC), 1975
Highest innings total against County   319 for 2 by Somerset (BHC), 1987
Lowest innings total for County   99 v. Kent (NWBT), 1984
Lowest innings total against County   82 by Wiltshire (GC), 1973
Highest individual innings for County   177 C.G. Greenidge v. Glamorgan (GC), 1975
Highest individual innings against County   155 n.o. M.D. Crowe for Somerset (BHC), 1987

Best bowling performance for County   7 for 30 P.J. Sainsbury *v.*
Norfolk (GC), 1965
Best bowling performance against County   6 for 13 M.J. Procter for
Gloucestershire (BHC), 1977

HOW TO GET THERE

Rail   Southampton Central, 1 mile
Bus   Hampshire Bus 47, 147 Southampton–Winchester and Solent
Blue Line 48 Southampton– Eastleigh all pass within ¼ mile of the
ground (Tel: 0962 52352)
Car   From north: M3 to junction 10, then follow A33 Southampton
and city centre, ground situated in Northlands Road off The
Avenue (A33) west of Southampton Common and ¾ miles north of
the city centre, or A3037 and A35 to city centre. From east: M27
junction 5, then follow signs Southampton and city centre, A35 and
A33, then as north. From west: M27 junction 3 then M271, A35 or
A3024 follow Southampton and city centre, then as north.

WHERE TO STAY AND OTHER INFORMATION

Northlands Hotel (0703 333871). Dolphin Hotel (0703 226178), The
Polygon (0703 330055), Post House Hotel (0703 330777)

Disabled Areas   No special area, request position
Local Radio Station(s)   BBC Radio Solent (96.1 MHz FM), Radio
Victory (95.0 MHz FM/1170 KHz MW)
Local Newspaper(s)   Evening Echo & Hampshire Chronicle,
Southern Evening Echo, The News, Southampton Advertiser,
Southampton Guardian, Portsmouth News

Basingstoke

The May's Bounty Ground is the home of Basingstoke and North
Hants C C founded in 1865, member of both the Thames Valley and
the Hampshire cricket leagues. Cricket has been played in Basingstoke since 1817, but the Folly or May's Bounty Ground was not used
for cricket until 1855. The club was created by John May as president
after the Gents of Basingstoke C C was disbanded in 1864, 24 years
after it was formed. Cricket has been played at May's Bounty ever
since. In 1880 John May purchased the land in order to prevent
building taking place on the ground and in 1885 the Basingstoke
Athletic Club was formed with cricket, football and cycling sections.
This reflected poor support for cricket, but in 1893 cricket interest
increased and the cricket club was reinstated. In 1901 the club's title
was changed to its present name. The ground was purchased in 1950

for £450 freehold and the cricket club became the proprietor of one of the finest cricket grounds in the county for an absurdly low price.

The original pavilion was built in 1877 and was a single-storey thatched building. It was replaced in 1901 by the present building which had subsequent additions in 1965, in 1974 (two squash courts), in 1979 (a further club room and kitchen) and in 1986 (a third squash court, committee/snooker room and a general office).

The ground is also used by London Welsh and Odiham hockey clubs through the winter months. During the cricket season matches have been staged for Victoria C C, Basingstoke Total Abstinence C C, Queen Mary's School and the Hampshire Police. Hampshire C C C first staged a match at May's Bounty in 1906 when Warwickshire were the visitors. Over thirty visits have been made since then, and eighteen limited-overs matches have been staged including a Gillette Cup match against Lincolnshire in 1967 and John Player Sunday League/Refuge Assurance Sunday League fixtures. Today Hampshire take one championship and one limited-overs match to this, the most northerly ground in the county, usually in early June. John Arlott, who was born in Basingstoke, witnessed his first cricket match at May's Bounty and in 1938 played his one and only game for the club.

In 1944 the top dressing for the square was said to have come from the local cemetery!

Crowds are good at May's Bounty, usually 3,500–4,500. The 4,300 crowd for the Warwickshire John Player Sunday League match in 1977 was possibly one of the largest. Records have included a 204 not out by Alan Jones for Glamorgan and bowling performances in an innings and match from another Welshman, Malcolm Nash. In 1974 Colin Cowdrey was hit while batting by West Indian Andy Roberts, after he mistimed a hook. He fell onto his stumps and retired from the match.

ADDRESS   Basingstoke and North Hants C C, May's Bounty, Bounty Road, Basingstoke, Hampshire
TELEPHONE PROSPECTS OF PLAY   0256 473646

DESCRIPTION OF GROUND AND FACILITIES

Closely hemmed in by housing and community buildings, this is a small ground to which access is gained either from Fairfields Road or through the car park in a playing field off Bounty Road. There is a small entrance on Bounty Road but no footpath and it is not used by many people.

The only permanent building is the pavilion which has been extended in recent years. The members' area in front of the pavilion provides a small area of tiered seating. The ground contains some benches but the vast majority of the seating is temporary and you are advised to bring your own seats to important matches. There is a small scoreboard on the east side of the ground but all other facilities are temporary. These include refreshment tents of various kinds, a press tent and scorers' tent, and a series of temporary toilets.

This is a small ground with a playing area of 120 metres by 115

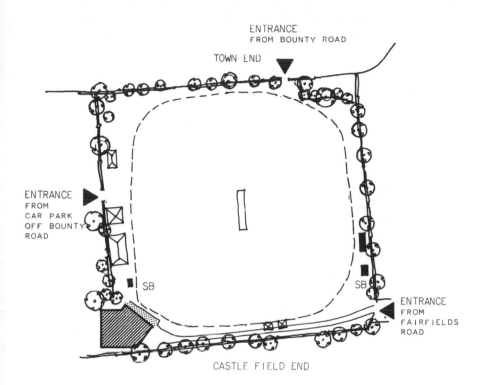

ENTRANCE
FROM BOUNTY ROAD

TOWN END

ENTRANCE
FROM
CAR PARK
OFF BOUNTY
ROAD

SB

SB

ENTRANCE
FROM
FAIRFIELDS
ROAD

CASTLE FIELD END

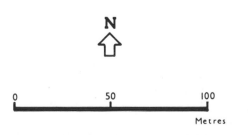

N

0	50	100

Metres

metres and the space behind the boundary boards is very limited on the east and north sides. There is, however, good tree planting on three sides of the ground, making it a pleasant venue at which to watch cricket.

Some old photographs are displayed in the pavilion, which is a two-storey building with a balcony for players to view the cricket.

GROUND RECORDS AND SCORES

FIRST-CLASS MATCHES
Highest innings total for County 401 for 5 dec. *v.* Surrey, 1986
Highest innings total against County 461 by Cambridge University, 1937
Lowest innings total for County 61 *v.* Nottinghamshire, 1936
Lowest innings total against County 64 by Surrey, 1986
Highest individual innings for County 172 J. Arnold *v.* Cambridge University, 1937
Highest individual innings against County 204 n.o. A. Jones for Glamorgan, 1980
Best bowling performance in an innings for County 8 for 67 A. Jaques *v.* Derbyshire, 1914
Best bowling performance in an innings against County 9 for 56 M.A. Nash for Glamorgan, 1975
Best bowling performance in a match for County 14 for 105 A. Jaques *v.* Derbyshire, 1914
Best bowling performance in a match against County 14 for 137 M.A. Nash for Glamorgan, 1975

LIMITED-OVERS MATCHES
Highest innings total for County 251 *v.* Glamorgan (JPL), 1974
Highest innings total against County 226 for 8 by Warwickshire (JPL), 1973
Lowest innings total for County 43 *v.* Essex (JPL), 1972
Lowest innings total against County 114 by Glamorgan (JPL), 1974
Highest individual innings for County 123 B.A. Richards *v.* Glamorgan (JPL), 1974
Highest individual innings against County 85 A.I. Kallicharran for Warwickshire (JPL), 1977
Best bowling performance for County 5 for 31 M.D. Marshall *v.* Kent (JPL), 1982
Best bowling performance against County 5 for 52 D.L. Williams for Glamorgan (JPL), 1974

HOW TO GET THERE

Rail Basingstoke, ¾ mile
Bus Hampshire Bus 322/3/4 from BR Basingstoke Station to within ¼ mile of ground (Tel: 0256 464501)
Car From north: M4 junction 11 then A33 follow signs Basingstoke or M4 junction 12 then A4 and A340 follow signs

Basingstoke, the ground is situated ½ mile from the town centre south-west of the town off the A30 Winchester Road in Bounty Road. From east: M3 junction 6 then follow signs Basingstoke and A30 Winchester Road, then into Bounty Road, or A30. From west: M3 junction 7 then follow signs Basingstoke, then as north. From south: A339 or A32 and A30 to Basingstoke then as north.

WHERE TO STAY AND OTHER INFORMATION

Crest Hotel (0256 468181), Red Lion Hotel (0256 28525)

Disabled Areas   No special area, request position
Local Radio Station(s)   Radio 210 (97 MHz FM/1431 KHz MW), County Sound (96.4 MHz FM/1476 KHz MW)
Local Newspaper(s)   Southern Evening Echo, The News, Basingstoke and North Hants Gazette

Bournemouth

The ground at Dean Park was laid out in 1869 and the first match took place in 1871. It was one of the oldest cricket grounds in the county but is now in Dorset. The first county match to be staged was with Somerset in 1882. In 1897 the initial first-class match took place; the Philadelphians were the opponents. A year later Somerset were the adversaries in the first county championship match. In all, 325 matches have been played on the ground and over 60 limited-overs matches by the county club.

In 1927 the county club formed a company to take over the lease of the Bournemouth ground from the Cooper-Dean family and in 1948 the ground was taken under direct control of the county club. Colonel R.A.W. Binny was appointed to manage the club facilities. Formerly part of the Cooper-Dean family estate, Dean Park was one of the few privately-owned cricket grounds. It is now named the Bournemouth Sports Club. The family continue to support the club and in 1974 Miss A. Ellen Cooper-Dean presented a new scoreboard. This is situated opposite the pavilion built in 1902. The ground, which is located in the northern suburb of the town, extends to about 4½ acres and is enclosed by fine trees, and houses. The entrances are from Cavendish Road which is not easily found by those who are strange to the area.

Bournemouth is one of the most pleasant of Hampshire grounds and the County today stage three championship and at least two limited-overs matches on the ground, a first visit in May and then a cricket week in August while the holidaymakers are at the south coast seaside resort. Dean Park was the ground where the County won the championship for the first time in 1961 and also where in 1978 they won the John Player Sunday League after beating Middlesex. No doubt players and supporters have fond memories of matches at Dean Park. The ground has been used by Dorset C C C for Minor County matches in recent years and should not be confused with Bournemouth C C which plays at Kinson Sports Ground in the Northbourne district of the town.

W.G. Grace played in the first festival on the ground in 1902. Such events at Bournemouth, however, tended to be less successful than the others of the time at Hastings and Scarborough. Ground records include big scores from R.H. Moore and Len Hutton, and some splendid bowling performances.

Bournemouth has seen good crowds with 5,000–6,000 expected for cricket weeks. The largest crowd was 15,000 for the visit of Gloucestershire in 1947.

ADDRESS   Bournemouth Sports Club, The Pavilion, Dean Park, Cavendish Road, Bournemouth, Dorset
TELEPHONE PROSPECTS OF PLAY   0202 25872

DESCRIPTION OF GROUND AND FACILITIES

Main access to the Bournemouth ground is from the western, Cavendish Road side of the ground where there are two entrances, one for members and cars and another for the public. The pavilion, press/scorers' building and players' dining room are the only permanent buildings, together with a new scoreboard and enclosure adjoining the pavilion and groundsman's stores. The members' enclosure is on the west side in front of the pavilion and dining area. The remainder of the ground is open to the public. All the seating from the press building southwards towards the sightscreen at the Town End is permanent open raised timber seating. Refreshments are available in the pavilion on the ground floor for members and in temporary mobile facilities to the east close to the new scoreboard and opposite the pavilion. A further refreshment area, Hampshire supporters' caravan and sponsors' tents can be found at the Winton End.

The ground is enclosed with trees and the surrounding housing, and is bounded by a tall hedge. The playing area is 140 metres by 135 metres, roughly circular, and defined by a rope and advertising boards. Spectators are advised to bring their own seats to popular matches but members' seating is adequate for large crowds. 65 per cent of seating is supplied, out of a ground capacity of 8,000. Toilets can be found in the pavilion and at the rear of the press building.

A fine view can be gained from the first floor of the pavilion next to the secretary's office, one of the two areas of covered accommodation for spectators. Members can park inside the ground and there is plenty of street parking in the area.

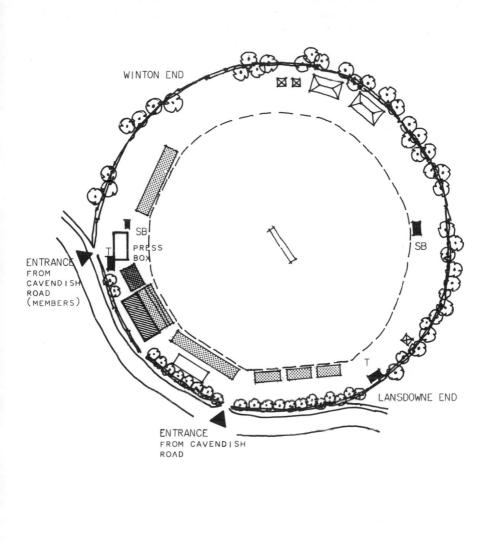

WINTON END

SB

T

PRESS
BOX

ENTRANCE
FROM
CAVENDISH
ROAD
(MEMBERS)

SB

T

LANSDOWNE END

ENTRANCE
FROM CAVENDISH
ROAD

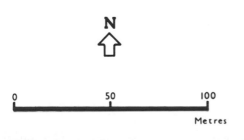

N

0   50   100

Metres

GROUND RECORDS AND SCORES

FIRST-CLASS MATCHES

Highest innings total for County   536 v. Warwickshire, 1928
Highest innings total against County   610 by Kent, 1906
Lowest innings total for County   31 v. Worcestershire, 1965
Lowest innings total against County   37 by Somerset, 1956
Highest individual innings for County   316 R.H. Moore v. Warwickshire, 1937
Highest individual innings against County   270 n.o. L. Hutton for Yorkshire, 1947
Best bowling performance in an innings for County   9 for 131 J.A. Newman v. Essex, 1921
Best bowling performance in an innings against County   9 for 93 S. Venkataraghavan for Indians, 1971
Best bowling performance in a match for County   14 for 99 D. Shackleton v. Warwickshire, 1965
Best bowling performance in a match against County   14 for 91 J.W.H.T. Douglas for Essex, 1921

LIMITED-OVERS MATCHES

Highest innings total for County   261 v. Yorkshire (GC), 1977
Highest innings total against County   250 for 9 by Derbyshire (GC), 1963
Lowest innings total for County   111 v. Derbyshire (JPL), 1978
Lowest innings total against County   77 by Lancashire (JPL), 1974
Highest individual innings for County   132 n.o. B.A. Richards v. Kent (JPL), 1970
Highest individual innings against County   119 n.o. N.E. Briers for Leicestershire (JPL), 1981
Best bowling performance for County   5 for 32 T.E. Jesty v. Middlesex (JPL), 1978
Best bowling performance against County   5 for 26 D.P. Hughes for Lancashire (JPL), 1970

HOW TO GET THERE

Rail   Bournemouth, 500m
Bus   Numerous local services to within ¼ mile
Car   From north: M27 junction 1 then follow A31 and A338 follow signs. Bournemouth ground is situated 1 mile north of the seafront, between the A347 Wimborne Road and B3064 Lansdowne Road. Dean Park is signposted from the A347 junction with the A338, or A348 and A341 to town centre then Wimborne Road for Dean Park. From east: A35 to town centre then as north or as north. From west: A31, A35, A350 or A341 to town centre then as north.

WHERE TO STAY AND OTHER INFORMATION

Carlton Hotel (0202 22011), Belvedere Hotel (0202 21080), Pavilion Hotel (0202 291266)

Disabled Areas No special area, request position
Local Radio Station(s) BBC Radio Solent (96.1 MHz FM/1359 KHz MW), Two Counties Radio (97.2 MHz FM/828 KHz MW), Ocean Sound (103.2 MHz FM/1557 KHz MW)
Local Newspaper(s) Bournemouth Evening Echo, Southern Evening Echo, The News

Portsmouth

The Burnaby Road Ground is the United Services Officers sports ground. It is used for Services matches, including matches with touring sides as it is now the only military ground used for first-class cricket. The ground is used by United Services Portsmouth C C established in 1880, who play in the Save and Prosper Southern Cricket League. The ground is also shared with US Portsmouth Rugby Football Club and there are facilities for tennis adjoining the club.

Hampshire's association with the United Services ground began in 1888 when they played Sussex. They did not use the ground again until they attained first-class status in 1895 when a solitary match was staged with Leicestershire. Since then matches have been played on the ground every year; a total of 293 first-class matches have been staged by the County and 40 limited-overs matches. Hampshire take two championship and one limited-over match to the ground each year, usually in July for a cricket week. The first ever first-class match was staged in 1882 when the Australians played Cambridge Past and Present. In 1893 the Australians scored 843 against Cambridge and Oxford Past and Present; the innings lasted into a third day which was a record for first-class cricket at the time and still remains the highest ever score made by an Australian team in this country. The scorecard of this match is still displayed in the pavilion.

Behind the pavilion and across the road the railway runs between the Town and Harbour Stations. Passing trains can be heard and seen from the ground. At the other end of the ground the Portsmouth Polytechnic buildings dominate the enclosed playing area, as does the US club which was built in 1950 as a recreational and residential centre for services sport, principally the Royal Navy.

Ground records for first-class matches include a number for Yorkshire, including Percy Holmes and Hedley Verity. Trevor Jesty hit 166 not out in a John Player Sunday League match against Surrey in 1983, a county he was later to join and captain. Subsequently he has moved to Lancashire who will visit Portsmouth in 1989. Bobby Parks took 10 catches in a match with Derbyshire in 1981. Derek

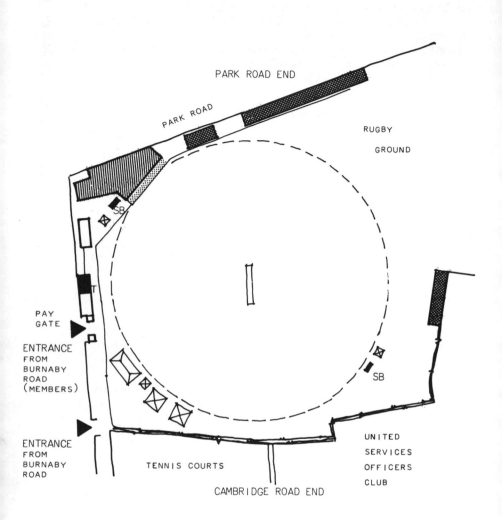

PARK ROAD END

PARK ROAD

RUGBY

GROUND

SB

PAY
GATE

ENTRANCE
FROM
BURNABY
ROAD
(MEMBERS)

T

SB

ENTRANCE
FROM
BURNABY
ROAD

TENNIS COURTS

UNITED

SERVICES

OFFICERS

CLUB

CAMBRIDGE ROAD END

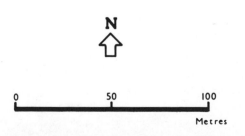

N

0   50   100

Metres

Shackleton holds the record for the most wickets taken for Hampshire on the ground, both in a season and in a career.

Crowds today are usually around 5,000. The highest was 10,000 for the match with Sussex in 1948.

ADDRESS United Services Portsmouth, United Services Officers Ground, Burnaby Road, Portsmouth, Hampshire

TELEPHONE PROSPECTS OF PLAY 0705 22351

DESCRIPTION OF GROUND AND FACILITIES

Access to the ground is from Burnaby Road and the King James Gate, one of the original city gates, which is the main entrance. The main permanent buildings are the pavilion and rugby club and two covered stands, but the latter are disposed in positions which only suit the rugby field. There is no car parking in the ground and it is necessary to leave one's car in adjoining streets (occasionally the Polytechnic can be used when the building is closed).

The members' area is on the north-west side of the ground on either side of the pavilion. The scoreboard adjoins the pavilion to the west and another temporary scoreboard is sited in the south-east corner. There is temporary seating for about 2,000 so it is advisable to take your own seats to important matches. The playing area is approximately circular and 145 metres in diameter. The pitch is in a north–south position at an angle of 40 degrees to the pavilion. The toilets are in a permanent structure but all other facilities are temporary. There are no specific facilities for disabled persons, who are advised to ask for a suitable position on the ground.

Portsmouth still boasts the heaviest of heavy rollers weighing some 5½ tons. The United Services Ground is a historic urban ground which is now overshadowed not only by the railway embankment to the north but by the buildings of the Portsmouth Polytechnic to the north-east and south-east, the latter building being the former Nuffield Officers' Club.

GROUND RECORDS AND SCORES

FIRST-CLASS MATCHES

Highest innings total for County 616 for 7 dec. v. Warwickshire, 1920

Highest innings total against County 585 for 3 dec. by Yorkshire, 1920

Lowest innings total for County 35 v. Middlesex, 1922

Lowest innings total against County 36 by Warwickshire, 1927

Highest individual innings for County 213 n.o. J.R. Gray v. Derbyshire, 1962

Highest individual innings against County 302 n.o. P. Holmes for Yorkshire, 1920

Best bowling performance in an innings for County 9 for 30 D. Shackleton v. Warwickshire, 1960

Best bowling performance in an innings against County 8 for 25
W. Andrews for Somerset, 1947
Best bowling performance in a match for County 13 for 86
M. Heath *v.* Sussex, 1958
Best bowling performance in a match against County 13 for 107
H. Verity for Yorkshire, 1935

LIMITED-OVERS MATCHES
Highest innings total for County 292 for 1 *v.* Surrey (JPL), 1983
Highest innings total against County 231 for 9 by Worcestershire
(JPL), 1976
Lowest innings total for County 113 *v.* Leicestershire (JPL), 1971
Lowest innings total against County 92 by Surrey (JPL), 1969
Highest individual innings for County 166 n.o. T.E. Jesty *v.* Surrey
(JPL), 1983
Highest individual innings against County 87 A. Kennedy for
Lancashire (JPL), 1975
Best bowling performance for County 5 for 13 M.D. Marshall *v.*
Glamorgan (JPL), 1979
Best bowling performance against County 6 for 22 R.R. Bailey for
Northamptonshire (JPL), 1972

HOW TO GET THERE

Rail Portsmouth & Southsea, 500m; Portsmouth Harbour, ½ mile
Bus From surrounding areas to The Hard Interchange, thence ½
mile
Car From north: A3 or M3(M) follow signs Portsmouth and IOW
Ferry Terminal, ground is situated in Old Portsmouth off the A3
London Road, close to the Guildhall and United Services' Sports
Club. The ground is shared with USO Portsmouth Royal Navy.
From east: A27 then A2030 signposted Portsmouth and Ferry
Terminal. From west: M27 junction 12 then M275 follow signs
Portsmouth harbour and Ferry Terminal, then as north.

WHERE TO STAY AND OTHER INFORMATION

Crest Hotel (0705 827651), Holiday Inn (0705 383151), Keppel's
Head Hotel (0705 833231)

Disabled Areas No special area, request position
Local Radio Station(s) BBC Radio Solent (96.1 MHz FM), Ocean
Sound (103.2 MHz FM/1557 KHz MW)
Local Newspaper(s) Southern Evening Echo & Hampshire
Chronicle, Portsmouth Evening News

KENT

KENT.

CANTERBURY

DARTFORD

FOLKESTONE

MAIDSTONE

TUNBRIDGE WELLS

Kent

The story of Kent is the story of cricket. Long before the marriage of the Canterbury and Maidstone clubs produced the offspring of the county club in 1870, the famous Kent XI were hailed as the champions and the biggest attraction in the growing game. In 1744 Kent were powerful enough to take on All-England. Indeed three years later they played England three times and beat them three times. Kent were Hambledon's most serious rivals, and many were the epic struggles with Surrey.

The Canterbury festival, the father of all cricket weeks, began in 1842, and, on the present St Lawrence ground, in 1847. The beautiful game with the beautiful name now had its most beautiful setting. A county's style and character is often the reflection of its environment, and, amid the marquees, tents and flowers of Canterbury, Maidstone, Tunbridge Wells and Dover Kent have paraded a glittering host.

From Alfred Mynn, the first of cricket's heroes, Fuller Pilch and Felix, whose real name was Nicholas Wanostrocht, to J.R. Mason, A.P.F. Chapman, Frank Woolley, Leslie Ames, Doug Wright, Godfrey Evans, Colin Cowdrey, Derek Underwood, Alan Knott and the Pakistani Asif Iqbal, Kent have had actors to do honour to their stage.

For sixty years Kent was dominated by the powerful personality of the 4th Lord Harris, a formidable autocrat of the old school and a pillar of the establishment. He captained Kent from 1871 to 1889, England in the first home Test in 1880 and in Australia in 1878–9, was chairman, president and secretary of Kent, and president and honorary treasurer of MCC. Apart from spells as Governor of Bombay, Under-Secretary for India and Under-Secretary for War, his life was devoted to cricket. He ruled both amateur and professional, strictly but with impartiality, but only Lord Harris could have sent a dismissal notice to a wretched bowler half-way through an over in a county match!

A dependence on amateurs often led to erratic results as they were unable to make consistent appearances, and one of the most significant events – matched later only by the alliance of Ames and Cowdrey – was the setting-up of the Tonbridge nursery in 1897, which supplied a stream of high professional quality and more settled sides. The products included Woolley, 'Tich' Freeman, Humphries, Fielder, Seymour, Hubble the wicket-keeper – a position always in safe hands in Kent – and Fairservice. At last Kent were champions in 1906, Woolley's first season, and again in 1909, 1910 and 1913. In between they were twice 2nd and once 3rd.

Apart from Mason the bowling was professional, headed by Fielder, fast, and Blythe, classical slow left arm, and the batting mainly amateur and aggressive. Fielder's extra celebration in 1906 was to take all 10 Gentlemen wickets, and in the following tour of Australia he had 25 wickets in the series.

In the sixteen seasons until he joined up in August 1914, never to

KENT COUNTY C.C.

C. BLYTHE (KENT).

return, Colin Blythe took 2,506 wickets, and in his last three seasons he headed the national averages. A violinist, he was of such sensitive nature that he was forbidden by doctors to play in Test cricket after he had taken 100 wickets in 19 matches at only 18.63. A memorial to a much-loved cricketer stands at Canterbury.

With Blythe and Woolley together Kent enjoyed unrivalled spin. It is hard to credit that a batsman of such elegant flair to be compared with Australia's Victor Trumper and scorer of 58,969 and 145 centuries – an aggregate of runs exceeded only by Hobbs – was in the upper tier of slow left arm bowlers. Yet Woolley gave up bowling at the age of 35 with 2,068 wickets, twelve more than Wright – a statistic designed not to belittle Wright, an unlucky genius, but to underline Woolley's contributions. A cast-off line is his 1,018 catches, a comfortable record.

Bowlers of the class of Tate and Constantine confessed they could not bowl to the tall willowy figure, such was the range and invention of his strokes, nor curb his aggressive approach. On no fewer than thirty-five occasions he was out between ninety and ninety-five. 'I never gave a thought to the "nervous nineties"' he said on his retirement in 1938. 'We were never allowed to play for averages in Kent sides.'

Leslie Ames played in forty-seven Tests to Woolley's sixty-four, and maintained the fashion of wicket-keeper–batsman. In both departments Ames was remarkably successful, scoring 102 centuries and collecting 1,121 victims behind the stumps. The combination of Ames and Freeman, the 5ft 2ins leg spinner, whose aggregate was bettered only by Rhodes, was irresistible, but Kent owed as much to Ames the team-building secretary-manager as Ames the player.

Kent had often been in the hunt between the wars, but were too inconsistent to unseat Yorkshire, and from 1946 there were more disappointments than successes. The halcyon years seemed to belong to a long-distant past, but a new dawn broke in 1957 when the new captain Cowdrey linked with Ames the manager.

A brilliant era began with the winning of the Gillette Cup in 1967. That year and the next Kent were runners-up, and appropriately in 1970, their centenary year, the title justly went to Cowdrey – remarkably as they were bottom on 1 July. Kent were in the thick of all the competitions, sharing the title with Middlesex under the Pakistani Asif Iqbal in 1977, and in the following season Ealham, a superb fielder, who had taken over from Iqbal, then with Packer, did even better with the championship and the Benson and Hedges Cup for the third time.

Mike Denness, the Scot who captained England and formed an outstanding opening partnership with Luckhurst, had five years as Cowdrey's successor, twice winning both the Sunday League and the Benson and Hedges Cup in the same season. He also took the Sunday League and the 2nd position in the championship in 1972. Five other appearances in Lord's finals from 1971 to 1986 were further proof of the county's brilliant adoption of single innings cricket.

There have been few better batsmen than Cowdrey – at his best perhaps another Hammond – and he ended his distinguished career with a record 114 Tests, twenty-two centuries for England, and having rekindled Kent's pride. Moreover he saw his son, Christopher, carry the torch as captain of Kent and England.

Cowdrey, Wright, Evans, Knott, who added five Test centuries to his wicket-keeping prowess, and Underwood, with 2,465 wickets, including 297 for England, more than upheld the standards set by the Kent titans of bygone days. [A.B.]

Founded 1870
Colours Maroon and white
Crest White horse on a red background
Chief Executive J. Woodhouse
Secretary D.B. Dalby FCA
Cricket administrator B.W. Luckhurst
Groundsman B.A. Fitch
Scorer J. Foley
Address St Lawrence Ground, Old Dover Road, Canterbury CT1 3NZ
Telephone 0227 456886
Cricketcall 0898 121421

Achievements:

County Championship Champions (6) 1906, 1909, 1910, 1913, 1970 and 1978; Joint Champions (1) 1977
Gillette Cup Winners 1967 and 1974; finalists 1971
National Westminster Bank Trophy Finalists 1983 and 1984
Benson & Hedges Cup Winners 1973, 1976 and 1978; finalists 1977 and 1986
John Player Sunday League Champions (3) 1972, 1973 and 1976
Refuge Assurance Sunday League Champions (0) 6th 1987
Fenner Trophy Winners 1971 and 1973
Tilcon Trophy Finalists 1980

Grounds:

Canterbury (St Lawrence Ground, Old Dover Road) Tunbridge Wells (Nevill Cricket Ground, Warwick Park) Folkestone (Sports

Aerial view of the St Lawrence ground, Canterbury

Ground, Cheriton Road)   Dartford (Hesketh Park, Pilgrims Way)   Maidstone (Mote Park, Willow Way).

Other grounds that have been used since 1969 are: Blackheath (Rectory Field, Charlton Road), Dover (Crabble Athletic Ground, Lewisham Road), Gillingham (Garrison Stadium, Marlborough Road), Gravesend (Bat & Ball Ground, Wrotham Road), New Beckenham (Midland Bank Sports Ground, Lennard Road).

Canterbury

The St Lawrence Cricket Ground in Old Dover Road was opened in 1847 and was known at that time as the Beverley cricket ground. This name came from the previous ground which was used by the club from 1841 to 1846 and was situated beyond the cavalry barracks. The ground has been used for housing close to Vauxhall Lakes and the nearby gravel quarry workings. The present name, the St Lawrence Ground, comes from the adjoining St Lawrence House which was originally the St Lawrence priory (founded in 1137). The St Lawrence Ground is the only cricket ground in Kent that is owned by the county club.

The pavilion was built in 1900 at a cost of £2,340, and refurbished and renamed the Stuart Chiesman Pavilion in 1970 as a result of the club centenary appeal. The Iron Stand was constructed in 1897 and renamed the Leslie Ames Stand in 1973. It now accommodates sixteen private boxes and a new enlarged scoreboard. The concrete stand was built in 1926–27 and renamed the Frank Woolley Stand. The most recent addition is the New Stand which was built in 1986 at a cost of £600,000 and comprises two levels containing a shop, public bar, dining room for members, an executive suite and raised seating. Much of the funds to build the New Stand came from the Kent C C C Project '85 appeal. A lime tree stands within the playing area on the Old Dover Road side of the ground and was once cleared by a hit from Learie Constantine the only player to accomplish this feat.

Originally the ground formed part of the Winter's Farm Estate, Nackington. It was bought from the landlord, Lord Sondes, for £4,500 in 1896. In addition to the games staged by Kent the ground is also used by the Beverley C C, the St Lawrence and Highland Court C C (formerly the St Lawrence C C established in 1864 with the specific purpose of making greater use of the ground) and the 'F' Division of the Kent Police. The first match of importance staged on the ground was in early August 1847 when Kent played England and won by 3 wickets. A Canterbury cricket festival is always held in early August (the first was organized in 1848), and in recent years the festival has included two championship matches and two limited-overs matches together with a tourists' match.

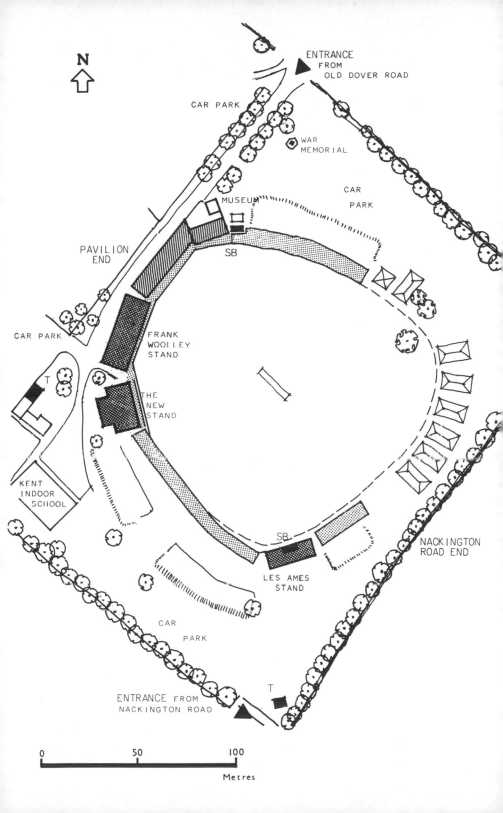

N

ENTRANCE
FROM
OLD DOVER ROAD

CAR PARK

WAR
MEMORIAL

CAR
PARK

MUSEUM

PAVILION
END

SB

CAR PARK

FRANK
WOOLLEY
STAND

T

THE
NEW
STAND

KENT
INDOOR
SCHOOL

SB

NACKINGTON
ROAD END

LES AMES
STAND

CAR
PARK

ENTRANCE FROM
NACKINGTON ROAD

T

0   50   100

Metres

Crowds at Canterbury are usually 7,500–8,500. The ground capacity is now set at 14,000, which is always reached for limited-overs matches of importance in whatever competition. Ground performances have included 344 by W.G. Grace for M C C in 1876 which was followed in matches against Nottinghamshire and Yorkshire with 177 and 318 not out respectively, a record of 839 in three consecutive innings which still stands today. His younger brother E.M. took 10 for 92 and scored 192 not out for M C C against the Gentlemen of Kent in 1862. Frank Woolley hit the highest individual innings on the ground for Kent and 'Titch' Freeman, Doug Wright and in recent years Derek Underwood also had many good performances on their home ground. Limited-overs records have included highest innings from Chris Tavare and Graeme Clinton (formerly a Kent player) and bowling spells from Derek Underwood and Don Wilson, now coach at Lord's M C C indoor school.

ADDRESS   St Lawrence Cricket Ground, Old Dover Road, Canterbury, Kent CT1 3NZ
TELEPHONE PROSPECTS OF PLAY   0227 457323

DESCRIPTION OF GROUND AND FACILITIES

There are three entrances to the St Lawrence Ground, which are located in Nackington Road and Old Dover Road for members and the public through the adjoining turnstiles. Ample car parking is available at most matches for members and the public (depending on weather conditions). During festival week and Benson & Hedges Cup or NatWest quarter- and semi-final ties space may be limited, and there is overflow car parking about 10 minutes walk from the ground. Space is limited on the banks and from the ring where cricket can be viewed from your own vehicle. The Leslie Chiesman pavilion, annexe, Leslie Ames enclosure, Frank Woolley Stand and the first floor of the New Stand are available to members only. The general public can sit anywhere else in the ground or members area after a transfer charge obtained from the ticket office. Disabled persons have a special area reserved in the ground floor of the Frank Woolley Stand, which includes an attendant and wheelchairs. Special provision for invalid cars is available on prior request. Seating is provided with approximately 6,000 plastic tip-up permanent seats, so spectators can bring their own seats to matches if they wish. Bar and refreshment facilities are available to members and the general public including light snacks and hot meals on the second floor of the New Stand and on the ground floor for fast food. Toilet facilities are available around the ground including a disabled facility at the rear of the Frank Woolley and annexe Stands. The supporters' souvenir Kent shop is sited at the rear of the New Stand and the scorecard/bookshop is close to the museum. The TV camera position is at the Nackington Road End, and the radio commentary box is on the top floor of the pavilion. The playing area is 150 metres by 135 metres and is defined by a rope and advertising boards. During a break in play a visit to the Kent museum at the rear of the annexe and to the cabinets in the pavilion Long Room will bring back memories of the county's past glory years and performers. On the Old Dover Road side of the ground near the drive entrance is the war memorial in memory of Colin Blythe, a former Kent player. A Kent C C C Howard Levett (indoor cricket) school is situated near the county offices at the top end of the drive. The ground capacity is 12,000, there is seating for 70 per cent available. Additional facilities are brought in for popular matches when required.

GROUND RECORDS AND SCORES

FIRST-CLASS MATCHES
Highest innings total for County 568 v. Sussex, 1906
Highest innings total against County 676 by Australians, 1921
Lowest innings total for County 46 v. Surrey, 1862
Lowest innings total against County 37 by Philadelphians, 1908
Highest individual innings for County 270 F.E. Woolley v. Middlesex, 1923
Highest individual innings against County 344 W.G. Grace for MCC, 1876
Best bowling performance in an innings for County 9 for 35 J. Jackson v. England, 1858
Best bowling performance in an innings against County 10 for 92 W.G. Grace for MCC, 1873
Best bowling performance in a match for County 15 for 94 A.P. Freeman v. Somerset, 1931
Best bowling performance in a match against County 15 for 147 W.G. Grace for MCC, 1873

LIMITED-OVERS MATCHES
Highest innings total for County 297 for 3 v. Worcestershire (GC), 1970
Highest innings total against County 293 for 8 by Surrey (NWBT), 1985
Lowest innings total for County 73 v. Middlesex (BHC), 1979
Lowest innings total against County 80 by Surrey (JPL), 1983
Highest individual innings for County 136 n.o. C.J. Tavaré v. Gloucestershire (JPL), 1978
Highest individual innings against County 146 G.S. Clinton for Surrey (NWBT), 1985
Best bowling performance for County 5 for 14 D.L. Underwood v. Surrey (JPL), 1983
Best bowling performance against County 6 for 18 D. Wilson for Yorkshire (JPL), 1969

HOW TO GET THERE

Rail   Canterbury East, 1 mile; Canterbury West, 1½ miles
Bus   East Kent 15–17 Canterbury Bus Station–Folkestone; C1/2/5 link BR Stations with the Bus Station (Tel: 0843 581333); also 339 from city centre
Car   From north: A290, A291 and A28 follow signs Canterbury and city centre, ground is situated ½ mile south of city centre off Old Dover Road. From east: A257 to Canterbury, then as north. From west: M2 to junction 7, then A2 to Bridge turnoff on Canterbury bypass, then A290 to Canterbury and Old Dover Road signposted. From south: A2, A28 and B2068 follow Canterbury signs and Old Dover Road signposted County Cricket.
Ample parking facilities on ground. Overflow car parks sometimes available within short distance of ground. No offstreet parking

WHERE TO STAY AND OTHER INFORMATION

County Hotel (0227 66266), Chaucer Hotel (0227 464427)

Disabled Areas   In Frank Woolley Stand and as requested elsewhere in the ground
Local Radio Station(s)   BBC Radio Kent (104.2 MHz FM/1035 KHz MW), Invicta Radio (103.1 MHz FM/1242 KHz MW)
Local Newspaper(s)   Evening Post, Kentish Gazette, Kent and Sussex Courier

Dartford

Hesketh Park is the third ground to be used by Kent for home matches in the town. The previous grounds were the Brent at Brent Lane close to East Hill (used from 1709 to 1793) and the Bowman's Lodge near to Dartford Heath (used in 1806). Dartford C C (founded in 1727) played at the Brent until 1905 when after the club had lost a lawsuit, the ground was sold for building development. Fortunately for the club Everard Hesketh, a well-known local person, gave the Hesketh Park ground 'for the free use of the inhabitants of Dartford for ever'. More important Hesketh stipulated the main playing area must be retained as a cricket ground. The ground was named after him. The first match staged on the ground was in 1906 between the Daily Telegraph XI and the Riverside Mills XI. Hesketh bowled the first over on the ground.

Since 1906 Dartford C C has been the tenant and rents the ground from the Dartford Borough Council. The first Kent match was staged in May 1956 when Essex were the visitors. Prior to the match a new pavilion was constructed to accommodate County members and of

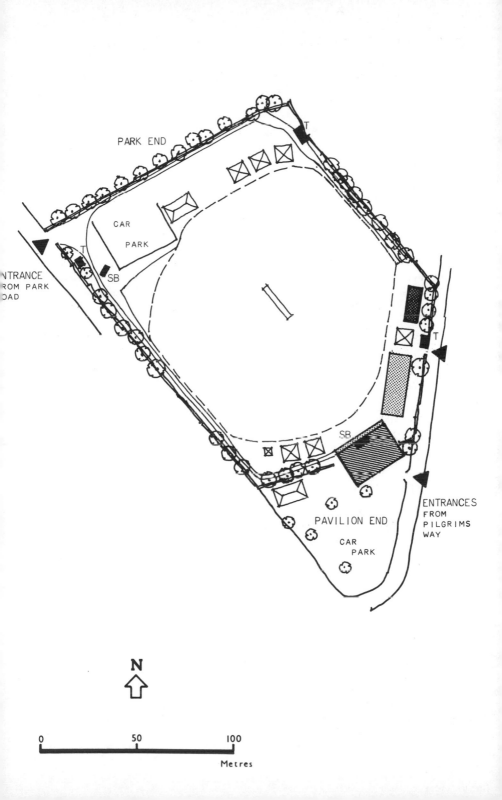

PARK END

CAR PARK

ENTRANCE FROM PARK ROAD

T

SB

SB

T

ENTRANCES FROM PILGRIMS WAY

PAVILION END

CAR PARK

N

0   50   100

Metres

course provide players' facilities. Hesketh Park is almost all that remains untouched by building development of the original Brent ground which was covered by houses in Rochester, Bedford and Carlton Roads close to the ground.

Kent Second XI first used the ground in 1947 and limited-overs matches have been staged with Essex in 1978 and 1981. The Old Pavilion still stands and is used as the press box for county matches. The ground is flat and is rather enclosed despite being close to the main A2 trunk road and within a mile of the M25 and Dartford Tunnel. Dartford C C field three XIs throughout the season and play in the Kent County League. The ground is also used by Dartford (Crackenfield) Ladies, Woolwich and New Ash Green hockey clubs during the winter months. In recent seasons Kent have usually played one championship match at Hesketh Park in May.

Cricketers who have graduated from Dartford to the county side have included Alan Dixon, Derek Ufton, Graham Dilley (now of Worcestershire) and Neil Taylor. Crowds at Hesketh Park are usually 3,000–3,500; the largest for a single day was 3,750 against Essex in 1985 when a total of nearly 10,000 watched the three days of championship cricket. Ground records include a double hundred from Alan Ormrod for Worcestershire and fine bowling from Frederick Ridgway for Kent in 1960. Clive Lloyd hit the fastest hundred on the ground and then went on to score 163 in 140 minutes for Lancashire in 1970. Nottinghamshire the then champions were dismissed for 65 in 1988.

ADDRESS   Dartford C C, Hesketh Park, Pilgrims Way, Dartford, Kent DA1 1ST
TELEPHONE PROSPECTS OF PLAY   0322 25152

DESCRIPTION OF GROUND AND FACILITIES

There are four entrances into Hesketh Park; from the south in Park Road and Pilgrim's Way, and two further access points, one to the north of the playing area in Park Road and the other off Watling Street. Car parking is available for players/officials and members at the rear of the main pavilion, on the tennis courts and at the rear of the marquees behind the sponsors' and Mayor's tents, at the northern end of the ground. The main pavilion is used by members for refreshment and, in addition to its use by players, also provides a secretary's office and toilet facilities. The scorers sit in a room in the roof of the pavilion and above this room is the T V camera position and the commentary box. Also, between the pavilion and the old pavilion are two temporary raised seating areas and a cricket net. However, much of the temporary seating is bench variety and at ground level. To the west of the pavilion is the Kent C C C souvenir shop, the scorecard printer's tents and two large public and members' refreshment areas. A scoreboard is located to the north-west corner, close to the tennis courts. A groundsman's tent is situated near the old pavilion, and toilet facilities are available to the north and south of the playing area. The members' enclosure is in front of the pavilion and is situated to the west of the pavilion, just to the east of the old pavilion. The playing area is 132 metres by 126 metres and is defined by a rope and advertising boards. Some 2,500 seats are provided so spectators who are not members may also bring seats.

Some historic photographs of Dartford are on view in the pavilion and are well worth viewing during a break in play.

GROUND RECORDS AND SCORES

FIRST-CLASS MATCHES
Highest innings total for County   476 for 9 v. Essex, 1985
Highest innings total against County   463 by Worcestershire, 1973
Lowest innings total for County   82 v. Essex, 1966
Lowest innings total against County   65 by Nottinghamshire, 1988
Highest individual innings for County   150 n.o. C.J. Tavaré v. Essex, 1985
Highest individual innings against County   204 n.o. J.A. Ormrod for Worcestershire, 1973
Best bowling performance in an innings for County   8 for 39 F. Ridgway v. Lancashire, 1960
Best bowling performance in an innings against County   8 for 84 Muhammad Munaf for Pakistan Eaglets, 1963
Best bowling performance in a match for County   12 for 101 F. Ridgway v. Lancashire, 1960
Best bowling performance in a match against County   10 for 89 R.G.M. Carter for Worcestershire, 1964

LIMITED-OVERS MATCHES
Highest innings total for County   226 for 4 v. Essex (BHC), 1978
Highest innings total against County   222 for 6 by Essex (BHC), 1978
Lowest innings total for County   162 for 2 v. Essex (BHC), 1981
Lowest innings total against County   161 by Essex (BHC), 1981
Highest individual innings for County   79 n.o. R.A. Woolmer v. Essex (BHC), 1981
Highest individual innings against County   73 G.A. Gooch for Essex (BHC), 1978
Best bowling performance for County   3 for 24 J.N. Shepherd v. Essex (BHC), 1978
Best bowling performance against County   2 for 25 S. Turner for Essex (BHC), 1978

HOW TO GET THERE

Rail   Dartford, 1 mile
Bus   Kentish Bus 1/3, 19 from BR Station (Tel: 0474 321300; London Transport 494, 499, 480, 486, 423 and 450
Car   From north: M25 junction 2, then follow signs Dartford, A2 and A225 Princes Road, the ground is situated adjoining Park Road

and Pilgrims Way ½ mile west of the M25 and ¾ mile east of
Dartford town centre. From east: A2, A296 follow signs Dartford for
Princes Road A225 for Park Road and Pilgrims Way. From west: A2,
A296, A225 and A206 to Dartford town centre, then as north for
Princes Road. From south: M25 junction 2 then as north or B258 to
Dartford then A225 Princes Road for ground.

WHERE TO STAY AND OTHER INFORMATION

Royal Victoria & Bull (0322 24415), Crest Hotel (0322 526900).
Princes Hotel (0322 20352)

Disabled Areas   No special area, request position
Local Radio Station(s)   BBC Radio Kent (104.2 MHz FM/1035 KHz
MW), Invicta Radio (103.1 MHz FM/1242 KHz MW)
Local Newspaper(s)   Evening Post, Kentish Times, Dartford &
Gravesend Reporter

Folkestone

The first matches staged by Kent in Folkestone were at the Sandgate
Hill ground, the original home of the Folkestone C C, in 1862 and
1863. Folkestone C C was established in 1856 and after searching for
a new ground at the turn of the century they were given a piece of
land, barely a mile from the town centre and close to the North
Downs, which was originally a part of the Earl of Radnor's Broad Mead
Farm in the Cheriton district. Once acquired thanks to the benevolent
Earl the ground was levelled and prepared under the supervision of
Alec Hearne a former Kent player for the inaugural match in 1905
when a local side played a Kent Club and Ground XI. Lord Harris
commented in his after-dinner speech at a reception given after the
match that first-class cricket should be staged on the ground.
Nevertheless the initial first-class match was not staged until twenty
years later in September 1925 when the Gentleman played the
Players. Following this match Kent played against the M C C and
hence the festival began. Matches were played intermittently from
1928 and since 1961 the Folkestone week has become a regular feature
in late August. In recent years, however, only one championship and
one limited-overs match has been staged. The home of a late-summer
cricket festival 1925–38, it has also been used by Kent Second XI since
1910.

The present pavilion and stands were built in 1926 at a cost of
£1,000, the cash being advanced from Lord Radnor. The buildings
were designed by architect R. Pope. The ground extends to some 30
acres, which includes the nearby Folkestone Town F C, tennis courts
and bowling greens. The ground is also used for hockey and both

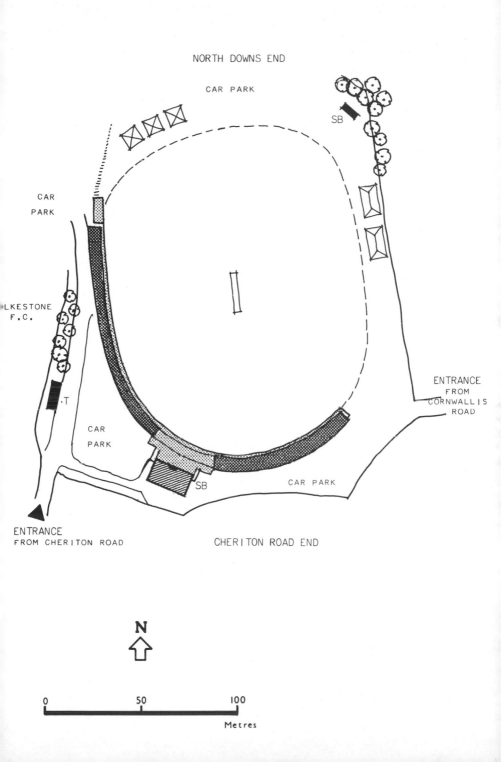

NORTH DOWNS END

CAR PARK

SB

CAR
PARK

LKESTONE
F.C.

.T

CAR
PARK

SB

ENTRANCE
FROM
CORNWALLIS
ROAD

CAR PARK

ENTRANCE
FROM CHERITON ROAD

CHERITON ROAD END

N

0   50   100

Metres

Folkestone men and ladies clubs use the recreation area facilities during the winter months. The ground is now very close to the Channel Tunnel development. This can be seen and machinery and plant can be heard from the ground. The ground was originally called the Municipal Sports Ground but since being taken over by Folkestone and Shepway Council, has been known as the Cheriton Road ground. The Folkestone C C play in the Woolwich Kent County League and field two teams.

Crowds at Folkestone are usually 4,000–4,500; the best crowd was 7,500 for a John Player Sunday League match with Essex in 1976. Major performances on the ground have included double centuries from two England opening batsman, Les Ames and Len Hutton. 'Titch' Freeman always enjoyed his visits to Cheriton Road as did Robin Marlar, who performed well with the ball for Cambridge University in 1953. Limited-overs records include a hundred from Chris Tavaré and 5 for 60 by John Jameson for Warwickshire in 1974, although he is remembered more as an opening batsman!

ADDRESS   Folkestone C C, Sports Ground, Cheriton Road, Cheriton, Folkestone, Kent CT19 5JU
TELEPHONE PROSPECTS OF PLAY   0303 53366

DESCRIPTION OF GROUND AND FACILITIES

From the south, entry to the ground is from Cheriton Road and from the east, via Cornwallis Avenue. Car parking for members is available on the polo ground but spectators can also view cricket from their cars at the northern end of the ground. The majority of permanent buildings are situated south of the playing area and include the pavilion with scoreboard and covered and open seating for members. There are also two covered stands on either side of the pavilion which surround the complete west and southern sides of the playing area. Toilets can be found in the pavilion and close to the car park at the rear of the pavilion. Entrance to this car park is from Cheriton Road or from Cherry Garden Avenue. Car parking is also available at the nearby Presto store, but only on Sundays.

At the opposite end of the ground to the pavilion there is a public catering marquee along with a scorecard printer's tent and Kent C C C shop (also in a tent). The main scoreboard is to the north-east of the ground. The east side of the playing area is bounded by sponsors' marquees and entertainment areas. The T V camera position is situated directly above and behind the sightscreen at the pavilion, Cheriton Road End and the radio point is situated on the roof of the pavilion, adjoining the press box room. The playing area is 134 metres by 170 metres and is defined by a rope and advertisement boards. The ground capacity is 8,000 and approximately 4,000 seats are provided so spectators are only advised to bring seats to popular matches. The members' enclosure is in front of the pavilion but the rest of the seating accommodation is available to both members and the public.

GROUND RECORDS AND SCORES

FIRST-CLASS MATCHES

Highest innings total for County   592 *v.* Gloucestershire, 1933
Highest innings total against County   528 by Hampshire, 1934
Lowest innings total for County   61 *v.* Essex, 1928
Lowest innings total against County   65 by Warwickshire, 1986
Highest individual innings for County   295 L.E.G. Ames *v.* Gloucestershire, 1933
Highest individual innings against County   230 H. Sutcliffe for Yorkshire, 1931
Best bowling performance in an innings for County   9 for 61 A.P. Freeman *v.* Warwickshire, 1932
Best bowling performance in an innings against County   8 for 32 R.G. Marlar for Cambridge University, 1953
Best bowling performance in a match for County   17 for 92 A.P. Freeman *v.* Warwickshire, 1932
Best bowling performance in a match against County   13 for 90 R.G. Marlar for Cambridge University, 1953

LIMITED-OVERS MATCHES

Highest innings total for County   281 for 5 *v.* Warwickshire (JPL), 1983
Highest innings total against County   223 by Warwickshire (JPL), 1983
Lowest innings total for County   84 *v.* Gloucestershire (JPL), 1969
Lowest innings total against County   118 by Derbyshire (JPL), 1976
Highest individual innings for County   122 n.o. C.J. Tavaré *v.* Warwickshire (JPL), 1983
Highest individual innings against County   86 by R.T. Robinson for Nottinghamshire (JPL), 1984
Best bowling performance for County   4 for 15 D.L. Underwood *v.* Gloucestershire (JPL), 1982
Best bowling performance against County   5 for 60 J.A. Jameson for Warwickshire (JPL), 1974

HOW TO GET THERE

Rail   Folkestone Central, ½ mile; Folkestone West, ½ mile
Bus   From surrounding areas to Bus Station, thence 1 mile – East Kent F1/3/6/9 link Bus & BR Central Station with ground (Tel: 0843 581333)
Car   From north: A260 to Folkestone, then follow signs Cheriton, ground is situated ½ mile west of town centre off (A20) Cheriton Road. From east: A20 to Folkestone, then west of town centre, as north. From west: M20 junction 12, then A20 to Cheriton district, ground situated off (A20) Cheriton Road.

WHERE TO STAY AND OTHER INFORMATION

Clifton Hotel (0303 41231), Burlington Hotel (0303 55301)

Disabled Areas No special area, request position
Local Radio Station(s) BBC Radio Kent (104.2 MHz FM/1035 KHz MW), Invicta Radio (103.1 MHz FM/1242 KHz MW)
Local Newspaper(s) Evening Post, Folkestone Dover People, Folkestone Hythe and Romney Marsh Herald

---

Maidstone

This cricket ground is located in the loveliest of settings: Mote Park within the Mote Estate of some 558 acres to the east of the town centre of the county town, Maidstone. The ground dates back to the thirteenth century and situated within the park is the Mote House, a late eighteenth-century building which is now a Cheshire Home. The cricket ground dates back to the formation of the Mote C C in 1857 and is one of the oldest clubs in the county. Sir Marcus Sammel, later the First Viscount Bearstead, the last private owner of the Mote Estate was responsible in 1908 for levelling the playing area. It is now on three terraces. At that time the wicket was moved 90 degrees, to its present layout.

The main pavilion was constructed in 1909–10. The smaller pavilion, the Tabernacle, which is one of cricket's architectural curiosities was originally Viscount Bearstead's private pavilion from which he viewed matches. The Tabernacle is used as an office by the Kent C C C during county matches. After his death, the Second Viscount Bearstead sold the estate in 1928 to its present owner, the Maidstone Borough Council, but the cricket ground was reserved and presented to the Mote C C after the sale.

The first Kent match at Mote Park was in June 1859 when an M C C team were the visitors. Further visits were made in 1861 and 1862 for matches against Surrey and Cambridgeshire but it was not until 1870 that Kent began to play regularly at Maidstone. A cricket festival week was granted in 1907 and has been a permanent feature since 1910. In recent years two championship and one limited-overs match have been staged usually in early July. Matches with touring sides have on occasions been played at Mote Park rather than at Canterbury and these have included Australians in 1890, Philadelphians and South Africans in 1897 and 1912 respectively. The Mote C C play in the Woolwich Kent County League and field four XI's on a Saturday and three on a Sunday throughout the season; they also run one mid-week team.

Crowds at Mote Park are usually 5,000–6,000; the best was 14,000 against Lancashire in the 1974 John Player Sunday League, a match which resulted in Kent becoming Sunday League Champions that

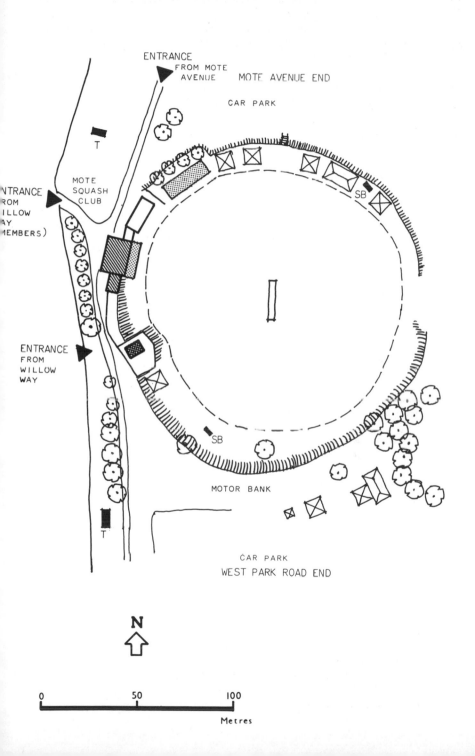

ENTRANCE FROM MOTE AVENUE

MOTE AVENUE END

CAR PARK

T

ENTRANCE FROM WILLOW WAY (MEMBERS)

MOTE SQUASH CLUB

SB

SB

ENTRANCE FROM WILLOW WAY

MOTOR BANK

T

CAR PARK

WEST PARK ROAD END

N

0   50   100

Metres

year. Ground performances have included double centuries from Percy Chapman against Lancashire and in recent years Graeme Fowler for the Red Rose county. A.P. 'Tich' Freeman, David Halfyard and Derek Underwood have all enjoyed fine bowling spells here for the County.

ADDRESS   The Mote C C, Mote Park, Willow Way, Maidstone, Kent ME15 7RN
TELEPHONE PROSPECTS OF PLAY   0622 54159/54545

DESCRIPTION OF GROUND AND FACILITIES

There are two entrances to the ground from Willow Way to the west of the ground and two areas for car parking: one to the north, down the bank and the other to the south, high above the playing area. The ground is on three levels and the cricket pitch is a flat, circular area. The pavilion, together with the Mote Squash Club and permanent raised seating, is situated on the west side of the ground. There is also a members' enclosure between the pavilion and the 'Tabernacle'. Close to the Tabernacle is a small area of sponsors' tents and a small scoreboard is located under the trees. Also, situated high above the bank at the West Park Avenue End, is the scorecard printer's, Kent C C C souvenir shop and a large refreshments marquee. The T V camera position and commentary position/radio point are situated directly above and behind the sightscreen. All the seating to the south-east of the playing area, as far as the main scoreboard, is made of temporary benches and nestle close to the bank and under the trees. The northern end of the ground comprises at least ten tents and marquees of various sizes. This includes a Kent C C S C marquee amongst others. Toilets are situated within the pavilion, at the rear, in a separate building and to the south. The members' enclosure is situated between the 'Tabernacle' to the south-west and in front of the pavilion and ends after the open raised seats to the north-west. The playing area is 136 metres by 135 metres and is defined by a rope and advertisement boards. The ground capacity is 8,000 and seating for roughly 85 per cent is provided. Spectators are advised to bring their own seating to popular matches.

The Mote Park is probably one of the finest grounds in the south and the pavilion has two levels. The scorers and press are in the roof and on the first floor respectively.

GROUND RECORDS AND SCORES

FIRST-CLASS MATCHES
Highest innings total for County   580 for 6 v. Essex, 1947
Highest innings total against County   502 by Essex, 1947
Lowest innings total for County   38 v. Lancashire, 1881
Lowest innings total against County   31 by Hampshire, 1967
Highest individual innings for County   260 A.P.F. Chapman v. Lancashire, 1927

Highest individual innings against County   226 G. Fowler for Lancashire, 1984
Best bowling performance in an innings for County   10 for 131 A.P. Freeman *v.* Lancashire, 1929
Best bowling performance in an innings against County   9 for 108 T.P.B. Smith for Essex, 1948
Best bowling performance in a match for County   15 for 117 D.J. Halfyard *v.* Worcestershire, 1959
Best bowling performance in a match against County   15 for 123 F.G. Roberts for Gloucestershire, 1897

LIMITED-OVERS MATCHES
Highest innings total for County   278 for 5 *v.* Gloucestershire (JPL), 1976
Highest innings total against County   254 for 5 by Sussex (JPL), 1982
Lowest innings total for County   86 *v.* Somerset (JPL), 1978
Lowest innings total against County   65 by Warwickshire (JPL), 1979
Highest individual innings for County   106 Asif Iqbal *v.* Gloucestershire (JPL), 1976
Highest individual innings against County   121 G.D. Mendis for Sussex (JPL), 1982
Best bowling performance for County   5 for 19 D.L. Underwood *v.* Gloucestershire (JPL), 1972
Best bowling performance against County   4 for 15 J. Birkenshaw for Leicestershire (JPL), 1977

HOW TO GET THERE

Rail   Maidstone East, 1 mile; Maidstone West, 1¼ miles
Bus   Boro' Line 85 from High Street (¼ mile from both BR Stations) (Tel: 0622 690060). Also routes 5 and 12.
Car   From north: M20 junctions 6 or 7 then either A229 or A249 to town centre signposted Maidstone, ground situated off Ashford Road A20 through Square Hill Road and Mote Road for Mote Park. From east: M20 junction 8, then A20 to town centre, then as north or A274 or A229 to town centre then as north. From west: M20 junction 5 then follow signs Maidstone and town centre, then as north. From south: A26, A229 or A274 to Maidstone and town centre, then as north.

WHERE TO STAY AND OTHER INFORMATION

Great Danes, Hollingbourne (0622 30022), Royal Star Hotel (0622 55721), Larkfield Hotel (0732 846858)

Disabled Areas   No special area, request position
Local Radio Station(s)   BBC Radio Kent (104.2 MHz FM/1035 KHz MW), Invicta Radio (103.1 MHz FM/1242 KHz MW)
Local Newspaper(s)   Evening Post, Kentish Gazette, East Kent Mercury, Maidstone Borough News

Tunbridge Wells

The Nevill Cricket ground is located at Nevill Gate and is the home of Tunbridge Wells C C (established in 1782) and Blue Mantles C C (established in 1895). Tunbridge Wells C C previously played at the Higher Common Ground in Fir Tree Road between 1786 and 1884 until its move to Nevil Gate in 1895. Kent also played on the Common from 1845 until 1884 and other clubs who played there included Linden Park C C and the Madhatters Hockey Club.

The Nevill Gate ground was acquired on a lease of 99 years from the Eridge Park Estate of the Marquess of Abergavenny (family name Nevill) to the Tunbridge Wells Cricket, Football and Athletic Club. The ground has been used for football, cycling racing, athletics, archery, hockey and tennis. Tennis courts border the ground on one side and a notable tennis tournament is staged, usually in August each year. The ground was opened in 1898 by the Marquess of Abergavenny and the first Kent match was in 1901 when Lancashire were the visitors. The present pavilion and additional buildings were constructed in 1903 at a cost of £1,200 but in 1913 when the suffragettes were campaigning, it suffered extensive fire damage and was rebuilt. After the 1914–18 War the ground became a picketing area for the cavalry; several hundred horses tethered over the playing area did little to improve the wickets! The ground is now owned by the Tunbridge Wells Borough Council which took control in 1946 and looks after its upkeep.

The Nevill Ground is probably one of the most beautiful grounds on the county circuit especially during festival week, which is usually staged in early June when the giant purple blooms of the rhododendrons curving around the playing arena form a superb setting for county cricket. Tunbridge Wells C C plays in the Woolwich Kent County League and has three XI's most weekends. Blue Mantles C C play friendly matches throughout the week and matches have been played with M C C in the past. In 1983 an international match was staged on the ground when the Prudential Cup match between India and Zimbabwe followed the usual Kent and Sussex championship match. Kapil Dev hit 175 not out in that competition, the highest individual innings in the history of the Prudential World Cup until beaten by Viv Richards in Karachi in 1987. Kent usually play a week of cricket at Tunbridge Wells and this includes two championship and one limited-overs match.

Crowds at the Nevill Ground are usually 5,000–5,500; the largest was in 1950 when 10,000 attended the two days with Lancashire. Players who have represented Tunbridge Wells and played first-class cricket include: Mike Willard of Cambridge University, Peter Hearn and Bob Woolmer (both Kent). Ground records at Tunbridge Wells have included double hundreds from James Seymour and Wally Hammond and fine bowling from A.P. 'Tich' Freeman for Kent. Colin Blythe once bowled 12 overs here against Sussex and gave only one run away in an hour.

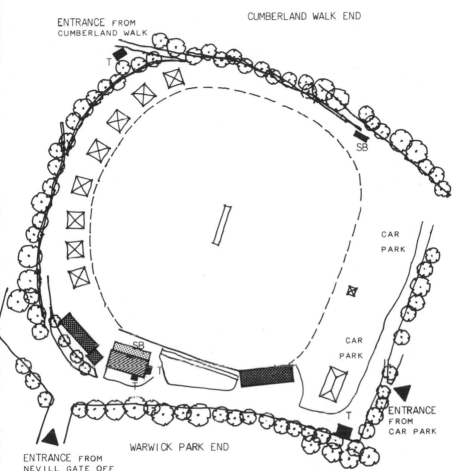

CUMBERLAND WALK END

ENTRANCE FROM
CUMBERLAND WALK

T

SB

CAR
PARK

CAR
PARK

SB

T

T

T

ENTRANCE
FROM
CAR PARK

WARWICK PARK END

ENTRANCE FROM
NEVILL GATE OFF
WARWICK PARK

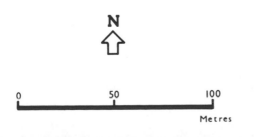

N

0   50   100

Metres

ADDRESS   Tunbridge Wells C C, Nevill Cricket Ground, Nevill Gate, Warwick Park, Tunbridge Wells, Kent TN2 5ES
TELEPHONE PROSPECTS OF PLAY   0892 20846

DESCRIPTION OF GROUND AND FACILITIES

Entrance to the Nevill Cricket Ground is from Nevill Gate off Warwick Park, and to the north of the playing area from Upper Cumberland Walk. Two further entrances to the ground, for pedestrians only, are from the path off Warwick Park and from the adjoining car park to the west of the playing area. Car parking is available within the ground for players, officials and some members on the tennis courts from where cricket may be viewed from parked cars. There is also a 4 acre field available for parking adjoining the ground and more in nearby streets. All the permanent buildings are located at the Warwick Gate End, where the scoreboard and scorers' room are situated on the roof of the main pavilion with the press box. There is seating for members in front of the pavilion and in the two other stands either side of the enclosure: the grandstand to the east and the covered enclosure, adjoining the Martlets private pavilion, to the west. To the west of the playing area, backing onto the tennis courts, are temporary seating areas plus a number of marquees which are sited around the whole playing area. A second scoreboard is situated in the north-east corner of the ground, on the east side of the playing area. The scorecard printers and Kent C C C souvenir tents are on the tennis courts. There is also a large catering area for the public and members, who also may take refreshment in the pavilion. Toilets are available in the north-west corner, south-east corner and at the rear of the members pavilion. The playing area which is 138 metres by 135 metres is flat, situated in fine grounds of trees and shrubs and is defined by a rope and advertising boards. The ground capacity is 5,500 and only 1,500 seats are provided so spectators would be well advised to bring their own seats to all matches.

GROUND RECORDS AND SCORES

FIRST-CLASS MATCHES
Highest innings total for County   519 for 6 v. Warwickshire, 1928
Highest innings total against County   563 by Gloucestershire, 1934
Lowest innings total for County   58 v. Leicestershire, 1938
Lowest innings total against County   25 by Worcestershire, 1960
Highest individual innings for County   214 J. Seymour v. Essex, 1914
Highest individual innings against County   290 W.R. Hammond for Gloucestershire, 1934
Best bowling performance in an innings for County   8 for 38 A.P. Freeman v. Northamptonshire, 1932
Best bowling performance in an innings against County   10 for 127 V.W.C. Jupp for Northamptonshire, 1932

Best bowling performance in a match for County 16 for 82
A.P. Freeman v. Northamptonshire, 1932
Best bowling performance in a match against County 14 for 141
A.E. Lewis for Somerset, 1910

LIMITED-OVERS MATCHES
Highest innings total for County 242 v. Sussex (GC), 1963
Highest innings total against County 314 for 7 by Sussex (GC),
1963
Lowest innings total for County 173 v. Sussex (BHC), 1972
Lowest innings total against County 120 by Surrey (JPL), 1970
Highest individual innings for County 127 P.E. Richardson v.
Sussex (GC), 1963
Highest individual innings against County 104 K.G. Suttle for
Sussex (GC), 1963
Best bowling performance for County 3 for 20 R.A. Woolmer v.
Surrey (JPL), 1970
Best bowling performance against County 2 for 22 D.L. Williams
for Glamorgan (JPL), 1972

HOW TO GET THERE

Rail Tunbridge Wells, ¾ mile
Bus From surrounding areas to Frant Road End, routes 280, 283,
254, 256, 252 and 791; also via Hawkenbury End, route 285
Car From north: A21, A26 or A227 to Tunbridge Wells, the
ground is situated ½ mile south of the town centre off A267
Hastings Road then into Roedean Road and Warwick Park. From
east and west: A264 to Tunbridge Wells then as north. From south:
A267 to Tunbridge Wells then as north.

WHERE TO STAY AND OTHER INFORMATION

Calverley Hotel (0892 36801), Russell Hotel (0892 44833)

Disabled Areas No special area, request position
Local Radio Station(s) BBC Radio Kent (104.2 MHz FM/1035 KHz
MW), Invicta Radio (103.1 MHz FM/1242 KHz MW)
Local Newspaper(s) Evening Post, Kent and Sussex Courier

LANCASHIRE

MANCHESTER – OLD TRAFFORD

LIVERPOOL

LYTHAM

SOUTHPORT

BLACKPOOL

Lancashire

In his *History of Lancashire*, John Kay, the county's foremost authority, boldly nominated the best team of players from 1864 when it all began from the seed planted by Manchester Cricket Club. His choice was: A.G. MacLaren, C. Washbrook, J.T. Tyldesley, C.H. Lloyd, E. Tyldesley, F.M. Engineer, J. Briggs, C.H. Parkin, S.F. Barnes, E.A. McDonald, J.B. Statham. 12th man, E. Paynter.

No A.N. ('Monkey') Hornby, authoritative captain and leading batsman, no R.H. Spooner, the epitome of batting grace, nor A.G. Steel, accomplished batsman and slow bowler, the pro batting stalwarts Barlow, Hallows, Watson and Makepeace, or fast bowler Brearley.

There is, of course, no way to judge the merits of Washbrook against Barlow, Hornby's opening partner. He played in 17 Tests against Australia, including 3 tours in which he played in every fixture, and opened both batting and bowling for England. It is also possible to imagine Hutton, who regarded Washbrook as his favourite partner, saying: 'I can't think Barlow could have been better than Washbrook.'

Kay includes three 'foreigners' – Lloyd, the West Indies captain, McDonald, one of Australia's finest fast bowlers, and the Indian wicket-keeper, Engineer. Presumably Engineer's batting wins him preference over Pilling, rated the best stumper of his day, and Duckworth.

Lancashire have never been thin-skinned about the geography of their recruits, and at one stage the Bolton-born Barlow was the only Lancastrian in the side, a state of affairs which led to acrimonious cards being exchanged with Nottinghamshire. Nottinghamshire's response to a cheeky Christmas card was a New Year's message which read:

LANCASHIRE COUNTY CRICKET

The only rules necessary for players in the County Eleven are that they shall neither have been born in, nor reside in, Lancashire.
Sutton-in-Ashfield will have the preference.

Since Johnny Briggs, a major all-rounder, came from Sutton-in-Ashfield, less than 20 miles from Trent Bridge, Nottinghamshire had cause to feel touchy. Only 5ft 5ins tall Briggs bowled left arm at slow to medium pace with uncanny accuracy and invention, and was an able enough batsman to have scored a century at Melbourne in one of his six visits to Australia. At Cape Town in 1888–9, under the captaincy of C.A. Smith – to become Sir Aubrey the Hollywood film actor – Briggs had 15 wickets for 28. Briggs was a jovial character, and once answered Hornby's charge of drunkenness with an exhibition of trick cycling. Unhappily he died from a mental disorder at the age of 39.

LANCASHIRE C.C.C

Lancashire's early teams comfortably eastablished the county as one of the Big Six, joining Yorkshire, Nottinghamshire, Surrey, Gloucestershire and Middlesex. They were the sides which dominated the championship almost up to the liberating 'sixties. Lancashire's share of the prizes were 6 championships, including a hat-trick from 1926 to 1928, and 3 shared.

Archie MacLaren, as captain and batsman, mirrored the Golden Age. He took 424 off Somerset at Taunton in 1895, still an English record, and there was batting of the highest class from J.T. Tyldesley, the elder brother by 16 years of Ernest, who more than upheld the family name. J.T.'s 31 Tests with 37,897 runs and 86 centuries stands beside Ernest's 14 Tests, 38,874 runs and 102 centuries: both pillars of strength.

Only once, in 1904, was MacLaren able to claim the championship, but Lancashire were invariably in contention, and his batting fired the imagination. His contribution to the romantic legends of the game was to take Sydney Barnes to Australia on the evidence of his bowling in the Old Trafford nets. Some contend there was never a better bowler, but Barnes had an estimation of his value which did not coincide with Lancashire's and he was lost to the Leagues.

Walter Brearley, like Barnes, would have been a godsend to today's media. After a dressing room dispute between the rival teams he fired a succession of high full tosses at Jessop. At Lord's he asked a luminary: 'Are you the manager of this 'ere bloomin' 'ipperdrome?' and, after being left out of a Test match, stationed himself below the box of Sir Henry Leveson Gower, chairman of selectors, and began a commentary which included 'Brearley for England,': 'I often get 6 wickets in an innings, and generally the leading batsmen', and 'I don't always trust the fieldsman so I clean bowl 'em.' The result was a gathering of curious spectators and a policeman arriving and telling Brearley to stop 'singing' as he was causing an obstruction!

The 'twenties saw a powerful side enriched by the dual purpose bowling of Parkin – another lost to the Leagues – Dick Tyldesley, a leg spinner of wide girth and dry humour ('he's no good to me' was his heartfelt summing up of Bradman during his 334 at Leeds in 1930), the magnificent McDonald, Duckworth and Ernest Tyldesley. All the diverse talents were welded into a team of champions by Leonard Green, a military man and firm believer in discipline and fairness. 'He gets on with his job and we get on with ours,' remarked Duckworth succinctly explaining the best of the old amateur captain–pro relationship.

Hallows hit 1,000 runs between 5 and 31 May in 1928, and the title returned to Old Trafford in 1930 and 1934. Though honours were shared with Surrey in 1950 Lancashire's standards fell below expectations after the war. Pride was abandoned when the club advertised in *The Times* for a captain. Yet in the course of time the evergreen Simmons, the hero of many a Cup tie, Statham and Bond demonstrated they knew all about the arts of captaincy. Simmons' achievements for Tasmania bordered on the miraculous, and Statham, a natural fast bowler if ever there was one, took 252 wickets in 70 Tests and formed a famous partnership with Trueman. In all Statham had 2,260 wickets.

Bond had modest recommendations as a batsman, but as a captain, inspiring his teams on the principles of fitness, loyalty and enjoyment, he enjoyed a remarkable five-year triumph. He had the luck to be positively supported by chairman Cedric Rhoades, to be in at the start of single-innings cricket and to have players singularly equipped for the new format, from Clive Lloyd to the long-serving David Hughes. As Bond took the Sunday League in its first two seasons and a hat-trick of the Gillette Cup from 1970 to 1972, there seemed to be a happy conspiracy between Bond and his two overseas stars, Clive Lloyd and Engineer, and his mainstays Simmons, Hughes, Wood, David Lloyd, Pilling, Peter Lever, Hayes and Sullivan.

The West Indies captain made a tremendous impact with his free hitting ('if I see it I hit it') and cover fielding, and both home and away Lancashire drew huge crowds. In the final game of the John Player Trophy against Yorkshire in 1970 the gates at Old Trafford were closed for the first time since 1948. When he retired *Wisden* said Bond 'managed' rather than led Lancashire from the depths of despair to the heights of success in one-day cricket. 'He created team spirit and guarded it jealously,' *Wisden* added. Sadly for Bond his wheel of fortune was to turn full circle.

David Lloyd, Bond's successor, again took the Cup, making four victories in five years, and in 1984 with John Abrahams in charge, Lancashire carried off the Benson and Hedges Cup, an achievement soured by a 16th position in the championship. For the first time in 110 years they had won only one game and, for the 9th successive year, they were in the bottom six. There was a brief glimpse of glory with a final place in the NatWest Trophy in 1986 when Clive Lloyd was one of Sussex bowler Reeves' four victims out for a duck. There were too many failures to stomach and at the season's end Lloyd was

WILL'S Cigarettes

J. BRIGGS, LANCASHIRE

KEN GRIEVES

OGDEN'S CIGARETTES

E. PAYNTER

replaced by Hughes as captain, and, while the playing staff was retained, manager Bond and coach Lever were dismissed.

A sad ending, but the days of Bond and Clive Lloyd will remain forever a saga of Old Trafford. [A.B.]

Founded 1864
Colours Red, green and blue
Crest Red rose
Secretary C.D. Hassell
Coaches J.A. Ormrod/J.A. Savage
Groundsman P. Marron
Scorers W. Davies/A. Lowe
Address Old Trafford, Talbot Road, Manchester M16 0PX
Telephone 061 848 7021
Cricketcall 0898 121469

Achievements:

County Championship Champions (8) 1881, 1897, 1904, 1926, 1927, 1928, 1930 and 1934; Joint champions (4) 1879, 1882, 1889 and 1950
Gillette Cup Winners 1970, 1971, 1972 and 1975; finalists 1974 and 1976
National Westminster Bank Trophy Finalists 1986
Benson & Hedges Cup Winners 1984
John Player Sunday League Champions (2) 1969 and 1970
Refuge Assurance Sunday League Champions (0) 3rd 1988
Refuge Assurance Cup Winners 1988
Fenner Trophy Finalists 1971 and 1972
Asda Trophy Winners 1983; finalists 1982, 1985 and 1987

Ward Knockout Cup   Semi-finalists 1988
Lambert & Butler Cup   (TCCB 7-a-side Floodlit Competition)
Winners 1981

Grounds:

Manchester (Old Trafford, Talbot Road)   Liverpool (Aigburth
Cricket Ground, Aigburth Road)   Southport (Trafalgar Road,
Birkdale)   Lytham (Church Road, Lytham)   Blackpool (Stanley
Park, West Park Drive).

Manchester – Old Trafford

Old Trafford has been the home of Lancashire cricket since 1857
when the new ground was opened. Lancashire play most of their
matches at Old Trafford and of course the ground also stages Test
Matches and limited-overs international matches.

Old Trafford is the third ground to be used in Manchester for
cricket. The first was at Moss Lane, Moss Side, Hulme. This ground
was closed in 1847 and play moved to Chester Road, Stretford where
matches were staged from 1848 until 1854 by the Manchester Cricket
Club. After the final move to the present ground, the Stretford ground
became the White City greyhound stadium.

Situated a short distance westwards, and still Sir Thomas de
Trafford's land, was Old Trafford. The first match staged was between
Manchester C C and Liverpool C C. The initial first-class match at
Old Trafford was between England and Another England XI in 1860.
Lancashire C C C was formed in 1864 and the first Lancashire match
was with Middlesex in 1865. The first Test Match was staged in 1884
when England played Australia.

The 18-acre ground was owned by de Trafford until 1898 when
Manchester C C purchased it from the de Trafford Estate for £24,082.
The pavilion was built in 1894, four years earlier. The pavilion was
used as a hospital during World War One and was bombed during the
Blitz of World War Two. Most of the buildings are located on the
Talbot Road side of the ground and much of the seating is permanent
and now of the plastic tip-up type. In 1982 a ground development
appeal raised £200,000 and in 1984 a further £47,000 was raised from
a Test Centenary Appeal. Much development has taken place with
this money, including some executive boxes and press/commentary
facilities. Other additions have included a Lancashire cricket museum
and a members' library in the pavilion. There are plenty of cricket
items in the pavilion, which was designed by A. Muirhead the same
architect who designed the Oval Pavilion. 1984 was the centenary of
Test cricket at Old Trafford and in 1989 Lancashire will celebrate its

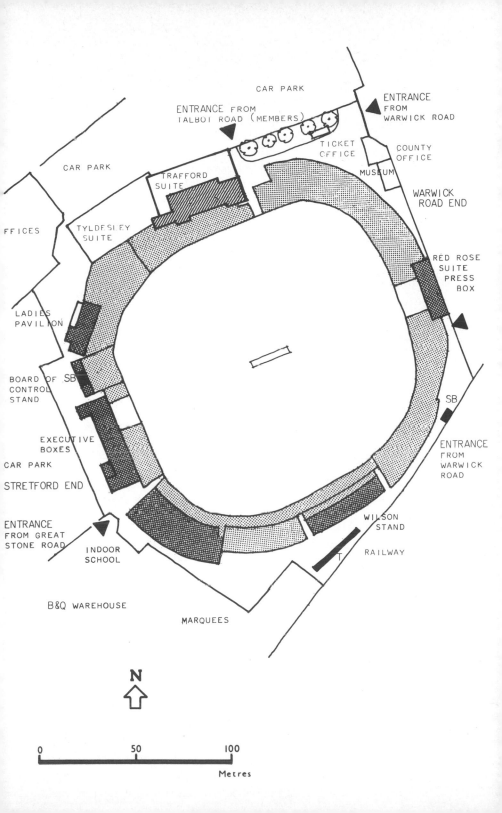

125th anniversary.

The ground is also used by Manchester C C and the Lancashire Club and Ground XI. Part of the ground at the Stretford End was leased to a D I Y store and garden centre during the 1980s. All the nearby government office towers are named after famous Lancashire cricketers; Statham, MacLaren, Duckworth and Washbrook.

Crowds at Old Trafford have always been large. The record attendance was 78,617 for the Roses Match in 1926 (46,000 on the first day), and for a limited-overs match 33,000 against Yorkshire in the John Player Sunday League in 1970. The current ground capacity of 20,000 is regularly attained for Test Matches and limited-overs internationals. The ground has staged all major county competitions as well as Prudential Trophy, Prudential Cup and Texaco Trophy competitions. Ground performances have included scores of 300 or more from Frank Watson against Surrey in 1928 and 311 by Bobby Simpson for Australia against England in 1964. Old Trafford was the ground where Jim Laker took 19 Australian wickets in 1956 and in recent years Viv Richards hit 189 not out in a Texaco Trophy match in 1984.

ADDRESS   Old Trafford Cricket Ground, Talbot Road, Manchester M16 6PX
TELEPHONE PROSPECTS OF PLAY   061-872 0261

DESCRIPTION OF GROUND AND FACILITIES

Situated in the Old Trafford district of Manchester, the ground is bounded by Talbot Road to the north, Warwick Road to the northeast, Great Stone Road to the west and to the south, the Altrincham to Manchester railway line. The main entrance is through the turnstiles next to the secretary's office in Warwick Road and there is access for cars from Talbot Road and Great Stone Road where car parking is available on the practice ground. This is also used for marquees and the chalet village during the Test Match. At weekends there is a car park in the government offices in Talbot Road. Once in the arena itself the members' enclosure stretches from the ladies' stand to the pavilion and in front of these two buildings. The pavilion comprises the Trafford suite, Tyldesley suite, Lancaster library and catering facilities as well as refreshments, toilets and changing rooms for players, and members seating both covered and uncovered. The stands are numbered A to K, circle the ground and comprise plastic and timber blue bench seats which are covered under the Red Rose suite at the Warwick Road End, the Wilson Stand (which includes a rather unusual light meter) and H Stand. The Executive Suites, together with T V camera and radio point positions, are sited on the roof at the Stretford End high above the playing area. Adjoining the executive suite is the board of control stand with scoreboard, scorer's room and TCCB boxes along with sponsors' seating. The ladies' pavilion includes the Jubilee Britannia suite and is only available to

Lady members and their husbands. Ladies are not allowed in the members' pavilion. At the Stretford End is the indoor cricket school with an area for marquees, erected during the Test Match. The main scoreboard is sited near the Warwick Road railway station, at the rear of the seating area in enclosure E. Toilet facilities are available throughout the ground as are bars, refreshment areas, a Lancashire club souvenir shop (which has several smaller outlets at popular matches) and a Lancashire cricket museum which is situated under A and B enclosures, near the main entrance. The press box is known as The Sir Neville Cardus Gallery and was opened by John Arlott OBE on the eve of the First Cornhill Test Match between England and Pakistan on 3rd June 1987. Restaurants are available to members and sponsors throughout the season. Other buildings include the groundsman's house in the Talbot Road car park, the ticket office (where transfers can be obtained), the secretary's office/Lancashire county offices and groundsman's equipment stores. A first aid room, toilets for the disabled and several disabled areas are available in enclosures A and B, the Wilson Stand and in the special wheelchair enclosure adjoining the ringside seats to the side of the E enclosure and Wilson Stand. The ground capacity is 20,000 and seating is provided for all. The playing area is flat and defined by a rope and advertising boards and by a white metal fence in front of the pavilion. The pitch is 143 metres by 149 metres and approximately circular in shape. Should poor weather end a match early or provide a lengthy break in play a visit to the Manchester United F.C. museum is recommended as it is only a short walk from the ground.

GROUND RECORDS AND SCORES

TEST MATCHES

Highest innings total for England   627 for 9 dec. v. Australia, 1934
Highest innings total against England   658 for 8 dec. by Australia, 1964
Lowest innings total for England   71 v. West Indies, 1976
Lowest innings total against England   58 by India, 1952
Highest individual innings for England   256 K.F. Barrington v. Australia, 1964
Highest individual innings against England   311 R.B. Simpson for Australia, 1964
Best bowling performance in an innings for England   10 for 53 J.C. Laker v. Australia, 1956
Best bowling performance in an innings against England   8 for 31 F. Laver for Australia, 1909
Best bowling performance in a match for England   19 for 90 J.C. Laker v. Australia, 1956
Best bowling performance in a match against England   11 for 157 L. Gibbs for West Indies, 1963

Highest innings total   295 by England *v.* Pakistan (PT), 1982
Lowest innings total   45 by Canada *v.* England (PC), 1979
Highest individual innings   189 n.o. I.V.A. Richards for West Indies *v.* England (TT), 1984
Best bowling performance   4 for 8 C.M. Old for England *v.* Canada (PC), 1979

FIRST-CLASS MATCHES

Highest innings total for County   676 for 7 dec. *v.* Hampshire, 1911
Highest innings total against County   597 by London County, 1903
Lowest innings total for County   25 *v.* Derbyshire, 1871
Lowest innings total against County   24 by Sussex, 1890
Highest individual innings for County   300 n.o. F. Watson *v.* Surrey, 1928
Highest individual innings against County   282 n.o. A. Sandham for Surrey, 1928
Best bowling performance in an innings for County   10 for 55 J. Briggs *v.* Worcestershire, 1900
Best bowling performance in an innings against County   10 for 79 A.P. Freeman for Kent, 1931
Best bowling performance in a match for County   17 for 137 W. Brearley *v.* Somerset, 1905
Best bowling performance in a match against County   16 for 65 G. Giffen for Australians, 1886

LIMITED-OVERS MATCHES

Highest innings total for County   317 for 5 *v.* Scotland (BHC), 1988
Highest innings total against County   314 for 5 by Worcestershire (BHC), 1980
Lowest innings total for County   76 *v.* Somerset (JPL), 1972
Lowest innings total against County   68 by Glamorgan (BHC), 1973
Highest individual innings for County   134 n.o. C.H. Lloyd *v.* Somerset (JPL), 1970
Highest individual innings against County   162 n.o. C.G. Greenidge for Hampshire (JPL), 1983
Best bowling performance for County   6 for 10 C.E.H. Croft *v.* Scotland (BHC), 1982
Best bowling performance against County   8 for 26 K.D. Boyce for Essex (JPL), 1971

HOW TO GET THERE

Rail   Warwick Road, adjacent from Manchester Piccadilly
Bus   GB Buses 115, 112, 113 and 720 from Piccadilly (Tel: 061-228 7811)
Car   From north: M61 then M63 junction 4, follow signs Manchester A5081, then after 2½ miles left into Warwick Road and

right into Talbot Road for Old Trafford. The ground is situated 2½ miles south-west of the city centre on the east side of the main A56 in the Old Trafford district. From east: M62 junction 17, then A56 follow signs Manchester, Old Trafford is signposted on your right in Talbot Road. From west: M62 then M63 junction 4, then as north. From south: M6 junction 19, then follow signs Stockport A556, then Altrincham A56, from Altrincham follow signs Manchester, Old Trafford is signposted on your right off Talbot Road.

WHERE TO STAY AND OTHER INFORMATION

Hotel Piccadilly (061-236 8414), Portland Thistle (061-228 3567), The Grand Hotel (061-236 9559), Post House Hotel (061-998 7090) and many others

Disabled Areas E Stand for wheelchairs, and members enclosure
Local Radio Station(s) Greater Manchester Radio (95.1 MHz FM), Radio Piccadilly (103 MHz FM/1152 KHz MW), BBC Radio Lancashire (104.5 MHz FM)
Local Newspaper(s) Manchester Evening News, North West Times, Sunday Pink

Liverpool

In the Aigburth district of the city barely 5 miles from the Liver Building is the Aigburth cricket ground, which has been the home of Liverpool C C since 1881. The club was founded in 1807 in the days of the Mosslake Cricket Society. Prior to this, cricket had been played at Mersey Bowman's Archery Ground but no organized cricket club existed until the Mosslake Society was formed in 1807. Liverpool C C emerged from this club and moved to Wavertree Road, Edgehill in 1829. This ground staged cricket between 1859 and 1872 including first-class matches between Gents of the North and Gents of the South. Three further moves took place due to housing needs and in 1877 Liverpool C C was without a ground. The Earl of Sefton rescued the club with an offer of a temporary ground at Croxteth Park until their present move to Aigburth in 1881.

Liverpool first staged a Lancashire match in 1881 when Cambridge University were the visitors. Since then first-class and in recent years limited-overs matches have been staged regularly. Liverpool is the county's oldest home venue outside Old Trafford. The ground is located on the corner of Aigburth Road and Riversdale Road which leads down to the River Mersey. The pavilion is located at the Aigburth Road End and is very grand for an out ground. During the 1880s when it was built, Liverpool was a thriving port and plenty of

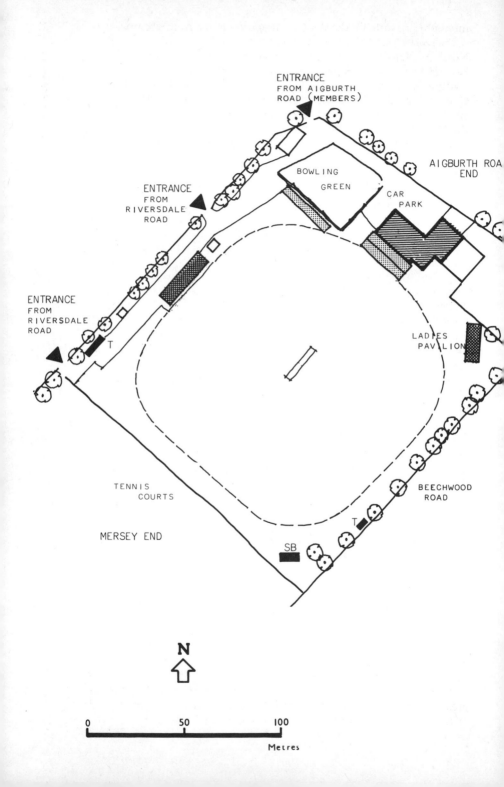

ENTRANCE
FROM AIGBURTH
ROAD (MEMBERS)

AIGBURTH ROA
END

ENTRANCE
FROM
RIVERSDALE
ROAD

BOWLING
GREEN

CAR
PARK

ENTRANCE
FROM
RIVERSDALE
ROAD

T

LADIES
PAVILION

TENNIS
COURTS

BEECHWOOD
ROAD

MERSEY END

T

SB

N

0   50   100

Metres

money was available thanks to generous support from members.

There are facilities for tennis and bowling, and in 1894 the Northern Lawn Tennis Tournament was staged on the ground. Hockey is played on the ground during the winter months.

Many famous players have represented Liverpool C C and the County including A.G. Steel, D.Q. Steel, E.C. Hornby, R.E. Barlow and J. White. Many tour matches have been played at Aigburth since the 1882 Australians visited the ground. Other tourists have been the South Africans, West Indians, Canadians, Philadelphians and the Parsees. Liverpool C C are founder members of the Youngers Liverpool and District Cricket Competition and field four XI's each season. Lancashire today play one championship and one limited-overs match at Aigburth usually in the early part of the season.

Crowds at Aigburth regularly number around 5,000–5,500. The largest was some 15,164 for the visit of Northamptonshire in 1948. The Aigburth Pavilion boasts possibly the largest dressing rooms on the county circuit, larger than at most Test grounds.

During Lancashire's long association with the Liverpool C C there have been many memorable performances on the ground. In 1903 J.T. Tyldesley scored 248 and 29 years later Wally Hammond scored 264 for Gloucestershire (still the highest ever score on the Aigburth ground). Records for Lancashire performances with the ball go to H. Dean and for the visitors to A.S. Kennedy and T.G. Wass. The records for first-class matches were made in the distant past and no doubt tax even the memories of older members. Notable performances at limited-overs matches have included 186 not out from Gordon Greenidge while batting for the West Indians in 1984 and 4 for 53 from Richard Hadlee.

In 1983 while batting for his county Hampshire, Greenidge scored 104 and 100 not out in a championship match and during a Sunday League match at Old Trafford he hit 162, giving him an aggregate of 366 runs over four days.

ADDRESS Liverpool C C, Aigburth Road, Grassendale, Liverpool L19 3QF
TELEPHONE PROSPECTS OF PLAY 051-427 2930

DESCRIPTION OF GROUND AND FACILITIES

Aigburth is entered from the corner of Aigburth Road and Riversdale Road. However, there are two additional pedestrian and vehicle access points in Riversdale Road. The extensive Liverpool pavilion would be a credit to any county ground and provides first class facilities for players and members alike, with large bars, refreshments and permanent seating. The pavilion balcony, high above the playing area and directly behind the sightscreen at the pavilion end, is used by the press and also as a radio point and T V camera position. To the side of the pavilion is the ladies' pavilion which includes restaurant and bar facilities. The main scoreboard is situated in the south corner of the ground and to the north-west is the covered stand with seats, groundsman's stores, toilet, bar and refreshment buildings. The scorers sit on this side, below the level of the playing area so it is probably one of the worst grounds at which to score (as most first class scorers will confirm). Temporary seating is provided and with the permanent bench seats, around 7,000 seats are provided which means 80 per cent of the ground capacity can be seated. The pavilion and the lawn in front of the ladies' pavilion is available to members only but the rest of the ground is open to the public. Temporary facilities include refreshment tents, the L C C C souvenir shop and sponsors' marquees all of which can be found at the Grassendale End of the ground, on the tennis courts. The playing area is 142 metres by 138 metres and is defined by a rope and advertising boards. Car parking is available within the ground for players/officials only but members may park on the lower ground adjoining the Merseyrail Electric track, off Riversdale Road and Beechwood Road. Street parking is also available within a short walk of the ground.

GROUND RECORDS AND SCORES

FIRST-CLASS MATCHES
Highest innings total for County   502 for 9 *v.* Leicestershire, 1929
Highest innings total against County   514 by Gloucestershire, 1932
Lowest innings total for County   28 *v.* Australians, 1896
Lowest innings total against County   22 by Glamorgan, 1924
Highest individual innings for County   248 J.T. Tyldesley *v.* Worcestershire, 1903
Highest individual innings against County   264 by W.R. Hammond for Gloucestershire, 1932
Best bowling performance in an innings for County   9 for 35 H. Dean *v.* Warwickshire, 1909
Best bowling performance in an innings against County   9 for 33 A.S. Kennedy for Hampshire, 1920
Best bowling performance in a match for County   17 for 90 H. Dean *v.* Yorkshire, 1913
Best bowling performance in a match against County   16 for 69 T.G. Wass for Nottinghamshire, 1906

LIMITED-OVERS MATCHES
Highest innings total for County   257 for 7 *v.* Derbyshire (BHC), 1988
Highest innings total against County   297 for 6 by West Indians (Tour), 1984
Lowest innings total for County   173 *v.* Warwickshire (JPL), 1980
Lowest innings total against County   162 for 4 by Derbyshire (BHC), 1975
Highest individual innings for County   94 G. Fowler *v.* West Indians (Tour), 1984
Highest individual innings against County   186 n.o. C.G.

Greenidge for West Indians (Tour), 1984
Best bowling performance for County   5 for 23 P. Lever v.
Northamptonshire (JPL), 1970
Best bowling performance against County   4 for 53 R. Hadlee for
Nottinghamshire (BHC), 1986

HOW TO GET THERE

Rail   Aigburth, ½ mile
Bus   Merseybus 82, Crosville X5, H25 from Lime Street (Tel: 051-
236 7676)
Car   From north: M6 junction 28, then follow signs Liverpool on
A48 and then A562 Aigburth, ground is situated south-east of the
city centre in the Aigburth and Grassendale district. From east: M6
21a then M62 to junction 4, then follow signs Aigburth or B5180
and A561 to ground. From west: Mersey Tunnel into Liverpool city
centre then follow A562 to Grassendale and Aigburth.

WHERE TO STAY AND OTHER INFORMATION

Holiday Inn (051-709 0181), Royal Hotel (051-928 2332), St George's
Hotel (051-709 7090)

Disabled Areas   No special area, request position
Local Radio Station(s)   BBC Radio Merseyside (95.8 MHz FM/1485
KHz MW), Radio City (96.7 MHz FM/1548 KHz MW)
Local Newspaper(s)   Liverpool Daily Post, Liverpool Echo,
Liverpool Star

Lytham

Church Road, Lytham receives one championship visit from Lancashire each year, usually in August, and this is always well supported
by the locals and people on holiday on the Fylde Coast. The ground
is the home of the Lytham Cricket and Sports Club and comprises a
pleasant ground of some 11¼ acres nestling in trees close to the
Preston–Blackpool (South) railway line. This passes through a cutting
at one end of the ground. The facilities are ample and shared with the
Lytham Hockey Club, Lytham Tennis Club and the Clifton Casuals
Football Club. Lytham C C play in the Manchester Association
Cricket League and also have teams represented in the Liverpool and
District Competition.

Lancashire made their initial visit to Church Road in 1985 for a
championship match with Northamptonshire which was affected by
rain. Since then visits have been made by Glamorgan, Sussex and
Nottinghamshire. In 1989 Essex are due to visit the seaside resort.

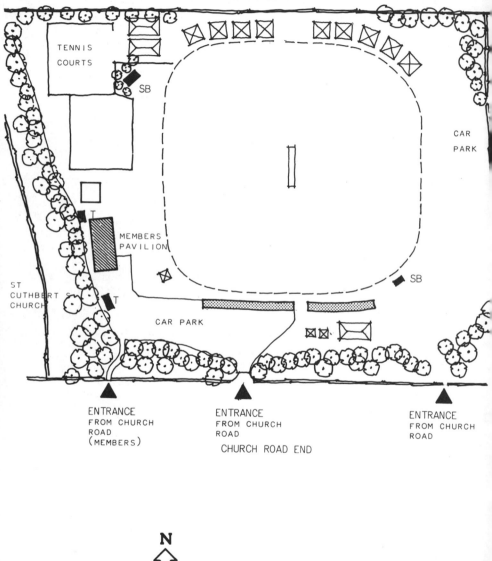

RAILWAY END

RAILWAY LINE

TENNIS
COURTS

SB

CAR
PARK

MEMBERS
PAVILION

ST
CUTHBERT'S
CHURCH

T

SB

CAR PARK

ENTRANCE
FROM CHURCH
ROAD
(MEMBERS)

ENTRANCE
FROM CHURCH
ROAD

CHURCH ROAD END

ENTRANCE
FROM CHURCH
ROAD

N

0   50   100

Metres

The only permanent buildings on the ground are the pavilion and club house located close to the parish hall and St Cuthbert's Church. An interesting old scoreboard is located under the trees near the tennis courts. The club house has a number of photographs and items of cricket interest including an aerial photograph of the first match in 1985.

The club has staged benefit matches for Lancashire players, the most recent for Clive Lloyd. Crowds at Church Road are usually around 3,000. The largest crowd for a single day was 3,500 against Glamorgan in 1986 and for the three days 6,750 against Sussex in 1987.

Performances at Lytham have included one achievement from a number 10 batsman: in 1985 against Northamptonshire David Makinson hit seven sixes off Richard Williams in his innings of 58 not out. Lytham has also seen some fine bowling performances from Mike Watkinson, Dermot Reeve (then of Sussex, now of Warwickshire) and Jack Simmons. No batsman has achieved a century on the ground, the highest score being 99 by John Abrahams in 1986.

ADDRESS Lytham C C, Lytham Cricket & Sports Club, Church Road, Lytham, Lancashire
TELEPHONE PROSPECTS OF PLAY 0253 734137

DESCRIPTION OF GROUND AND FACILITIES

The main entrance for spectators and vehicles is from Church Road. There are additional pedestrian entrances off Church Road and, for members and sponsors car parking, from Upper Westby Street. Car parking is also available in nearby streets and in a council car park only 250 yards from the main entrance. All the permanent buildings are to the west of the pitch and include a clubhouse/pavilion for members where there is a bar/refreshment area, the building used by players, and a scoreboard/groundsman store under the trees near to the tennis courts. Members' dining marquees and seats are situated on this side of the ground. Hospitality marquees are located at the railway End and to the east, general temporary public seating, a temporary scoreboard and car parking are to be found. At the South Church Road End, there are permanent open raised timber seating areas together with refreshment tents. A press tent is sited near the clubhouse/pavilion and the scorers sit in the main score-board. The playing area is 136 metres by 131 metres and is defined by a rope and some advertising boards. A Lancashire souvenir shop is also sited in a tent at the Church Road End. Permanent and temporary toilets are located around the ground. The ground capacity is 6,000 and 2,500 seats are provided so spectators are advised to bring their own seats to matches. A radio point is in the clubhouse/pavilion.

GROUND RECORDS AND SCORES

FIRST-CLASS MATCHES

Highest innings total for County 225 *v.* Northamptonshire, 1985
Highest innings total against County 272 by Nottinghamshire, 1988
Lowest innings total for County 121 *v.* Nottinghamshire, 1988
Lowest innings total against County 96 by Sussex, 1987
Highest individual innings for County 99 J. Abrahams *v.* Glamorgan, 1986
Highest individual innings against County 64 D.A. Reeve for Sussex, 1987
Best bowling performance in an innings for County 7 for 25 M. Watkinson *v.* Sussex, 1987
Best bowling performance in an innings against County 7 for 37 D.A. Reeve for Sussex, 1987
Best bowling performance in a match for County 10 for 145 J. Simmons *v.* Glamorgan, 1986
Best bowling performance in a match against County 7 for 74 R.C. Ontong for Glamorgan, 1986

HOW TO GET THERE

Rail Lytham, ½ mile
Bus From surrounding areas to town centre, thence ½ mile. 11A to Lytham, 167 St Anne's to Preston and 193 St Anne's to Kirkham also pass ground
Car From north: M6 junction 32, then follow M55 to junction 3, then A585 to Kirkham and B5259 signposted Lytham, ground is situated in Church Road ¼ mile west of Lytham town centre and the seafront. From east: A583 and A584 to Lytham, or as north.

WHERE TO STAY AND OTHER INFORMATION

Clifton Arms Hotel (0253 739898), Fernlea Hotel (0253 726726), St Ives Hotel (0253 720011)

Disabled Areas No special area, request position
Local Radio Station(s) BBC Radio Lancashire (104.5 MHz FM), Red Rose Radio (97.3 MHz FM/999 KHz MW)
Local Newspaper(s) Lancashire Evening Telegraph, Lancashire Evening Post, Lancashire Evening Gazette, Lytham St Anne's Express

Southport

The Trafalgar Road cricket ground is the home of the Southport and Birkdale C C, which was founded in 1859. The ground was purchased in 1884, with agreement from the Weld-Blundell family and the Birkdale Park Land Company, when the Birkdale Cricket Ground Company was established. Originally the ground was largely an area of waste and sandhills to the south of the Southport to Liverpool railway line but in 1850 much development took place in the area thanks to a Mr J. Aughton an enterprising builder from Preston. In 1881 the present pavilion was erected for about £300 and this stood until 1965 when it was rebuilt as the facilities were no longer satisfactory, nor adequate for the annual county visit. Birkdale C C was founded in 1874 and the club merged with the Southport C C in 1901.

The new pavilion built in 1965 cost £28,000 and was opened by Lord Derby in that year. The fixture with Derbyshire was staged in the same year and Lancashire disposed of the visitors in two days, which perhaps was just as well as it rained heavily on the third day. The Ladies Pavilion was erected in 1958 along with a bowling green. The ground was used in 1957 by the Minor Counties and has been used for schoolgirl hockey, and by Southport Hockey Club, the County Police and the Australian Ladies Cricket Team.

The first Lancashire visit was in 1959 when Worcestershire were the visitors for a championship match, although there was a previous visit for a Brian Statham benefit match. Since then championship cricket has been played each summer, usually in June, and in 1969 the first limited-overs match was staged with Glamorgan in the John Player Sunday League. Other limited-overs matches have followed, the most recent a Benson and Hedges Cup match with Scotland. The initial limited-overs match was televised and some 10,500 people attended: this is still a record for a match on the ground. Crowds usually are, 4,500–5,000 daily for championship matches.

Southport and Birkdale C C play in the Liverpool and District Cricket Competition and in recent years has spent considerable money on a new scoreboard and tiered terracing, which accommodates 2,000. The ground is entered from Trafalgar Road and the pavilion is close to the entrance. The railway embankment runs along the far side of the ground. The Birkdale area is known more for golf than cricket, for Royal Birkdale Golf Club is only a short distance from the ground.

Performances at Southport have included 142 by Ken Grieves for Lancashire in the first county match and 254 a career best from Warwickshire wicketkeeper Geoff Humpage during a 470 run fourth-wicket stand shared with Alvin Kallicharran who hit 234 not out. Other notable performances have included one by Graeme Fowler, who scored 126 and 128 not out in 1982 when batting in both his innings with a runner. Bowling performances have included wickets from Ian Folley, Ken Palmer (now a first-class umpire) Jack Simmons

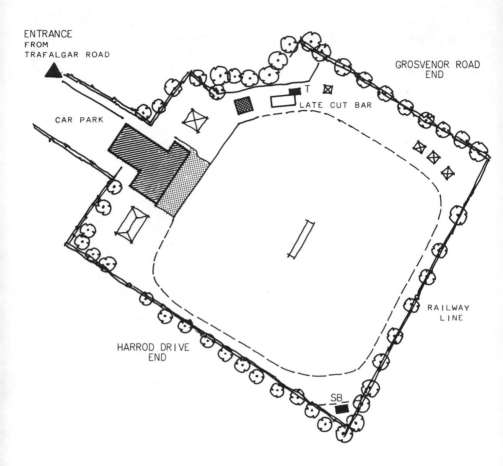

ENTRANCE
FROM
TRAFALGAR ROAD

GROSVENOR ROAD
END

T

LATE CUT BAR

CAR PARK

RAILWAY
LINE

HARROD DRIVE
END

SB

N

0   50   100

Metres

and Eddie Hemmings. In the limited-overs game only one century has been scored – by David Lloyd against Essex.

ADDRESS   Southport & Birkdale C C, Trafalgar Road, Birkdale, Southport, Merseyside PR8 2HF
TELEPHONE PROSPECTS OF PLAY   0704 69951

DESCRIPTION OF GROUND AND FACILITIES

The only entrance to the ground is from Trafalgar Road, to the north-west, as the ground is enclosed and surrounded by housing and, on the east side, by the railway line. The only permanent buildings on the ground are the pavilion, ladies' pavilion, 'Late Cut' bar and a scoreboard, together with several out-buildings used as a grounds-man's store and toilets. These are all located on the north-west side of the playing area, except for the scoreboard which is sited in the south-east corner, near the railway line. With the exception of the raised, permanent terrace seating in front of the scoreboard, all the seating is temporary and consists of plastic seats or benches. The members' enclosure is on the Trafalgar Road side and has a dining tent, refreshments, toilets, L C C souvenir tent and secretary's office in addition to the permanent buildings. At the Grosvenor Road End is the press tent, first aid tent, mobile tea cabin and some limited car parking for members. Public seating is available throughout the rest of the ground and is all uncovered. All seating is at ground level except the terrace area which is about 8 feet above the playing area. The ground is well tree-lined and rather confined compared with other Lancashire home venues. Car parking for players/officials and members is available in the main entrance car park, off Trafalgar Road and space is also available in Harrod Drive to the south of the ground and in the public car park on the Birkdale Royal Golf Course, off the main A565 trunk road some 10 minutes walk from the ground. The radio point and T V camera position are at the Harrod Road End. The playing area is 121 metres by 126 metres and is defined by a rope and some advertisement boards. The capacity is 6,000 and seating is providing for 75 per cent. Spectators need only take seats to popular matches.

GROUND RECORDS AND SCORES

FIRST-CLASS MATCHES
Highest innings total for County   422 for 9 v. Worcestershire, 1959
Highest innings total against County   523 for 4 dec. by Warwickshire, 1982
Lowest innings total for County   70 v. Northamptonshire, 1984
Lowest innings total against County   70 by Essex, 1978
Highest individual innings for County   142 K.J. Grieves v. Worcestershire, 1959

Highest individual innings against County 254 G.W. Humpage for
Warwickshire, 1982
Best bowling performance in an innings for County 7 for 15
I. Folley *v.* Warwickshire, 1987
Best bowling performance in an innings against County 7 for 56
K.E. Palmer for Somerset, 1966
Best bowling performance in a match for County 12 for 133
J. Simmons *v.* Gloucestershire, 1983
Best bowling performance in a match against County 10 for 175
E.E. Hemmings for Nottinghamshire, 1986

LIMITED-OVERS MATCHES
Highest innings total for County 195 for 2 *v.* Essex (JPL), 1974
Highest innings total against County 218 for 6 by Warwickshire
(BHC), 1979
Lowest innings total for County 162 for 9 *v.* Derbyshire (BHC),
1976
Lowest innings total against County 110 by Derbyshire (BHC),
1976
Highest individual innings for County 101 D. Lloyd *v.* Essex (JPL),
1974
Highest individual innings against County 71 I.L. Phillip for
Scotland (BHC), 1987
Best bowling performance for County 5 for 12 B. Wood *v.*
Derbyshire (BHC), 1976
Best bowling performance against County 5 for 30 M. Hendrick
for Derbyshire (BHC), 1976

HOW TO GET THERE

Rail Birkdale, ½ mile; Hillside, ½ mile
Bus Merseybus 16, 105, 284 from Southport Monument to within
¼ mile of ground (Tel: 051-236 7676); also 10 and 17
Car From north: A565 follow signs Southport, Then Birkdale and
Royal Birkdale Golf Club for Trafalgar Road ground, the ground is 1
mile south of Southport town centre and seafront. From east: M6
junction 26, then M58 and A570 to Southport, then as north. From
south: A565 to Birkdale or as from east, then as from north.

WHERE TO STAY AND OTHER INFORMATION

Prince of Wales Hotel (0704 36688), Royal Clifton Hotel (0704
33771)

Disabled Areas No special area, request position
Local Radio Station(s) BBC Radio Merseyside (95.8 MHz FM/1485
KHz MW), Red Rose Radio (97.3 MHz FM/999 KHz MW), BBC
Radio Lancashire 104.5 MHz FM)
Local Newspaper(s) Daily Post, Liverpool Echo, Southport Visitor

Blackpool

Cricket has been played in Blackpool since 1890 when there was a ground close to the Royal Palace Gardens. The present ground at Stanley Park, formerly Whitegate Park, was donated to the club in 1924 by Sir Lindsay Parkinson who required that the ground should be owned by Trustees comprising one member of the Blackpool Corporation, one member of the Blackpool C C and either himself or another member of his family. Another condition was that the club should erect a stand for spectators; the present pavilion was built in 1925 to satisfy this condition. The ground covers an area of around 5 acres and is enclosed within the park. In 1957 an additional stand was built costing £6,000 as well as a scoreboard and groundsman's store.

During late summer, Blackpool C C has staged festivals which comprised a county match, followed by a tourists' match and then club games. The club has staged four games with the Indians, South Africans and the West Indians. In 1961, when the Australians were unable to attend, a match was staged between the North and the South. The main festival was abandoned in 1961 but in 1988 after a lapse of ten years cricket returned with a Refuge Assurance Sunday League match with Middlesex. Blackpool C C was founded in 1888 and they play in the Northern Cricket League. In 1988 they celebrated their centenary. The initial first-class match was staged in 1905 when the North played the South. Lancashire first played on the present ground in 1904 against an England XI. In order to prolong the match the laws of cricket were not adhered to in the later stages of the game and the match was ruled not to be first-class. Lancashire today play one Sunday League match at Blackpool. Many benefit matches have been staged on the ground including one for Geoff Boycott and Ian Botham in 1984.

Blackpool C C is rather a long walk from the seafront and most holiday residential areas. As it is located within a large park there are ample facilities for other recreations including putting and tennis. The Blackpool club has a great tradition of having cricket professionals with Test Match status. These have included: E.A. McDonald, C.S. Dempster, H. Larwood, W.E. Alley, R.B. Kanhai, Hanif Mohammad, Cammie Smith, J. Parks (Sen.), P. Roy, Mushtaq Mohammad and M. Singh who was pro in 1988. Two Lancashire players have played for Blackpool: Bernard Reidy and Jack Simmons.

Many of the permanent buildings on the ground have been dedicated to officials. These include members' seating adjoining the pavilion 'dedicated to Winnie and Fred Dawson for their lifetime work for the club', the scorebox 'thanks to donations from Mr W.B. Corry' in 1954 and in 1979 in 'memory of past chairman Mr J. Holden – funds raised by the ladies committee'.

Ground attendances are usually 5,000–6,500 but the best was 13,782 for the championship match with Glamorgan in 1950 and 12,000 for the limited-overs John Player Sunday League match with Sussex in 1976.

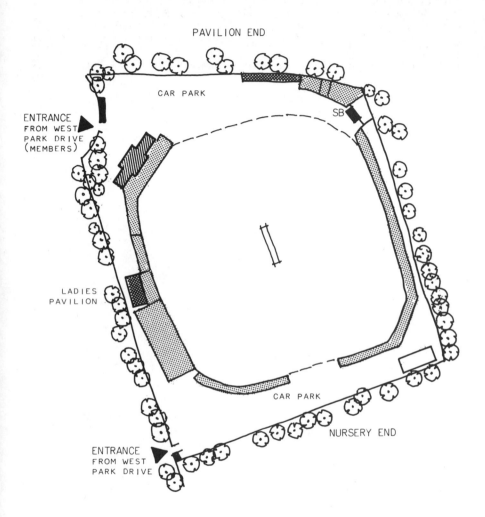

PAVILION END

CAR PARK

ENTRANCE
FROM WEST
PARK DRIVE
(MEMBERS)

SB

LADIES
PAVILION

CAR PARK

NURSERY END

ENTRANCE
FROM WEST
PARK DRIVE

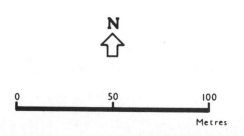

N

0   50   100

Metres

Ground performances have included double hundreds from Ken Grieves showing his liking for visits to the north-west coast, (he has the highest score at Southport as well) and from Peter Kirsten of Derbyshire. Bowling performances include those of R. Berry, T.B. Mitchell, C.H. Parkin and D.L. Underwood.

ADDRESS Blackpool C C, The Pavilion, Stanley Park, West Park Drive, Blackpool, Lancashire
TELEPHONE PROSPECTS OF PLAY 0253 33347/301950

DESCRIPTION OF GROUND AND FACILITIES

There are two entrances for members to Stanley Park from West Park Drive, through the main gates/turnstiles at the rear of the clubhouse/pavilion and a further entrance, for the public, to the south-west of the ground. The pavilion, which is used by members for refreshments as well as seating, is situated to the north-west of the ground. The west side of the ground is the members enclosure but the rest of the ground is for the public. The ladies' pavilion, and open seating on the terrace, provides a fine view of the playing area for members. South of the playing area there are deep concrete steps which are used for seating. At the top of the bank there is the facility for car parking and for people to view cricket from their vehicles. Further car parking is available in Stanley Park and in surrounding streets. An area for disabled vehicles is available at the northern end of the ground by prior arrangement. Ample seating is available for about 75 per cent of the ground capacity of 9,000. Spectators are advised only to bring seats to very popular matches. There are both permanent and temporary refreshments and toilets available around the ground for spectators' use. The main scoreboard is sited to the north-east of the playing area and to the north there is more car parking as well as the groundsman's store and some more seating which, although rather distant from the pitch, still provides a reasonable view. The ground is completely enclosed by a wall and trees on all four sides. The playing area is flat, and is defined by a rope and some advertisement boards. The playing area is 131 metres by 126 metres.

Some photographs of Blackpool C.C. history and past professionals can be found in the pavilion bar.

GROUND RECORDS AND SCORES

FIRST-CLASS MATCHES
Highest innings total for County 494 v. Essex, 1948
Highest innings total against County 478 for 7 dec. by Essex, 1948
Lowest innings total for County 62 v. Kent, 1966
Lowest innings total against County 39 by Hampshire, 1967
Highest individual innings for County 202 n.o. K.J. Grieves v. Indians, 1959
Highest individual innings against County 204 n.o. P.N. Kirsten for Derbyshire, 1981

Best bowling performance in an innings for County 10 for 102
R. Berry v. Worcestershire, 1953
Best bowling performance in an innings against County 8 for 38
T.B. Mitchell for Derbyshire, 1933
Best bowling performance in a match for County 15 for 95
C.H. Parkin v. Glamorgan, 1923
Best bowling performance in a match against County 10 for 68
D.L. Underwood for Kent, 1966

LIMITED-OVERS MATCHES
Highest innings total for County 207 v. Middlesex (RAL), 1988
Highest innings total against County 155 by Middlesex (RAL),
1988
Lowest innings total for County 155 for 1 v. Sussex (JPL), 1976
Lowest innings total against County 154 for 9 by Sussex (JPL),
1976
Highest individual innings for County 86 G.D. Mendis v.
Middlesex (RAL), 1988
Highest individual innings against County 50 J.E. Emburey for
Middlesex (RAL), 1988
Best bowling performance for County 4 for 17 M. Watkinson v.
Middlesex (RAL), 1988
Best bowling performance against County 3 for 43 S.P. Hughes for
Middlesex (RAL), 1988

HOW TO GET THERE

Rail Blackpool North, 1 mile
Bus Blackpool Transport 26 and 16 from Talbot Square (adjacent
BR Blackpool North), to within ¼ mile of ground (Tel: 0523 23931)
Car From north: M6 junction 32, then follow M55 to junction 4
Blackpool and Seafront, the ground is located off the (A583) in West
Park Drive adjoining Stanley Park which is ½ mile south east of
the town centre, or A584, A587, A586 or A587 to town centre.
From east: M6 junction 32, then follow M55 to junction 4
Blackpool and Seafront, then as north. From south: A584, A583 or
B5261 to Blackpool town centre, then as north.

WHERE TO STAY AND OTHER INFORMATION

Imperial Hotel (0253 23971), Savoy Hotel (0253 52561) and many
guest houses

Disabled Areas No special area, request position
Local Radio Station(s) Red Rose Radio (97.3 MHz FM/999 KHz
MW), BBC Radio Lancashire (104.5 MHz FM)
Local Newspaper(s) Lancashire Evening Telegraph, Lancashire
Evening Post, West Lancs Evening Gazette, Blackpool Evening
Gazette

LEICESTERSHIRE

LEICESTER

HINCKLEY

Leicestershire

Cricket in Leicestershire can be traced back to 1744, and the present club to 1879, but the hunting shire did not make its presence felt until the best part of a century later with the arrival from Worcestershire of Charles Palmer.

When Palmer was appointed secretary-captain in 1950 Grace Road was still council property and, for the most part since first-class status was gained in 1895, it was a struggle to keep pace with the pack. The highest-ever position was 5th in 1905. The former schoolmaster's formidable task was to rebuild and change the image of the club, and in his third season Leicestershire were 6th, and 3rd in the next but, if patchy results followed, a foundation was laid.

Palmer's own batting qualities – he twice went on MCC's tours – set more ambitious standards and he was more than a useful bowler. When Surrey were at their peak he took 8 for 7 against them when his intention was to bowl an over to change his bowlers round. All 8 wickets were taken without conceding a run, and the crowd urged him to take himself over to ensure breaking Jim Laker's record of 8 for 2. By fate Laker was next in, and he managed a boundary!

After seven years Palmer passed the captaincy to Yorkshire's Willie Watson, who found a new lease of life, but it was another distinguished import, Tony Lock, then also captaining Western Australia, who fired Leicestershire to 8th and then on to equal 2nd with Kent.

An aura of confidence engulfed Grace Road, which now belonged to the club. Mike Turner, a former player, who had been secretary since 1960 was appointed secretary-manager in 1969, and of his mountain of achievements the Everest must have been the signing of Ray Illingworth, who left Yorkshire after years of sterling service.

In the next decade the Turner–Illingworth partnership, a fusion of enterprise and tactical skill, worked like a charm. The county's first-ever title, the Benson and Hedges Cup, was won in 1972, and the Sunday League taken in 1974 and 1977. Twice more the Benson and Hedges Cup went to Grace Road, the 3rd time in 1985 under David Gower, but the biggest fish of all was the championship in 1975. It was the culmination of 96 years of endeavour. A double was the cause of double celebration, and Illingworth rightly said it was a magnificent team effort. In the last decisive match at Chesterfield Balderstone, another acquisition from Yorkshire, scored an unusual century. At the end of the second day he was 51 not out, and at stumps was rushed to Doncaster to play in a Football League match. The next morning he completed his century.

One of Illingworth's gifts was to get his side working for him. He had two gifted overseas men in Graham McKenzie, Australia's fast bowler, and Davison, from Bulawayo, one of the most punishing batsmen anywhere. Higgs, Steele and McVicker were untiring bowlers, but it would have been a supreme test for the captain who

MR.C.E.DE TRAFFORD,
LEICESTERSHIRE

brought the Ashes back from Australia to have made much of many of the older Leicestershire sides.

They did not lack fine individualists, but there weren't enough of them. C.E. ('Noisy') De Trafford, a noted hitter, led Leicestershire into first-class cricket and to a sensational victory over the champions, Surrey, in the first match. De Trafford was in charge for sixteen years both in second and first-class levels.

Bowling was the main strength in the early days with Woodcock, one of the fastest of his time, and Pougher, who topped the national averages. There was Knight, a devout lay preacher, who prayed before each innings, studied Greek and Latin and played for England, and C.J. Wood shared a record with W.G. Grace in carrying his bat seventeen times. At Bradford in 1907 he did it in both innings and put up such a stout defence that George Hirst said: 'Next time, Maister Wood, we'll bring a gun to get tha out!'

Ewart Astill was the first pro to be appointed the regular captain of any county in 1935, and the brilliant New Zealand batsman, C.S. Dempster, followed Astill. Alec Skelding, that irrepressible character, was distinctly sharp and became an umpire with remarks that have become part of the game.

Les Berry and Hallam were dependable and free-scoring openers, and the Australians, Jackson and Walsh, did much to put Leicestershire on the road to success. But George Geary and David Gower evoked the warmest local pride. Geary was fast-medium pace with an easy rhythm, Leicestershire's mainstay. In 14 Tests he took 46 wickets and played a notable role in Australia and South Africa – on the mat he was compared to Sydney Barnes. At home he had 100 wickets in 11 seasons, and a useful batsman he notched 8 hundreds.

For natural talent Gower was one of the brightest discoveries of post-war cricket, and was an immediate success on every rung of the ladder to the top. But perhaps, like Cowdrey, he set himself too high a standard too soon and he gave the impression of being too relaxed and laid back. His sense of timing and stroke range makes batting look easy, but he surrendered both the Leicestershire and England captaincy, though in 1988 he regained the former.

Willey, from Northamptonshire succeeded him as captain in the late 1986 season, and was yet another player to find pastures new to his liking. Tolchard, also a nimble-footed batsman, was one of the county's best wicket-keepers. [A.B.]

Founded 1879
Colours Dark green and scarlet
Crest Gold running fox on green ground
Chief Executive F.M. Turner MA
Coach K. Higgs
Groundsman L. Spencer
Scorer G.R. Blackburn
Address County Ground, Grace Road, Leicester LE2 8AD
Telephone 0533 831880
Cricketcall 0898 121442

Achievements:

County Championship Champions (1) 1975
Gillette Cup Semi-finalists 1977
National Westminster Bank Trophy Semi-finalists 1987
Benson & Hedges Cup Winners 1972, 1975 and 1985; finalists 1974
John Player Sunday League Champions (2) 1974 and 1977

COUNTY CRICKETERS.

MR. W. W. ODELL,
LEICESTERSHIRE.

M. R. HALLAM

LEICESTERSHIRE

Refuge Assurance Sunday League   Champions (0) 12th 1987
Fenner Trophy   Winners 1979
Tilcon Trophy   Winners 1984 and 1986
Lambert & Butler Cup   (TCCB 7-a-side Floodlit Competition):
Finalists 1981

Grounds:

Leicester (County Ground, Grace Road)   Hinckley (Sports Ground,
Leicester Road).

Other grounds that have been used since 1969 are: Coalville
(Snibston Colliery Ground, Owen Street), Loughborough (Park Road,
Loughborough) and Hinckley (Coventry Road).

Leicester

Cricket in Leicester is said to have begun in about 1780 at Saint
Margaret's Pasture, between the River Soar and the canal, but it was
in 1877 that the Leicestershire Cricket Ground Company purchased
some 16 acres of land bordered by Grace, Milligan and Hawkesbury
Roads. It is from Grace Road that the ground takes its name, not the
famous cricketer W.G. Grace.

The greater part of this area was laid out and prepared for cricket
and the first match took place in April 1878. The first first-class
match was with Yorkshire in 1894 and the first county match in 1895.
The county club used the ground from 1879 but after five years of
county championship cricket it was thought in 1900 that a more
accessible ground was needed closer to the city. The county club
moved to Aylestone Road and in the same year the company sold
most of its land.

County cricket continued at Aylestone Road ground until 1939, but
during the World War Two the ground was damaged and partly used
for industrial developments. Improvements in public transport suggested a return to Grace Road and once again the County moved to
the ground they had left forty-six years earlier. At this time the ground
was owned by the local education authority and was the sports ground
of the City of Leicester School. The County brought with them from
Aylestone Road the pavilion known as the Meet and a heavy roller.
In 1966 the ground was finally purchased and later years have seen
considerable development with the erection of a new pavilion,
dressing rooms and the facilities in winter of an indoor cricket school.
Situated about two miles from the city centre the ground remains
rather inaccessible being closely surrounded by residential property.
It is perhaps one of the best equipped grounds on the county circuit
other than the Test Match grounds.

Crowds at Grace Road in recent years have reached 12,000, which is the ground capacity. The record attendance was 16,000 in 1948 when the Australians were the visitors.

A Prudential Cup match was staged in 1983 between India and Zimbabwe. Outstanding performances have included double hundreds by Maurice Hallam and Keith Miller while in limited-overs matches Ken Higgs, the present county coach, holds the record for the best bowling performance.

ADDRESS   County Cricket Ground, Grace Road, Leicester LE2 8AD
TELEPHONE PROSPECTS OF PLAY   0533 836236

DESCRIPTION OF GROUND AND FACILITIES

Access to the ground is via the Milligan and Curzon Road entrances, the latter being used by all entering the car park (where there is space for some 500 cars). Members enter by a narrow roadway leading from Park Hill Drive. Once inside, one quickly perceives the general spaciousness of the ground, which is partly due to the fact that it is surrounded only by two-storey houses. Generally the northern part of the ground, including the pavilion, the Fernie and Quorn suites and the tiered seating above, are reserved for members and visiting members as is the Geary Stand on the east side. In the north-west corner is the Meet which, while looking rather like a barn with its barrel-vaulted roof, is now much changed since it was brought from Aylestone Road in 1946. It now provides refreshment facilities on the first floor for members and on the ground floor for the public. A good view of play can be obtained from the first floor of the Meet while taking refreshments.

A white boundary fence runs all round the perimeter of the playing area which measures some 151 metres by 133 metres. The pitch is disposed in a north–south direction providing a view from behind the wicket from the first floor of the pavilion. The Fox Bar in the pavilion displays a collection of many photographs as well as caps and ties. More photographs can be found in the first floor of the Meet.

The main scoreboard is on the east side of the ground. In 1987 a memorial clock tower surmounted by a running fox weathervane was added to the building, as a result of a bequest in the will of Cecily Williams, widow of the late Bishop of Leicester.

The rest of the ground has tiered seating and the south-east corner is also covered. Adequate toilets are available in the Meet, within the pavilion and in a separate building in the car park area. Areas are set aside for handicapped persons in the members' enclosure and at the southern end of the ground. It is possible to view the cricket from a limited number of cars in the car park area if you get to the ground early, but the reflection of the sun off the windscreens can cause problems to players in the afternoon. There is an excellent view from all parts of the ground. The main T V camera position is on the pavilion roof at the northern end of the ground.

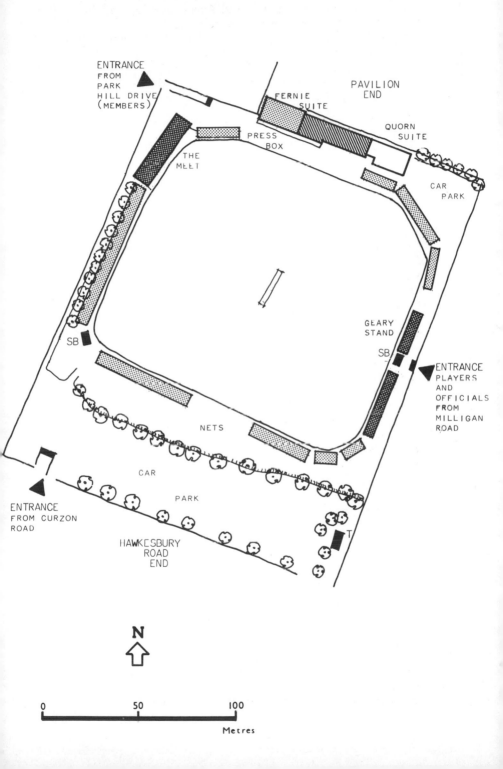

GROUND RECORDS AND SCORES

FIRST-CLASS MATCHES

Highest innings total for County 608 for 8 dec. *v.* Sussex, 1900
Highest innings total against County 694 for 6 for Australians,
1956
Lowest innings total for County 28 *v.* Australians, 1899
Lowest innings total against County 24 for Glamorgan, 1971
Highest individual innings for County 210 M.R. Hallam *v.*
Glamorgan, 1959
Highest individual innings against County 281 n.o. K.R. Miller for
Australians, 1956
Best bowling performance in an innings for County 9 for 29
J. Cotton *v.* Indians, 1967
Best bowling performance in an innings against County 9 for 68
G.G. Walker for Derbyshire, 1895
Best bowling performance in a match for County 15 for 136
A. Woodcock *v.* Nottinghamshire, 1894
Best bowling performance in a match against County 15 for 108
J.B. Statham for Lancashire, 1964

LIMITED-OVERS MATCHES

Highest innings total for County 326 for 6 *v.* Worcestershire (GC),
1979
Highest innings total against County 314 for 4 for Gloucestershire
(GC), 1975
Lowest innings total for County 36 *v.* Sussex (JPL), 1973
Lowest innings total against County 62 for Northamptonshire
(GC), 1974
Highest individual innings for County 156 D.I. Gower *v.*
Derbyshire (NWBT), 1984
Highest individual innings against County 158 Zaheer Abbas for
Gloucestershire (NWBT), 1983
Best bowling performance for County 6 for 17 K. Higgs *v.*
Glamorgan (JPL), 1973
Best bowling performance against County 6 for 22 M.K. Bore for
Nottinghamshire (BHC), 1980

HOW TO GET THERE

Rail Leicester Midland, 2 miles; South Wigston, 2¼ miles
Bus Midland Fox 68, 73 from Belvoir Street (¼ mile from BR
Leicester Station) (Tel: 0533 511411). Leicester Corporation Bus 23
from city centre
Car From north: M1 junction 22 or A46, A607 into Leicester city
centre, follow signs to Rugby into Almond Road, then into
Aylestone Road and follow signs County Cricket to Park Hill Drive
for County Ground. From east: A47 into Leicester city centre, then
as north. From west: M69 to junction with M1 or A50 to city
centre then as north or south. From south: M1 junction 21 or M69

then A46 signposted Leicester, A426 then Park Hill Drive for County Ground signposted County Cricket. The ground is located 1½ miles south of the city centre south of the B582 which links the A426 and A50.

WHERE TO STAY AND OTHER INFORMATION

Grand Hotel (0533 555599), Post House (0533 896688), Holiday Inn (0533 531161)

Disabled Areas   No special area, request position. A limited amount of space is set aside for disabled cars at the southern end of the ground
Local Radio Station(s)   BBC Radio Leicester (95.1 MHz FM/837 KHz MW), Leicester Sound (103.2 MHz FM/1260 KHz MW)
Local Newspaper(s)   Leicester Mercury, Leicester Mail, Leicester Trader

Hinckley

Hinckley Town C C was formed in 1841 and the home ground has been a venue for county cricket since 1911. The present ground on the north side of Leicester Road is the third ground in the town to have been used for first-class cricket (Ashby Road 1911–37, Coventry Road 1951–64).

The present ground was formed from an area of farmland and adjoins the town rugby club with which it shares the clubhouse and car parking facilities. It was opened in 1968. It was not until 1981 that Leicestershire returned to Hinckley for a championship match against Nottinghamshire. The County team now travel the 10 miles from Grace Road, Leicester once a season for a single championship match at Hinckley. The ground is regularly used for Leicestershire Second XI fixtures. Only one limited-overs Sunday League match has been played, against Essex in 1984.

Crowds at Hinckley have been in the region of 2,000 to 2,500 but for the return of the County in 1981, some 3,000 attended. Outstanding performances at the ground have included fine bowling by George Ferris and hundreds from Brian Davison and Graham Gooch.

The ground is about 2 miles from the centre of Hinckley on Leicester Road.

ADDRESS   Hinckley Town C C, The Tavern, Leicester Road, Hinckley, Leicestershire
TELEPHONE PROSPECTS OF PLAY   0455 615336

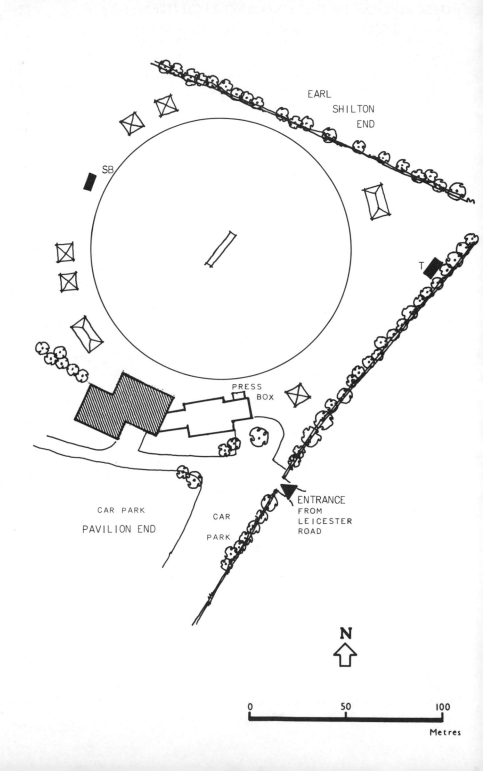

EARL SHILTON END

SB

T

PRESS BOX

CAR PARK
PAVILION END

CAR PARK

ENTRANCE
FROM
LEICESTER
ROAD

N

0   50   100

Metres

DESCRIPTION OF GROUND AND FACILITIES

Approached through a single entrance on Leicester Road, the cricket ground is to the right and the rugby ground to the left. Between these areas are the two main permanent buildings on the site, the clubhouse and the Tavern Bar. Car parking is available adjoining the entrance and on the rugby field, providing in all some 500 car spaces. The area available for members is around the clubhouse and the Tavern Bar (which also houses the press box). It extends westwards around the ground to the excellent new scoreboard that has been erected on the north-west side in recent years.

The playing area is circular, approximately 136 metres in diameter, and is defined by a low wooden fence. The pitch is situated in a north-east to south-west position.

Additional facilities provided for Leicestershire C C C matches include refreshment tents and tents for sponsors, as well as adequate temporary toilets. The ground capacity is set at 3,000 and members of the public are advised to bring their own seats as only 800 seats are set aside by the club for three-day matches and 1,600 seats for Sunday matches. Space is available for handicapped persons and a suitable position should be requested.

GROUND RECORDS AND SCORES

FIRST-CLASS MATCHES

Highest innings total for County 431 for 8 dec v. Nottinghamshire, 1981
Highest innings total against County 354 for Nottinghamshire, 1981
Lowest innings total for County 223 v. Somerset, 1988
Lowest innings total against County 109 for Glamorgan, 1983
Highest individual innings for County 123 B.F. Davison v. Nottinghamshire, 1981
Highest individual innings against County 113 G.A. Gooch for Essex, 1984
Best bowling performance in an innings for County 7 for 42 G.J.F. Ferris v. Glamorgan, 1983
Best bowling performance in an innings against County 6 for 64 R.C. Ontong for Glamorgan, 1983
Best bowling performance in a match for County 10 for 104 G.J.F. Ferris v. Glamorgan, 1983
Best bowling performance in a match against County 6 for 95 R.J. Doughty for Surrey, 1986

LIMITED-OVER MATCHES

Highest innings total for County 118 v. Essex (JPL), 1984
Highest innings total against County 148 for 7 by Essex (JPL), 1984
Highest individual innings for County 51 P. Willey v. Essex (JPL), 1984

Best bowling performance for County   2 for 25 P. Willey *v.* Essex (JPL), 1984
Highest individual innings against County   51 G.A. Gooch for Essex (JPL), 1984
Best bowling performance against County   2 for 5 J.K. Lever for Essex (JPL), 1984

HOW TO GET THERE

Rail   Hinckley, 2½ miles
Bus   Midland Fox Cub from The Borough (600m from BR Hinckley Station) (Tel: 0533 511411)
Car   From north: M1 junction 21, then M69 to junction 2, then A5070 signposted Hinckley, ground is situated off (A47) Leicester Road between Hinckley and Earl Shilton, or A447 and A47 signposted Hinckley then as above. FRom east: B4069 to M69 junction 2, then as north. From west: A47 or A5 signposted Hinckley then as north. From south: M1 junction 18, then A5 signposted Hinckley, then as north, or M6 junction 2, then M69 junction 2 then as north.

WHERE TO STAY AND OTHER INFORMATION

Sketchley Grange Hotel (0455 634251), or stay in Leicester

Disabled Areas   No special area, request position
Local Radio Station(s)   BBC Radio Leicester (95.1 MHz FM/837 KHz MW), Leicester Sound (103.2 MHz FM/1260 KHz MW)
Local Newspaper(s)   Leicester Mercury, The Hinckley Times

MIDDLESEX

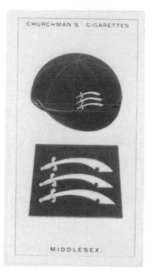

MIDDLESEX.

LONDON – LORD'S

UXBRIDGE

Middlesex

A provisional committee circulated a letter to newspapers in 1863 which began with a challenge: 'Middlesex being the only cricketing county in England that has no county club . . .' Its birth, a year later, coincided with the acceptance of over-arm bowling, and the first edition of John Wisden's *Cricketers' Almanack.*

The Walker brothers of Southgate, all seven of them, were prime movers in the launch and long continued to be influential on and off the field. When the championship was won in 1920, Sir Plum Warner's last season, the president was R.D. Walker, who had been a member of the 1866 champions.

Three different grounds at Islington, West Brompton and Kensington were used before Middlesex accepted an invitation by MCC in 1876 to play at Lord's. Middlesex have been identified with Lord's ever since, and it has proved, a century later, to be no disadvantage to take part in knock-out finals on their home ground. In eight finals they have won either the Gillette or the NatWest Trophy in four out of five attempts, and the Benson and Hedges Cup twice with one defeat.

Middlesex's early reputation was identified with the dashing amateur batsman. The Fords, Studds and Lytteltons set a fashion of family links which continued with the Manns, Comptons and the Robins, father and son. The Hearne cousins from Bucks gave years of brilliant professional service. In one of his 12 Tests in 1899 at Leeds John Thomas performed the famous hat-trick dismissing Hill, Gregory and Noble, and John William ('Young Jack') bowled his googlies like an angel and formed with Elias ('Patsy') Hendren one of the most illustrious batting partnerships in county cricket. He scored 96 centuries, took 1,839 wickets, and played in 24 Tests.

Among the captains to score in the grand manner was A.E. Stoddart, who led England in two of his four tours of Australia. His approach was summed up in a single word when Aussie propaganda tried to persuade him Monty Noble's flight was a problem for England. 'Rats,' he snorted.

A wealth of talent was available up to 1914 including such names as Warner, Bosanquet, the inventor of the googly which he called the 'twisti-twosti,' A.J. Webbe, player, captain, honorary secretary and president over sixty-one years, Sir T.C. O'Brien, and the two Australian pros, Albert Trott and Frank Tarrant. Gregor MacGregor was regarded as the finest wicket-keeper of his, or maybe, any period.

Trott qualified after being omitted from his brother Harry's party to England in 1896, despite outstanding form against Stoddart's side in 1894–5. In his 2nd and 3rd seasons he had over 200 wickets and 1,000 runs, and in 1899 straight drove over the Lord's pavilion, a feat never accomplished before or since. In the end it did him no good as he often lost his wicket trying to repeat the shot.

His benefit in 1907 was ruined ending on the second day when he

WILLS'S CIGARETTES.

MIDDLESEX C.C.C.

F. A. TARRANT (MIDDLESEX).

took 4 wickets with successive deliveries, and polished off the Somerset innings with a second hat-trick. 'I bowled myself into the workhouse,' he lamented. Brilliant though he was, there was a feeling that he could have been even better and his skipper MacGregor told him: 'If you had a head instead of a turnip, Alberto, you'd be the best bowler in the world.'

Tarrant, slow to medium left arm, averaged 100 wickets and 1,200 runs over a decade, and his ally J.W. Hearne provided Warner with a fine attack and runs. They did not reappear together after the war when Warner enriched his long career for England and county with Middlesex's 2nd championship. Warner was carried off the field in the last exciting match with Surrey.

Warner's life was given to cricket and his beloved Lord's, and only Sir George Allen can match the length, fidelity and variation of his stewardship. Gentlemen v Players, a fixture long before Test matches were thought of, was the love of his sporting life, because it represented the fabric of first-class cricket in England. 'I pray and believe it will never die,' wrote Warner. Fate decreed that he should die (in 1963), the day before the decision was taken to do away with the distinction between amateur and professional, which meant a traditional match, started in 1806, was no longer played.

F.T. Mann succeeded Warner in 1921 and led the championship race from starter's pistol to tape, but despite being able to call on the high talents of amateurs Allen, Stevens, Robins, Peebles, Haig, Enthoven, Killick and Owen-Smith, Middlesex had to wait until the Compton–Edrich run orgy of 1947 to taste victory again. The inability of the leading amateurs to play regularly, plus their absence on Test call, possibly cost Middlesex the honours, as they were 3rd in 1935, and runners-up in the four years up to 1939, a position retained in the first season after the war.

Hendren, with 170 centuries and 57,611 runs, and a splendid record in fifty-one Tests, was not merely a superb batsman and entertainer, but a personality who left a trail of warmth wherever he performed. Middlesex were singularly blessed when Compton and Edrich took over the mantle of Hendren and Hearne.

Compton, also an Arsenal footballer, collector of a Cup winners medal and a war-time international, was the most glamorous sportsman of his day. He batted as if it was fun and not a grim technical exercise, and few bowlers succeeded in shackling his genius. Mere figures seem intruders within the radius of his unique skills which had no affinity with the coaching manuals. But for a football injury he would have improved on his record of 123 centuries. Seventeen of these were for England, and a record 18, with 3,816 runs, came in the fabulous summer of 1947 when the visiting South Africans also felt the whiplash of his remarkable form. 'Far from feeling tired I wished it could have gone on forever with the season never ending,' Compton confessed. He served a demanding captain in Robins who asked for quick runs so as to leave time to bowl out his opponents twice. The first four in the Middlesex order – the thoroughbred Robertson, Brown, Edrich and Compton – responded with consistent brilliance. Centuries peeled from their bats, and remarkably Compton and Edrich augmented the bowling which included the high-class spin of Sims and Young. Middlesex have rarely had a more eventful season.

One of Middlesex's finest spinners, Titmus, collected 2,830 wickets with his off spin, and was a leading all-rounder in fifty-three Tests. Fast bowlers Moss, Warr, Price, Cowans and Daniel made a considerable impact as did the spinners, Emburey and Edmonds. Parfitt was invariably in the runs for both club and country, and Murray, 1,527 victims, Leslie Compton and Downton stand high in wicket-keeping ratings.

Brearley, a man of scholarship and understanding, was a captain of rare talent. As a batsman he was perhaps half a class short of Test match requirements, but he made useful scores, caught superbly at slip and was worth his weight in gold as a leader.

Gatting travelled the same road without the benefit of Brearley's apprenticeship of captaincy at Cambridge. He, too, returned from Australia a winning captain and was firmly established as England's No 3, but his patience was over-taxed in Pakistan and he lost the captaincy. He was a victim of the pernicious practice of planting a microphone on the pitch and an altercation with an umpire was relayed to the world. Such are the pitfalls of modern international captaincy. [A.B.]

Founded 1864
Colours Blue
Crest Three seaxes
Secretary Lt. Col. P.F. Packham MBE

County coach D. Bennett
Assistant coach C.T. Radley
Groundsmen M.J. Hunt (Lord's); R. Ayling (Uxbridge)
Scorer H.P.H. Sharp
Address Lord's Cricket Ground, St John's Wood Road, London
NW8 8QN
Telephone 01-289 1300/1310
Cricketcall 0898 121414

Achievements:

County Championship Champions (9) 1866, 1903, 1920, 1921,
1947, 1976, 1980, 1982 and 1985; Joint Champions (2) 1949 and
1977
Gillette Cup Winners 1977 and 1980; finalists 1975
National Westminster Bank Trophy Winners 1984 and 1988
Benson & Hedges Cup Winners 1983 and 1986; finalists 1975
John Player Sunday League Champions (0) 2nd 1982
Refuge Assurance Sunday League Champions (0) 4th 1988
Refuge Assurance Cup Semi-finalists 1988

Lord's

For history and description of ground and facilities, see MCC section.

GROUND RECORDS AND SCORES

FIRST-CLASS MATCHES
Highest innings total for County   612 for 8 dec v.
Nottinghamshire, 1921
Highest innings total against County   665 by West Indies, 1939
Lowest innings total for County   20 v. MCC, 1864
Lowest innings total against County   35 by Somerset, 1899
Highest individual innings for County   277 n.o. E.H. Hendren v.
Kent, 1922
Highest individual innings against County   316 n.o. J.B. Hobbs for
Surrey, 1926
Best bowling performance in an innings for County   10 for 40
G.O.B. Allen v. Lancashire, 1929
Best bowling performance in an innings against County   9 for 38
R.C. Robertson-Glasgow for Somerset, 1924
Best bowling performance in a match for County   15 for 47
F.A. Tarrant v. Hampshire, 1913
Best bowling performance in a match against County   15 for 122
A.P. Freeman for Kent, 1933

LIMITED-OVERS MATCHES
Highest innings total for County   280 for 8 v. Sussex (GC), 1965
Highest innings total against County   272 for 4 by Gloucestershire
(JPL), 1983
Lowest innings total for County   97 v. Northamptonshire (BHC),
1976
Lowest innings total against County   80 by Surrey (JPL), 1980
Highest individual innings for County   158 G.D. Barlow v.
Lancashire (NWBT), 1984
Highest individual innings against County   140 n.o. S.R. Waugh for
Somerset (RAL), 1988
Best bowling performance for County   7 for 22 J.R. Thomson v.
Hampshire (BHC), 1981
Best bowling performance against County   6 for 33 V.A. Holder for
Worcestershire (JPL), 1972

Uxbridge

Uxbridge C C, founded in 1789, claims to be the oldest club in
Middlesex. Its ground at Park Road was only inaugurated in 1971, but
cricket in the Uxbridge district is said to date from about 1730 and

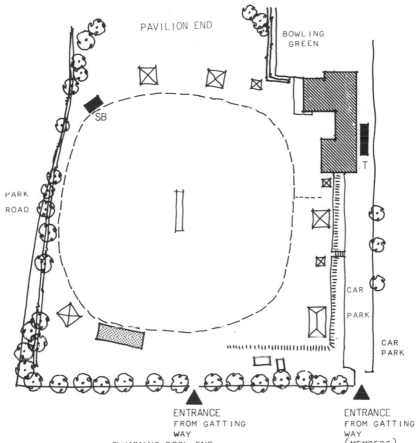

PAVILION END

BOWLING GREEN

SB

PARK ROAD

T

CAR PARK

CAR PARK

ENTRANCE FROM GATTING WAY

ENTRANCE FROM GATTING WAY (MEMBERS)

SWIMMING POOL END

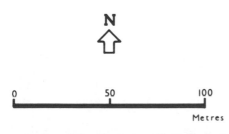

N

| 0 | 50 | 100 |

Metres

the previous grounds used were the Moor, Uxbridge Common (opposite the present ground) and from 1858 the site in Cricketfield Road. The latter was vacated after 112 years' use at the end of the 1970 season in order to make way for the building of the new Civic Centre in the town centre.

Middlesex played their first game at Uxbridge in August 1980 against Derbyshire. The venue was chosen primarily to free Lord's to allow preparations to be made for the Centenary Test Match against Australia and the Gillette Cup Final which Middlesex won beating Surrey. A single first-class match was played in 1981 and again in 1982 but since 1983 Middlesex have made this an annual visit of two championship games, providing Uxbridge with a mini festival week? There have been two limited-overs matches on the ground: the NatWest Bank Trophy against Cumberland in 1985 and against Nottinghamshire in 1987.

The ground is part of a large sports complex providing facilities for tennis and bowls as well as a swimming pool and a dry ski slope all with ample car parking adjoining. The pavilion has been extended since it was first built in 1971 to include squash courts. Approaching off Park Road through Gatting Way, the observant visitor will also notice Brearley Close in the neighbouring housing estate. Uxbridge C C fields four elevens and one midweek side during a season and plays in the Thames Valley Cricket League.

The ground capacity has been described as 3,000 but to date the largest crowd recorded was 5,750 for the NatWest Bank Trophy match against Notthinghamshire. Ground records have included 200 for Clive Radley (a career best) and 10 for 59 a best bowling performance in a match by Vincent van der Bijl, the tall South African from Natal. In recent years Nick Faulkner of Surrey (now of Sussex) scored his maiden first-class century on the ground and Colin Metson (now of Glamorgan) made 96, a career best, against Gloucestershire.

ADDRESS Uxbridge C C, Gatting Way, Park Road, Uxbridge, Middlesex
TELEPHONE PROSPECTS OF PLAY 0895 37571

DESCRIPTION OF GROUND AND FACILITIES

Although Park Road is one of the main access roads from Uxbridge town centre to the M40 motorway, the ground is screened from the road by high hedges and there is therefore no distraction to watching the cricket. The ground is approximately level and the playing area is near circular and 124 metres by 122 metres. The pitch is in a north–south disposition. Access to the ground is from Gatting Way and in the adjoining area at the end of the street there is parking for about 400 cars. A few cars are allowed into the ground and can be parked on the south side of the ground from which the cricket can be viewed.

The pavilion/clubhouse, a good modern building complex, is situated in the north-east corner of the ground furthest from the entrance, while the scoreboard is in the north-west corner – these are the only permanent buildings on the ground. Many additional temporary facilities are provided for the visits of Middlesex C C C and these are normally sited on the east side between the main entrance and the pavilion. Sponsors' tents are positioned on the north side on either side of the sightscreen. The members' enclosure is sited around the front of the pavilion/clubhouse and usually extends to the scoreboard position. Other provisions like press and radio positions are included in this area. Some temporary tiered seating is also provided for the public in the south-west corner and there is plenty of seating in all areas so it is usually unnecessary to bring your own seats.

No special facilities exist for disabled persons so it is advisable to ask for a suitable position.

GROUND RECORDS AND SCORES

FIRST-CLASS MATCHES

Highest innings total for County   567 for 8 v. Northamptonshire, 1985
Highest innings total against County   411 by Surrey, 1981
Lowest innings total for County   159 v. Surrey, 1986
Lowest innings total against County   121 by Hampshire, 1983
Highest individual innings for County   200 C.T. Radley v. Northamptonshire, 1985
Highest individual innings against County   148 J.C. Balderstone for Leicestershire, 1982
Best bowling performance in an innings for County   6 for 48 P.H. Edmonds v. Hampshire, 1982
Best bowling performance in an innings against County   6 for 32 N.G.B. Cook for Leicestershire, 1982
Best bowling performance in a match for County   10 for 59 V.A.P. van der Bijl v. Derbyshire, 1980
Best bowling performance in a match against County   7 for 115 M.D. Marshall for Hampshire, 1982

LIMITED-OVERS MATCHES

Highest innings total for County   283 for 9 v. Cumberland (NWBT), 1985
Highest innings total against County   279 by Nottinghamshire (NWBT), 1987
Lowest innings total for County   219 v. Nottinghamshire (NWBT), 1987
Lowest innings total against County   152 by Cumberland (NWBT), 1985
Highest individual innings for County   98 W.N. Slack v. Cumberland (NWBT), 1985
Highest individual innings against County   79 R.T. Robinson for Nottinghamshire (NWBT), 1987

Best bowling performance for County   4 for 28 P.H. Edmonds *v.*
Cumberland (NWBT), 1985
Best bowling performance against County   3 for 39 R.A. Pick for
Nottinghamshire (NWBT), 1987

HOW TO GET THERE

Rail   Uxbridge Underground (Metropolitan/Piccadilly line), ¾ mile
Bus   LRT 223 from Uxbridge & West Ruislip Underground Stations
(Tel: 01-222 1234); also LRT 128 and 129
Car   From north: M25 junction 16, then M40 to junction 1, then
follow A412 Uxbridge, ground is situated off (A412) Park Road in
Gatting Way 1 mile north of town centre. From east: A40 Western
Avenue from Central London to junction 1 of M40 (roundabout),
then A412 signposted Uxbridge for ground, as north. From west:
M40 junction 1 then follow signs Uxbridge A412 for ground as
north. From south: M25 junction 16, then as north or M4 junction
4, then A412 signposted Uxbridge.

WHERE TO STAY AND OTHER INFORMATION

The Guest House (01-574 3977). Master Brewer Hotel (0895 51199)
or central London/Heathrow Airport hotels

Disabled Areas   Space available – request suitable position
Local Radio Station(s)   Greater London Radio (94.9 MHz FM/1458
KHz MW), Capital Radio (95.8 MHz FM/1548 KHz MW), LBC (97.3
MHz FM/1152 KHz MW)
Local Newspaper   Evening Standard

NORTHAMPTONSHIRE

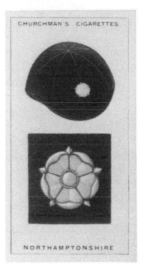

NORTHAMPTON

LUTON

WELLINGBOROUGH

FINEDON

TRING

Northamptonshire

Promotion to first-class status in 1905 was gained on the persuasive talents of George Thompson, the first from Northamptonshire to be selected by England and regarded as the finest local-born cricketer. As *Wisden* observed at the time: 'Thompson, to a greater extent than all the other members of the side put together, rendered the promotion possible.' *Wisden* might not have done justice to William East, another medium pace bowler and able batsman, but the combined excellence of Thompson, who scored 125 against the Gentlemen while still in the Minor Counties and East, was impressive.

On the whole the new ranking was justified up to 1914, despite the county's small population and moderate standard of club cricket. The unpleasant experience of being dismissed for a record low total of 12 at Gloucester Spa in 1907 ('come home to mother' telegraphed the secretary) was banished in 1912 when, with a settled pool of only twelve, Northamptonshire were runners-up to Yorkshire. Nine of the side, captained by G.A.T. Vials, played in every match, including the Denton twins, S.G. Smith, a white West Indian and the first of the line of overseas players.

Wounded in the war, Thompson was never again the same force, the pre-war side crumbled, and the cold facts of the club's frugal resources caused financial embarrassment and a sharp decline in playing strength. As late as the 'fifties a committee minute was recorded that the life span of the club was no more than two years unless the situation improved.

In the twenty-four years between 1919 and 1948 Northamptonshire were bottom ten times, bottom-but-one in six others, and four seasons passed between May 1935 and May 1939 without a single championship victory. When the ice was broken the crowd, such as it was, assembled in front of the pavilion in celebration.

The threadbare existence was punctuated by public appeals, and on more than one desperate occasion it was admitted there were simply not the means to support first-class cricket. Many and varied were the fund-raising schemes. Sir Thomas Beecham took his orchestra to the town free of charge with the proceeds of the concert divided between the club and the local YMCA, and the Northamptonshire Regiment, serving in India, had a 'voluntary' collection familiar to most servicemen.

Fortunately there were two fairy godfathers; Albert Cockerill, who presented the ground in trust to the club – previously they had played on the old Racecourse – and Stephen Schilizzi. In post-war years the Herculean efforts of secretary Kenneth Turner turned the accounts from red to black and created facilities only dreamed of through football competitions, discos and rock concerts. Without him Northamptonshire would assuredly have gone to the wall.

Founded in 1878, when Northamptonshire won the Gillette Cup in 1976, their first ever success, it was with a side largely built on the

NORTHAMPTONSHIRE C.C.C

T. L. LIVINGSTON

profits from rock and disco. 'If only the crowds queuing to get into the ground for the concerts had been to watch cricket I would have been a happy man' said Turner. The side also took 2nd place in the championship. Captained by Mushtaq Mohammad, and including his fellow Pakistani, Sarfraz Nawaz, and Bishen Bedi, the Indian captain and classic slow left arm bowler, this was by general consent Northamptonshire's strongest-ever team. Other captains, Brookes and Andrew, who also achieved runner-up positions, stand comparison, and Peter Watts added more distinction to a once-humble club with the Benson and Hedges Cup in 1980.

Northamptonshire had capable players in the dark days of the calibre of Vallance Jupp, wooed from Sussex as player-secretary, Timms, Bakewell, Brookes, Walden, Clark, and Claude Woolley, Frank's brother, but there was no in-depth strength. Clark and Capel followed Thompson as local-born Test players. Clark, fast left arm, had a firebrand reputation, and was one of the first cricketers to be used in a national advertising campaign. Shown in the eye-catching moment of delivering the ball, he was paid the princely sum of £100.

Clark had a lot to put up with. One morning after a second slip catch had been spilled he suddenly stopped on the way back to his bowling mark, looked at a skylark in full song overhead, and roared: 'What the — have you got to sing about?'

Both Bakewell and Milburn, two England batsmen, were tragically victims of car crashes at the peak of their careers. Bakewell, at 27, never played again while Milburn, one of the biggest crowd-pullers and most popular figures in the game, valiantly but briefly returned with only one eye.

Dennis Brookes, JP, a former chairman of the Northampton bench, scored 30,874 runs with 71 centuries, and served as batsman, captain, coach, assistant secretary and president with equal distinction. His ability deserved more than one cap and, typical of his tardy recognition, was to be told by the captain, Hammond, to get measured for his kit for the Australian tour of 1946–7 only to be passed over once again.

The escape from the post-war gloom dated from the inspired recruitment of F.R. Brown, who had virtually retired from first-class cricket. Never was there a better investment. Brown's direct and honest approach gave Northamptonshire new purpose and hope. England, too, had cause to be grateful for the resurrection of his career. What he did for his adopted county, he did for his country.

Tyson, and the immaculate wicket-keeper Andrew, seemingly unwanted by Lancashire, were the first of the county's pros to be selected for an Australian tour, and 'Typhoon' Tyson's part in Hutton's triumph is history. Yet but for Northampton Brown and Tyson, such successes in Australia, might have faded out of first-class cricket.

Overseas stars have included Lamb, Kapil Dev, Harper, Davis and Dennis Lillee, and from a wide choice Turner rates Mushtaq and the Australian googly left arm bowler Tribe as the two most gifted. Raman Subba Row was another successful captain from Surrey, and the Australian, Livingston, was a heavy scorer and an invaluable link with the northern Leagues when Turner's recruitment drive was in full swing.

As assistant secretary Turner shrewdly assessed the needs of county cricket, and, as secretary from 1958, he put his ideas into practice. A backroom staff of Brookes, Mercer and Davis scoured the country for talent, and the policies were so successful that by his retirement no fewer than nine first-time Test caps had been won – Milburn, Larter, Prideaux, Larkins, Geoff Cook, Lamb, Steele, Willey and Subba Row. Many were coached by Brookes and Bailey, capped in 1988, was also taken on by Turner. Reynolds was also a first-rate coach.

Inevitably there were set-backs. The centenary season began with the building of a new £100,000 pavilion and ended with an injury-ridden side at the bottom, Bedi and a groundsman took the club to Industrial Courts alleging wrongful dismissal but lost their claims, and three Lord's finals, including two in 1987, ended in defeats. Yet it could be said in truth there was a time when Northamptonshire would have been wild outsiders to win anything but sympathy from the more fortunate clubs. [A.B.]

Founded 1878
Colours Maroon
Crest Tudor rose
Secretary/Manager S.P. Coverdale MA, LLB,
Coach R.M. Carter
Groundsman R. Bailey
Scorer B.H. Clarke
Address County Cricket Ground, Wantage Road, Northampton NN1 4NJ

RAMAN SUBBA ROW

GEORGE TRIBE

PLAYER'S CIGARETTES

A. H. BAKEWELL (NORTHAMPTONSHIRE)

Telephone 0604 32917
Cricketcall   0898 121450

Achievements:

County Championship   Champions (0) 2nd 1912, 1957, 1965 and 1976
Gillette Cup   Winners 1976
National Westminster Bank Trophy   Finalists 1981 and 1987
Benson & Hedges Cup   Winners 1980; finalists 1987
John Player Sunday League   Champions (0) 4th 1974
Refuge Assurance Sunday League   Champions (0) 10th 1987
Fenner Trophy   Winners 1978
Tilcon Trophy   Winners 1982 and 1983; finalists 1981

Grounds:

Northampton (County Cricket Ground, Wantage Road)   Wellingborough (Wellingborough School, London Road)   Luton (Wardown Park, Old Bedford Road)   Tring (Pound Meadow, Station Road)   Finedon (Dolben Cricket Ground, Avenue Road).

   Other grounds that have been used since 1969 are: Peterborough (Baker Perkins Sports Ground), Kettering (Northampton Road), Brackley (off Buckingham Road), Bedford (Bedford School, Burnaby Road), Milton Keynes (Manor Fields, Bletchley) and Horton (Horton CC).

Northampton

The ground was formed from land in the Abingdon district on the east side of Northampton and laid out by the Northampton County Cricket and Recreation Grounds Co. Ltd in 1885 for £2,000 under the guidance of H.H. Stephenson, an old Surrey cricketer who captained the first ever England team to visit Australia. The county club moved to this venue in 1886 having previously played at the Northampton Racecourse before being forcibly ejected. The ground is shared with Northampton Town F C and association football has been played on the ground since 1897, which restricts cricket games at the beginning and end of the season. The Old Pavilion was originally shared with the football and bowling clubs but is now in the sole use of cricket club and members. In 1968 a new stand was built for members, which provides a press box as well as, on the ground floor, space for indoor nets in the winter. In 1979 a new pavilion was erected in place of the old Ladies Pavilion. It now houses facilities for both players and members as well as administration and was added to in 1987 and 1988.

The ground has struggled for recognition and praise over the years; although it is now owned by the cricket club's trustees, major redevelopment has yet to take place. Alfred Cockerill guaranteed the cricket club possession of the ground in perpetuity – something they could not have managed themselves – and in 1923 handed it over for a small rent for 1,000 years. The whole area of 8½ acres is used jointly with the football club although the overlap between pitches is little more than twenty metres or so. Crowds of 4,500 are usual and, popular one-day matches sometimes attract 7,500 spectators. The record crowd for a single day was 21,770 against the Australians in 1953 and 31,000 for the three days.

Ground records at the county ground include double centuries for Raman Subba Row and J.R. Freeman along with fine bowling spells from George Tribe, the Australian, for Northamptonshire and Colin Blythe for the visitors. The fastest century scored in first-class cricket until equalled recently by Steve O'Shaugnessey was scored at Northampton by Percy Fender of Surrey in 1920. On that occasion this remarkably free hitter not only scored his first century in first-class cricket, but it only took him 35 minutes. Another batting feat at the ground was in 1973 when Glenn Turner scored his 1000th run in May 1973, while with the touring New Zealanders, off the bowling of Bishen Bedi, the Indian Test spinner.

ADDRESS County Cricket Ground, Wantage Road, Northampton NN1 4NJ
TELEPHONE PROSPECTS OF PLAY 0604 37040

DESCRIPTION OF GROUND AND FACILITIES

The main access to the ground is from Wantage Road, off the Wellingborough Road, but there is also pedestrian access from

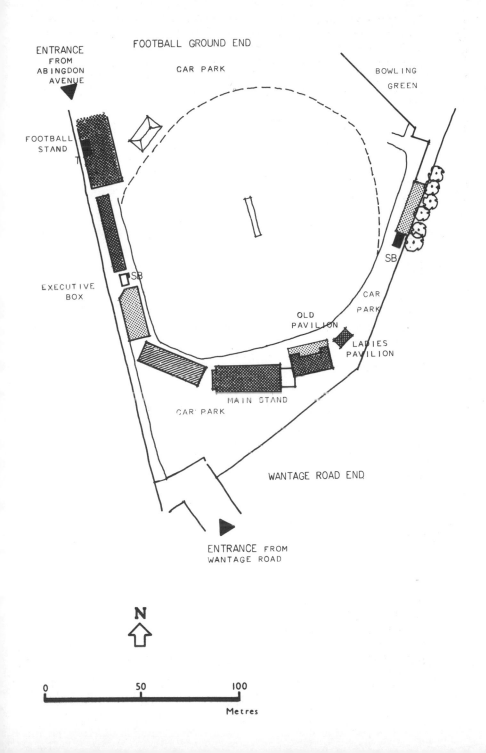

ENTRANCE
FROM
ABINGDON
AVENUE

FOOTBALL GROUND END

CAR PARK

BOWLING
GREEN

FOOTBALL
STAND

EXECUTIVE
BOX

SB

OLD
PAVILION

CAR
PARK

SB

LADIES
PAVILION

MAIN STAND

CAR PARK

WANTAGE ROAD END

ENTRANCE FROM
WANTAGE ROAD

N

0   50   100

Metres

Abington Avenue through the Northampton Town football club entrance. Car parking within the ground is limited but there is ample space in adjoining streets. The main permanent buildings are the old pavilion (a timber structure of which the upper part is now restricted to vice presidents of the club), the new stand (which provides public refreshment facilities and the club shop on the ground floor and on the first floor seating for members and provision for the press) and the new pavilion (which provides refreshment facilities for members). These three buildings comprise the section of the ground that is primarily used by members.

Seating is available on the east and west of the ground for the public and around 2,000 seats in all are provided. It is advisable to bring your own seats to popular matches. Disabled persons are advised to request a suitable position to view the cricket. Permanent toilets are available in the new stand (ground floor) and at the rear of the old pavilion and the west football stand.

The playing area is approximately 133 metres by 132 metres; the northern part extends across the football field, where a number of cars are allowed to park in a position to enable viewing the cricket. Cover during rain showers is limited to the ground floor of the new stand, which houses the indoor cricket school in winter and an area for refreshments during the summer. The club offices together with the players' changing room are to be found on the first floor of the new pavilion. The T V camera is normally sited on the first floor of the new stand adjoining the press box.

Watching cricket at the Wantage Road ground one feels that the future development of cricket will forever be overshadowed by the football stands and floodlight pylons.

GROUND RECORDS AND SCORES

FIRST-CLASS MATCHES

Highest innings total for County   532 for 6 dec. v. Essex, 1952
Highest innings total against County   631 for 4 dec. by Sussex, 1938
Lowest innings total for County   15 v. Yorkshire, 1908
Lowest innings total against County   33 by Lancashire, 1977
Highest individual innings for County   260 n.o. R. Subba-Row v. Lancashire, 1955
Highest individual innings against County   286 J.R. Freeman for Essex, 1921
Best bowling performance in an innings for County   9 for 43 G.E. Tribe v. Worcestershire, 1958
Best bowling performance in an innings against County   10 for 30 C. Blythe for Kent, 1907
Best bowling performance in a match for County   15 for 31 G.E. Tribe v. Yorkshire, 1958
Best bowling performance in a match against County   17 for 48 C. Blythe for Kent, 1907

Highest innings total for County   259 *v.* Middlesex (NWBT), 1986/ *v.* Warwickshire (JPL), 1979
Highest innings total against County   303 for 7 by Middlesex (BHC), 1977
Lowest innings total for County   41 *v.* Middlesex (JPL), 1972
Lowest innings total against County   69 by Hertfordshire (GC), 1976
Highest individual innings for County   134 R.J. Bailey *v.* Gloucestershire (BHC), 1987
Highest individual innings against County   129 G.D. Barlow for Middlesex (BHC), 1977
Best bowling performance for County   7 for 37 N.A. Mallender *v.* Worcestershire (NWBT), 1984
Best bowling performance against County   6 for 22 C.E.B. Rice for Nottinghamshire (BHC), 1981

HOW TO GET THERE

Rail   Northampton, 2 miles
Bus   Northampton Transport 1 from BR Station to within 200m of ground (Tel: 0604 51431); also numbers 6, 8 and 15 from town centre
Car   From north: M1 junction 16, then A45 follow signs Northampton and town centre, then follow A43 signposted Kettering, then follow signs County Cricket into Abingdon Avenue for County Ground. From east: A45, A4500 or A428 signposted Northampton then follow signs County Cricket for Abingdon Avenue and County Ground. From west: A45 or A43 to town centre then as north. From south: M1 junction 15, then follow signs A508, then A43 for Wellingborough Road and Wantage Road for County Ground, follow signs County Cricket.

WHERE TO STAY AND OTHER INFORMATION

Westone Moat Hotel (0604 406262), Northampton Moat House Hotel (0604 22441), Graid Hotel (0604 34416)

The only first-class ground in the country shared with a professional league football club
Disabled Areas   None specified. Plenty of freedom of movement throughout the ground
Local Radio Station(s)   BBC Radio Northampton (104.2 MHz FM/ 1107 KHz MW), Hereward Radio (96.6 MHz FM/1557 KHz MW), Chiltern Radio (96.9 MHz FM/792 KHz MW)
Local Newspaper(s)   Chronicle and Echo, Northampton Post, Sports Pink (Saturday), Mercury & Herald, Northamptonshire Image

Luton

Founded in 1906 the Luton Town C C is probably one of the strongest club sides in the county and fields three XI's throughout the season. The club plays in the Bryan-Grasshopper Hertfordshire Cricket League. The ground was first used by Northamptonshire in 1973 for a John Player Sunday League match with Nottinghamshire and each season thereafter for Sunday League matches. This was so successful that in 1986 first-class cricket was staged on the ground. The inaugural fixture was with Yorkshire, and now four days of the County's season is spent on this attractive club ground.

The ground was formed from an area in the north of Wardown Park and the town gardens; the club has played here since its establishment. The ground has been used by Bedfordshire C C C for Minor County fixtures including the Gillette Cup and National Westminster Bank Trophy first round matches. The Luton Nomads C C and Bedfordshire Eagles Hockey Club also use the club's fine facilities.

Crowds of 4,000–5,000 are usual on fine days. The record crowd was for a benefit match in 1961 for Tom Clark of Surrey when 6,000 people were present. Wardown Park was the place where Worcestershire's Tom Graveney attended one of his benefit matches on the rest day of the first England v. West Indies Test at Old Trafford, Manchester in 1969, and as a result lost his test match place.

Ground records at Wardown Park include a double century by Robert Bailey in the inaugural first-class match in 1986, and a sparkling knock in the Sunday League (a career best) by Wayne Larkins in 1983.

ADDRESS Luton Town C C, Wardown Park, Old Bedford Road, Luton, Bedfordshire
TELEPHONE PROSPECTS OF PLAY 0582 27855

DESCRIPTION OF GROUND AND FACILITIES

Entry to the ground is from Wardown Park and pedestrians can approach from either Old Bedford Road or New Bedford Road. All cars are required to enter Wardown Park from the New Bedford Road and park on the grass. The pavilion is a new extension of an existing building; the latter still houses the players changing rooms.

This is a very pleasant tree-enclosed ground which has been levelled so that a raised area exists to the east backed by trees and the Old Bedford Road. This provides a most advantageous position for the public to view the cricket. To the west of the ground is the scoreboard (now with digital numbering) and an area given over for sponsors' tents. The members' area is on either side of the pavilion and contains a small section of tiered seating. A good number of seats are provided so it is not always necessary to take your own. Public toilets adjoin the south end of the ground. The playing area is defined only by a

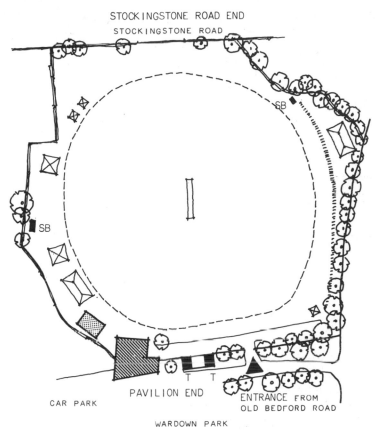

STOCKINGSTONE ROAD END

STOCKINGSTONE ROAD

SB

SB

PAVILION END

CAR PARK

ENTRANCE FROM
OLD BEDFORD ROAD

WARDOWN PARK
AND MUSEUM

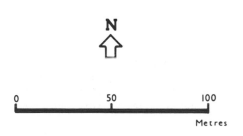

N

0   50   100

Metres

rope and boards and is approximately circular and 131 metres in diameter. Refreshment facilities and the N C C C shop are housed in tents. T V cameras are normally sited on the west and south sides of the ground. In the event of rain or bad light, an hour or so can be spent visiting Wardown House Museum which adjoins the ground; here one can learn the methods and history of hat-making in Luton.

GROUND RECORDS AND SCORES

FIRST-CLASS MATCHES

Highest innings total for County   385 for 4 dec. v. Yorkshire, 1986
Highest innings total against County   314 for 6 dec. by Yorks, 1986
Lowest innings total for County   193 for 7 dec. v. Yorkshire, 1986
Lowest innings total against County   174 by Warwickshire, 1987
Highest individual innings for County   200 n.o. R.J. Bailey v. Yorkshire, 1986
Highest individual innings against County   151 A.A. Metcalfe for Yorkshire, 1986
Best bowling performance in an innings for County   5 for 46 R.A. Harper v. Warwickshire, 1987
Best bowling performance in an innings against County   4 for 58 A.R.C. Fraser for Middlesex, 1988
Best bowling performance in a match for County   5 for 46 R.A. Harper v. Warwickshire, 1987
Best bowling performance in a match against County   4 for 76 A.R.C. Fraser for Middlesex, 1988

LIMITED-OVERS MATCHES

Highest innings total for County   298 for 2 v. Warwickshire (JPL), 1983
Highest innings total against County   264 for 8 by Warwickshire (JPL), 1983
Lowest innings total for County   113 v. Nottinghamshire (JPL), 1973
Lowest innings total against County   138 for 6 by Kent (JPL), 1980
Highest individual innings for County   172 n.o. W. Larkins v. Warwickshire (JPL), 1983
Highest individual innings against County   105 n.o. M.W. Gatting for Middlesex (RAL), 1988
Best bowling performance for County   5 for 30 R.G. Williams v. Warwickshire (JPL), 1983
Best bowling performance against County   4 for 20 K.D. Boyce for Essex (JPL), 1975

HOW TO GET THERE

Rail   Luton Midland, 1 mile
Bus   Luton & District 26 from Mill Street (200m from BR Station) (Tel: 0582 404074); and 6 from town centre
Car   From north: M1 junction 11, then follow signs Luton A505

into Dunstable Road for town centre. A6 from town centre to New Bedford Road for Wardown Park and ground which is ½ mile out of town centre. From east: A505 signposted Luton, from town centre follow New Bedford Road for Wardown Park. From west: A505 signposted Luton, then as north. From south: M1 junction 10/10a, follow signs Luton and town centre, then A6 for New Bedford Road.

WHERE TO STAY AND OTHER INFORMATION

Chiltern Hotel (0582 575911), Strathmore Thistle Hotel (0582 34199)

Disabled Areas Within the enclosure
Local Radio Station(s) Chiltern Radio (96.9 MHz FM/792 KHz MW), BBC Radio Bedfordshire (95.5 MHz FM/1161 KHz MW)
Local Newspaper(s) Luton News, The Herald

Wellingborough

This is the school ground of Wellingborough School, which was founded in 1595, and has been used for first-class cricket since 1946 when Hampshire were the visitors. The first limited-overs match was in 1970 when Worcestershire were the opponents. The pavilion is an attractive thatched roofed building with a clock tower. It was built in 1929. The steps of the pavilion include the stone that was once the threshold to the Downend home of Dr W.G. Grace in Bristol. The stone is inscribed 'Not of an age, but for all time' and was laid on 10 July 1940 by Henry Grierson, the founder of the Forty Club 'XL'. Beneath the pitch bottles have been buried for posterity on Hallowe'en to record the names of every county player to appear at the school ground, including their signatures and a scorecard.

Northamptonshire abandoned the wicket for one year in 1982 due to its poor condition but returned a year later. This is the second ground to be used in the town for county cricket; in 1929 the County played at the Town Ground for one season. Northamptonshire usually take four days of cricket to the school ground in August at a time when the County headquarters is undergoing changes for the start of Northampton Town F C football season. Crowds of 4,000 are usual. The largest of recent years was for the visit of Somerset in the John Player League when 7,000 attended and were rewarded by Ian Botham despite a rain-interrupted game. The record attendance was 24,000 against Yorkshire in 1949 over three days.

It is a small ground by first-class standards but nevertheless a historic ground. C.B. Fry's footprints were once to be found in concrete close to the school chapel. In recent times Ian Botham's innings of 175 not out in a 1986 Sunday League fixture will be long remembered by those who saw it. Possibly the most well known of

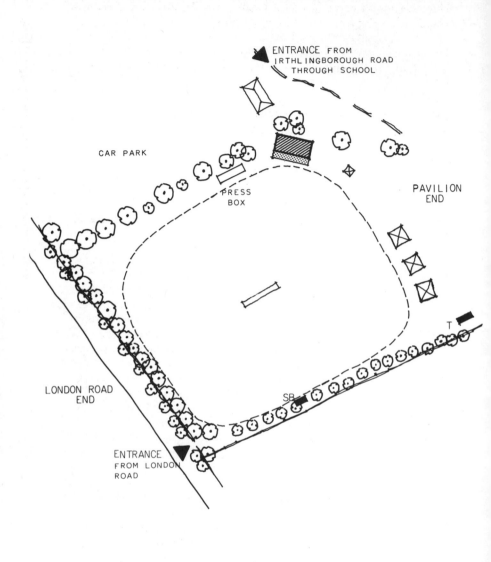

ENTRANCE FROM
IRTHLINGBOROUGH ROAD
THROUGH SCHOOL

CAR PARK

PRESS
BOX

PAVILION
END

LONDON ROAD
END

SB

T

ENTRANCE
FROM LONDON
ROAD

N

0   50   100

Metres

Old Wellingburians was George Thompson who played for the county club. Others were the Denton twins, Jack Timms, T.E. Manning, G.A.T. Vials, R.O. Raven, A.H. Bull and W.C. Brown.

Ground records include significant scores from Jock Livingston and Len Hutton. Bowling records belong to Frank Tyson and Bishen Bedi for Northamptonshire, and Jack van Geloven and Derek Shackleton for the visitors.

ADDRESS Wellingborough School, Irthlingborough Road, Wellingborough, Northamptonshire NN8 2BX

TELEPHONE PROSPECTS OF PLAY 0933 223705/222427

DESCRIPTION OF GROUND AND FACILITIES

While pedestrians can enter the ground from London Road, it is necessary for all cars and other vehicles to enter through the school entrance in Irthlingborough Road. Car parking is permitted on the football fields.

The cricket ground is to the south of the school, and the only permanent structures are the pavilion in the north-east corner and a shed to the north which is used by press and scorers. The scoreboard is on the south side of the ground. All other facilities are temporary and housed in tents. Enclosed by trees and close to the London Road, the ground is quite small, no more than 113 metres by 133 metres defined by a rope, with limited space for spectators except to the north and east sides. The area provided for members is on the north and east sides in the area from the pavilion and including the shed and space in front of the trees which separate the cricket and football fields. You are advised to bring your own seats as only 1,200 are provided. Ladies' toilets are provided only in the school premises while men's toilets are in temporary accommodation.

This is a very pleasant ground to watch cricket providing there is not too great a crowd; and it is one of only three school grounds now used for county cricket.

GROUND RECORDS AND SCORES

FIRST-CLASS MATCHES

Highest innings total for County 395 v. Warwickshire, 1976
Highest innings total against County 523 for 8 by Yorkshire, 1949
Lowest innings total for County 80 v. Leicestershire, 1962
Lowest innings total against County 62 by Middlesex, 1977
Highest individual innings for County 172 n.o. L. Livingston v. Essex, 1955
Highest individual innings against County 269 n.o. L. Hutton for Yorkshire, 1949
Best bowling performance in an innings for County 7 for 46 F. Tyson v. Derbyshire, 1956
Best bowling performance in an innings against County 6 for 28 J. van Geloven for Leicestershire, 1962

Best bowling performance in a match for County   11 for 107
B.S. Bedi *v.* Middlesex, 1977
Best bowling performance in a match against County   11 for 104
D. Shackleton for Hampshire, 1963

LIMITED-OVERS MATCHES
Highest innings total for County   234 for 1 *v.* Leicestershire (JPL),
1979
Highest innings total against County   272 for 5 by Somerset (JPL),
1986
Lowest innings total for County   114 *v.* Hampshire (JPL), 1980
Lowest innings total against County   132 by Yorkshire (JPL), 1 81
Highest individual innings for County   111 W. Larkins *v.*
Leicestershire (JPL), 1979
Highest individual innings against County   175 n.o. I.T. Botham
for Somerset (JPL), 1986
Best bowling performance for County   3 for 8 B. Crump *v.*
Worcestershire (JPL), 1970
Best bowling performance against County   4 for 24 T.M. Tremlett
for Hampshire (JPL), 1980

HOW TO GET THERE

Rail   Wellingborough, 1¼ miles
Bus   United Counties 46 from Church Street (¾ mile from BR
Station) (Tel: 0604 36681)
Car   From north: A509 signposted Wellingborough and town
centre, follow signs for London Road and Wellingborough School is
situated off this road next to the Dog and Duck Pub. The school
ground is situated south-east of the town centre. From east: A45 or
A510 to Wellingborough then as north. From west: A45 or A4500
signposted Wellingborough, then as north. From south: M1 junction
14 then follow A509 signposted Wellingborough, then as north.

WHERE TO STAY AND OTHER INFORMATION

Hind Hotel (0933 222827), High View Hotel (0933 78733)

Disabled Areas   No special area, request position
Local Radio Station(s)   BBC Radio Northampton (104.2 MHz FM/
1107 KHz MW), Hereward Radio (96.6 MHz FM/1557 KHz MW),
Chiltern Radio (96.9 MHz FM/792 KHz MW)
Local Newspaper(s)   The Evening Telegraph, The Chronicle and
Echo

Finedon

Founded in 1836, Finedon Dolben C C has always been an active venue for cricket and over the years has produced some fine players. Foremost of these was without doubt A.G. Henfrey who played for the County from 1886 to 1889 and captained the County in 1894–5. Henfrey also represented England at football on five occasions. Other Finedon cricketers who reached first-class level were R.W. Clarke, who was also a top-class footballer, J. Minney and Rev. H.H. Gillet.

The fact that Finedon has always been a strong club, by local standards, must to some extent be due to the fine ground, which is the home of the village cricket club Dolben. For approximately a century, minus the few years lost to ironstone excavation close to the ground, cricket has been played at Avenue Road. The ironstone workings are why the ground is some 15 feet below road level. In the early 1920s the ground was purchased from the Ebbw Vale Mining Company and in recent years a number of improvements have been made. These have not gone unnoticed by the county club which has played a number of Second Eleven matches at the ground.

In 1986, to celebrate the club's 150th birthday, a number of special fixtures were arranged. Visitors included M C C, a County Select League eleven and Tring Park C C. The highlight was a John Player Sunday League match with Derbyshire which attracted a good crowd of 4,400. With this show of support the county club has returned each season for one Sunday League match. The match with Sussex in 1988 was rearranged to Northampton because the Finedon ground was waterlogged. The club play in the Northamptonshire County Cricket League and also has teams represented in the Higham and District Youth League, which is a source of raw material for the Club's ongoing youth policy. A benefit match was arranged for Wayne Larkins in 1986 and was well supported.

Ground records at Dolben include 97 by Allan Lamb, and 5 for 7 by Duncan Wild, both against Derbyshire in the inaugural match.

ADDRESS Finedon Dolben C C, Dolben Cricket Ground, Avenue Road, Finedon, Northants NN9 5JJ
TELEPHONE PROSPECTS OF PLAY 0933 681117

DESCRIPTION OF GROUND AND FACILITIES

The ground is entered off Avenue Road; some 360 car parking spaces are available in the ground through this entrance and additional car parking is available in the adjoining field. An area is set aside for invalid cars which can be parked in a position to see the cricket.

The only permanent building is the pavilion, which is in the north-east corner. To one side provision is made in temporary accommodation for the press and scorers. The area in front of the pavilion is reserved for members, whilst the rest of the ground is available to the public. In total some 2,000 seats are provided, which

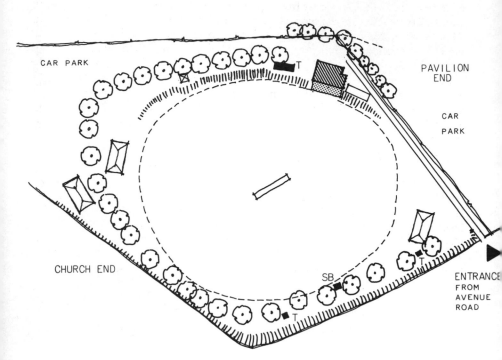

CAR PARK

PAVILION
END

CAR
PARK

CHURCH END

T

SB

T

T

ENTRANCE
FROM
AVENUE
ROAD

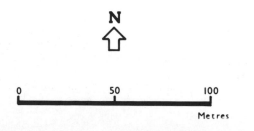

N

0   50   100

Metres

is about one-third of the ground capacity. The ground, being in a natural bowl or saucer surrounded by trees on three sides, provides excellent views of the cricket from all sides. The pitch is oval-shaped, about 130 metres by 119 metres, and defined by a rope and boards. The scoreboard is on the south side; the north side provides the best view of the cricket as here the ground is banked higher than on the other sides.

Refreshment tents, sponsors' areas and other temporary accommodation are disposed around the ground, mainly on the north side. The surrounding lime trees help to give this ground its individual character.

GROUND RECORDS AND SCORES

LIMITED-OVERS MATCHES

Highest innings total for County   242 for 6 v. Derbyshire (JPL), 1986
Highest innings total against County   145 by Derbyshire (JPL), 1986
Lowest innings total for County   170 for 8 v. Gloucestershire (RAL), 1987
Highest individual innings for County   97 A.J. Lamb v. Derbyshire (JPL), 1986
Highest individual innings against County   46 K.J. Barnett for Derbyshire (JPL), 1986
Best bowling performance for County   5 for 7 D.J. Wild v. Derbyshire (JPL), 1986
Best bowling performance against County   2 for 38 J.W. Lloyds for Gloucestershire (RAL), 1987

HOW TO GET THERE

Rail   Wellingborough, 3 miles
Bus   United Counties 45/7 from Church Street, Wellingborough (¾ mile from BR Station) (Tel: 0604 36681)
Car   2 miles north-east of Wellingborough. From north: A6 or A510 signposted Finedon, ground situated off Avenue Road on north-western outskirts of village. From east: as north. From west: A510 signposted Finedon, then as north. From south: A6 or A510 signposted Finedon, then as north.

WHERE TO STAY AND OTHER INFORMATION

Tudor Gate Hotel, High Street (0933 680408), or stay in Wellingborough

Disabled Areas   Made available if requested in advance
Local Radio Station(s)   BBC Radio Northampton (104.2 MHz FM/ 1107 KHz MW), Hereward Radio (96.6 MHz FM/1557 KHz MW), Chiltern Radio (96.9 MHz FM/792 KHz MW)
Local Newspaper(s)   The Evening Telegraph, The Chronicle and Echo

Tring

Cricket may well have been played in Tring prior to the club's foundation in 1836. The players of that time consisted of ten farmers and workers on the Rothchild's Tring Park Estate. Before the move to the present ground, previously known as Knuckle Stile Close in 1873, two other grounds were used: at Tring Grove Park and in the area of Tring Park to the west of Hastoe Park. A footpath to Pendley was closed when the new road to Tring railway station was made.

Northamptonshire's association with the Tring Park C C began in 1955 when a benefit match was staged for Australian left-hander Jock Livingstone. Since 1956 ten benefit matches have been staged for County players including George Tribe, Dennis Brookes, Frank Tyson, Keith Andrew and Geoff Cook. In 1974 when Northamptonshire decided to take cricket outside the county, Tring were fortunate to be asked to participate in the venture. The first match was a John Player Sunday League visit by Middlesex.

Crowds of 4,000 are quite usual; the largest was for a visit by Kent in 1977 which attracted 5,500 spectators plus B B C T V cameras. The ground is owned by the club and it fields four XI's during the season. They participate in the Bryan-Grasshopper Hertfordshire Cricket League and the Thames Valley Cricket League. The county boundary is less than a mile from the ground, and over the years club members have represented both Hertfordshire and Buckinghamshire.

The club has hosted Minor County matches for Hertfordshire and friendly matches with the M C C and Tannon's XI, captained by Harry Sharp the Middlesex scorer between 1964 and 1982.

Ground records have included fine hundreds from Wayne Larkins and Peter Willey, who scored the first century (107) on the ground in 1976 against Hampshire. No visitor has scored a hundred. Pakistan quick bowler Sarfraz Nawaz (5 for 31 against Middlesex) holds the bowling record for Northamptonshire and Norman Graham for the visitors.

ADDRESS Tring Park C C, The Pavilion, Station Road, Tring, Herts
TELEPHONE PROSPECTS OF PLAY 044282 3080

DESCRIPTION OF GROUND AND FACILITIES

Access can be gained either from London Road (A41) adjoining the pavilion or from entrances on Station Road to the north of the ground. Car owners are required to park in the fields on the south side of Station Road on either side of the cricket ground. The only permanent building is the small pavilion. There is no permanent seating, and you are advised to bring your own seats as the club only provide seats for about 20 per cent of the 8,000 capacity.

The small scoreboard is in the south-east corner and the members' area extends from the pavilion on the south side around to the scoreboard. All other facilities are provided in temporary tents; they

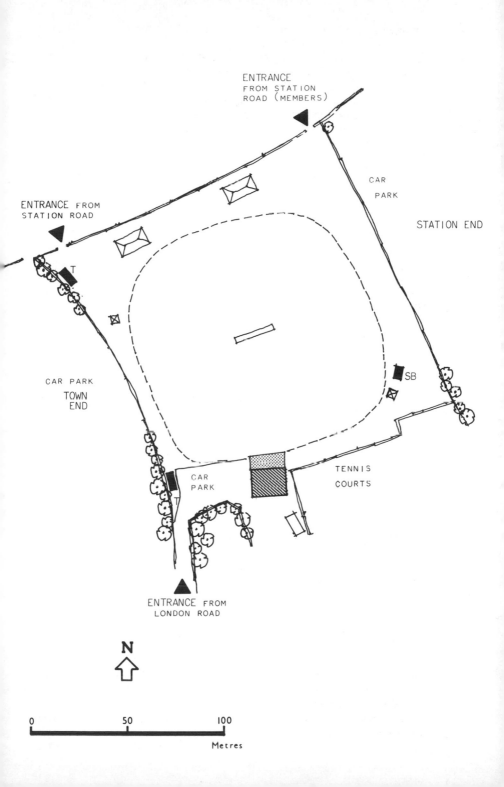

ENTRANCE
FROM STATION
ROAD (MEMBERS)

CAR
PARK

ENTRANCE FROM
STATION ROAD

STATION END

T

CAR PARK
TOWN
END

SB

CAR
PARK

TENNIS
COURTS

ENTRANCE FROM
LONDON ROAD

N

0   50   100

Metres

include refreshments and a N C C C shop. The playing area is about 124 metres by 125 metres and is defined only by a rope and advertisement boards. Toilets except in the pavilion are in temporary accommodation on the west side of the ground. T V cameras are normally sited at the west (town) end of the ground by the sightscreen.

This is a pleasant park-like ground enclosed by hedges and trees and close to Tring centre.

GROUND RECORDS AND SCORES

LIMITED-OVERS MATCHES
Highest innings total for County   290 for 6 v. Lancashire (RAL), 1987
Highest innings total against County   236 by Lancashire (RAL), 1987
Lowest innings total for County   59 v. Middlesex (JPL), 1974
Lowest innings total against County   119 for 4 by Middlesex (JPL), 1974
Highest individual innings for County   107 n.o. W. Larkins v. Surrey (JPL), 1978
Highest individual innings against County   88 M.R. Benson for Kent (JPL), 1984
Best bowling performance for County   5 for 31 Sarfraz Nawaz v. Middlesex (JPL), 1981
Best bowling performance against County   5 for 7 J.N. Graham for Kent (JPL), 1975

HOW TO GET THERE

Rail   Tring, 2 miles
Bus   Luton & District 27 links BR Station with town centre; also 61 Aylesbury–Luton (Tel: 0296 84919) and London Country (NW) 501, 768 Aylesbury–Hemel Hempstead (Tel: 0923 673121) pass ground
Car   10 miles north-west of Hemel Hempstead on the (A41) to Aylesbury. From north: M1 junction 11, then follow A505, B489 and B488 for Tring, then follow A41 Tring town centre, ground situated off main High Street at eastern end. From east: M1 junction 8 then follow A41 to Tring, ground situated off (A41) on southern outskirts of town. From west: A41, A4011, A413 signposted Tring, then as north. From south: A41 signposted Tring as east.

WHERE TO STAY AND OTHER INFORMATION

Royal Hotel, Tring station (044282 7616). Rose and Crown (044282 4071), Hamblings Hotel, Northchurch

Disabled Areas   In front of club car park close to Pavilion
Local Radio Station(s)   BBC Radio Bedfordshire (95.5 MHz FM/792 KHz MW), Chiltern Radio (96.9 MHz FM/792 KHz MW), Greater London Radio (94.9 MHz FM/1458 KHz MW)
Local Newspaper(s)   Bucks Herald, Bucks Advertiser and Aylesbury News, Berkhamsted and Tring Gazette

NOTTINGHAMSHIRE

NOTTINGHAM – TRENT BRIDGE

WORKSOP

Nottinghamshire

By happy chance, Nottinghamshire began 1988 celebrating the 150th anniversary of Trent Bridge as the reigning champions and holders of the NatWest Trophy. A hat-trick was missed by 2 points in the Sunday League. With timely opportunism a £150,000 appeal was launched to spend on ground improvements, including a plan for a stand named after William Clarke, founder of Trent Bridge.

Inter-city contests with Sheffield and other neighbours, which stimulated interest, commenced as early as 1771, and it was William Clarke who first spotted the commercial possibilities of cricket by founding and captaining the All-England Eleven in 1846. The cream of the professionals toured the country in what was realistically a money-making enterprise, but it served to widen cricket's appeal. Clarke was astute but tight-fisted, and a group broke away called the United All-England Eleven. Once the novelty of the touring sides faded, and the clubs became better organized, county cricket came into its own. Opinions on Clarke are mixed, but he left his county a magnificent centre, which has staged Test matches since 1899, and a quality of players more than ready to accept any new challenge. Nottinghamshire were the first of the northern sides to end southern supremacy and, starting from 1865 to 1889, they were champions ten times, and co-champions in five other seasons.

Famous names live on – Richard Daft, Alfred Shaw, often seen as the bowler of the century, and George Parr, whose leg sweep battered a tall elm tree. 'Parr's tree' became a Trent Bridge landmark. When Parr was asked why he played cricket for a living he replied: 'Because I don't like work!'

Arthur Shrewsbury was a master of back play and Grace's favourite. 'Give me, Arthur,' said the Doctor to the selectors, 'and you pick the rest.'

The Gunns, William, and his two nephews, and the Hardstaffs, Joe Snr and Joe Jr are celebrated names. William Gunn refused to tour Australia because of the unattractive terms offered to the pros, putting his time to the benefit of his growing sports business of Gunn and Moore. He left £60,000. After providing for his widow and daughter the rest went to employees who had helped to build up the enterprise.

George lightened the scene for thirty years with a whimsical, almost eccentric outlook, batting according to the mood of the moment. One innings would be the last word in classical execution, the next would produce dazzling shots off the best ball and a dead bat to the worst. He had the scorn of the truly gifted for the second rate. Going to Australia for health reasons in 1907–8 he was pressed into service when the captain, Arthur Jones, fell ill, and he scored 119 and 74 in the opening Test at Sydney. In the later stages of his century he complained his concentration was affected by a flat cornet playing in a band. Gunn's series average of 51 was above Hobbs and his county teammate Joe Hardstaff.

NOTTINGHAMSHIRE C.C.C.

W. W. KEETON (NOTTINGHAMSHIRE)

COUNTY CRICKETERS.

E. ALLETSON,
NOTTINGHAMSHIRE.

MR. A. O. JONES (NOTTS.).

WILLS'S CIGARETTES.

PLAYER'S CIGARETTES

WILLS'S Cigarettes.

A. SHREWSBURY,
NOTTINGHAMSHIRE.

On his 50th birthday he scored a memorable 164 not out against
Worcestershire, and the records have the statistic – G. Gunn (183) and
G.V. Gunn (100 not out) at Birmingham in 1931. It is the only
instance of father and son each scoring a century in the same innings
of a first-class match. Gunn was over 50 when he toured the West
Indies, and not only scored well in all four Tests, but baited the fast
bowler Learie Constantine by going down the pitch and putting his
tongue out at him. This extraordinary by-play was all very well but
his batting partner, Sandham, remarked: 'George didn't stay all that
long and I was left to deal with some very irate bowlers!'

Gunn would have found a soul-mate in Randall, who delighted
crowds – particularly in India – with his enthusiasm and sheer
brilliance at cover point. Though his fidgety movements at the crease

worried the purists and enraged Lillee and Co, he scored 2,470 runs in 47 Tests with 7 centuries, including 174 brave and skilful runs in the Melbourne centenary Test.

The bowling of Wass and Hallam played a significant part in the championship success of 1907, and the captaincy of A.W. Carr, who was a considerable batsman, produced a high level of consistency from 1919 to 1934 – the title in 1929, three 2nd places and always in single-figures.

Harold Larwood and Bill Voce, who started as a left arm spinner, formed as menacing a fast bowling partnership as county cricket has seen. They were the instruments of Jardine's leg theory, or bodyline, which caused so much trouble and was rightly outlawed. The last match of 1932 was used by Larwood and Voce as a rehearsal for the theory and holds a coveted niche in Glamorgan's folklore. Far from being intimidated Turnbull (205) and Dai Davies feasted on the short-pitched attack and added 220 for the 3rd wicket, a county record to stand until Emrys Davies and Willie Jones took 310 off Essex in 1946.

That night at Cardiff the Notts players left the pavilion after quaffing some beer and walked across the ground towards their hotel. On the way they relieved their frustrations on the pitch, much to the outrage of groundsman Trevor Preece when he made the discovery of the tainted wicket the next morning. Lord's decided it was a matter for the captains, Turnbull and Carr, and Turnbull unsurprisingly said it was no concern of his as Notts were due to bat. The match was drawn.

After the bodyline tour Larwood was left with an injury to his left foot, and the mental scars of an affronted scapegoat. The only solace for him was to settle happily in Sydney on the sponsorship of Jack Fingleton, Australia's opening bat in the ill-fated 1932–3 series. Larwood deserves to be chiefly remembered for the poetry of his co-ordinated movements, his speed and accuracy and the perfect follow-through which had his knuckles brushing the turf.

Nottinghamshire spent too many of the post-war years in the discouraging exercise of evading the wooden spoon – they were bottom five times between 1958 and 1966 – and the lack of in-depth strength was even too much for such eminent performers as Simpson, Hardstaff, who retired with 83 centuries in 1955, and Sir Gary Sobers, who joined in 1968 and was engaged in the teeth of fierce competition.

Simpson was the pride of post-war Nottinghamshire scoring four centuries for England and showing how fast bowling should be played and bumpers avoided. The Australian Dooland took 770 wickets for Nottinghamshire with his leg breaks and scored 4,782 runs for the county in five years.

Sobers was captain of the West Indies when he accepted a contract worth around £5,000 a season in 1968. He worked wonders for South Australia, and in his first season at Trent Bridge there was a rise from 15th to 4th, and his 6 sixes in an over at Swansea was a sensation. Unfortunately for his county Sobers was lost for half the next season on Test call, and in his third came an unexpected duty to lead the

Rest of the World in a hastily-arranged rubber to replace the cancelled visit by South Africa. The fates seemed to conspire against him, and the sheer grind of county cricket was really not to his taste. He was the man for the big occasion.

The long-awaited revival came with the Springbok Clive Rice and the Kiwi Richard Hadlee. The championship was won under Rice in 1981 with Hadlee taking 105 wickets. The batting of Randall and the experienced bowling of Hemmings also played a substantial part. Rice's initial triumph broke a 52-year barren spell, and in 1987 came the double of the championship and the NatWest Trophy.

Hadlee emerged as one of the world's foremost all-rounders. In eight years he headed the national bowling averages five times, and was twice 2nd. In 1984 he was the first to complete the double since the championship programme was reduced in 1969, and as Rice and Hadlee passed into the legends Franklyn Stephenson, from Barbados, also completed the double in 1988. [A.B.]

Left: William Clarke, founder of Trent Bridge

Right: A bat made from the wood of Parr's tree

Founded   1841
Colours   Green and gold
Crest   Coat of arms of the City of Nottingham
Secretary   B. Robson
Cricket Manager   K.A. Taylor
Groundsman   R. Allsopp
Scorer   L. Beaumont
Address   County Cricket Ground, Trent Bridge, Nottingham NG2 6AG
Telephone 0602 821525
Cricketcall   0898 121460

Achievements:

County Championship   Champions (14) 1865, 1868, 1871, 1872, 1875, 1880, 1883, 1884, 1885, 1886, 1907, 1929, 1981 and 1987; joint champions (5) 1869, 1873, 1879, 1882 and 1889
Gillette Cup   Semi-finalists 1969
National Westminster Bank Trophy   Winners 1987; finalists 1985
Benson & Hedges Cup   Finalists 1982
John Player Sunday League   Champions (0) 2nd 1984
Refuge Assurance Sunday League   Champions (0) 2nd 1987
Tilcon Trophy   Winners 1977; finalists 1984 and 1985

Grounds:

Nottingham (Trent Bridge, West Bridgford)   Worksop (Town Ground, Central Avenue).
   Other grounds that have been used since 1969 are: Nottingham (John Player & Sons Sports Ground, Aspley Lane), Newark-On-Trent (RHP Limited Ground, Elm Avenue) and Cleethorpes (Sports Ground, Chichester Road).

Nottingham – Trent Bridge

Truly the definitive home of cricket in Nottinghamshire, Trent Bridge became a cricket ground due to the enterprise of William Clarke. He moved from the Bell Inn, still to be found in the main city square, to the Trent Bridge Inn and laid out a cricket ground at the back of his new home. By trade a bricklayer, William Clarke was also the organizer of the Nottingham First XI in the 1830s. In late 1837 he married Mrs Chapman, the landlady and lessee of the Trent Bridge Inn (known today to locals as the TBI) and the open ground behind the building.
   On 10 July 1838 he organized the first cricket match on the ground

behind the Inn between T. Baker's Side and W. Clarke's Side. In July 1840 the first county match was staged, with Sussex the visitors.

William Clarke left Nottingham to move to London in 1846 and was succeeded by his stepson John Chapman. It was not until 1881 that the owners, the Chaworth-Musters family, signed a 99-year lease for both the inn and ground with the county club. In 1919 the county cricket club purchased both the inn, which they later sold, and the ground which has been in their sole ownership since that date.

The present pavilion was built in 1886 and designed by H.M. Townsend of Peterborough. It has since been altered and extended but much of its original character remains. Developments have continued to take place at the ground over the intervening years so that Trent Bridge is one of the best grounds in the country. The most recent addition, in 1985, was the Larwood and Voce Stand and Tavern on the Fox Road side of the ground.

The ground has been used for soccer by both Nottingham Forest and Notts. County, both of whose grounds are within walking distance of Trent Bridge on either side of the nearby River Trent. In 1988 the club celebrated 150 years of Trent Bridge. Proceeds will go towards the rebuilding of the Parr Stand and the west side of the Ground.

The first Test Match at Trent Bridge was played in 1899 against Australia. In recent years the ground has seen many limited-overs international matches including Prudential Cup games and limited-overs matches with the tourists. In 1978–79 the new squash courts and club offices were built by the Dixon Gates, the members' entrance.

Much has been written and spoken of Parr's Tree, which stood close to the Bridgford Road side of the ground behind the Parr Stand and was blow down in a gale in January 1976. It was an elm tree which gained its name in the last century from the frequency with which George Parr (1826–91, Nottinghamshire 1845–70) managed to hit balls into its branches. Mini bats have been made from the tree and, indeed, close to the ground is the home of bat making: the Gunn and Moore bat factory is only five minutes away by car.

Over 1,200 Nottinghamshire matches have been staged on the ground and all Test nations have played on the hallowed turf. The county have played on four other grounds in the city; the most recent journey from the headquarters was to the John Player & Sons Sports Ground at Aspley Lane in 1973 for a Sunday League match with Gloucestershire. Crowds at Trent Bridge tend to be 5,000–6,000 these days with limited-overs matches and Test matches attracting the greatest crowds. One of the largest was 35,000 against Surrey in 1948 for a single day's play, and 35,000 in 1938 during the England v. Australia Test Match.

Ground records have included scores of over 200 from Charlie Macartney, A.O. Jones, Denis Compton and Frank Worrell. Tom Graveney took 258 off the West Indies during the 1950s. In recent years, a 232 from Viv Richards against England in 1976 graced this historic venue. Nottingham has seen some great players in action

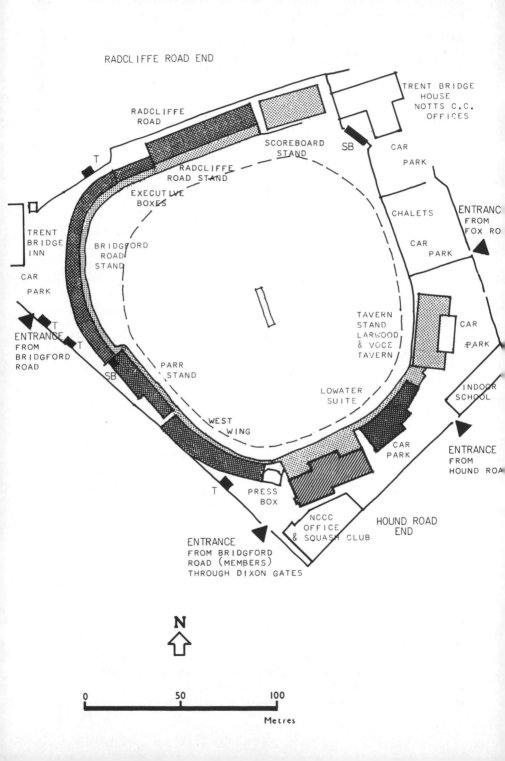

RADCLIFFE ROAD END

TRENT BRIDGE
HOUSE
NOTTS C.C.
OFFICES

RADCLIFFE
ROAD

SCOREBOARD
STAND

SB

CAR
PARK

T

RADCLIFFE
ROAD STAND

EXECUTIVE
BOXES

CHALETS

ENTRANC
FROM
FOX RO

TRENT
BRIDGE
INN

BRIDGFORD
ROAD
STAND

CAR
PARK

CAR
PARK

T

ENTRANCE
FROM
BRIDGFORD
ROAD

T

TAVERN
STAND
LARWOOD
& VOCE
TAVERN

CAR
PARK

SB

PARR
STAND

LOWATER
SUITE

INDOOR
SCHOOL

WEST
WING

ENTRANCE
FROM
HOUND ROA

CAR
PARK

T

PRESS
BOX

NCCC
OFFICE
& SQUASH CLUB

HOUND ROAD
END

ENTRANCE
FROM BRIDGFORD
ROAD (MEMBERS)
THROUGH DIXON GATES

N

⇧

0   50   100

Metres

including Clarke, Parr, Shaw, Carr, Voce, Larwood, Simpson, Sobers, Rice, Randall, and Hadlee and Stephenson.

ADDRESS   County Cricket Ground, Trent Bridge, Bridgford Road, Nottingham NG2 6AG
TELEPHONE PROSPECTS OF PLAY   0602 822753

DESCRIPTION OF GROUND AND FACILITIES

Entry to the ground for members and the public is made from Bridgford Road but there are further entrances in Hound Road and Fox Road. Some car parking is available within the ground on normal county cricket days but for Test Matches this space is allocated and car parking must be sought in the adjoining streets. All seating is available in permanent buildings and additionally, for Test Matches and International One Day Matches, temporary seating is provided in front of the main scoreboard and adjoining the temporary hospitality suites erected on the car park next to the office tower, on the Fox Road side of the ground. The areas restricted to members include not only the pavilion and the west wing stand on Bridgford Road side but also the Tavern Stand and the area in front of the Lowater suite which also includes a Ladies' Stand as well as the Boundary restaurant. These areas together extend to the whole of the southern half of the ground. However, there is still more than adequate accommodation for the public in the Parr Stand, Bridgford Road Stand and the Radcliffe Road and scoreband stands which also provide a large area of covered seating. There is ample space for disabled spectators and they should ask for a suitable position. As is to be expected of a Test Match venue there are ample refreshment facilities as well as toilets. This is a large ground with a playing area extending to 160 metres by 150 metres but this is restricted on match days to about 141 metres by 144 metres. A Club shop is to be found close to the main gates from Bridgford Road and the pavilion houses a library and various cricket memorabilia which can be inspected on request.

This is an excellent ground which provides a good view of cricket from every position. The most recent building, the Larwood and Voce Tavern Stand, is an excellent structure providing good seating and a tavern building in keeping with the traditions of the area. The Trent Bridge Inn remains open to the cricket spectators for refreshment with direct access from the ground.

GROUND RECORDS AND SCORES

TEST MATCHES
Highest innings total for England   658 for 8 dec. *v.* Australia, 1938
Highest innings total against England   558 by West Indies, 1950
Lowest innings total for England   112 *v.* Australia, 1921
Lowest innings total against England   88 for South Africa, 1960

Highest individual innings for England   278 D.C.S. Compton *v.* Pakistan, 1954

Highest individual innings against England   261 F.M.M. Worrell for West Indies, 1950

Best bowling performance in an innings for England   8 for 107 B.J.T. Bosanquet *v.* Australia, 1905

Best bowling performance in an innings against England   7 for 54 W.J. O'Reilly for Australia, 1931

Best bowling performance in a match for England   14 for 99 A.V. Bedser *v.* Australia, 1953

Best bowling performance in a match against England   11 for 129 W.J. O'Reilly for Australia, 1934

LIMITED-OVERS INTERNATIONALS

Highest innings total   330 for 6 by Pakistan *v.* Sri Lanka (PC), 1975

Lowest innings total   138 by Sri Lanka *v.* Pakistan (PC), 1975

Highest individual innings   118 A.J. Lamb for England *v.* Pakistan (PT), 1982

Best bowling performance   6 for 39 K.H. MacLeay for Australia *v.* India (PC), 1983

FIRST-CLASS MATCHES

Highest innings total for County   739 for 7 dec. *v.* Leicestershire, 1903

Highest innings total against County   706 for 4 dec. by Surrey, 1947

Lowest innings total for County   13 *v.* Yorkshire, 1901

Lowest innings total against County   16 by Derbyshire, 1879

Highest individual innings for County   296 A.O. Jones *v.* Gloucestershire, 1903

Highest individual innings against County   345 C.G. Macartney for Australians, 1921

Best bowling performance in an innings for County   9 for 19 J. Grundy *v.* Kent, 1864

Best bowling performance in an innings against County   9 for 32 J.T. Hearne for Middlesex, 1891/M.S. Nichols for Essex, 1936

Best bowling performance in a match for County   17 for 89 F.C. Matthews *v.* Northamptonshire, 1923

Best bowling performance in a match against County   16 for 122 C.L. Townsend for Gloucestershire, 1895

LIMITED-OVERS MATCHES

Highest innings total for County   271 *v.* Gloucestershire (GC), 1968

Highest innings total against County   306 for 2 by Essex (JPL), 1983

Lowest innings total for County   81 *v.* Derbyshire (JPL), 1972

Lowest innings total against County   84 by Surrey (JPL), 1974

Highest individual innings for County   123 D.W. Randall *v.* Yorkshire (RAL), 1987

Highest individual innings against County   171 G.A. Gooch for Essex (JPL), 1985
Best bowling performance for County   6 for 12 R.J. Hadlee *v.* Lancashire (JPL), 1980
Best bowling performance against County   7 for 41 A.N. Jones for Sussex (JPL), 1986

HOW TO GET THERE

Rail   Nottingham Midland, 1 mile
Bus   Nottingham City 12, 69, 85, 90–7 and Trent Buses link BR Station with ground (Tel: 0602 503665)
Car   From north: M1 junction 26, follow signs Nottingham A610, follow signs to Melton Mowbray, Trent Bridge A606, cross river and ground is ahead of you. From east: A52 signposted Nottingham into West Bridgford, then follow Bridgford Road for ground. From south: M1 junction 24, then follow signs Nottingham (South) for Trent Bridge, then into Bridgford Road for Trent Bridge. From west: A52 follow signposts Nottingham, then follow signs Melton Mowbray, then Trent Bridge as north

WHERE TO STAY AND OTHER INFORMATION

Albany Hotel (0602 470131), Victoria Hotel (0602 419561), Royal Hotel (0602 414444)

Disabled Areas   Ample room on boundary edge, request suitable position
Local Radio Station(s)   BBC Radio Nottingham (95.5 MHz FM/1584 KHz MW), Radio Trent (96.2 MHz FM/999 KHz MW)
Local Newspaper(s)   Nottingham Evening Post, Nottingham Trader

---

Worksop

The first match staged at Worksop was in November 1880 (Nottingham against the Twenty-two of Sheffield) but the initial first-class county match at the present Central Avenue ground was in 1921 when neighbours Derbyshire were the visitors. The ground which is situated only minutes from the town centre, is the home of Worksop Town C C which play in the Bassetlaw Cricket League. The land for the cricket ground was given to the cricket club in 1900 by William Allen, director of a local brewery, who also financed the building of the original pavilion. The previous ground was situated south of the River Ryton, which bounds the ground at the Central Avenue End, in Bridge Street where the main bus station is now built.

The present ground, a valuable piece of land close to the town centre was previously agricultural land and before cricket could be played levelling of the ground had to take place. Some locals said at the time that an error was made as the pitch now lies 4 to 5 feet below the water level of the nearby river. The ground tends to hold the dampness and as it is shared with the Worksop Town Football Club the outfield on the east side of the playing area tends to be quite rough.

The original pavilion was opened in 1901 prior to a match between Worksop and Notts. Club and Ground but the match was washed out by rain. The pavilion was replaced in 1972 by a new structure which includes squash facilities as well as room for cricketers. In 1986–87 the cricket club decided to have its own pavilion. The extension is neat, has ample facilities, and includes a players' area in the front overlooking the playing area. The pavilion and the scoreboard are the only permanent buildings for cricket but on the football ground side are stands and terrace facilities. These are sufficiently distant from the playing area not to be used much by cricket spectators, except during poor weather. Other facilities are limited compared with the county's headquarters but despite this the county club visits Worksop for one championship match each season usually in July. This is invariably with Yorkshire as the ground is only a few miles from the county boundary.

The number of Yorkshire visits is significant in that a careful look at the ground records shows that no less than three belong to Yorkshire, including a double hundred from Geoff Boycott, and 8 wickets from Fred Trueman. Crowds at Worksop are usually around 4,000–4,500. The largest was in 1966 when some 7,000 saw the Yorkshire match. Two limited-overs matches have been staged at the ground, in 1970 and 1971, both in the John Player Sunday League.

Geoff Boycott will have good memories of Central Avenue for he has scored over 900 runs on the ground, averaging well over 100. In 1986 three Nottinghamshire batsmen scored centuries against Yorkshire: Chris Broad (122), Tim Robinson (105) and Paul Johnson (105 not out). In 1988 Phil de Freitas scored a fast 113 for Leicestershire which was his career best in 82 minutes. Over the years many famous players have represented Worksop Town C C including Les Jackson the Derbyshire bowler, Ken Farnes who taught at Worksop College, Bill Voce and Wilfred Rhodes (before he joined Yorkshire).

This is the only ground currently used by Nottinghamshire other than Trent Bridge. However in 1989 it is hoped to stage a Second Eleven match at Chesterfield Road, Mansfield with a view to possibly taking county cricket to the ground in the future.

ADDRESS Worksop Town C C, The Pavilion, Central Avenue, Worksop, Nottinghamshire
TELEPHONE PROSPECTS OF PLAY 0909 472681

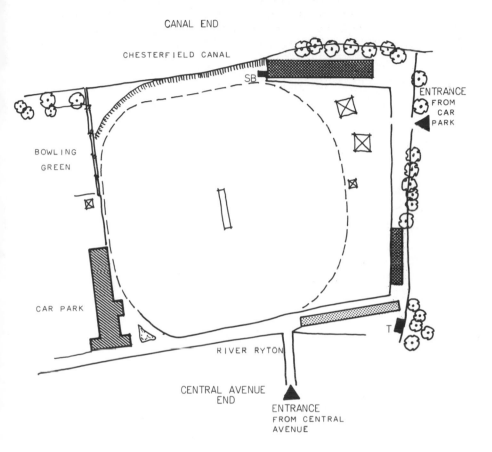

CANAL END

CHESTERFIELD CANAL

SB

ENTRANCE
FROM
CAR
PARK

BOWLING
GREEN

CAR PARK

T

RIVER RYTON

CENTRAL AVENUE
END

ENTRANCE
FROM CENTRAL
AVENUE

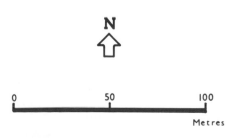

N

| 0 | 50 | 100 |

Metres

DESCRIPTION OF GROUND AND FACILITIES

Entry to the ground for members, players and officials is from Central Avenue and adjoining the rear of the football stand near the car park of the Netherholme Shopping Centre for the public. The ground is within minutes of Worksop's main shopping street and is bounded to the north by the now disused Chesterfield Canal and to the south by the River Ryton. The pavilion and sports building is west of the playing area and close to the bowling greens. The northern end has a steep bank where temporary seating can be found for members, and the scoreboard is situated. To the north and west, the stands and dressing rooms of the Worksop Football Club are located. Much of the seating is temporary and spectators are advised to bring their own to all matches as only 2,500 seats are provided for a ground capacity of some 7,000. The east side of the ground houses, in tents, the press and scorers as well as facilities for refreshments. Near to the pavilion, on the opposite side of the playing area, is the Nottinghamshire C C C souvenir tent. The members' area is in front of the pavilion and on the north side of the ground. The playing area is 126 metres by 123 metres and is quite flat. The playing area outfield to the east is on the football pitch and it is on this side of the ground that the only covered accommodation can be found which is a fair distance from play! Car parking at the rear of the pavilion is for 100 cars but ample parking can be found in nearby car parks, close to the shops. The playing area is defined by a rope with a number of advertising boards transported from Trent Bridge for the three days.

GROUND RECORDS AND SCORES

FIRST-CLASS MATCHES

Highest innings total for County   540 *v.* Worcestershire, 1934
Highest innings total against County   434 by Yorkshire, 1983
Lowest innings total for County   67 *v.* Northamptonshire, 1975
Lowest innings total against County   54 by Derbyshire, 1980
Highest individual innings for County   223 W.W. Keeton *v.* Worcestershire, 1934
Highest individual innings against County   229 n.o. A.S.M. Oakman for Sussex, 1961
Best bowling performance in an innings for County   7 for 66 H.J. Butler *v.* Glamorgan, 1935
Best bowling performance in an innings against County   8 for 84 F.S. Trueman for Yorkshire, 1962
Best bowling performance in a match for County   12 for 130 F. Barratt *v.* Worcestershire, 1923
Best bowling performance in a match against County   11 for 174 D.S. Steele for Derbyshire, 1980

LIMITED-OVERS MATCHES

Highest innings total for County   161 for 6 *v.* Sussex (JPL), 1971

Highest innings total against County   273 for 4 by Sussex (JPL), 1971
Lowest innings total for County   125 for 8 *v.* Derbyshire (JPL), 1970
Lowest innings total against County   162 for 7 by Derbyshire (JPL), 1970
Highest individual innings for County   39 S.B. Hasson *v.* Derbyshire (JPL), 1970
Highest individual innings against County   121 M.A. Buss for Sussex (JPL), 1971
Best bowling performance for County   4 for 39 D.J. Halfyard *v.* Derbyshire (JPL), 1970
Best bowling performance against County   3 for 33 J. Denmon for Sussex (JPL), 1971

HOW TO GET THERE

Rail   Worksop, ¾ mile
Bus   Numerous services link BR Station with town centre – close to ground. South Yorkshire Traction to/from Sheffield, Doncaster, Rotherham, Mansfield, Nottingham and Chesterfield
Car   From north: M1 junction 31, then follow A57 signposted Worksop, ground is situated close to town centre off Central Avenue. From east: A57 or B6079 from A1 signposted Worksop then as north. From west: A619 follow signs Worksop then as north. From south: M1 junction 30, then follow A619 signposted Worksop, then as north, or A60 or B6005 then as north.

WHERE TO STAY AND OTHER INFORMATION

The Lion Hotel (0909 2179), Ye Olde Bell, Barnby Moor/Retford (0777 705121)

Disabled Areas   No special area, request position
Local Radio Station(s)   BBC Radio Nottingham (95.5 MHz FM/1584 KHz MW), Radio Trent (96.2 MHz FM/999 KHz MW)
Local Newspaper(s)   Nottingham Evening Post, Worksop Guardian, Sheffield Star

SOMERSET

TAUNTON

BATH

WESTON-SUPER-MARE

Somerset

At one time the image of Somerset was of Jack ('Farmer') White wheeling down his deceptive left arm slows, and Harold Gimblett smiting one of his career's 265 sixes – an astonishing number for an opening bat. The picture changed with a business-like restructuring of county finances and the instant registration of overseas stars.

Taunton, Bath and Weston-super-Mare might have been regarded as charming backwaters of the game, but not when they became the stage for Viv Richards, the most fluent West Indies batsman since Sir Gary Sobers, Joel ('Big Bird') Garner, the fast bowler, and England's own Ian Botham.

Once the dressing room was full of amateurs – the club couldn't run to many pros – and there was always the chance of laughter when R.C. ('Crusoe') Robertson-Glasgow, a man of letters and good swing bowler, was in the team. It was noticed in one match only ten of Somerset took the field, but 'Crusoe' suddenly emerged from behind a sightscreen with an ice cream cone in each hand.

Bill Andrews, new ball partner of Wellard the mighty hitter, camped out at Maidstone and Clacton to save expenses – carefully selecting a site next to the beer tents – and persuaded the police at Warrington to let him pass a night in a cell.

Only Somerset could found their club in Devon in 1875, the Gentlemen of Somerset being on tour at the time, and only Somerset could have had the nerve to pluck Australian Bill Alley from League club Colne at the age of 38, and chortle four years' later when his season's haul was 3,019 runs and 62 wickets. Alley gathered 19,612 runs, 31 centuries, and 768 wickets after most players have retired.

No cricketer has made a more startling début than Gimblett, a 20-year-old from Bicknoller, a tiny village near Watchet where he was a farmer's boy. Going in at 107 for 6 he hit 123 out of 175 in 79 minutes at Frome, and won the Lawrence Trophy for the fastest century of 1935. *Punch* was not lost for a suitable rhyme:

> How comes it that this agricultural youth
> Can meet the wiliest ball and freely scotch it?
> Simple and elementary is the truth,
> His Gimblett eye enables him to Watchet.

Though Gimblett totalled 21,142 runs in fourteen seasons he gained only three pre-war caps, a disappointment which might have contributed to the self-doubts later to assail him. He was perhaps a victim of his sensational start, and the war robbed him of his prime years, but he had better claims than many selected for post-war teams and tours. Even Gimblett never matched Botham's 80 sixes in 1985, nor Wellard's 66 in 1935. Wellard, discarded by Kent, was one of the old school of bowlers who delighted in a tail-end slog, and he hit 50 or more sixes in a season four times. He was one of the best opening bowlers in the country.

COUNTY CRICKETERS.

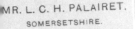

MR. L. C. H. PALAIRET.
SOMERSETSHIRE.

SOMERSET C.C.C.

R. C. ROBERTSON GLASGOW

WILLS'S CIGARETTES.

J. C. WHITE

A. YOUNG.

133-C SOMERSET

99-C SOMERSET

Somerset, awarded first-class ranking in 1891, creditably justified their status and have invariably had compulsive crowd pullers. Viv Richards had peak years with Somerset, who have made good use of their overseas registrations with such notables as Greg Chappell, McCool, O'Keeffe, Garner, Stephen Waugh and Martin Crowe. One of their first major personalities, S.M.J. (Sammy) Woods, was born in Sydney, and played for both Australia and England. But for an injury he would have been in the 1902 England side against Australia. An old-style Cambridge Corinthian games player – he was an outstanding rugby forward – Woods steered Somerset through the difficult transition from second- to first-class cricket with aggressive inclinations. Once, when it was suggested Somerset's only hope was to play for a draw, he snorted: 'Draws, draws – they're only fit for bathing in.' He was secretary from 1894 to 1923 and captain from 1894 to 1906.

His successor as captain was the graceful bat, L.C.H. Palairet, and one of the county's best-known pros was Len Braund, an attractive stroke-maker, leg spinner and superb slip catcher. Unwanted by Surrey he played in twenty Tests against Australia and in three against South Africa.

Somerset's most famous bowler until the advent of the all-rounder Botham was White, who, over 28 summers, divided his hours between his farm at Combe Florey and the cricket field where he found 2,356 victims. His success was founded on flight and length and, if some eminent wicket-keepers who stood up to him are to be believed, he never consciously spun the ball in his career. His flight played a large part in England's victory in Australia in 1928–9, and when he returned jubilant supporters pulled his car with ropes all the way from Taunton station to his home. He was also accepted as a shrewd and wise tactical captian.

Tremlett, who suffered from a surfeit of praise early in his career through no fault of his own, was Somerset's first pro captain. Ken Palmer could hardly have been a more consistent bowler, and Stephenson carried the dual responsibility of wicket-keeper and captain for five years with much credit. Another top-ranking wicket-keeper was Taylor. In recent years batsman Roebuck and all-rounder Marks made splendid contributions. Marks' tight bowling in single-innings competitions was often a feature of Somerset's success.

After leading Yorkshire to 4 championships and the Gillette Cup in seven seasons, and serving England as captain, Brian Close accepted a new challenge at Somerset at the age of 40 in 1971, becoming captain in 1972, and in 1978 handed on to Brian Rose a strong side able to cope with the demands of the various competitions. To Somerset's satisfaction Close was recalled by England at the age of 45 – twenty-seven years after his first cap – to face the West Indies battery of speed.

In his second term Rose took Somerset to their first-ever success, a double in two days. The Gillette Cup was the first prize in 104 years with Richards scoring 117 and Garner taking 6 for 29. The Sunday League was won the next day.

The year of their double triumph, however, was marred by Somerset's expulsion from the Benson and Hedges Cup for the 'shame' (Wisden's word) of declaring at Worcester after one over with the score at one, a no-ball. The home side took 2 singles to win, and the farcical proceedings ended after 17 balls. Somerset already had 9 points in their Group against 6 by Glamorgan and Worcestershire. They also had the advantage of a faster wicket-taking rate than either of the other two teams, but, by declaring, Worcestershire were not given the chance to improve their wicket-taking rate.

Somerset were within the laws of the competition – hastily amended – but the Test and County Cricket Board were not prepared to allow its spirit to be so fragrantly breached and by a majority of 17 to 1 replaced Somerset with Glamorgan. Two years later Somerset won the same competition, Richards overwhelming Surrey with 132 not out, and retained the Cup by 9 wickets against Nottinghamshire.

In 1985 Somerset enhanced their reputation for the unexpected by finishing bottom of the championship, despite Botham's staggering average of 100 (5 centuries) and Richards' 76.50 (9 centuries) and 3,047 runs between them.

Botham resigned the captaincy that autumn, giving as his reason his many outside interests, and was replaced by Roebuck, and in late August 1986 the contracts of Richards and Garner, who had been at the core of Somerset's surge of success, were not renewed. There were cricketing reasons, as the West Indies were due to tour England the following summer but, despite protests, the committee survived a no-confidence vote at a Special General Meeting. Botham resigned and left for Worcestershire. A sad ending to Somerset's proudest years. [A.B.]

A commemorative plate of Viv Richards' 322 at Taunton

Founded 1875
Colours Black, white and maroon
Crest Wessex Wyvern
Secretary P. Anderson
Cricket Manager J. Birkenshaw
Senior coach P.J. Robinson
Groundsman P. Frost
Scorer D.A. Oldham

Address   The County Ground, St James's Street, Taunton TA1 1JT
Telephone: 0823 272946/253666/254287
Cricketcall   0898 121424

Achievements:

County Championship   Champions (0) 3rd 1892, 1958, 1963, 1966 and 1981
Gillette Cup   Winners 1979; finalists 1967 and 1978
National Westminster Bank Trophy   Winners 1983
Benson & Hedges Cup   Winners 1981 and 1982
John Player Sunday League   Champions (1) 1979
Refuge Assurance Sunday League   Champions (0) 4th 1987
Tilcon Trophy   Finalists 1976

Grounds:

Taunton (The County Ground, St James's Street)   Bath (Recreation Ground, William Street)   Weston-Super-Mare (Clarence Park, Walliscote Road).

   Other grounds that have been used since 1969 are: Bristol (Imperial Ground, West Town Lanes), Yeovil (Westland Sports Ground, Westbourne Close), (Johnson Park, Boundary Close), Glastonbury (Morlands Athletic Ground, Street Road), Torquay (Recreation Ground), Weston-Super-Mare (Devonshire Road Park Ground), Brislington (Ironmold Lane), Street (Millfield School) and Frome (Agricultural Showgrounds).

Taunton

The County Ground, St James's Street has been the headquarters of Somerset cricket since 1882, although admission to the county championship was not granted until 1891. The county club acquired the ground from the Taunton Athletic Company and secured a lease for the ground in 1885. The club has shown an interest in improving facilities at the ground by the River Tone ever since 1891 when a running track was built around the perimeter of the cricket pitch. The track was later used for greyhound racing. The Old Pavilion was erected together with the Ridley Stand which is situated under the shadow of St James's Church. The River Stand was built thanks to funds generated from the supporters' club. The ground is used by Taunton C C and the Somerset Stragglers who both have small separate pavilion facilities on the ground. The past decade has produced a major advance for the club as a result of the achievements in limited-overs competitions and money has been spent to build a new pavilion, executive boxes, a scoreboard which was presented by Saab U K in 1981 and a cricket museum. More recently the club has secured a number of barns on the Priory Bridge Road side of the ground. These will be redeveloped into stores, offices and refreshment areas.

The initial first-class match staged on the ground was in 1891. Lancashire were the visitors. Crowds of over 8,500 have been known for popular limited-overs matches in recent years. The ground record of 10,000 was established in 1948 when the Australians visited this the most westerly county ground on the county circuit.

Taunton will certainly be remembered as the stage where, in 1925, Jack Hobbs scored his 126th and 127th centuries to surpass Dr W.G. Grace's record. Grace completed his century of centuries on this ground too, in 1895, and went on to score 288 for the visitors. Two more recent innings will be remembered by spectators: Viv Richards (who took 322 off Warwickshire in 1985) and Graeme Hick the Worcestershire batsman (who scored 405 not out in 1988 and so nearly reached the record 424 scored by A.C. MacLaren of Lancashire in 1895).

Somerset play the majority of matches at Taunton, though two cricket weeks are spent at Bath and Weston-super-Mare. It was often said by local followers, 'If you can see the Quantock Hills it is going to rain and if you can't see them it is already raining.' However the new pavilion has its back to the hills and the members can no longer see them! The ground was used for international cricket in 1983 when the Prudential Cup match between England and Sri Lanka was staged.

ADDRESS County Cricket Ground, St James's Street, Taunton, Somerset TA1 1JT
TELEPHONE PROSPECTS OF PLAY 0823 70007

DESCRIPTION OF GROUND AND FACILITIES

The past ten years has seen so many improvements that the visiting spectator will find few familiar sights. Entry to the ground is gained from Priory Bridge Road as well as from the old entrance in St. James's Street, and access is still available through the car park and mower shed, off Coal Orchard in the south-west corner of the ground. There is no car parking available in the ground for the public. The main permanent building is now the new pavilion on the north side of the ground but all the former pavilion buildings on the south side of the ground remain and are still restricted to members. There are now, therefore, two separate members' areas on the ground. Seating for the public is available on the east and west sides of the ground as well as the covered stand to the north side. A large proportion of the 8,000 capacity can be accommodated on the permanent seating although there is space available for those that may wish to bring their own seats. There are ample facilities for refreshments and all other facilities are now much improved. The club shop is at the St. James's Street entrance and proposals are afoot to provide a museum for the club's collection, some of which can now be viewed in the pavilion. The playing area is approximately 127 metres by 140 metres and is an uneven oval shape. The shorter dimension is in the direction of the wicket so that a straight hit over the bowler's head will frequently fall in the River Tone barely 90 metres from the batsman.

GROUND RECORDS AND SCORES

FIRST-CLASS MATCHES
Highest innings total for County   592 v. Yorkshire, 1892
Highest innings total against County   801 by Lancashire, 1895
Lowest innings total for County   48 v. Yorkshire, 1954
Lowest innings total against County   37 by Gloucestershire, 1907
Highest individual innings for County   322 I.V.A. Richards v. Warwickshire, 1985
Highest individual innings against County   424 A.C. MacLaren for Lancashire, 1895
Best bowling performance in an innings for County   10 for 49 E.J. Tyler v. Surrey, 1895
Best bowling performance in an innings against County   10 for 42 A.E. Trott for Middlesex, 1900
Best bowling performance in a match for County   15 for 96 E.J. Tyler v. Nottinghamshire, 1892
Best bowling performance in a match against County   15 for 131 A.W. Mold for Lancashire, 1891

LIMITED-OVERS MATCHES
Highest innings total for County   307 for 6 v. Gloucestershire (BHC), 1982
Highest innings total against County   299 for 5 by Hampshire (NWBT), 1985
Lowest innings total for County   63 v. Yorkshire (GC), 1965
Lowest innings total against County   68 by Combined Universities (BHC), 1978
Highest individual innings for County   139 n.o. I.V.A. Richards v. Warwickshire (GC), 1978
Highest individual innings against County   154 n.o. M.J. Proctor for Gloucestershire (BHC), 1972
Best bowling performance for County   5 for 11 J. Garner v. Kent (GC), 1979
Best bowling performance against County   6 for 15 F.S. Trueman for Yorkshire (GC), 1965

HOW TO GET THERE

Rail   Taunton, ½ mile
Bus   From surrounding areas to Bus Station, thence 500m; also shuttle from town centre
Car   From north and east: M5 junction 25, then follow A358 from

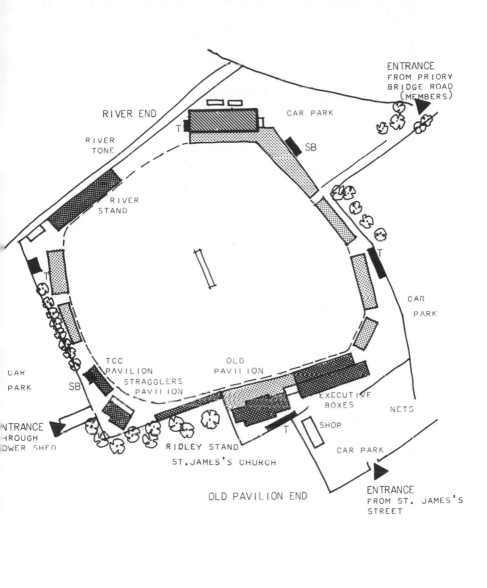

ENTRANCE
FROM PRIORY
BRIDGE ROAD
(MEMBERS)

RIVER END

CAR PARK

RIVER
TONE

T

SB

RIVER
STAND

T

CAR
PARK

T

CAR
PARK

TCC
PAVILION

OLD
PAVILION

STRAGGLERS
PAVILION

SB

EXECUTIVE
BOXES

NETS

ENTRANCE
THROUGH
LOWER SHED

T

SHOP

RIDLEY STAND

CAR PARK

ST. JAMES'S CHURCH

OLD PAVILION END

ENTRANCE
FROM ST. JAMES'S
STREET

N

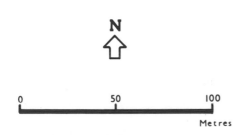

0   50   100

Metres

Creech Castle roundabout to town centre. At next roundabout take exit signposted County Ground. Ground situated close to main shopping street in St James's Street and Priory Bridge Road. From west: M5 junction 26 then follow A38 Taunton and town centre, then follow signs County Cricket for County Ground in St James's Street. From south: A358 or B3170 then as north.

WHERE TO STAY AND OTHER INFORMATION

Castle Hotel (0823 72671), County Hotel (0823 87651)

Disabled Areas In front of Old Pavilion
Local Radio Station(s) BBC Radio Bristol (95.5 MHz FM/1548 KHz MW), BBC Radio Devon (103.4 MHz FM/801 KHz MW)
Local Newspaper(s) Somerset County Gazette, West Somerset Free Press, Western Daily Press

Bath

The Recreation Ground is situated almost in the middle of the Roman city; it lies in the very bottom of the hollow in which Bath nestles, next to the River Avon and close to Bath Abbey. The ground is shared with the Bath Rugby Football Club who play in the national Courage Club League. The Bath Sports Centre, located at the North Parade Road end of the ground, once caused the players to be called from the field on a sunny day when the batsmen were blinded by rays of sunlight reflected from the glass roof. The ground can be approached by William Street from Great Pultney Street through a fine architectural turnstile or via the rugby entrance by the river. The pavilion is the only permanent feature on the ground. There are ample facilities for lawn tennis, croquet and bowls on the Pultney Street side. In 1977 when Somerset hosted the touring Australians at Bath, two silver birch trees were planted to the west of the pavilion by captains Brian Close and Greg Chappell (who himself played for Somerset in the early 1970s).

The first county match was staged in 1898 when Yorkshire were the visitors; a match with Sussex was staged in 1880 but was not of first-class status. The ground is maintained by the City of Bath Leisure Services Department.

During the winter, hockey and rugby are played but cricket provides the Recreation Ground's history. Two ground records stand out for Somerset here: the highest innings total ever for the County (against Hampshire in 1924) and the bowling performances by J.C. White in 1919 and 1932. Warwick Armstrong, the Australian captain, in 1905 scored his career best innings of 303 not out in an innings total of 609 for 4 declared. In recent years Mike Gatting of Middlesex has shown

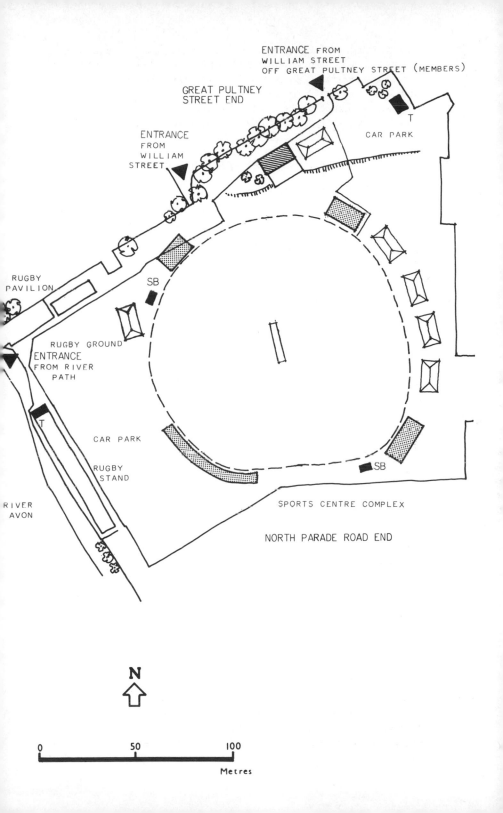

ENTRANCE FROM
WILLIAM STREET
OFF GREAT PULTNEY STREET (MEMBERS)

GREAT PULTNEY
STREET END

ENTRANCE
FROM
WILLIAM
STREET

CAR PARK

T

RUGBY
PAVILION

SB

RUGBY GROUND
ENTRANCE
FROM RIVER
PATH

T

CAR PARK

RUGBY
STAND

RIVER
AVON

SB

SPORTS CENTRE COMPLEX

NORTH PARADE ROAD END

N

0   50   100

Metres

a liking for the wicket at the Recreation Ground: in 1986 he made his career best score of 258 and then made a 196 on his next visit in 1987.

The Bath cricket festival always attracts good crowds (usually 5,000 plus each day) and attendances are boosted for limited-overs matches. The ground is not to be confused with Bath C C who play on the other side of North Parade Road or Lansdown C C who have used the ground but only play a limited number of games these days.

ADDRESS   Recreation Ground, William Street, off Great Pultney Street, Bath, Avon
TELEPHONE PROSPECTS OF PLAY   0225 25180

DESCRIPTION OF GROUND AND FACILITIES

The main access to the ground is from William Street although there is also an entrance through the rugby field side from Spring Gardens Road, adjoining the River Avon. The only permanent buildings are the small cricket pavilion close to the entrance from William Street and a block of toilets in the north-west corner of the ground. The rugby stands are some 70 metres from the playing area and provide little benefit other than as a shelter in bad weather. Car parking is available within the ground for members whilst the public must seek parking in the city centre car parks. All facilities are temporary and include a tiered seating stand for members and two tiered stands for the public at the southern end of the ground, adjoining the site screen. The members' area is to the north side of the ground and facilities are provided for disabled spectators. The ground capacity is 8,000 and seats are provided for approximately 80 per cent. Spectators may therefore need to bring their own seats to popular matches. The playing area is approximately 133 metres by 131 metres and has a near circular boundary defined by advertisement boards.

The ground is now somewhat overshadowed by the new sports centre to the south and has lost some of its charm, as an urban sports ground within sight of Bath Abbey and the buildings of the city centre. Being a local authority ground the cricket square is wedged between the hockey, football and rugby pitches, a part of each serving as the cricket out field in summer.

GROUND RECORDS AND SCORES

FIRST-CLASS MATCHES
Highest innings total for County   675 for 9 dec. v. Hampshire, 1924
Highest innings total against County   609 for 4 dec. by Australians, 1905
Lowest innings total for County   35 v. Yorkshire, 1898
Lowest innings total against County   37 by Derbyshire, 1919
Highest individual innings for County   198 A. Young v. Hampshire, 1924

Highest individual innings against County 303 n.o. W.W. Armstrong for Australians, 1905
Best bowling performance in an innings for County 9 for 51 J.C.White v. Glamorgan, 1932
Best bowling performance in an innings against County 9 for 77 H. Dean for Lancashire, 1910
Best bowling performance in a match for County 16 for 83 J.C. White v. Worcestershire, 1919
Best bowling performance in a match against County 16 for 80 D.V.P. Wright for Kent, 1939

LIMITED-OVERS MATCHES
Highest innings total for County 262 for 5 v. Lancashire (JPL), 1978
Highest innings total against County 241 for 7 for Nottinghamshire (JPL), 1986
Lowest innings total for County 61 v. Hampshire (JPL), 1973
Lowest innings total against County 72 by Nottinghamshire (JPL), 1982
Highest individual innings for County 131 D.B. Close v. Yorkshire (JPL), 1974
Highest individual innings against County 130 n.o. J.A. Hopkins for Glamorgan (JPL), 1983
Best bowling performance for County 5 for 27 J. Garner v. Yorkshire (JPL), 1985
Best bowling performance against County 5 for 44 E.E. Hemmings for Nottinghamshire (JPL), 1982

HOW TO GET THERE

Rail Bath Spa, ½ mile
Bus Badgerline 4, 18 link BR Station with ground (Tel: 0225 64446); also from surrounding areas to Bus Station, thence ½ mile
Car From north: M4 junction 18 then follow A46 signposted Bath, the ground is situated off Great Pulteney Street (A36) to the east of the city centre by the River Avon and adjoining the rugby club. From east: M4 junction 18, then as north or M4 junction 17 then A429 and A4 to Bath then as north. From west: A4, A431, A36 to Bath then as north. From south: A367 or A36 to Bath then as north.

WHERE TO STAY AND OTHER INFORMATION

Royal Crescent Hotel (0225 319090), Fernley Hotel (0225 61603), The Francis Hotel (0225 24257), The Bath Spa (opening '89)

Disabled Areas Seating area in front of members area. Car park on rugby field
Local Radio Station(s) BBC Radio Bristol (95.5 MHz FM/1548 KHz MW), Great Western Radio (96.3 MHz FM/1260 KHz MW)
Local Newspaper(s) Bath Chronicle, Evening Post and Echo

Weston-Super-Mare

Clarence Park is located very close to the coast of Somerset's popular family holiday resort. The County travel there during the holiday season in August, usually playing two championship and one Sunday League fixture. The park was given to the town in 1882 as a gift from Rebecca Davies the landowner in memory of her husband Henry. The pavilion, which is a single storey and painted white and green, dates from 1882 and is the only permanent building on the ground. The County made their first visit to Clarence Park in 1914 when the consideration of facilities failed to include the pitch – Yorkshire won by 140 runs and Essex by 10 wickets. The third match, with Northamptonshire, was cancelled due to the outbreak of World War One and not until 1922 did county cricket return to Clarence Park. The County have made annual visits ever since. The County played several limited-overs matches at Devonshire Park Road, home of Weston-super-Mare C C during the early 1970s.

Clarence Park is a public park and is only used for the Somerset festival cricket weeks; no other matches are played on the square. If you visit the ground when the festival is not in full swing, you will find the square fenced off, to protect it from ballgames or holidaymakers in the summer months and from hockey pitches flanking it on two sides in the winter months. Weston Hockey Club use the ground and pavilion facilities for matches. The pitch is prepared by the county groundsman from Taunton and the park grounds are maintained by Woodspring District Council.

The ground has had its fair share of records including the County's ninth and tenth wicket record partnerships. Individual record performances are plentiful: M.M. Walford's 264 was the highest innings on the ground. In recent years Ian Botham's 134 against Northamptonshire in 1985 included ten sixes. Clarence Park was where Viv Marks scored his maiden century. Batting records cannot be concluded without mention of A. Hyman, playing for a scratch team against Thornbury C C in 1902 (Graces included) who scored 359, of which 192 came in sixes off the bowling of 62-year-old E.M. Grace. No doubt holidaymakers enjoy watching cricket at Weston each annual holiday in the hope of seeing a repetition of that innings! Bowling records don't come much greater than that of visitor to the ground Alonzo Drake, of Yorkshire and Sheffield United F C, who took all ten Somerset wickets for 35 in the first festival visit. On a sad note, however, this was the ground where Viv Richards jumped over an advertising hoarding, prompted by racial abuse from the visiting crowd.

ADDRESS Clarence Park East, Walliscote Road, Weston-super-Mare, Somerset
TELEPHONE PROSPECTS OF PLAY temporary line installed each year. Refer to B T Directory Enquiries

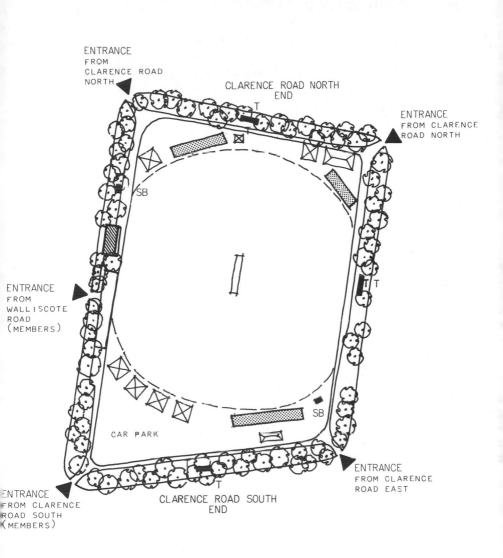

ENTRANCE
FROM
CLARENCE ROAD
NORTH

CLARENCE ROAD NORTH
END

ENTRANCE
FROM CLARENCE
ROAD NORTH

T

SB

ENTRANCE
FROM
WALLISCOTE
ROAD
(MEMBERS)

T

SB

CAR PARK

ENTRANCE
FROM CLARENCE
ROAD SOUTH
(MEMBERS)

CLARENCE ROAD SOUTH
END

T

ENTRANCE
FROM CLARENCE
ROAD EAST

N

0   50   100

Metres

DESCRIPTION OF GROUND AND FACILITIES

This is a public park and entry is gained from each corner of the rectangular space. The only permanent buildings are the pavilion on the west side, which is used by players and officials, and a block of toilets on each of the other sides of the ground. All other facilities are temporary. Car parking is only available for sponsors and disabled persons. Seating areas are allocated to members on the west and north sides of the ground while temporary seating for the public is provided on the other two sides. Areas are allocated for disabled persons in both the members' and public areas. Refreshment facilities are numerous and may vary from year to year as one would expect from a seaside resort! The capacity is 6,000 persons of which 80 per cent can be accommodated on seats provided. The county also brings a temporary souvenir shop to the ground. The playing area is approximately 118 metres by 134 metres and therefore has relatively short, square boundaries.

This ground provides what must be a good representation of the atmosphere of a match held in the early years of the century.

GROUND RECORDS AND SCORES

FIRST-CLASS MATCHES

Highest innings total for County   507 for 6 dec. v. Surrey, 1946
Highest innings total against County   514 by Middlesex, 1937
Lowest innings total for County   36 v. Surrey, 1965
Lowest innings total against County   47 by Sussex, 1936
Highest individual innings for County   264 M.M. Walford v. Hampshire, 1947
Highest individual innings against County   222 n.o. Nawab of Pataudi (sen) for Worcestershire, 1933
Best bowling performance in an innings for County   9 for 26 B.A. Langford v. Lancashire, 1958
Best bowling performance in an innings against County   10 for 35 A. Drake for Yorkshire, 1914
Best bowling performance in a match for County   15 for 54 B.A. Langford v. Lancashire, 1958
Best bowling performance in a match against County   16 for 88 J.A. Newman for Hampshire, 1927

LIMITED-OVERS MATCHES

Highest innings total for County   197 v. Middlesex (JPL), 1982
Highest innings total against County   288 for 5 by Hampshire (JPL), 1975
Lowest innings total for County   109 v. Lancashire (JPL), 1976
Lowest innings total against County   99 by Surrey (JPL), 1984
Highest individual innings for County   80 V.J. Marks v. Derbyshire (RAL), 1988
Highest individual innings against County   102 C.G. Greenidge for Hampshire (JPL), 1975

Best bowling performance for County   4 for 11 V.J. Marks *v.* Surrey (JPL), 1984
Best bowling performance against County   4 for 22 B.J. Griffiths for Northamptonshire (JPL), 1977

HOW TO GET THERE

Rail   Weston-Super-Mare, ½ mile
Bus   Badgerline 5 links BR Station with ground (Tel: 0934 621201); also from surrounding areas to town centre, thence ½ mile
Car   From north: M5 junction 21 then follow A370 signposted Weston-Super-Mare and seafront, ground situated at Clarence Park East in Walliscote Road signposted from seafront. From east: A370 or A368 signposted Weston-Super-Mare then as north. From south: M5 junction 22 then A370 to Weston-Super-Mare, then as north.

WHERE TO STAY AND OTHER INFORMATION

Berni Royal Hotel (0934 23601), Albert Hotel (0934 21363), and many guest houses

Disabled Areas   Special enclosure in south-west corner of ground
Local Radio Station(s)   BBC Radio Bristol (95.5 MHz FM/1548 KHz MW), Great Western Radio (96.3 MHz FM/1260 KHz MW)
Local Newspaper(s)   Weston Mercury, Weston Daily Press

SURREY

LONDON – FOSTER'S OVAL

GUILDFORD

Surrey

If the convivial meeting at 'The Horns' tavern, Kennington, in October 1845 had been granted the power to see the outcome of their decision to provide Surrey cricket with a 'local habitation and a name' there would have been both awe and satisfaction. The sight of a packed house at The Oval on a great occasion, a Jack Hobbs–Tom Hayward first-wicket stand, Peter May in full attacking flight, a bowling burst from Tom Richardson, overs from Alec Bedser, Jim Laker and co and the fielding during those incredible seven championship seasons, would have exceeded all expectations.

No county can boast a longer or richer history – mention of the game at Guildford goes back to 1550 – and The Oval, once a 10-acre market garden, has an honoured place ever since it staged the first home Test against Australia in 1880.

The first county fixture was on 25 and 26 June 1846, when Kent were defeated, and the vision of Harrovian Charles Alcock, the county's first paid secretary, put the ground firmly on the sporting map. Not only did he have the initiative to arrange the first Test match in England, but in his joint role as secretary of the Football Association, he dreamed up the FA Challenge Cup. Its first final, and the first home soccer internationals with Scotland and Wales, were played at The Oval, and, for good measure, the first rugby internationals against Scotland and Ireland. Packer had nothing on Alcock.

A century on and it was imperative to embark on big-scale developments on the west side, and to undertake general improvements. After much negotiation and disappointment involving even government departments, Elders IXL, the brewery group, in the name of their Foster's brand lager, offered and agreed a sponsorship package by which the famous old ground became 'The Foster's Oval' for the 15-year duration of the sponsorship from October 1988. This sponsorship, together with donations raised through the Ken Barrington Appeal and Save The Oval Appeal, will enable the south-west corner of the ground to be redeveloped. This will include a sports centre/indoor cricket school, new changing rooms, press box, bars, executive boxes and groundstaff headquarters as well as some 1,700 terraced seats for members and public. The only alternative to sponsorship would have been the unthinkable loss of The Oval as a Test centre, or, at worst, the ground itself. It remains, of course, part of the lands of the Duchy of Cornwall. Edward, then Prince of Wales, jokingly made that plain when he saw a note pinned to the door of the Australian dressing room in 1930 forbidding entry without the manager's permission. 'You can't keep me out,' was his response. 'I'm your landlord!'

Surrey have often been the pacemakers. H.H. Stephenson captained the first side to Australia, and in the late 'eighties and 'nineties they were seldom off the top. Shuter was one of many outstanding captains of Surrey – general agreement is that Percy Fender was the finest of

SURREY COUNTY C.C.

all and a length in front of Jardine – and was the first to declare an innings closed.

The roll of honour of distinguished players and their deeds for England and Surrey could fill a fat volume, but the pride of place belongs to John Berry Hobbs, the first professional cricketer to be knighted. 'The Master' enobled the art of batting, conquered all forms of newly-invented bowling from swing to the googly, and left a string of records which could stand for all time. He scored 197 centuries, 98 coming after the age of 40, and 61,760 runs, and as a natural No. 1, shared in 166 first-wicket stands of 100 or more, including 66 with Andy Sandham and 40 with Hayward. Twenty-eight of the stands passed 200, and in one week he shared opening partnerships of 428, 182, 106 and 123 before a wicket fell.

In 61 Tests he had 15 centuries, 12 of which were against Australia, and 23 opening stands of 100 or more, 15 with Herbert Sutcliffe, 8 with Wilfred Rhodes. At Melbourne in 1911–12 Hobbs and Rhodes realized 323. In the words of Fender, Hobbs was simply the best in all conditions of all time; indeed he made runs on old-style Australian gluepots and had to an astonishing degree, that quality which separates the great from the very good, of being able to score off the good ball.

Hobbs came from Cambridge where his idol Tom Hayward lived. Hayward was the first to follow Grace with 100 centuries, and was one of the elite scoring 1,000 runs in twenty seasons – before the end of May in 1900 – and totalled 3,170 in 1904 and 3,518 two years later. A classical batsman he came from a family of cricketing perfectionists, who played for Surrey XIs. The young Hobbs could have had no better mentor, and no better tribute can be imagined than to say he was even better than Hayward.

Only Surrey can boast of four batsmen with over 100 centuries. After Hobbs, comes Sandham with 107, Hayward 104 and John Edrich 103. To find Edrich, the efficient left hander in such company is perhaps surprising, but he had all the merits and determination of his Norfolk clan and was effective for both Surrey and England. No doubt May, the one genuinely great batsman of England since 1946, and Barrington, a high-ranker with 20 Test centuries and an average of almost 60 from 76 hundreds would have joined the elite club if they had played longer. May's dual responsibilities as leading batsman and captain in 41 Tests eventually took its toll, and Barrington, without an enemy in the world, suffered a second and fatal heart attack while serving as assistant manager to England at Barbados in 1981.

Way back in the 'eighties The Oval took little Bobby ('The Gov'nor') Abel to its heart – no-one has overtaken his 357 not out in 1899 – and Tom Richardson, who used to walk to his home at Mitcham carrying his bag after a day's fast bowling, was one of the game's greatest fast bowlers. Herbert Strudwick, the famed wicket-keeper, recommended to The Oval by a Sunday School mistress, always said Richardson never wittingly bowled a short pitcher in his life. The Richardson–Lockwood partnership was much feared, and George Lohmann and Tom Crawford, who quarelled with the club and went to Australia, were outstanding.

For all Fender's ingenuity Surrey, handicapped by the quality of home pitches and sometimes by the inability to take the catches off the potent fast bowling of Alf Gover, could not manage a championship between the wars. The first tangible success after the 1914 victory was to share the title in 1950, but it was then very clear that Surrey were on the brink of high achievement. Before he started his captaincy in 1952 Stuart Surridge wrote in his diary: 'Surrey will be champions for the next five years.' How right he proved to be.

Surridge was born within two miles of The Oval, and one important reason for Surrey's success was that he had grown up with many of his team; the Bedser twins, McIntyre, a superb wicket-keeper, Constable and the hitter Whittaker. His attack of Alec Bedser, an all-time great, Loader, and the spinners Laker and Lock was virtually England's, and as a back-up all-rounder Eric Bedser was close to that class as an off spinner. The fielding was dramatic, and Surrey played with such fire and purpose that they expected to take a wicket with every ball. Some of Surridge's declarations were so audacious that they seemed to be acts of folly, but they invariably came off, and the psychological pressure alone was often too much for the opposition.

Surrey raced to championships with bowlers who stood out at Test level, let alone at county. Laker was arguably the best off spinner of all time with 19 wickets against Australia at Old Trafford, a record never likely to be beaten. When Surridge retired in triumph May extended the run to seven championships and in 1971 Micky Stewart, later England's team manager, completed Surrey's 18th outright success. [A.B.]

Founded 1845
Colours Chocolate and silver
Crest Prince of Wales' Feathers
Secretary D.G. Seward
Coach G.G. Arnold/C.E. Walker
Groundsman H. Brind
Scorer T. Billson
Address The Foster's Oval, Kennington, London SE11 5SS
Telephone 01-582 6660
Cricketcall 0898 121433

Achievements:

County Championship Champions (18) 1864, 1887, 1888, 1890, 1891, 1892, 1894, 1895, 1899, 1914, 1952, 1953, 1954, 1955, 1956, 1957, 1958 and 1971; Joint Champions (2) 1889 and 1950
Gillette Cup Finalists 1965 and 1980
National Westminster Bank Trophy Winners 1982
Benson & Hedges Cup Winners 1974; finalists 1979 and 1981
John Player Sunday League Champions (0) 5th 1969 and 1980
Refuge Assurance Sunday League Champions (0) 5th 1988
Tilcon Trophy Finalists 1978

Grounds:

London (The Foster's Oval, Kennington) Guildford (Woodbridge Road, Guildford).
   Other grounds that have been used since 1969 are: Byfleet (BAC Ground, Byfleet), Sunbury-on-Thames (Kenton Court Meadow, Lower Hampton Road), Leatherhead (St John's School), Sutton (Cheam Road), Godalming (Charterhouse School), Tolworth (Decca Sports Ground), East Molesey (Metropolitan Police Sports Ground, Imber Court), Croydon (Old Whitgiftians) and Banstead (Avenue Road).

The Foster's Oval

The formation of Surrey C C C was precipitated by the removal of the Montpelier Club, one of the strongest clubs in South London, from their ground at Walworth. The Walworth ground was bought in 1844 and left the club without a ground, but a member, Mr William Baker, came to the club's assistance. He suggested that Kennington Oval, a market garden and the property of the Duchy of Cornwall, might be used for cricket. The Duchy was willing to let it for the purpose of a cricket ground and a lease of thirty-one years was granted at one hundred and twenty pounds per year, with taxes which amounted to a further twenty pounds. At the time of its conversion to a cricket ground, Kennington Oval was mainly an open space with a small hedge surrounding it, and it takes its name from the surrounding streets rather than the shape of the playing area itself. The original turf came from Tooting Common and was laid in March 1845 by Mr M. Turtle of Clapham Road for three hundred pounds.

The first match on the ground is recorded as having been played on 13 May 1845 between Mr Fould's XI and Mr Houghton's XI. The first Surrey match was on 21 and 22 August 1845 between the Gentlemen of Surrey and the Players of Surrey. Following the meeting of the Montpelier Club on 22 August at the Horns Tavern, Kennington, more than a hundred members of different clubs in the county proposed the formation of a club for the County of Surrey. The resolution was carried amidst cheering and the formal inauguration took place at the Horns Tavern on 18 October 1845. The first Surrey C C C match was staged with neighbours Kent in 1846, while the first County Championship match was in 1873 against Sussex and the first Test Match with Australia in 1880.

During the first Test Match Dr W.G. Grace scored 152 for England and W.L. Murdoch replied for Australia with 153 not out. The ground was used for association football in the 19th century and was the venue for the FA Cup Final in 1872 and again between 1874 and 1892. The pavilion was built in 1896 and was designed by the architect Mr A. Muirhead who was also responsible for the Old Trafford pavilion. Although much altered in subsequent years it still retains much of its original character. The Mound Stand, along with a number of fine executive boxes, was rebuilt during the 1980s. The nets and the West Stand were demolished after the 1988 season to make way for the new West development. This includes the Ken Barrington Cricket Centre, which has been financed by the 'Save the Oval Fund' with assistance from Foster's Australian brewery. The ground is now known as the Foster's Oval and, as well as cricket during the summer months, a highlight of the autumn sporting calendar in recent years has been Australian Rules football, which has been staged between the two top Australian sides for the Foster's Challenge Cup. Other tournaments staged at the Oval have included an International Batsman of the Year competition in 1979.

There are many famous paintings and items of cricket interest in the various parts of the pavilion as well as in the library. The world-famous Hobbs Gates form the main entrance to the ground, at the rear of the pavilion. Like most Test Match grounds the facilities for members are good and, except for the Peter May Enclosure and the West Terrace, other parts of the ground are covered. A new press box and executive boxes were constructed in 1988 at the Vauxhall End. A large T V screen was installed high above the Vauxhall Stand to view action replays of the cricket, like those at some Australian grounds, but this remained only for part of one season in 1983.

One of the main cricket records at the Oval is of course Len

Hutton's 364 against Australia in 1938. Well remembered also is the occasion in 1948 when Don Bradman was bowled for a duck on his last appearance in Test cricket by Eric Hollies of Warwickshire, so finishing with a Test Match average of 99.94. Surrey records have included their highest total of 811 against Somerset in 1899 which included 357 not out from Bobby Abel. The ground has staged matches in all the major competitions for Surrey and England as well as other international matches (not including England), for matches in the Prudential Cup were staged in 1975, 1979 and 1983. Middlesex have even staged home matches at the Oval when unable to use Lord's. Crowds at the Oval are restricted to the present ground capacity of 15,205 but the largest attendance over three days was 80,000 for the visit of Yorkshire in 1906.

ADDRESS   The Foster's Oval, Kennington, London SE11 5SS
TELEPHONE PROSPECTS OF PLAY   01-582 6660

DESCRIPTION OF GROUND AND FACILITIES

The main entrances are in Kennington Oval with additional public entrances in Harleyford Road. All buildings on the ground are permanent and work is currently in progress on the new west development (which replaces the nets and the west stand) and should be completed for the 1990 season. This development will include a sports complex (The Ken Barrington Cricket Centre).

The centre piece is the pavilion, little changed since it was built and still a credit to the ground that first provided a venue for Test Cricket in England. All members' accommodation and facilities are in the buildings which span the south-east side of the ground: the Taverners Stand, the pavilion and the future west development (yet to be named). All the remaining areas are available to the public with the exception of the new executives boxes and new press box recently erected at the rear of part of the Vauxhall Stands. The only covered area available to the public is the centre Vauxhall Stand. Refreshments are available in several parts of the ground including the bar at the rear of the Tavern as well as the Banqueting Suite and the Tavern itself. An excellent souvenir and book shop is also available at the rear of the pavilion. The playing area is very large extending to 170 metres by 150 metres, within which the actual playing area is defined by a rope stretched to the appropriate dimensions depending on the position of the playing strip being used, but usually about 137 metres by 140 metres.

There is only a limited amount of car parking in the ground for members and only at certain times. Car owners must seek to park in neighbouring streets, where permitted. There are facilities for disabled persons both in the pavilion and in the public areas. The current ground capacity is 15,200 (probably to be amended on completion of the west development) and all can be accommodated on modern plastic seating.

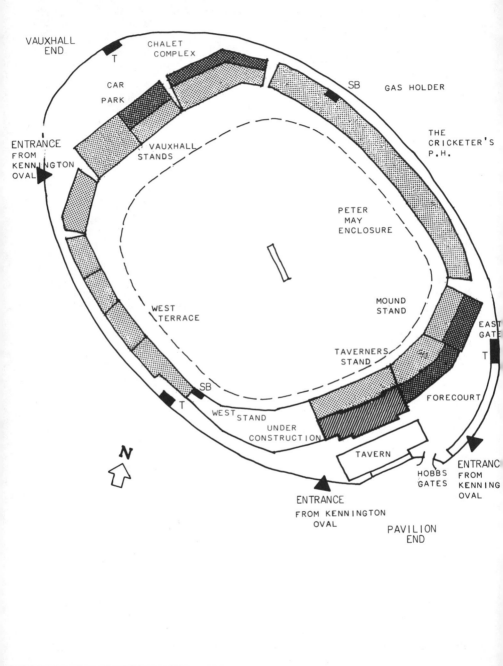

VAUXHALL
END

CHALET
COMPLEX

CAR
PARK

T

SB

GAS HOLDER

THE
CRICKETER'S
P.H.

ENTRANCE
FROM
KENNINGTON
OVAL

VAUXHALL
STANDS

PETER
MAY
ENCLOSURE

WEST
TERRACE

MOUND
STAND

EAST
GATE

T

TAVERNERS
STAND

FORECOURT

SB

T

WEST STAND

UNDER
CONSTRUCTION

TAVERN

HOBBS
GATES

ENTRANCE
FROM
KENNING
OVAL

N

ENTRANCE
FROM KENNINGTON
OVAL

PAVILION
END

0   50   100

Metres

This is very much an urban situation overshadowed as it has been for so many years by the gas holders and blocks of flats, but still retaining, from the upper part of the pavilion, a view of the tower of the Palace of Westminster.

GROUND RECORDS AND SCORES

TEST MATCHES

Highest innings total for England   903 for 7 dec. v. Australia, 1938
Highest innings total against England   708 by Pakistan, 1987
Lowest innings total for England   52 v. Australia, 1948
Lowest innings total against England   44 by Australia, 1896
Highest individual innings for England   364 L. Hutton v. Australia, 1938
Highest individual innings against England   291 I.V.A. Richards for West Indies, 1976
Best bowling performance in an innings for England   8 for 29 S.F. Barnes v. South Africa, 1912
Best bowling performance in an innings against England   8 for 65 A. Trumble for Australia, 1902
Best bowling performance in a match for England   13 for 57 S.F. Barnes v. South Africa, 1912
Best bowling performance in a match against England   14 for 90 F.R. Spofforth for Australia, 1882

LIMITED-OVERS INTERNATIONALS

Highest innings total   328 for 5 by Australia v. Sri Lanka (PC), 1975
Lowest innings total   154 by Pakistan v. England (PT), 1978
Highest individual innings   125 n.o. G.S. Chappell for Australia v. England (PT), 1977
Best bowling performance   5 for 31 M. Hendrick for England v. Australia (PT), 1980

FIRST-CLASS MATCHES

Highest innings total for County   811 v. Somerset, 1899
Highest innings total against County   704 by Yorkshire, 1899
Lowest innings total for County   16 v. Nottinghamshire, 1880
Lowest innings total against County   20 by Kent, 1870 (1 man absent)
Highest individual innings for County   357 n.o. R. Abel v. Somerset, 1899
Highest individual innings against County   300 R. Subba-Row for Northamptonshire, 1958
Best bowling performance in an innings for County   10 for 45 T. Richardson v. Essex, 1894
Best bowling performance in an innings against County   10 for 28 W.P. Howell for Australians, 1899
Best bowling performance in a match for County   15 for 83 T. Richardson v. Warwickshire, 1898

Best bowling performance in a match against County   15 for 57
W.P. Howell for Australians, 1899

LIMITED-OVERS MATCHES
Highest innings total for County   304 for 6 v. Warwickshire (JPL),
1985
Highest innings total against County   300 for 9 by Warwickshire
(JPL), 1985
Lowest innings total for County   86 v. Gloucestershire (JPL), 1969
Lowest innings total against County   65 by Glamorgan (JPL), 1969
Highest individual innings for County   129 M.A. Lynch v.
Durham (NWBT), 1982
Highest individual innings against County   123 n.o. R.T. Virgin for
Somerset (JPL), 1970
Best bowling performance for County   6 for 25 Intikhab Alam v.
Derbyshire (JPL), 1974
Best bowling performance against County   7 for 15 A.L. Dixon for
Kent (GC), 1967

HOW TO GET THERE

Rail   Oval Underground (Northern Line) 200m; Vauxhall; BR and
Underground (Victoria Line), 600m
Bus   LRT 3, 36, 36A, 36B, 59, 95, 109, 133, 155/9, 185, 196 (Tel:
01-222 1234)
Car   From north: From Edgware Road A5 follow signs Marble
Arch, then take A202 Park Lane to Grosvenor Place, then follow
signs Vauxhall Bridge using Vauxhall Bridge Road, after passing
over the Thames go under the railway bridge and turn right down
Harleyford Road for Kennington and The Foster's Oval. The ground
is located south of the Thames at Kennington close to the A3, A23
and A202 trunk roads from Central London. From east: Follow
A202 to Kennington district, take Harleyford Road and follow signs
for The Oval and County Cricket. From west: M4/M3 or A23, A24
follow signs Central London, then signs Kennington, or as north.
From south: From M25 junctions 6, 7, 8 or 9 then on A22, A23,
A24 or A243 signposted London, then follow signs Kennington for
The Foster's Oval.

WHERE TO STAY AND OTHER INFORMATION

London Park Hotel, London SE1 (01-735 9191), or any London hotel

No parking at the ground. Street parking in surrounding area or NCP
Disabled Areas   Pavilion area if member, or two special areas for public
Local Radio Station(s)   Greater London Radio (94.9 MHz FM/1458
KHz MW), Capital Radio (95.8 MHz FM/1548 KHz MW), LBC (97.3
MHz FM/1152 KHz MW)
Local Newspaper(s)   The Evening Standard, South London Press,
Surrey Advertiser

Guildford

The earliest known reference to the playing of cricket, within the borders of Surrey is in a document of 1598 relating to a dispute over a plot of land at Guildford. The document speaks of a John Derrick a scholar in the Free School of Guildford and states that 'he and several of his fellows did run and play there at cricket'. The Guildford C C was founded in 1862 by two brothers W. and J. Stevens in 1866 and the first mention of cricket at Guildford was in the *James Lillywhite Cricket Annual of 1873.* J. Stevens scored 191 in 1874. At that time the ground was located on the cattle market which is now close to the law courts and car parks at the rear of the Guildford Sports Centre. Two famous players scored heavily in club matches here – C.T. Studd made 222 not out for Horsham against Guildford in 1881 and in the same year W.W. Read scored 263 for Reigate Priory.

The present Woodbridge Road Ground was given to the town by Sir Harry Waechter-Bart in 1911 for cricket, cycling, military parades and charitable purposes. Guildford C C disbanded between 1914 and 1922, though after 1918 the club's players played under the name Guildford Wanderers. In May 1922 players donned the club colours of claret, pink and black again when Guildford played its first home match since 1914, against Woking. The famous amateur football club the Guildford Pinks had the same colours and shared the Woodbridge Road sports ground until their demise in the early 1950s.

Covering some 8 acres the ground is lush and green with trees around most of the perimeter. The busy Woodbridge Road runs along the east side of the tree-lined area. At the far end from the pavilion brief glimpses of the trains can be seen through the poplars and beeches. The only permanent buildings on the ground are the pavilion, the scoreboard (which was built along the lines of the original famous Sydney version in Australia) and the groundsman's stores. Woodbridge Road is reputed to be one of the few level playing areas in the city.

The first visit to Guildford by Surrey was in 1938 when Hampshire were the visitors; the first two days attracted a total of 10,000 spectators. Except for occasional breaks, since the inaugural match 50 years ago the ground has been regularly used for championship cricket and in recent years limited-overs matches. In 1988 the Guildford club celebrated a jubilee of county cricket at the county town. Other matches staged have included a one-day match between the Club Cricket Conference and the touring South Africans in 1947 when a total of 715 runs were scored in a single day's play by the two sides. In 1957 the Queen and the Duke of Edinburgh attended a match with Hampshire and met both sides.

Guildford C C play in the Surrey Championship sponsored by Eve Construction. The current president is David Frith (the editor of *Wisden Cricket Monthly*), who is ably supported by Charles Woodhouse, the chairman.

Crowds at Guildford are usually around 4,500–5,000; the best for a single day was 7,000 against Hampshire in 1938. Ground records include a 200 not out from Gordon Greenidge and fine bowling performances by Tony Lock and Derek Shackleton. In limited-overs matches Allan Lamb hit the highest score (132 not out) for Northamptonshire in 1985.

The majority of matches on the ground have been staged with Hampshire or Sussex, the two neighbouring counties. In recent years rather than four days' cricket over a weekend, the Guildford festival has been extended to six days, starting on a Wednesday.

ADDRESS   Guildford C C, Woodbridge Road, Guildford, Surrey
TELEPHONE PROSPECTS OF PLAY   0483 572181

DESCRIPTION OF GROUND AND FACILITIES

Entry to the ground is from Woodbridge Road with the members' entrance at the junction of Wharf Road. Car parking is available to the north of the cricket field towards the railway embankment. The only permament buildings are the two storey cricket pavilion and some terrace seating on either side of it. This area of the ground is restricted to members. The scoreboard is in the north-west corner of the cricket field. All seating is temporary and the northern side of the ground is allocated to sponsors' tents and refreshment tents for the public. Members' refreshments are provided in the pavilion and in an adjoining tent. Provision is made for disabled spectators and a toilet is provided at the rear of the pavilion. Temporary toilets are provided although there are permanent toilets to the north of the car park area near the railway bridge. The capacity of the ground is 7,000 and seats for over half of that number are provided. However, it is appropriate to bring your own seats to popular matches. The playing area is approximately 113 metres by 119 metres.

A pleasant ground with ample tree planting on three sides.

GROUND RECORDS AND SCORES

FIRST-CLASS MATCHES
Highest innings total for County   504 v. Hampshire, 1948
Highest innings total against County   446 for 7 by Worcestershire, 1979
Lowest innings total for County   77 v. Derbyshire, 1939
Lowest innings total against County   48 by Hampshire, 1946
Highest individual innings for County   172 H.T. Barling v. Hampshire, 1946
Highest individual innings against County   200 n.o. C.G. Greenidge for Hampshire, 1977
Best bowling performance in an innings for County   9 for 77 G.A.R. Lock v. Oxford University, 1960
Best bowling performance in an innings against County   7 for 34 D. Shackleton for Hampshire, 1958

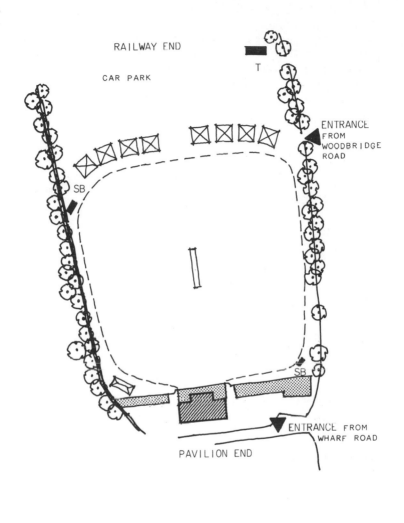

RAILWAY END

CAR PARK

T

ENTRANCE
FROM
WOODBRIDGE
ROAD

SB

SB

ENTRANCE FROM
WHARF ROAD

PAVILION END

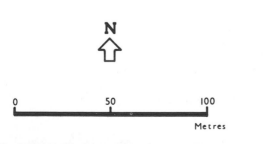

N

0   50   100

Metres

Best bowling performance in a match for County   12 for 148
G.A.R. Lock v. Oxford University, 1960
Best bowling performance in a match against County   9 for 125
A.C.S. Pigott for Sussex, 1987

LIMITED-OVERS MATCHES
Highest innings total for County   270 for 6 v. Worcestershire (JPL),
1983
Highest innings total against County   306 for 2 by
Northamptonshire (JPL), 1985
Lowest innings total for County   89 v. Gloucestershire (JPL), 1978
Lowest innings total against County   133 by Gloucestershire (JPL),
1980
Highest individual innings for County   87 R.D.V. Knight v.
Worcestershire (JPL), 1983
Highest individual innings against County   132 n.o. A.J. Lamb for
Northamptonshire (JPL), 1985
Best bowling performance for County   4 for 31 I.R. Payne v.
Northamptonshire (JPL), 1977
Best bowling performance against County   5 for 28 A.C.S. Pigott
for Sussex (JPL), 1982

HOW TO GET THERE

Rail   Guildford or London Road, both ¾ mile
Bus   Greenline buses from surrounding areas to Bus Station,
thence ½ mile
Car   From north: A320 follow signs Guildford and town centre,
ground situated north of town centre off (A320) Woodbridge Road.
From east: M25 junction 10, then follow A3 signposted Guildford
and town centre, then as north, or A25 signposted Guildford, then
as north. From south: A281 or A3100 follow signs Guildford and
town centre, then take A320 for Woodbridge Road, north of town
centre. From west: A3 or A31 follow signs Guildford and town
centre, then as north.

WHERE TO STAY AND OTHER INFORMATION

Angel Hotel (0483 64555), White Horse Hotel (0483 64511)

Disabled Areas   No special area, request position
Local Radio Station(s)   County Sound (96.4 MHz FM/1476 KHz
MW), Radio 210 (102.9 MHz FM/1431 KHz MW)
Local Newspaper(s)   Surrey Advertiser, Surrey Times

SUSSEX

HOVE

EASTBOURNE

HASTINGS

HORSHAM

Sussex

In 1903, a year after playing full back for Southampton in an FA Cup final and scoring 82 on the following Monday against Surrey, C.B. Fry touted his idea of a cricket knock-out competition. Believing the counties needed a new impetus and would benefit financially from pooled gate receipts he wrote to W.G. Grace, m'Lords Hawke and Harris among others. All agreed in principle, but when it came to the crunch the traditionalists prevailed.

Fry would have been well gratified if sixty years on he had seen not only the adoption of his plan – and broadly for the same reasons – but his own county of Sussex take the Gillette Cup in the first two years of its inception, and led by another Corinthian spirit, Ted Dexter.

Sussex also won the competition in 1978 and 1986, and were beaten finalists on three other occasions, but seven Lord's finals in twenty-three years, and the Sunday League in 1982 by a record margin, is something to shout about. In contrast, though belonging to the original nine counties in 1873, Sussex have failed to land the championship. There have been seven near-misses in 2nd place, including three in succession from 1932 to 1934 under Kumar Shri Duleepsinhji, nephew of the batting magician Ranji, hard-hitting Robert Scott and Alan Melville, who later captained South Africa in England.

At the turn of the century Ranjitsinhji, HH the Maharajah Jam Sahib of Nawanagar, finished runner-up in successive seaons, but powerful as he was in batting he did not have the balance enjoyed in the other two near-misses by David Sheppard, who became the Anglican Bishop of Liverpool and the first priest to play in Test cricket, and the Etonian John Barclay.

As a general rule Sussex captains have shared the common problem of batting outshining bowling, but it is an oddity that the championship has proved so elusive for, since the foundation in 1839 – making Sussex the oldest first-class club – no county can assemble a gallery of such notable captains. Going back to C. Aubrey Smith, who tramped the New York streets flat broke in his sixties, and went on to earn £17,000 a year in Hollywood and a knighthood, Sussex can boast of a team of Test captains.

W.L. Murdoch, Australia's captain in the original Test at The Oval and later an England wicket-keeper in South Africa, preceded Ranji and Fry, and there has been the ever-popular A.E.R. Gilligan and his brother A.H.H., Duleep (dubbed Smith at Cambridge), Melville, Sheppard, the Nawab of Pataudi, a second generation captain of India, Dexter and Greig, whose association with Packer cost him the England captaincy. For all that he was an outstanding leader and all-rounder. S.C. Griffith, an accomplished wicket-keeper, is the only England player to have scored his maiden first-class century in his first Test in 1947–8 at Port of Spain – some years before he became secretary of MCC.

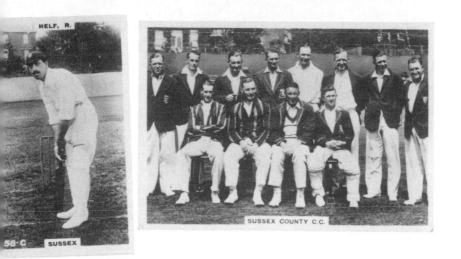

RELF, R.

58-C SUSSEX

SUSSEX COUNTY C.C.

Imran Khan divided his brilliant all-round talents between captaining Pakistan and lifting Sussex. His pretensions to the crown worn by the top world all-rounder were genuine.

Sussex were awash with runs with Ranji and Fry, two of the jewels of the Golden Age of amateur batting. As the Australians said of Ranji after his first innings against them: 'He's no cricketer. He's a conjurer, an Eastern juggler.' Ranji's natural gifts of an eagle eye, nimble feet, supple wrists and instant judgement, were assiduously cultivated by day-long sessions in the nets, and not only was he glorious to watch but he vastly extended the techniques of batting. Fry, the Oxford classicist who applied his academic mind to all his sporting activities – he held the world record long jump for twenty-one years and was a soccer international – admitted he did not become a true England batsman until he learned from Ranji during their eight years at Hove.

In 1899 Ranji totalled 3,159 runs and 3,065 the next season with 5 double centuries, and such was the faith of the Sussex pros in him that after a hard day against Somerset they told him he must reply with a triple century. His response was 285 not out though he spent the whole night fishing!

Fry hit 94 centuries, including 6 in succession in 1901, and his aggregate of 30,886 averaged 50 an innings. He was particularly strong on the on side.

Sussex have always been a family club. There were 4 generations of Lillywhites, and the Tates, Gilligans, Langridges, Coxes, Parkes, Griffiths, Busses, Lenhams, Oakeses have made telling contributions. Duleep, as Ranji's nephew, also qualifies, and he positively dazzled until felled by ill health. Between 1929 and 1931 he scored 7,791 runs, more than any other batsman, and how he scored them! He murdered slow bowling, and 'christened' a new scoreboard at Hove with an even time innings of 333 against Northamptonshire.

Sheppard was a record-breaking batsman at Cambridge, and took

Sussex from 13th to 2nd in 1953. He scored a century in 'Laker's match' against Australia. Inevitably David was the subject of good-natured leg pulling. On his second Australian tour he had a rash of dropped catches, which prompted Freddie Trueman to growl: 'If the reverend gentleman cannot put his hands together, what hope is there for the rest of us?' In another Test at Manchester Sheppard was dismissed as the light deteriorated. Soon play was suspended and as umpire Frank Lee came off he was confronted by the batsman. 'I would like you to know the light had nothing to do with my getting out,' said David.

The Arthur Gilligan–Maurice Tate fast-bowling partnership was formidable. Together they dismissed South Africa for 30 at Birmingham. Gilligan, who was really fast, took 6 for 7 and after a couple of wickets he turned to Maurice and pointed to the visitors balcony. There were seven batsmen with their pads on.

Tate, like his father, Fred, started as an off spinner, and his progress was so moderate that there were elements within the club who wanted him to abandon bowling in favour of his aggressive batting – he scored 23 centuries on top of his 2,784 wickets. Fortunately for England, for whom he took 155 wickets in 39 Tests, there were opposing batsmen – notably Ernest Tyldesley – who were victims of his faster ball and advised him to change his methods. He became the best fast-medium bowler of his age.

John Snow had 202 wickets from 49 Tests, and was Illingworth's key fast bowler in the 1970–71 campaign. A poet and self-confessed rebel Snow had several clashes with the club, but, in the mood, he was high in post-war international rankings.

The Langridges and the Parkses were of more placid nature. James Langridge would have been followed in the England team by brother John but for Hitler's war – a first-class slip he scored 1,000 and over seventeen times – and Jim Parks, whose father and uncle gave sterling

WILLS'S CIGARETTES.

G. COX (SUSSEX)

E. H. BOWLEY

SUSSEX

TATE

service, had a spell as captain. He appeared in 46 Tests, and hit 51 centuries. The family tradition is maintained by his son, Robert, the Hampshire wicket-keeper. [A.B.]

Founded   1839
Colours   Dark blue, light blue and gold
Crest   County arms of six martlets (in shape of inverted pyramid)
Secretary   N. Bett
Coach   N. Gifford
Groundsman   P. Eaton
Scorer   L.V. Chandler
Address   County Ground, Eaton Road, Hove BN3 3AN
Telephone 0273 732161
Cricketcall   0898 121414

Achievements:

County Championship   Champions (0) 2nd 1902, 1903, 1932, 1933, 1934, 1953 and 1981
Gillette Cup   Winners 1963, 1964 and 1978; finalists 1968, 1970 and 1973
National Westminster Bank Trophy   Winners 1986
Benson & Hedges Cup   Semi-finalists 1982
John Player Sunday League   Champions (1) 1982
Refuge Assurance Sunday League   Champions (0) 14th 1987
Tilcon Trophy   Winners 1979

Gounds:

Hove (County Ground, Eaton Road)   Horsham (Cricket Field Road, Horsham)   Hastings (Central Cricket Ground, Priory Meadow, Queens Road)   Eastbourne (Eastbourne Saffrons Sports Club, The Saffrons).
     Other grounds that have been used since 1969 are: Arundel (Castle Park) and Pagham (Pagham CC, Pagham).

Hove

The Sussex cricket headquarters has been at Eaton Road since 1872. Previously the club played on the Royal Brunswick cricket ground, which opened in 1848 and was sited where Fourth Avenue now lies. The land was leased in 1858 to Tom Box, the wicket-keeper, who also managed the local hotel, but in 1863 the lease was transferred to the county club, providing it with its own ground for the first time. The last important match was played there in August 1871. When the Club moved to Eaton Road, the Brunswick turf was removed, transported and relaid there.

The initial first-class match staged by Sussex was against Gloucestershire in June 1872 and county matches have been played at Eaton Road ever since. Today Sussex play most of their matches at Hove, but games are also staged at Eastbourne, Hastings and Horsham. The pavilion was built in the 1880s, with extensions in 1921, and the upper pavilion was reconstructed in 1961. The Gilligan Stand was opened in 1971 and houses cricket nets for indoor practice by youngsters. Sussex is the oldest county club and many historic items can be found in the pavilion and club library.

The ball can be lost against the stands or flats which surround the ground on two sides, and the sea mist or 'fret' at Hove can provide differing conditions. The ground is entered from Eaton Road through the Tate Gates. A plaque marking the Centenary of cricket at Hove can be found in the ground. Sussex and Hove was the home of William Lillywhite, James Dean and John Wisden founder of the *Wisden Cricketers' Almanack*. The scoreboard which dates from the 1930s was paid for by the Harmsworth family. Visitors will also notice large eggs around the ground: these are sponsored by Stonegate County Eggs Co., which offers £3,000 to players who hit an egg while batting. Paul Parker hit one in 1986 when they were located at the Saffrons but no one has hit one at Hove. A new East Stand was built in 1988 and has taken the place of the Cowshed, which was demolished the previous year much to the displeasure of locals. A squash rackets club exists in the ground and this is managed by Tony Pigott, the club's fast bowler.

Ground records have included scores of over 300 by K.S. Duleepsinhji for the County against Northamptonshire, and by Eddie Paynter against the County for Lancashire. J.E.B.B.P.Q.C. Dwyer and A.P. 'Tich' Freeman hold the bowling records. In the limited-overs game, Graham Gooch holds the competition record of 198 not out for Essex, scored in the 1982 Benson and Hedges Cup. Michael Holding's 8 for 21 in the NatWest Bank Trophy is the best spell of bowling in a limited-overs match in this country.

Crowds at Hove are usually about 4,500–5,000 with more for popular limited-overs games. The largest was 14,500 for the Australians in 1948. Many great players have played at Hove including Ranji, Fry, Duleepsinhji, Tate, the Gilligans and the Langridges but no one will forget Ted Alletson who, playing for Nottinghamshire, in 1911 threatened the ground with demolition with 189 in 90 minutes, the last 142 coming in 40 minutes after lunch. He hit Killick for 34 in one over. This latter record was not beaten until Sobers scored 36 off Malcolm Nash at Swansea in 1968.

ADDRESS County Cricket Ground, Eaton Road, Hove, East Sussex BN3 3AN
TELEPHONE PROSPECTS OF PLAY 0273 772766

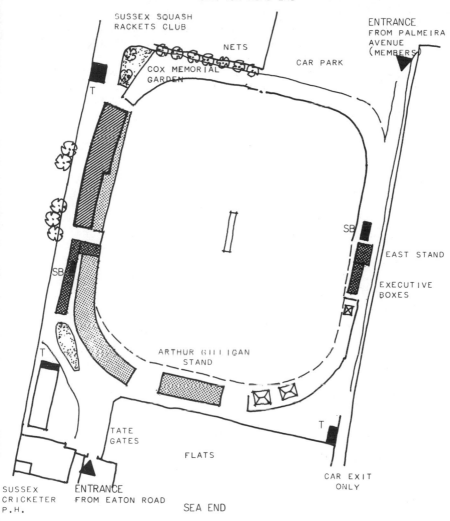

COMPTON ROAD END

SUSSEX SQUASH
RACKETS CLUB

NETS

ENTRANCE
FROM PALMEIRA
AVENUE
(MEMBERS)

CAR PARK

COX MEMORIAL
GARDEN

T

SB

EAST STAND

SB

EXECUTIVE
BOXES

T

ARTHUR GILLIGAN
STAND

T

TATE
GATES

CAR EXIT
ONLY

FLATS

SUSSEX
CRICKETER
P.H.

ENTRANCE
FROM EATON ROAD

SEA END

N
⇧

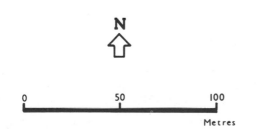

0   50   100

Metres

DESCRIPTION OF GROUND AND FACILITIES

There are two entrances to the County Ground: from Eaton Road by the 'Sussex Cricketer' public house, for members and their cars only and from Palmeira Avenue. The ground is entered by members and the public through the Tate Gates at the Sea End. The pavilion, Wilbury Stand, press box, library, secretary's and general offices can be found to the west of the playing area and at right angles to the wicket. To the south at the Sea End, is the Arthur Gilligan Stand and indoor school together with the club shop and, sometimes, a number of marquees for sponsors. To the east is the main scoreboard, East Stand, sponsors' boxes and disabled car park area. To the north, at the Cromwell Road End, are the outdoor nets, members' car park, the George Cox Memorial Garden and the Sussex County Squash Rackets Club. Much of the seating to the north is deckchairs and to the west, in the pavilion and terrace enclosures, are plastic tip-up seats in blue and white colours together with some benches. The T V camera position and radio point are located in the Arthur Gilligan Stand, behind the bowler's arm. Ample refreshment bars and permanent toilet facilities are available around the ground for both members and the public. The playing area is 130 metres by 150 metres and is defined by a rope and advertising boards. The pitch slopes towards the sea end and there is also a plastic wicket within the square for practise use. A second scoreboard is situated near the library and scorer's box in the Wilbury Stand. The ground capacity is 6,000 and about 4,500 seats are provided. Spectators are therefore advised only to bring their own seats to popular matches. The ground is surrounded by houses and multi-storey flats in the Hove district of Brighton.

There is a good, comprehensive history of the ground for members, a little cricketana and some pictures in the pavilion despite much having been sold by the club in the early 1980s to raise funds. A pleasant ground to view cricket and enjoy the local surroundings.

GROUND RECORDS AND SCORES

FIRST-CLASS MATCHES

Highest innings total for County ' 670 for 9 dec. v. Northamptonshire, 1921

Highest innings total against County   703 for 9 dec. by Cambridge University, 1890

Lowest innings total for County   19 v. Nottinghamshire, 1873

Lowest innings total against County   23 by Kent, 1859

Highest individual innings for County   333 K.S. Duleepsinhji v. Northamptonshire, 1930

Highest individual innings against County   322 E. Paynter for Lancashire, 1937

Best bowling performance in an innings for County   9 for 35 J.E.B.B.P.Q.C. Dwyer v. Derbyshire, 1906

Best bowling performance in an innings against County   9 for 11

A.P. Freeman for Kent, 1922
Best bowling performance in a match for County   16 for 100
J.E.B.B.P.Q.C. Dwyer *v.* Derbyshire, 1906
Best bowling performance in a match against County   17 for 67
A.P. Freeman for Kent, 1922

LIMITED-OVERS MATCHES
Highest innings total for County   305 for 6 *v.* Kent (BHC), 1982
Highest innings total against County   327 for 2 by Essex (BHC), 1982
Lowest innings total for County   61 *v.* Middlesex (BHC), 1978
Lowest innings total against County   86 by Gloucestershire (GC), 1969
Highest individual innings for County   141 n.o. G.D. Mendis *v.* Warwickshire (GC), 1980
Highest individual innings against County   198 n.o. G.A. Gooch for Essex (BHC), 1982
Best bowling performance for County   6 for 14 M.A. Buss *v.* Lancashire (JPL), 1983
Best bowling performance against County   8 for 21 M.A. Holding for Derbyshire (NWBT), 1988

HOW TO GET THERE

Rail   Hove, ½ mile; Brighton, 1 mile
Bus   Brighton & Hove 7 BR Brighton Station–BR Hove Station passes ground (Tel: 0273 206666); also 1, 2, 3, 5, 5B, 6, 19, 26, 33, 37, 43, 43A, 46, 49 and 59
Car   From north: M25 junction 7, then follow M23 and A23 signposted Brighton, follow signs Pyecombe and Hove after entering Brighton, then follow signs County Cricket for County Ground. From east: A27 follow signs Brighton and town centre, then Worthing, for Hove and County Ground, or take seafront (Kingsway) to Second Avenue, then cross the A277 into Wilbury Road and Eaton Road is then the first turning on the right for County Ground. From west: A27 follow signs Hove for County Ground or A259 seafront (Kingsway) to Second Avenue then as east.

WHERE TO STAY AND OTHER INFORMATION

Alexandra Hotel (0273 202722), Imperial Hotel (0273 731121), The Dudley Hotel (0273 736266), and many guest houses

Disabled Areas   Special area plus car spaces opposite main pavilion, north of scoreboard. Entrance from Palmeira Avenue
Local Radio Station(s)   BBC Radio Sussex (104.5 MHz FM/1161 KHz MW), Southern Sound (103.4 MHz FM/1332 KHz MW)
Local Newspaper(s)   Evening Argus, Brighton and Hove Leader

Eastbourne

The Saffrons ground is the home of Eastbourne C C, which was founded in 1855 and plays in the Sussex League. The outfield is shared with Eastbourne United F C. The complex is known today as the Eastbourne Saffrons Sports Club and Saffrons celebrated its centenary in 1986. Cricket has been played in Eastbourne for about 245 years, a fact which may surprise many followers of the game, but the Saffrons has not always been the venue. The earliest ground was at Paradise, now the Royal Eastbourne Golf Club. The Dental Estimates Board offices now stand on the second ground and the third at Ashford Road was on the site now occupied by the multi-storey car park near the railway station. The Aboriginals played on this ground in 1868. In 1870 Dr W.G. Grace visited with a United South of England XI and played an Eastbourne team of XVIII. The club moved in 1874 to Devonshire Park (given to the town by the Duke of Devonshire) and cricket was played there until the turn of the century. A move to the Saffrons was made in 1884 but Sussex did not play on the ground until 1897 when Middlesex were the visitors.

The main pavilion was destroyed by fire in 1947 and replaced by the existing building, which was itself damaged by fire in 1977. Plans are in hand at present for refurbishment of the pavilion and car parking area; squash courts have already been built. On the old white pavilion known as the War Memorial Pavilion and squash courts is a plaque bearing the name of the illustrious D.R. Jardine. The other pavilion on the ground is the Harry Bartlett Pavilion, which is also at the Meads Road End.

The name 'the Saffrons' originates from the use to which the land was put over a century ago, when saffron was grown for dyeing and medicinal purposes. The part of the ground known as Larkin's Field dates from the 1700s when a saddler named Larkin rented the ground there to graze the cattle he raised for their hides.

Most of the famous players appeared at the Saffrons: the Hide brothers both Eastbourne men, Maurice Tate when a Sussex colt and W.G. Grace, but Jack Hobbs only played once in a festival match. Archie MacLaren's Young Amateurs defeated the formidable Australians in 1921 at the Saffrons; this is possibly the most famous match on the ground. Sussex have played limited-overs matches on the ground – the first was in 1969 – and the ground has also been used for tourist matches by Sussex, Derek Robins XI, H.D.G. Leveson-Gower's XI and Col. L.C. Stevens' XI.

Ground records have included 272 not out by R.R. Relf against Worcestershire in 1909 and 310 by Harold Gimblett for Somerset in 1948. In 1972 Pat Pocock captured 7 wickets for 4 runs in his last two overs for Surrey. His earlier figures were 14-1-67-0, but he ended up with 16-1-71-7.

The club has been served well by groundsmen notably Wilf Wooller for 54 years from 1922 to 1976 and his father for 50 years from 1884

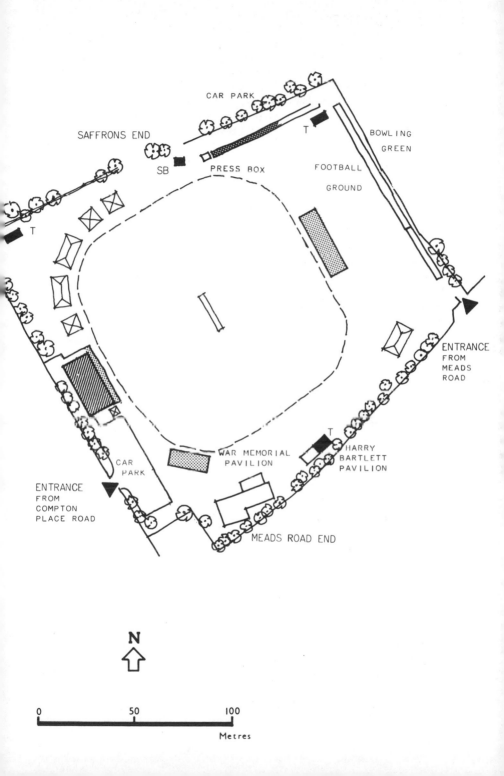

CAR PARK

SAFFRONS END

SB

PRESS BOX

T

BOWLING GREEN

FOOTBALL GROUND

ENTRANCE FROM MEADS ROAD

T

HARRY BARTLETT PAVILION

WAR MEMORIAL PAVILION

CAR PARK

ENTRANCE FROM COMPTON PLACE ROAD

MEADS ROAD END

T

N

0   50   100

Metres

to 1934. Between them they prepared over 5,000 wickets.

The most recent men to have played at the club and then played first-class cricket are former Sussex captain John Barclay and Bobby Parks of Hampshire.

Crowds at the Saffrons have been in the region of 4,000–5,000. the largest was 8,000 for a Sunday League match with Kent in 1978. And 25,000 watched cricket during the 1981 festival week when some fine cricket was played. Sussex take two championship and one limited-overs match to the Saffrons each year, usually in early August to attract the holiday crowds.

ADDRESS   Eastbourne C C, Eastbourne Saffrons Sports Club, The Saffrons, Compton Place Road, Eastbourne, East Sussex
TELEPHONE PROSPECTS OF PLAY   0323 24328

DESCRIPTION OF GROUND AND FACILITIES

There are two entrances to the ground; for members in Compton Place Road and for the public and disabled persons, in Meads Road. There is a large car park available at the rear of the football stands which is entered from Old Orchard Road and Saffrons Road, close to the bowling greens. The only permanent buildings on the ground are the pavilion, to the west of the playing area, which comprises the changing facilities for players, members' bar and refreshments and, in front of the playing area, a members' enclosure. Refreshments are available in a number of tents for the public. Also, to the south is the War Memorial pavilion and the Harry Bartlett pavilion. A scoreboard is situated on the north football ground side with a groundsman's store and a press box below. The football stands and terraces are too far away from the cricket field and only provide shelter during poor weather. The seating is all temporary and is made up of large, raised open seats, semi-raised areas and plastic seats, as well as a number of deckchairs. The west side of the ground is the members' enclosure and includes an area for sponsors' marquees, the S C C C committee tent, the secretary's office and Sussex C C C caravan, car parking for players/officials and temporary members' stands. On the east football ground side, directly behind the sightscreen is the T V camera position and radio point, plus a Sussex souvenir shop in the Harry Bartlett pavilion a first aid tent, temporary seating for the public, an area for disabled vehicles and public deckchair seating areas. The ground capacity is 8,000 and usually 3,000 seats are provided for all matches so spectators would be advised to bring their own seats only to very popular matches. Toilet facilities are both permanent and temporary. The playing area is 120 metres by 130 metres and defined by a rope on one side and, on the other, by some advertisement boards.

The ground is enclosed and a view of Eastbourne Town Hall, with its fine clock tower and dome can be seen from the pavilion.

FIRST-CLASS MATCHES

Highest innings total for County   540 for 6 dec. *v.* Glamorgan, 1938

Highest innings total against County   586 by Gloucestershire, 1936

Lowest innings total for County   38 *v.* Hampshire, 1950

Lowest innings total against County   57 by Nottinghamshire, 1962

Highest individual innings for County   272 n.o. R.R. Relf *v.* Worcestershire, 1909

Highest individual innings against County   310 H. Gimblett for Somerset, 1948

Best bowling performance in an innings for County   8 for 41 A.F. Wensley *v.* Leicestershire, 1933

Best bowling performance in an innings against County   9 for 62 A.G. Nicholson for Yorkshire, 1967

Best bowling performance in a match for County   12 for 86 J. Langridge *v.* Hampshire, 1950

Best bowling performance in a match against County   14 for 106 R.G. Robertson-Glasgow for Somerset, 1923

LIMITED-OVERS MATCHES

Highest innings total for County   227 for 8 *v.* Gloucestershire (JPL), 1975

Highest innings total against County   206 for 7 by Nottinghamshire (JPL), 1980

Lowest innings total for County   146 *v.* Nottinghamshire (JPL), 1980

Lowest innings total against County   63 by Minor Counties (East) (BHC), 1978

Highest individual innings for County   109 R.D.V. Knight *v.* Leicestershire (JPL), 1976

Highest individual innings against County   93 n.o. C.E.B. Rice for Nottinghamshire (JPL), 1980

Best bowling performance for County   5 for 28 A.N. Jones *v.* Essex (JPL), 1984

Best bowling performance against County   4 for 21 S. Oldham for Derbyshire (JPL), 1983

HOW TO GET THERE

Rail   Eastbourne, ½ mile

Bus   From surrounding areas to within ½ mile of ground; 8B passes Meads Road

Car   From north: A22 follow signs Eastbourne and town centre, then take A259 to Grove Road and then Saffrons Road. Meads Road is then the first turning on the right for Saffrons Ground. The ground is situated ½ mile from town centre and town hall. From east: A259 follow signs Eastbourne and town centre, then as north. From west: A259 follow signs Eastbourne and town centre, then as north.

WHERE TO STAY AND OTHER INFORMATION

Grand Hotel (0323 22611), Chatsworth Hotel (0323 30327), The Wish Tower (0323 22676) and many guest houses

Disabled Areas Football ground side of playing area
Local Radio Station(s) BBC Radio Sussex (104.5 MHz FM/1161 KHz MW), Southern Sound (103.5 MHz FM/1323 KHz MW)
Local Newspaper(s) Eastbourne News, Eastbourne Gazette and Herald

Hastings

Cricket at Hastings Priory Meadow started in 1864. The Central Cricket and Recreation Ground, as it is known today, is the home of Hastings and St Leonards Priory C C. The club was established in 1957 and play in the Sussex League. The first Hastings cricket festival took place in 1887 and the first County match in 1895 against Yorkshire. The ground is nominally owned and managed by a group of trustees for the benefit of the townspeople. It is occasionally used for activities other than cricket, but because the ground is at sea level and subject to flooding, it cannot be used for sport during the winter months. At present Sussex play one championship and one limited-overs match here in late June or early July. The Sussex Second XI play matches on the ground as well.

The players' pavilion suffered fire damage in September 1985, the bar area being destroyed along with many historic photographs. Part of the roof of the visitors' dressing room was also severely damaged. In 1986 Hastings Council announced that the ground would be developed into a major shopping centre development. Work is due to start in late 1989. The last visit will be made by Middlesex in 1989 for four days' cricket and will no doubt be a sad event. The ground, which is steeped in cricket history, was laid out in 1864 by the estate of the Cornwallis family. Situated close to the seafront and the town's main shopping streets the ground is sited in a bowl-like depression. It is surrounded by houses of every description and to the east is Hastings Castle. The pavilion and much of the older stands date back to the 1880s but have had extensions and improvements in recent years.

Ground records have been numerous and include for Sussex their highest ever total in a first-class match (705 for 8 declared against Surrey), and a 246 by K.S. Duleepsinhji against Kent in 1929. Traditionally the Hastings Festival always took place in September and many records have been made during these fixtures. The first name that comes to mind is Gilbert Jessop who scored seven centuries on the ground, six during festivals. In 1947 Denis Compton scored 101 for South of England against the South Africans, his seventeenth century of the season, passing the previous record held by Jack Hobbs since 1926. C.T.B. Turner took 17 wickets for 50 runs on the ground (8 for 13 and 9 for 37) for the Australians against an England XI during the second festival. This is still the best bowling feat achieved on the ground. Recent records include a 203 by Ted Dexter in 1968 against Kent, his only double hundred for Sussex, and in 1975 Tony Greig scored 226 against Warwickshire. The traditional visitors to Hastings have been Kent and in 1972 and 1973 each side had a large victory, Sussex by 10 wickets and Kent by an innings and 161 runs. Derek Underwood will have fond memories of Hastings for in 1964 he took 9 for 28 and in 1984 scored his maiden century of 111.

Crowds have been 20,000 capacity for festival matches. Against Kent in 1932 the crowd was 6,889 for the first day; in all 20,000 watched the match over the three days. In recent years crowds of 4,500–5,000 have been usual. With the shopping centre development due to start after the 1989 season, the council was responsible for finding a new ground for the club at Bohemia Road, St Leonards, close to the fire station. This has been developed since 1986. It is hoped that cricket will be played by Sussex at this ground in the future.

ADDRESS Hastings and St Leonards Priory C C, Central Cricket and Recreation Ground, Priory Meadow, Queens Road, Hastings, East Sussex TN34 1RP
TELEPHONE PROSPECTS OF PLAY 0424 424546

DESCRIPTION OF GROUND AND FACILITIES

The ground can be entered from Station Road where there is limited car parking for players/officials and members, via Queens Parade, through the Coach Station which is used for car parking, and for pedestrians only, from the south terrace. The members' pavilion houses refreshment facilities, a bar, the secretary's office and a press box. Next to this is the main scoreboard, groundsman's equipment store and, fenced off, the players' pavilion and enclosure. Also adjoining this is the grandstand which is situated directly behind the sightscreen at the South Terrace End. Situated on the Queens Parade side of the ground is the Cantilever Stand which provides open seating high above the playing area, at the rear of the houses and shops. A secondary small scoreboard is also situated at the southern end of this enclosure which is only available to members. The T V camera position is at the Station Road End and sponsors' marquees can be found at the opposite end of the ground, on the Queens Parade side. The ground capacity is 7,000 and about 3,500 seats are provided so spectators are advised to bring their own seats to popular matches. The playing area is 122 metres by 127 metres and is defined by a rope and advertising boards. The Sussex club provides a souvenir caravan and ample, temporary refreshment facilities. Toilets are available.

The members' pavilion has a good collection of cricket photographs and a small library which can be viewed by appointment.

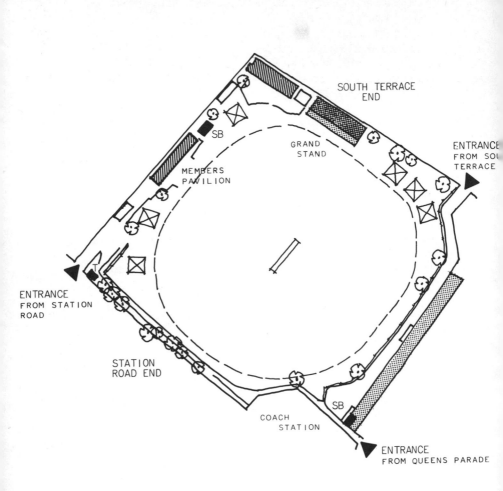

SOUTH TERRACE
END

GRAND
STAND

ENTRANCE
FROM SOU
TERRACE

MEMBERS
PAVILION

SB

ENTRANCE
FROM STATION
ROAD

T

STATION
ROAD END

COACH
STATION

SB

ENTRANCE
FROM QUEENS PARADE

N

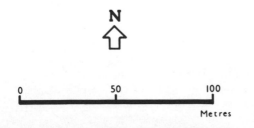

```
0          50          100
```
Metres

FIRST-CLASS MATCHES

Highest innings total for County   705 for 8 dec. *v.* Surrey, 1902
Highest innings total against County   552 for 8 by Surrey, 1923
Lowest innings total for County   56 *v.* Derbyshire, 1963
Lowest innings total against County   66 by Kent, 1955
Highest individual innings for County   246 K.S. Duleepsinhji *v.*
Kent, 1929
Highest individual innings against County   228 n.o.
K.W.R. Fletcher for Essex, 1968
Best bowling performance in an innings for County   8 for 40
G.R. Cox *v.* Warwickshire, 1912
Best bowling performance in an innings against County   9 for 28
D.L. Underwood for Kent, 1964
Best bowling performance in a match for County   13 for 194
M.W. Tate *v.* Kent, 1929
Best bowling performance in a match against County   15 for 173
D.V.P. Wright for Kent, 1947

LIMITED-OVERS MATCHES

Highest innings total for County   267 for 5 *v.* Essex (JPL), 1980
Highest innings total against County   259 for 8 by Essex (JPL),
1980
Lowest innings total for County   100 *v.* Northamptonshire (JPL),
1986
Lowest innings total against County   113 by Warwickshire (JPL),
1974
Highest individual innings for County   121 n.o. P.W.G. Parker *v.*
Northamptonshire (JPL), 1983
Highest individual innings against County   136 K.S. McEwan for
Essex (JPL), 1980
Best bowling performance for County   4 for 25 A. Buss *v.*
Worcestershire (JPL), 1974
Best bowling performance against County   6 for 12
D.L. Underwood for Kent (JPL), 1984

HOW TO GET THERE

Rail   Hastings, ¼ mile
Bus   Maidstone & District and Hastings Bus Co. from surrounding
areas to town centre, adjacent ground
Car   From north: A21 and A2101 follow signs Hastings and
seafront, then take Station Road or Queens Road for Central
Cricket Ground, the ground is situated close to the Bus/Coach
Station and Town Hall. From east: A259 follow signs Hastings and
town centre, then as north. From west: A259, A269 or A2100
follow signs Hastings and town centre, then as north.

WHERE TO STAY AND OTHER INFORMATION

Burlington Hotel (0424 424303), and many guest houses

Disabled Areas   No special area, request position
Local Radio Station   BBC Radio Sussex (104.5 MHz FM/1161 KHz MW)
Local Newspaper(s)   Evening Argus, Hastings Observer and Hastings News

Horsham

Sussex first appeared at Horsham as a representative side in 1853 but not on the present ground at Cricket Field Road, which is the home of Horsham C C, founded in 1771, who play in the Sussex league and share facilities with Horsham Caledonians C C, founded in 1949. Four other grounds in the town have been used for cricket: the Artillery Ground (the first site), the Common in North Parade at the south side of the junction with Hurst Road, Denne Park, and Stanford's or the 'new' ground. The County have played on the present Cricket Field Road ground since 1908 when the first first-class match was staged with Essex. Matches have been played during the following periods: 1908–10, 1912–14, 1920–39 and 1946–56. The County visited in 1971 and 1974 against University sides but not until 1983 did championship cricket return to Horsham. The County have made thirteen visits to this delightful, rural setting during the 1970s and 1980s for limited-overs Sunday League fixtures. The Horsham club has hosted a festival week but in recent years this has only been one championship and one limited-overs match, usually over a weekend in June. The club celebrated its 200th anniversary in 1971 with a visit from Cambridge University C C. Horsham C C has played on the ground since 1851.

The first pavilion was situated close to the footbridge crossing the railway but was demolished. The present pavilion was built in 1921. There are facilities for tennis and ample space surrounding the playing area. Along the banks of the River Arun which runs close to the ground are willow trees planted by Ben Warsop the former cricket bat manufacturer. The ball has been hit into the river once, by 'Jacko' Watson the mightiest of Sussex hitters. At the southern end of the ground is a railway line and B R Southern Region trains can often be heard. So can the more pleasing sound of bells ringing from the local St Mary's Church close by. Horsham C C owns the ground and there has been talk in recent years of improving the facilities to attract more County matches.

Cricket Field Road has its fair share of ground records including a 176 by E.H. Bowley against Warwickshire. C.P. Mead, probably John Arlott's favourite Hampshire batsman, hit 224 for Hampshire in 1921. Limited-overs records include 147 by Glenn Turner for Worcester-

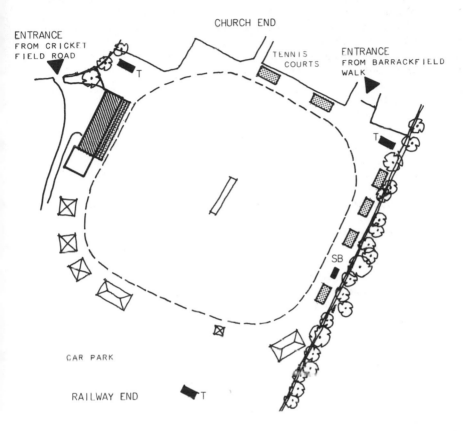

CHURCH END

ENTRANCE
FROM CRICKET
FIELD ROAD

TENNIS
COURTS

ENTRANCE
FROM BARRACKFIELD
WALK

T

T

SB

CAR PARK

RAILWAY END

T

N

| 0 | 50 | 100 |

Metres

shire, and Sussex's highest total in the Sunday League (in the same match). The ground witnessed the departure from county cricket of one of England's greatest ever batsmen, Jack Hobbs, who after scoring 79 in 1934 retired from the game after the Horsham Week. In recent years Garth Le Roux's swashbuckling knock against Hampshire to set up victory in a Sunday League match is also remembered by locals. Viv Richards kept wicket here for Somerset one Sunday in 1985 after Trevor Gard was injured warming up on the slippery outfield.

Cricket here attracts crowds of 4,500 to 5,000. Probably the largest attendance was 6,500 against Worcestershire for the John Player Sunday League match in 1980.

ADDRESS Horsham C C, Cricket Field Road, Worthing Road, Horsham, West Sussex
TELEPHONE PROSPECTS OF PLAY 0403 54628

DESCRIPTION OF GROUND AND FACILITIES

The main entrance to the ground is from Cricket Field Road which is a narrow road off Worthing Road (A24) although there is another pedestrian access off a footpath from St Mary's Church yard. There is a large area for car parking to the south and east of the ground. The only permanent building is the large pavilion/club house which has been extended by adding two storeys. It is situated on the west side of the ground, the whole of which is given over to members. All other areas are available to the public and a number of small groups of tiered bench seats are provided for the public. The capacity of the ground is about 5,500 of which only about 20 per cent can be accommodated on the seats provided so you are advised to bring your own. Bars and refreshments are available to members in the pavilion and to the public in tents on the ground. There are no special arrangements for disabled persons so they should ask for suitable accommodation. The playing area is approximately 126 metres by 122 metres and is bounded by advertisement boards.

This is a pleasant club ground although the facilities for the public on popular match days are limited. The county club bring a club shop to the ground and there is usually a number of sponsors' tents in the south-east corner of the ground.

GROUND RECORDS AND SCORES

FIRST-CLASS MATCHES
Highest innings total for County 519 v. Leicestershire, 1921
Highest innings total against County 438 by Surrey, 1938
Lowest innings total for County 35 v. Glamorgan, 1948
Lowest innings total against County 51 by Leicestershire, 1924
Highest individual innings for County 176 E.H. Bowley v. Warwickshire, 1927

Highest individual innings against County 224 C.P Mead for Hampshire, 1921

Best bowling performance in an innings for County 9 for 50 G.R. Cox v. Warwickshire, 1926

Best bowling performance in an innings against County 9 for 48 V. Broderick for Northamptonshire, 1948

Best bowling performance in a match for County 17 for 106 G.R. Cox v. Warwickshire, 1926

Best bowling performance in a match against County 10 for 154 V. Broderick for Northamptonshire, 1948

LIMITED-OVERS MATCHES

Highest innings total for County 293 for 4 v. Worcestershire (JPL), 1980

Highest innings total against County 261 by Worcestershire (JPL), 1980

Lowest innings total for County 171 for 8 v. Leicestershire (JPL), 1971

Lowest innings total against County 136 for 8 by Somerset (JPL), 1978

Highest individual innings for County 106 n.o. P.W.G. Parker v. Worcestershire (JPL), 1980

Highest individual innings against County 147 G.M. Turner for Worcestershire (JPL), 1980

Best bowling performance for County 4 for 32 D.A. Reeve v. Nottinghamshire (JPL), 1985

Best bowling performance against County 4 for 26 A.M. Ferreira for Warwickshire (JPL), 1981

HOW TO GET THERE

Rail Horsham, 1 mile

Bus London Country (SW) H1/2/5 link BR Station with ground (Tel: 01-668 7261)

Car From north: M25 junction 9, then A24 follow signs Horsham and town centre, then take Worthing Road and turn into Cricketfield Road for Horsham CC. The ground is situated close to the River Arun and Church. From east: A264 follow signs Horsham and town centre, then as north. From west: A281 or A264 follow signs Horsham and town centre, then as north. From south: A24 or A281 follow signs Horsham and town centre, then as north.

WHERE TO STAY AND OTHER INFORMATION

Ye Olde King's Head (0403 53126)

Disabled Areas No special area, request position

Local Radio Station(s) BBC Radio Sussex (104.5 MHz FM/1161 KHz MW), Radio Mercury (102.7 MHz FM/1521 KHz MW)

Local Newspaper(s) West Sussex County Times, Crawley Observer, West Sussex Gazette

WARWICKSHIRE

CHURCHMAN'S CIGARETTES

WARWICKSHIRE.

BIRMINGHAM - EDGBASTON

NUNEATON

Warwickshire

When Warwickshire outpaced Kent to become the first outside the Big Six to win the championship in 1911, *Punch* celebrated an event, which stunned English cricket by its audacious brilliance, with a full-page cartoon. Frank Foster, the dashing 22-year-old captain from Small Heath, was shown with another with a Warwickshire qualification, William Shakespeare. 'Tell Kent from me she hath lost,' says Foster. The Bard replies, 'Warwick, thou art worthy.'

Warwickshire in post-war years have twice won the championship and the Gillette Cup, and, as a bonus, the Sunday League, and boast of such renowned bowlers as Field, Foster's partner, Hollies, Howells, Willis, Cartwright, Small and the West Indian off spinner Gibbs, but the exploits of Foster and his unfancied side – 14th out of 16 the previous year – is the most vivid page in the annals of the club.

There have also been distinguished captains of the calibre of Calthorpe, Wyatt, Cranmer, Dollery, M.J.K. Smith, A.C. Smith and Brown, yet Foster remains unique, a meteor flashing across the cricket sky in a briefly sad career lasting from 1908 to 1914. It was all over in 1915 when he was crippled for life in a motor cycle crash.

His epic season began with him twice changing his mind before accepting the captaincy – typically his decision came after a two-day innings defeat at The Oval and an announced intention to retire from first-class cricket – and ended in triumph after a nerve-wracking night spent playing cards. *Wisden* described him as the best young captain since W.G. Grace, and A.H. Altham, the cricket historian, wrote: 'There was about all his cricket an atmosphere of supreme confidence and inexhaustible vitality that acted as a wonderful inspiration to his side.'

Foster, whose first two victims in London were Hobbs and Hayward, was established as the country's leading all-rounder taking 116 wickets with his fast-medium left arm attack directed at the leg stump, and 1,383 runs from his aggressive batting. Field was his perfect foil, and together they dismissed Yorkshire, beaten twice that year, for 58 at Scarborough. Decades passed before the estimable Cartwright emulated Foster's 'double', and with Septimus Kinneir and wicket-keeper Jim ('Tiger') Smith adding to Foster's automatic selection Warwickshire had three representatives in one of the most powerful sides to visit Australia.

Australia, beaten 4–1, declared Barnes, who had one unremarkable outing for Warwickshire, and Foster to be the finest opening bowling pair ever sent there, a view endorsed by the captain Warner. Barnes had 34 wickets at 22.88, and Foster 32 at 21,62. Foster had the extra recommendation of a batting place among Hobbs, Woolley, Gunn, J.W. Hearne, Mead and Douglas. Unrelated to the Fosters of Worcestershire he was indeed some cricketer.

There were so many variations and paces of his bowling that Smith, who had just succeeded the outstanding Test wicket-keeper Lilley at

WARWICKSHIRE C.C.C

COUNTY CRICKETERS.

S. P. KINNEIR,
WARWICKSHIRE.

Edgbaston, now found himself ahead of Strudwick because his knowledge of Foster's methods and signals was essential. 'Tiger', who had a 75-year love affair with Edgbaston, used to say that the only Australian able to detect a signal was an observant Sydney tram conductor who rightly interpreted a foot shuffle to warn a slower ball was coming up!

One of Foster's batting stalwarts was the model stylist Willy Quaife, the smallest man ever to play for England. If he lacked inches he was not short of staying power for he was 56 when he made the last of his 72 centuries. Warwickshire also had J.H. Parsons, a future Canon who played for both Gentlemen and Players, and Percy Jeeves, whose name was adopted by P.G. Wodehouse as his fictional butler after watching the county at Cheltenham.

A shortage of penetrative bowling found success hard to come by in the Calthorpe and Wyatt years, but Wyatt's 4th position in 1934 was the highest since 1911. Wyatt, with 85 centuries and 40 Test appearances, including 16 as captain, was as good a batsman, and possibly the best technically equipped, as Warwickshire have produced, an opinion Amiss would be entitled to challenge.

Cranmer, the rugby international, had his problems in the seasons straddling the Second World War, but he was never deterred and put Warwickshire on to the road of the title in 1951 by Dollery's all-pro side. The strength was built around Dollery the batsman and Hollies, the spin bowler, reinforced by New Zealander Pritchard and Grove with the new ball, Spooner a batsman–wicket-keeper, Ord, Gardner and Townsend. The superb left hander, Donnelly, was also briefly available but left before the championship year.

The most famous of Hollies' 2,323 dismissals (2,201 for Warwickshire) deprived Sir Don Bradman of a Test average of 100, and he extended his services to the county by taking the captaincy for a year while M.J.K. Smith, from Leicestershire, qualified. Smith had an uncanny knack of leadership, both for England and Warwickshire, and his eleven years were marked by his own run-getting, superb close-in catching and near-misses in the championship, a losing final and the taking of the Gillette Cup in 1966.

After Smith came another Smith, Alan, the winner of the Man of the Match award in the 1968 Gillette Cup final. Lord's was a fitting place for the future chief executive of the TCCB to shine. Warwickshire, nourished by the hugely successful Supporters' Association, by now had the brilliant West Indians, Gibbs and Kanhai, and backed to the hilt Smith's determination to go for the championship. He almost did it in 1971 when Surrey, with the same number of points, took the title by virtue of more victories. Another West Indian, Kallicharran, as run-hungry as Kanhai, was secured and in 1972 Warwickshire ended undefeated and 36 points in front of Kent. They were also beaten finalists in the Gillette Cup. Willis, from Surrey, came in midway through the season as the main support to Brown.

Willis was captain when the Sunday League was won in 1980 and the eight home games were watched by 46,000 spectators – a proper response to a magnificent Test-ranking ground which stands as a compliment to the initiative of former secretary Leslie Deakins and the husband and wife team of David Blakemore and Winnie Crook of the Supporters' Association.

Brown, as fast bowler and captain and subsequently team manager, and Amiss, who ended with 43,423 runs and in the company of the greats with 102 centuries in twenty-eight seasons, could hardly have given better service. From 1972 to 1974 Amiss was England's most prolific batsman averaging 71 over 20 Tests. His rearguard action scoring 262 not out at Kingston in 1973–74 was an epic innings of skill and concentration. Other equally masterful scores were 174 and 118. He ended the series with an average of 82.87, and added to his high reputation with a double century against the West Indies at The Oval in 1976. Like Hollies, who broke all the county's bowling records, Amiss, 11th in the list of all-time batsmen, set new batting standards for Warwickshire. He was the first local-born player to hit a century for England. [A.B.]

Founded   1882
Colours   Blue, gold and silver
Crest   Bear and ragged staff
Secretary   D.M.W. Heath
Cricket manager/senior coach   R.M.H. Cottam
Youth development officer and coach   R.N. Abberley
Groundsman   B. Franklin
Scorer   S.P. Austin
Address   County Ground, Edgbaston, Birmingham B5 7QU
Telephone 021 440 4292
Cricketcall   0898 121456

Achievements:

County Championship   Champions (3) 1911, 1951 and 1972
Gillette Cup   Winners 1966 and 1968; finalists 1964 and 1972
National Westminster Bank Trophy   Finalists 1982
Benson & Hedges Cup   Finalists 1984
John Player Sunday League   Champions (1) 1980
Refuge Assurance Sunday League   Champions (0) 10th 1988
Fenner Trophy   Finalists 1974
Tilcon Trophy   Winners 1985; finalists 1986 and 1988

Grounds:

Birmingham (County Ground, Edgbaston)   Nuneaton (Griff & Coton Sports Ground, Heath End Road).
   Another ground that has been used since 1969 is: Coventry (Courtaulds Sports Ground, Lockhurst Lane).

Birmingham – Edgbaston

Edgbaston is the third ground in Birmingham used by the Warwickshire County Cricket Club. The other grounds were at Aston Lower Grounds, Trinity Road, close to Aston Villa Football Club, where just one match was staged in 1884 and the Mitchell and Butlers' Ground at Portland Road and City Road, where matches were staged from 1931 until the last match in 1961 with Cambridge University. Mitchell and Butlers are the club's sponsors and their ground has since been used for Second XI matches. The first County match on the Edgbaston ground was played against Kent in 1894. However the initial match was between an England XI and the Australians in 1886. M C C also played in that year, but not until 1895 when the club was admitted to the County Championship did matches take place frequently.

   The main part of the ground was acquired by the reorganized Warwickshire County Cricket Club in 1886 and the freehold land has been added to piecemeal at intervals since then. It has now been developed into one of the best-equipped grounds in the country. In 1902 the ground was recognized as suitable for Test Matches when England met Australia in the First Test of the series. Test Matches continued to be played until 1929, but there was a gap until 1946, since when it has remained a regular venue.

   The ground was originally a 'meadow of rough grazing land' and belonged to Lord Calthorpe until he allowed the club to lease it for cricket purposes. The original pavilion still remains but so much alteration has taken place that, except for the distinctive, red-tiled roof, it is difficult to recognize it among all the new additions at the

Pavilion End. The William Ansell Stand was built during the 1950s from funds raised by the Warwickshire C C S A and the stand was named after the first key figure in Warwickshire and Edgbaston's history. In 1975 an executive suite was added to the Ansell Stand and in recent years more sponsors' rooms and tip-up plastic seats have been installed to improve the facilities. Edgbaston is still one of the few grounds where the press box is immediately behind the sight screen at the opposite end of the ground to the pavilion. In 1988–89 the club moved the existing Thwaite Scoreboard and rebuilt it close by to allow further seating to be constructed at the City End.

All the bars around the ground are named after fielding positions and there are a number of fine cricket items to be viewed in the club museum. On the Edgbaston Road frontage of the ground the observant will note the site of the Sydney Barnes Wicket Gate. The Warwickshire Indoor Cricket School is located on the ground and the most interesting innovation at Edgbaston has been the installation of a large mechanically operated pitch cover known as the 'Brumbreller'.

In 1989 as part of the ground development at Edgbaston, some key county names are to be perpetuated: the executive club will be known as the Cyril Goodway Suite; the members' bar/lounge, the Tom Dollery Lounge; the Rea Bank Stand, the Eric Hollies Stand; the West Wing Stand, the Ryder Stand; and the East Wing Stand, the Leslie Deakins Stand, acknowledging the service to the County Club of the two Secretaries during the years 1889–1976.

Crowds at Edgbaston have always been good: the record was 28,000 against Lancashire in 1951 for a championship match. The current ground capacity is 17,500 and this gate has been achieved in recent years for Test Matches, limited-overs internationals and county competitions including the recent Refuge Assurance Cup Final which was staged at Edgbaston in 1988. Notable performances at Edgbaston are plentiful – these have included double centuries from Percy Holmes, S.P. Kinneir, Alvin Kallicharran, Peter May and Zaheer Abbas amongst many others. In addition to staging county matches the ground has been used for all limited-overs matches by the county and international matches including Prudential Trophy, Prudential Cup and Texaco Trophy matches.

Edgbaston is certainly a most welcoming ground to enter after a journey of some distance with its fine facilities, covered accommodation and permanent seating, and Lords is really its only superior in Britain.

ADDRESS County Ground, Edgbaston Road, Edgbaston, Birmingham B5 7QU

TELEPHONE PROSPECTS OF PLAY 021-440 3624

DESCRIPTION OF GROUND AND FACILITIES

This is one of the premier cricket grounds in the country – perhaps it is now more of a stadium, being surrounded on most sides by tiers

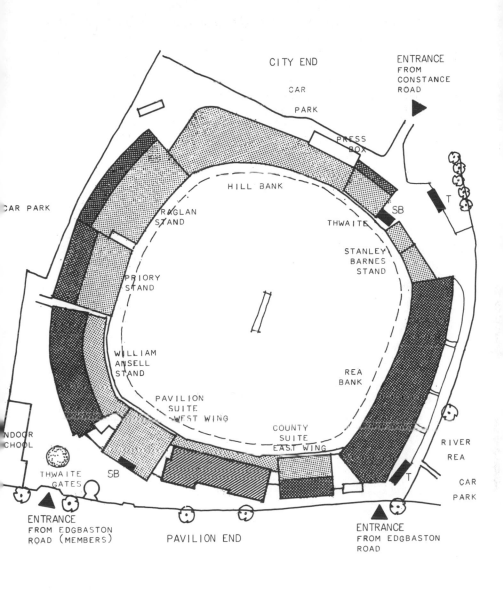

CITY END

ENTRANCE FROM CONSTANCE ROAD

CAR PARK

PRESS BOX

CAR PARK

HILL BANK

RAGLAN STAND

THWAITE

SB

STANLEY BARNES STAND

PRIORY STAND

WILLIAM ANSELL STAND

REA BANK

PAVILION SUITE WEST WING

COUNTY SUITE EAST WING

INDOOR SCHOOL

RIVER REA

CAR PARK

THWAITE GATES

SB

ENTRANCE FROM EDGBASTON ROAD (MEMBERS)

PAVILION END

ENTRANCE FROM EDGBASTON ROAD

T

T

N

0   50   100
Metres

of raised seats. Nevertheless a backcloth of trees is still visible in many areas.

The main access to the ground is gained from Edgbaston Road but there are also entrances on Pershore and Constance Roads. There are substantial areas for car parking adjoining the ground, mainly for members' cars. For important matches, additional car parks are available on the opposite side of Edgbaston Road adjoining Edgbaston Park.

The capacity is 17,500 and all seating is in permanent stands providing excellent views of the playing area. The areas of seating in the William Ansell Stand, the Pavilion Centre and East and West wings above the pavilion and County Suits are available to members and visiting members (except that on occasions parts of the centre pavilion are restricted to Warwickshire members only). The remainder of the ground is open to the public but on Test Match days and other ticket matches all seats are allocated. An area in front of the Thwaite scoreboard is reserved for disabled persons.

Ample toilets are available at the rear of most stands, including facilities for disabled persons. Excellent provisions for obtaining refreshments exist in all parts of the ground. Members are well served by the bar in the William Ansell Stand, the County Suite and several other bars in the members' areas. The general public is well catered for at the Press Box Stand and in the Long On (south-east corner) and Third Man (north-west corner) bars.

T V camera positions are usually above the pavilion area and Press Box Stand and at a lower level in front of the pavilion and Priory Stand. The members' club room houses items of cricket history.

This is a large ground, the total playing area being 148 metres by

Aerial view of Edgbaston

145 metres. The actual playing area for a particular match will depend on the position of the playing strip selected and boundaries defined by ropes may vary, though Test Match boundaries will only vary between 68 metres and 70 metres.

Substantial entertainment facilities are available in executive boxes. On Test Match days a virtual tented city is developed at the rear of the Hill Bank and Press Box Stands.

GROUND RECORDS AND SCORES

TEST MATCHES

Highest innings total for England 633 for 5 dec. v. India, 1979
Highest innings total against England 608 for 7 dec. by Pakistan, 1971
Lowest innings total for England 101 v. Australia, 1975
Lowest innings total against England 30 by South Africa, 1924
Highest individual innings for England 285 n.o. P.B.H. May v. West Indies, 1957
Highest individual innings against England 274 Zaheer Abbas for Pakistan, 1971
Best bowling performance in an innings for England 7 for 17 W. Rhodes v. Australia, 1902
Best bowling performance in an innings against England 7 for 49 S. Ramadhin for West Indies, 1957
Best bowling performance in a match for England 12 for 119 F.S. Trueman v. West Indies, 1963
Best bowling performance in a match against England 9 for 108 J. Garner for West Indies, 1984

LIMITED-OVERS INTERNATIONALS

Highest innings total 320 for 8 by Australia v. England (PT), 1980
Lowest innings total 70 by Australia v. England (PT), 1977
Highest individual innings 171 n.o. G.M. Turner for New Zealand v. East Africa (PC), 1975
Best bowling performance 5 for 18 G.J. Cosier for Australia v. England, 1977

FIRST-CLASS MATCHES

Highest innings total for County 657 for 6 dec. v. Hampshire, 1899
Highest innings total against County 887 by Yorkshire, 1896
Lowest innings total for County 35 v. Yorkshire, 1963
Lowest innings total against County 15 by Hampshire, 1922
Highest individual innings for County 268 n.o. S. Kinneir v. Hampshire, 1911
Highest individual innings against County 250 P. Holmes for Yorkshire, 1931
Best bowling performance in an innings for County 10 for 49 W.E. Hollies v. Nottinghamshire, 1946
Best bowling performance in an innings against County 10 for 67 E.A. Watts for Surrey, 1939
Best bowling performance in a match for County 14 for 93

T.L. Pritchard *v*. Glamorgan, 1951
Best bowling performance in a match against County   15 for 154
H. Young for Essex, 1899

LIMITED-OVERS MATCHES
Highest innings total for County   392 for 5 *v*. Oxfordshire (NWBT), 1984
Highest innings total against County   283 for 3 by Glamorgan (GC), 1976
Lowest innings total for County   86 *v*. Surrey (JPL), 1979
Lowest innings total against County   74 by Yorkshire (JPL), 1972
Highest individual innings for County   206 A.I. Kallicharran *v*. Oxfordshire (NWBT), 1984
Highest individual innings against County   163 n.o. C.G. Greenidge for Hampshire (JPL), 1979
Best bowling performance for County   7 for 32 R.G.D. Willis *v*. Yorkshire (BHC), 1981
Best bowling performance against County   5 for 18 J.K. Lever for Essex (JPL), 1972

REFUGE ASSURANCE CUP FINAL
Highest innings total   201 for 5 by Lancashire *v*. Worcestershire (RAC), 1988
Lowest innings total   149 by Worcestershire *v*. Lancashire (RAC), 1988
Highest individual innings   59 T.E. Jesty for Lancashire *v*. Worcestershire (RAC), 1988
Best bowling performance   4 for 46 A.N. Hayhurst Lancashire *v*. Worcestershire (RAC), 1988

HOW TO GET THERE

Rail   Birmingham New Street, 1¾ miles
Bus   West Midlands Travel 45/7 link New Street with ground (Tel: 021-200 2601); also 41 from John Bright Street to Pershore Road; 61, 62 and 63 from Navigation Street to Bristol Road; 1 from city centre to Edgbaston Road
Car   From north: M6 junction 6, follow A38 city centre and pass through city centre and tunnels. 1½ miles south of city centre, take left at traffic lights into Priory Road, cross Pershore Road traffic lights and the entrance to the ground is then on the left off Edgbaston Road. Follow signs County Cricket once south of city centre area. From east: A45, A41 or A34 follow signs Birmingham and city centre, then Edgbaston for County Ground, or as north. From west: M5 junction 4, follow A38 city centre, pass through Selly Oak and then follow signs Edgbaston and County Cricket for County Ground in Edgbaston Road. From south: A441, A435, A34, A41 or A45 follow signs Birmingham and city centre, then Edgbaston and County Cricket for County Ground, or as north.

WHERE TO STAY AND OTHER INFORMATION

Beech House Hotel (021-373 0620), Wentsbury Hotel, Selly Park (021-472 1258) – all local. Also The Albany (021-631 2528), Post House Hotel (021-357 7444), and several others

Disabled Areas In front of main scoreboard, and by special arrangement in other areas
Local Radio Station(s) BBC Radio WM (95.6 MHz FM/1468 KHz MW), BRMB (96.4 MHz FM/1152 KHz MW)
Local Newspaper(s) Birmingham Post, Birmingham Evening Mail, Birmingham Despatch, Daily News, Sports Argus

Nuneaton

Within the geographical triangle defined by Birmingham, Coventry and Nuneaton lie the former Warwickshire coalfields and just 1½ miles from the Nuneaton town centre was the village of Chivers Coton, where Griff Colliery was located. The land, which also included the Griff & Coton C C ground, was owned by Sir Francis Newdegate, the Governor of Tasmania and Western Australia between 1917 and 1924. The ground at Heath End Road has been used for cricket since the early 1900s and was known to locals as the Chivers Coton Ground. When the land came under the ownership of Griff Colliery, sheep were allowed to graze on the outfield during weekdays.

The ground was and still is a miners' social welfare club and has changed very little since Warwickshire made their initial visit in 1930, when neighbours Leicestershire were the visitors. After 1934 the ground was not used again by the County until 1960 when (thanks to F.G. Watson, a local building contractor who loved his cricket, and a donation of £1,000 from the Warwickshire C C S A) improvements and development took place. The effort to attract County matches again was successful, cricket returned and a year later in 1961 the colliery closed down, as it had become uneconomic to continue mining. Today there is little to remind the visitor that this was once a colliery ground. Nuneaton is Warwickshire's only venue away from Edgbaston nowadays (visits to Courtaulds Ground, Coventry ceased in 1982) and one championship match is staged at Nuneaton each year.

The colliery bandstand is still situated on the ground and a football field can still be viewed from the pavilion. There are facilities for bowling and tennis behind the scoreboard. The only permanent buildings are the players pavilion, a pavilion and social club, the scoreboard and groundsman's store. Seating is provided for county matches and the record crowd was 6,000 for a John Player Sunday League match with Lancashire in 1970. Crowds are usually around

2,500–3,500 for championship matches. Warwickshire have staged championship cricket at one other ground in the town, Weddington Road home of Nuneaton C C, where three matches were staged between 1912 and 1914.

Ground records at Griff & Coton have included two double centuries, 210 by Tom Cartwright who also took 9 for 40 in an innings and 221 not out by Bill Alley the Australian while batting for Somerset, his career best.

Alan Smith and Tom Cartwright shared a partnership of 244 in just under three hours in 1962 against Middlesex. This is still a record for the ground. In limited-overs matches between 1969 and 1980, the highest score was by Dennis Amiss and best bowling by Tom Cartwright. In recent years Alvin Kallicharran has always enjoyed scoring heavily on the ground and in 1982 Bob Willis hit 62 not out against Gloucestershire which was his career best with the bat!

ADDRESS Griff & Coton C C, The Pavilion, Griff & Coton Sports Club Ground, Heath End Road, Nuneaton, Warwickshire
TELEPHONE PROSPECTS OF PLAY 0203 386798

DESCRIPTION OF GROUND AND FACILITIES

The ground is entered from Heath End Road to the south. A car park immediately adjoins the road and there is an additional area for car parking on the football field to the west. The playing area, which is oval and quite narrow is 108 metres by 130 metres and is enclosed by a two-railed timber fence. The pavilion to the south is a substantial single-storey building with dormers but provides no raised seating. The players' dressing room is a small pavilion in the south-east corner surmounted by a clock and weathervane. The scoreboard is on the opposite side of the ground and affixed to it is a plaque to the memory of Jack Smart (Warwickshire 1919–36 and subsequently a first-class umpire and groundsman at Nuneaton). The members' area adjoins the pavilion to the south and east of the ground. The remainder is available to the public, who are advised to bring their own seats as only about 2,500 are available on the ground.

Nuneaton is a somewhat featureless ground now rather dominated by the backs of the semi-detached houses to the east, but attempts are being made to provide a tree screen on this boundary. Perhaps the most interesting feature is the bandstand just to the west of the playing area, which is usually within the area set aside for a sponsors' tent.

GROUND RECORDS AND SCORES

FIRST-CLASS MATCHES
Highest innings total for County 387 v. Middlesex, 1962
Highest innings total against County 395 for 5 dec. by Derbyshire, 1960

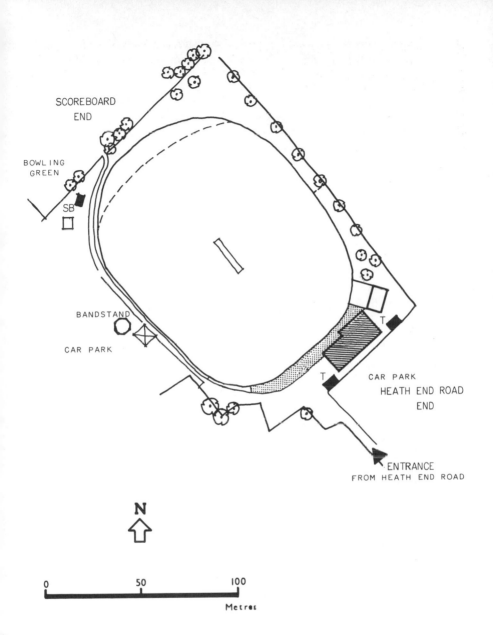

SCOREBOARD
END

BOWLING
GREEN

SB

BANDSTAND

CAR PARK

T

T

CAR PARK
HEATH END ROAD
END

ENTRANCE
FROM HEATH END ROAD

N

0   50   100

Metres

Lowest innings total for County   70 *v.* Hampshire, 1979
Lowest innings total against County   34 by Nottinghamshire, 1964
Highest individual innings for County   210 T.W. Cartwright *v.*
Middlesex, 1962
Highest individual innings against County   221 n.o. W.E. Alley for
Somerset, 1961
Best bowling performance in an innings for County   7 for 50
R.L. Savage *v.* Glamorgan, 1977

Best bowling performance in an innings against County 8 for 47
A. Brown for Kent, 1963
Best bowling performance in a match for County 9 for 40
T.W. Cartwright *v.* Nottinghamshire, 1964
Best bowling performance in a match against County 10 for 97
A. Brown for Kent, 1963

LIMITED-OVERS MATCHES
Highest innings total for County 234 for 5 *v.* Northamptonshire
(JPL), 1980
Highest innings total against County 208 for 7 by
Northamptonshire (JPL), 1980
Lowest innings total for County 153 *v.* Lancashire (JPL), 1969
Lowest innings total against County 204 for 5 by Lancashire (JPL),
1969
Highest individual innings for County 81 D.L. Amiss *v.*
Northamptonshire (JPL), 1980
Highest individual innings against County 69 R.G. Williams for
Northamptonshire (JPL), 1980
Best bowling performance for County 3 for 31 T.W. Cartwright *v.*
Lancashire (JPL), 1969
Best bowling performance against County 2 for 17 J. Sullivan for
Lancashire (JPL), 1969

HOW TO GET THERE

Rail Nuneaton, 1½ miles
Bus Midland Road (South) N1 links BR Station with ground (Tel:
0203 553737)
Car From north: M6 junction 3, follow A444 signposted
Nuneaton, at first roundabout take left into Bridge Street, which
leads into Heath End Road for Griff & Coton Sports Ground, or
A44, A47 or M69 junction 1 then A5 and A47 signposted Nuneaton
and town centre for Griff & Coton Sports Ground. From east, west
and south: M6 junction 3, follow A444 signposted Nuneaton, then
as north.

WHERE TO STAY AND OTHER INFORMATION

Longshoot Hotel (0203 329711)

Disabled Areas No special area, request position
Local Radio Station(s) BBC Radio WM (95.6 MHz FM/1468 KHz
MW), Mercia Sound (97 MHz FM/1359 KHz MW)
Local Newspaper(s) Nuneaton Evening Tribune, Coventry Evening
Telegraph

WORCESTERSHIRE

WORCESTER

KIDDERMINSTER

HEREFORD

Worcestershire

Worcestershire are a prime example of the changes brought about by the up-dating of the format of county cricket. Cinderella's rags have been well and truly cast aside. After almost winding up in 1914 and years of amiable failure between the wars – four wooden spoons and ten times clamped in the bottom four – twenty-five exciting seasons of transformation from 1963 have brought four championships, the John Player League in 1971 and the first two years of the Refuge Assurance League, 1987 and 1988, plus five Lord's finals, albeit all ending in defeat.

Frankly Worcestershire were not up to first-class strength, but in 1988 Botham's claim that theirs was 'far and away the strongest team' was not only hard to refute but graphically illustrated the change of power since the emancipating 'sixties. The achievement of the 'double' of the championship and the retention of the Sunday League was all the more meritorious as Botham was absent injured for the best part of the season. It might well have been a hat-trick with the prize of the NatWest Trophy if skipper Phil Neale had not made his only error of his triumphant season by losing the toss which led to Worcestershire being put in and committed to bat on a damp pitch. Maybe that was Gatting's one piece of luck in his traumatic year.

As the championship pennant, plus cheque, was parachuted in, Neale was deservedly re-appointed captain for the 8th time, and, to crown all the achievements were the deeds of Graeme Hick, a batting nugget to fall in Worcestershire's lap from Zimbabwe's distant sky. Not since the days of Hutton, Compton, May and Cowdrey has a young batsman been so universally praised. He became the 9th, and the youngest since Bradman, to score 1,000 before the end of May. His 1,019 came from only 1,343 balls, including 600 in boundaries, and was highlighted by a mammoth 405 not out against Somerset, the highest innings in county cricket since McLaren's record 424 in 1895, also at Taunton.

Another of Worcestershire's distinguished imports, Glenn Turner, scored 1,018 before the end of May, but it was on behalf of the touring New Zealanders! Hick also equalled Turner's county record of 10 centuries in a season, and in 1988, when he confirmed his high class, he totalled 2,713 runs in 37 first-class innings. Like Turner, Hick found his way to Worcester because other clubs had their quota of overseas players – Warwickshire recommended Turner and Leicestershire Hick – and within two years he broke Hutton's 49-year-old record as the youngest to reach 2,000 in an English season. Hick was 20, Hutton 21. In 1986 Hick and Curtis scored an undefeated 287 to improve on the previous county record for the second wicket set up 53 years before by the Nawab of Pataudi Snr and Gibbons. In due course Hick might set ambitious eyes on the 287, then an individual record Test score, made by R.E. Foster at Sydney in 1903–4. Foster was one of the leading three or four batsmen in the early years of the

C. F. ROOT

WORCESTERSHIRE C.C.C.

century, and was the most gifted of the seven brothers. Four appeared in one game, and it was hardly surprising that the county was dubbed 'Fostershire'.

Reginald captained England in the home series with South Africa in 1907, the year Worcestershire were runners-up, a heady position not equalled until 1962 when the modern era of professionalism was already entrenched. In his short life – he died from diabetes at 36 – Foster was also a renowned soccer international.

Arnold, an early all-rounder of note, went to Australia with Foster and was highly successful, and in the run-up to the first war Simpson-Hayward, the last of the famous under-arm bowlers, was captain. As relatively late as 1910–11 he took 6 South African wickets for 42 on the Johannesburg mat. Strudwick kept wicket to him and volunteered to bat early against him for Surrey as he could 'read' him. Struddy used to make the grinned confession that he was immediately out to him – to a full toss! Chester, the finest of all umpires, started at Worcester at the age of 14 and was marked for the highest honours. By 1914 he had hit 4 centuries – one against Essex of 178 not out included 4 sixes off Douglas – and was praised by W.G. Grace. He lost his right hand in Salonika in 1917.

Worcestershire, though never far from the wrong end of the table between the wars, were often indebted to the skills of Bowley, scorer of 276 in a day off Hampshire, Root, the deadly exponent of leg theory swing bowling, the batting of the Nawab of Pataudi, the graceful Test opener and secretary from Glamorgan, Walters, and Nichol and Gibbons. 'Doc' Gibbons – so named because he first appeared on the ground carrying an old-style doctor's bag – was one of the best batsmen never to have been capped by England.

The emergence of fast bowler Perks, 2,233 wickets, the first pro captain and twenty-seven sterling years, and the spinners, Howorth and Jenkins, was important in Worcestershire's next phase in the building-up of the Kenyon-led championship sides. Appointed captain in 1959, some years after he had failed to do himself justice at Test level, Kenyon brilliantly bridged the old and new Worcestershire. In his 39th year he all but took the title finishing 4 points behind Yorkshire, but that 1962 disappointment proved but a rehearsal for Worcestershire's first success in sixty-five years.

Coming in 1964 it was but a few months of the club's centenary. However, that event was celebrated in style with the retention of the championship in a thrilling dash for the post. Ten wins in the last 11 matches took Kenyon's able side to the top for the first time in the season in the closing overs. As D'Oliveira pointed out, it was the only time it really mattered!

Though Peter Richardson, who had reached 1,000 Test runs in fewer innings than any previous Englishman, had departed for Kent, Kenyon had exceptional fire power. Graveney was on a high in the second lease of his career, D'Oliveira was collecting his 43 centuries and 44 caps – and considerable respect for his dignity amid the crisis he innocently provoked over his native South Africa – and Headley, Ormrod and Dick Richardson were consistent run-getters. The bowlers came up trumps led by Flavell, Coldwell, Gifford, Slade, Carter and Brain. The all-rounders, D'Oliveira and Horton, were vital cogs in an impressive side.

The experience of D'Oliveira was influential when Gifford captained Worcestershire to a 3rd victory in 1974. Now assisted by Turner, one of the world's leading batsmen who flowered at Worcester, and fast bowler Holder, Gifford led what *Wisden* described as a triumph of team participation adding, 'there is no reason why this performance should be rated below that of Kenyon's possibly more gifted champions.' Gifford also took the Sunday League in 1971, and extended his own successful career with Warwickshire.

Whether Neale, with Hick, Curtis, the two Test fast bowlers, Dilley and Newport, and even Botham sidelined, had the strongest of the title-winning teams could be an endless argument, but it was all a far cry from the days when Worcestershire managed to dismiss Yorkshire for 99 at Bradford and still lost by an innings! [A.B.]

Founded 1865
Colours Dark green and black
Crest Shield argent bearing fess between three pears stable
Secretary Rev. M.D. Vockins
Senior coach B.L. D'Oliveira
Groundsman R. McLaren
Scorer J.W. Sewter
Address County Cricket Ground, New Road, Worcester WR2 4QQ
Telephone 0905 422694
Cricketcall 0898 121455

DON KENYON

TOM GRAVENEY

OGDEN'S CIGARETTES

R. T. D. PERKS

Achievements:

County Championship   Champions (4) 1964, 1965, 1974 and 1988
Gillette Cup   Finalists 1963 and 1966
National Westminster Bank Trophy   Finalists 1988
Benson & Hedges Cup   Finalists 1973 and 1976
John Player Sunday League   Champions (1) 1971
Refuge Assurance Sunday League   Champions (2) 1987 and 1988
Refuge Assurance Cup   Finalists 1988
Tilcon Trophy   Winners 1981

Grounds:

Worcester (County Cricket Ground, New Road)   Hereford
(Racecourse Ground, Grandstand Road)   Kidderminster (Offmore
Lane, Chester Road).
   Other grounds that have been used since 1969 are: Dudley (The
County Ground, Tipton Road), Stourbridge (Stourbridge War
Memorial Ground, Amblecote), Stourport-on-Severn (Parsons
Controls Holdings Limited, The Chainwire Club Sports Ground,
Minster Road) and Halesowen (Halesowen Sports Ground, Grange
Road).

Worcester

The County Cricket Ground at Worcester is situated in New Road, west of the bridge crossing the River Severn and within walking distance of the city centre. Worcester is probably the most attractive county ground in England and was the property of Worcester Cathedral until purchased by the club in 1976 for £30,000. The view of the playing area from the pavilion has as its backcloth the fourteenth-century Cathedral. This scene is illustrated frequently in books on cricket. The county club moved to New Road in 1899 from Boughton Park and the initial first-class match staged on the ground was with Yorkshire in May of that year. So urgent were the preparations that the sightscreen was still being painted by ground staff on the morning of the match. The pavilion was built in 1898–99 and remains today little different externally, although internal alterations have taken place. Since 1951 when Worcestershire C C Supporters' Association was founded by the Lord Lieutenant of the county, Admiral Sir William Tennant, much money has been raised to improve the ground. Changes have included the addition of new seating in 1952 on the popular side of the ground, a scoreboard in 1954 and two years later a ladies pavilion. In 1965 the championship year, the Severn Bar on the east side was rebuilt and in the 1973–74 closed season major additions were made to the New Road Stand, notably a roof, a press box and the secretary's office. In 1984–85 further development was undertaken when an executive suite was built on the site of the old supporters' association offices, scorers' room and press box. The scorers and press have now been moved to the other end of the New Road Stand, near to the pavilion. The supporters' association is now housed in the offices of the Club's marketing department.

Regular floods from the nearby River Severn have on occasions introduced fishing, boating, swimming and even ice skating to the County Ground! In the pavilion, there is a brass plate showing the highest water level in 1947 – some 3½ feet above the floor and several feet above the playing area outside. The flooding usually occurs around Christmas but in 1987 flooding took place only a few weeks before the start of the season.

The ground has staged Test trial and international matches including the following: 1983 Prudential World Cup (West Indies and Zimbabwe), Young England and Young Australia in 1980, the 1979 I C C Trophy final between Sri Lanka and Canada and more recently a ladies' Test Match in 1984 with New Zealand (this was the third ladies Test on the ground). Since the restructuring of the Minor Counties cricket competition in 1983 the winners of the two sections East and West meet in the final. This has been staged at New Road since 1983, but will be staged at Lord's in 1989 for the first time. For many years, Worcester was traditionally the first county match for the touring side, but this has altered in recent years.

Ground records include Glenn Turner's 311 not out against

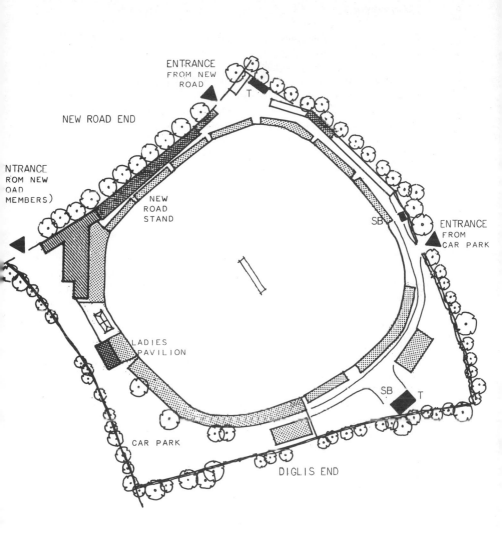

ENTRANCE
FROM NEW
ROAD

NEW ROAD END

T

NTRANCE
ROM NEW
OAD
MEMBERS)

NEW
ROAD
STAND

SB

ENTRANCE
FROM
CAR PARK

LADIES
PAVILION

SB

T

CAR PARK

DIGLIS END

N

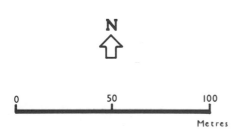

0   50   100

Metres

Warwickshire, which was his 100th hundred. Another cricketer who achieved this feat at Worcester was Tom Graveney when he scored 132 against Northamptonshire in 1964.

In 1987 Worcestershire scored 404 for 3 against Devon in the NatWest Bank Trophy, the highest innings total in the 60-overs game. Graeme Hick made 172 not out during the match. Crowds at Worcester have been good and in recent years limited-overs matches have attracted large attendances. The largest crowd for a match was probably 14,000 against the Australians in 1948. Sunday League matches attract 8,000 for popular games.

ADDRESS County Cricket Ground, New Road, Worcester WR2 4QQ
TELEPHONE PROSPECTS OF PLAY 0905 422011

DESCRIPTION OF GROUND AND FACILITIES

There are two entrances in New Road, one for members and their cars, at the rear of the pavilion and a second, adjoining the offices of the marketing department. Car parking is available in the ground and in the field adjoining the Diglis End close to the river. Street parking and nearby car parking is within a short walk over the bridge and into the city centre. Much of the covered accommodation for members is at the northern New Road End and in addition to the New Road Stand, pavilion and ladies' pavilion, the remainder of the ground is uncovered. All the terracing of plastic seats and benches are available to the public on the Severn side of the ground. For popular matches large banks of temporary, raised seating is erected at the Diglis End and these provide attractive views of the playing area. There is no need to bring your own seating as seating is provided for the capacity of 8,000. The main radio point is in the New Road Stand and the T V camera position is at the Diglis End. The members' enclosure stretches from the Diglis End sightscreen westwards to the sponsors' balcony area adjoining the New Road Stand – at least half the ground. There is a Worcestershire supporters shop on the Severn side adjoining a bar and refreshment area. Other refreshments can be obtained from under the main scoreboard and in the tent between the main pavilion and ladies' pavilion as well as in the New Road Stand. The press box and scorers sit in the New Road Stand, close to the secretary's office and players' dining area. The ground falls slightly towards the west side and is defined by a rope and advertising boards. The playing area is 145 metres by 136 metres and is roughly circular in shape. A fine view of the Cathedral across the beautiful county ground can be seen from the members' pavilion and enclosure.

GROUND RECORDS AND SCORES

FIRST-CLASS MATCHES
Highest innings total for County 633 v. Warwickshire, 1906

Highest innings total against County   701 for 4 dec. by Leicestershire, 1906
Lowest innings total for County   40 v. Leicestershire, 1971 (only 8 wickets fell, two batters absent hurt) 47 v. Derbyshire, 1936/v. Cambridge University, 1955
Lowest innings total against County   30 by Hampshire, 1903
Highest individual innings for County   311 n.o. G.M. Turner v. Warwickshire, 1982
Highest individual innings against County   331 n.o. J.D.B. Robertson for Middlesex, 1949
Best bowling performance in an innings for County   9 for 23 C.F. Root v. Lancashire, 1931
Best bowling performance in an innings against County   10 for 51 J. Mercer for Glamorgan, 1936
Best bowling performance in a match for County   15 for 106 R.T.D. Perks v. Essex, 1937
Best bowling performance in a match against County   15 for 175 J.C. White for Somerset, 1921

LIMITED-OVERS MATCHES
Highest innings total for County   404 for 3 v. Devon (NWBT), 1987
Highest innings total against County   284 for 6 by Derbyshire (BHC), 1982
Lowest innings total for County   81 v. Leicestershire (BHC), 1983
Lowest innings total against County   59 by Lancashire (GC), 1963
Highest individual innings for County   172 n.o. G.A. Hick v. Devon (NWBT), 1987
Highest individual innings against County   142 G. Boycott for Yorkshire (BHC), 1980
Best bowling performance for County   6 for 14 J.A. Flavell v. Lancashire (GC), 1963
Best bowling performance against County   6 for 14 H.P. Cooper for Yorkshire (JPL), 1975.

HOW TO GET THERE

Rail   Worcester Foregate Street, ½ mile; Worcester Shrub Hill, 1 mile
Bus   Midland Red West 23-6, 33 link Angel Place (200m from BR Foregate Street Station) with ground (Tel: 0345 212 555)
Car   From north: M5 junction 5, then follow A38 signposted Worcester and city centre, then take A44 for New Road and County Cricket, the ground is situated south of the city centre and south of the River Severn close to Bridge Street; or A443, A449 to city centre, then as above. From east: A422 or A44 follow signs Worcester and city centre, then as north. From west: A44, A4103 or A419 follow signs Worcester and city centre, then as north. From south: M5 junction 7, follow A44 signposted Worcester and city centre, then as north.

WHERE TO STAY AND OTHER INFORMATION

Giffard Hotel (0905 27155), Star Hotel (0905 24308), Bredon Manor (0684 72293)

Disabled Areas   Two viewing points on ground accessible to wheelchairs. Toilet facilities for disabled. Unfortunately, owing to flooding, most buildings are 6–8 ft. above ground and are accessible only by steps.
Local Radio Station(s)   Radio Wyvern (102 MHz FM/1530 KHz MW), BBC Radio WM (95.6 MHz FM/1468 KHz MW)
Local Newspaper(s)   Worcester Evening News, Birmingham Post, Birmingham Mail, Express and Star, Berrow's Worcester Journal

Kidderminster

The Chester Road ground was established in 1870 but cricket has been played in the town since 1850. The present Kidderminster club was formed in 1890 and its ground is located close to the main Chester Road. The club played at Worcester Road until the land was purchased for a steeplechasing racecourse. For two years they played at Comberton Road, on a field provided by the grammar school but then the club had to be on the move again. This time the club were more fortunate and rented some land close to Offmore farm which was part of the Earl of Dudley's estate. The ground opened on 20 August 1870 and is still the home of the club today. By 1896 the club had secured the lease direct from the Earl of Dudley and this was renewed annually until 1918 when the Dudley property was sold by auction. A local carpet manufacturer, Michael Tomkinson, the then President of the club purchased the freehold for £1,287 10s. on 31 December 1918 with a view to taking over when finances permitted. Still owned by the club the Old Pavilion was brought from the Worcester Road ground and rebuilt on its present site. The new pavilion was built in 1925 at a cost of £886 suscribed by members to commemorate winning the league in 1924. Close to this is a recreation and tea room with ample bar facilities for members, known as the Long Room.

The first Worcestershire match staged at Kidderminster was in 1921 when Glamorgan were the visitors. After 46 matches in 1973 with a game against Northamptonshire, the run ended – possibly because Worcestershire were bowled out for 63. In 1987, however, first-class cricket returned with Nottinghamshire the visitors and one championship match has been staged each season since. Kidderminster C C is a member of the Birmingham Cricket League which it joined in 1895. The club won the league championship in 1899 and on ten occasions since. The ground has been used by the County for Second XI fixtures. I C C Trophy matches have been staged on the ground

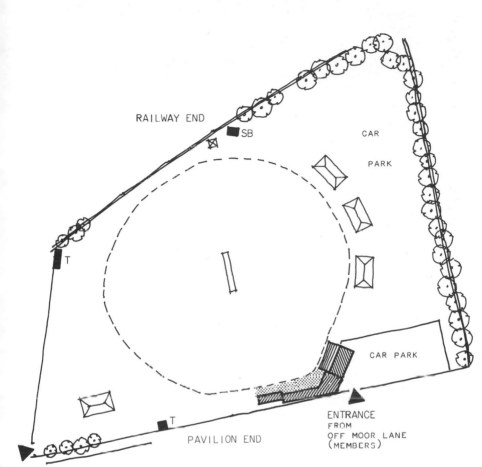

RAILWAY END

SB

CAR

PARK

T

CAR PARK

ENTRANCE
FROM
OFF MOOR LANE
(MEMBERS)

T

PAVILION END

NTRANCE FROM
ESTER ROAD

N

0   50   100

Metres

since 1979, with Denmark, Malaysia (twice) and Bangledesh taking part. Only one limited-overs match was staged, in 1969. In 1984 the association between Kidderminster C C, the Kidderminster Hockey Club and the Old Carolians was formalized with the creation of the Chester Road Sporting Club, in which the land and buildings are now vested. Crowds have been in the region of 4,500 to 5,500. The largest attendance was 7,000 for Yorkshire in 1956.

Ground records have included 259 from Don Kenyon against Yorkshire in 1956 and fine bowling performances from Jack Flavell and Alf Gover. Duncan Fearnley the cricket bat manufacturer will no doubt remember Chester Road well, for he scored his only first-class century there, 112 against Derbyshire in 1966.

The association between the club and the County has meant that players of the calibre of Laddie Outschoorn, Fred Rumsey, Basil D'Oliveria and latterly Graeme Hick have represented the club.

ADDRESS Kidderminster C C, Chester Road Sporting Club, Offmore Lane, Chester Road, Kidderminster, Worcestershire DY10 1TH
TELEPHONE PROSPECTS OF PLAY 0562 4175

DESCRIPTION OF GROUND AND FACILITIES

Entrance to the ground is from Chester Road where the main entrance is situated. The entrance in Offmore Lane adjoining the car park is for members and sponsors only. The pavilion, Long Room where refreshment facilities for members are provided and the Old Pavilion are situated at the Offmore Lane End south of the playing area. The members' enclosure is in front of the pavilion and on the terracing adjoining the building, and in front of the Long Room. The scoreboard is at the Lyndholm Road End close to the railway cutting. Sponsors' tents and refreshment facilities can be found to the east side and temporary seating for the public is on the west side of the playing area. There are refreshment tents and temporary toilets on the west side of the ground.

The playing area is 131 metres by 121 metres and defined by a rope and advertising boards. The Chester Road side of the ground is bounded by housing on the main A449 trunk road, whilst to the north and east are plenty of trees. The ground is very flat with a slight fall towards Chester Road in the direction of the main entrance. There is no fixed seating except near the pavilion. The ground capacity is 5,500 but seating is provided for only about one-third of that number. Spectators are therefore advised to bring their own seats.

Several old photographs and prints in the pavilion and Long Room bar relate to Kidderminster cricket and the history of the ground.

GROUND RECORDS AND SCORES

FIRST-CLASS MATCHES
Highest innings total for County 477 *v.* Northamptonshire, 1946

Highest innings total against County 551 for 7 by Leicestershire, 1929
Lowest innings total for County 63 v. Northamptonshire, 1973
Lowest innings total against County 71 by Leicestershire, 1933
Highest individual innings for County 259 D. Kenyon v. Yorkshire, 1956
Highest individual innings against County 200 n.o. W.E. Bates for Warwickshire, 1927
Best bowling performance in an innings for County 9 for 56 J.A. Flavell v. Middlesex, 1964
Best bowling performance in an innings against County 7 for 35 A.R. Gover for Surrey, 1938
Best bowling performance in a match for County 13 for 96 J.A. Flavell v. Somerset, 1965
Best bowling performance in a match against County 14 for 85 A.R. Gover for Surrey, 1938

LIMITED-OVERS MATCHES
Highest innings total for County 116 for 9 v. Middlesex (JPL), 1969
Highest innings total against County 56 by Middlesex (JPL), 1969
Highest individual innings for County 45 B.L. D'Oliveira v. Middlesex (JPL), 1969
Highest individual innings against County 11 C.T. Radley for Middlesex (JPL), 1969
Best bowling performance for County 3 for 8 N. Gifford v. Middlesex (JPL), 1969
Best bowling performance against County 3 for 14 J.S.E. Price for Middlesex (JPL), 1969

HOW TO GET THERE

Rail Kidderminster, ½ mile
Bus Midland Red from surrounding areas to Bus Station, thence ¾ mile; Midland Red 7 passes ground
Car From north: M5 junction 3, then follow A456 signposted Kidderminster, then take junction with A449 bypass for Offmore Lane and County Cricket close to railway line, or A449, A442 to Kidderminster, then as above. From east: A456 or A448 signposted Kidderminster, then as north. From west: A456 or A451 signposted Kidderminster, then as north. From south: M5 junction 6, then follow A449 signposted Kidderminster, then as north.

WHERE TO STAY AND OTHER INFORMATION

Gainsborough House Hotel (0562 754041), Cedars Hotel (0562 745869)

Disabled Areas No special area, request position
Local Radio Station(s) BBC Radio WM (95.6 MHz FM/1468 KHz

MW), Beacon Radio (97.2 MHz FM/990 KHz MW), Radio Wyvern (102 MHz FM/1530 KHz MW), BRMB (96.4 MHz FM/1152 KHz MW)

Local Newspaper(s) Berrow's Worcester Journal, Kidderminster Shuttle, Kidderminster Chronicle

Hereford

The Hereford cricket ground is part of the Hereford racecourse complex and has been the home of the town club since 1909. The club was founded in 1836 and played at Widemarsh Common until the move to the present ground. The club notched up 150 years in 1986. Celebrations included a tour of Barbados and a visit from the Worcestershire county club for a John Player Sunday League match with Gloucestershire. The ground is now the only one in Britain used for first-class cricket which is within a racecourse, now that the County Cricket Ground, Derby, formerly the Racecourse Ground, no longer shares that distinction.

Widemarsh Common and the Westfield racecourse were the same area until separated by a new road. The original pavilion was built at the common in 1889 and is still in use today. The initial first-class match staged was in 1919 when Worcestershire played H.K. Foster's XI and the game was part of the County's programme after they decided not to re-enter the County Championship after World War One. Hereford hosted later matches for H.K. Foster's XI, including a game with the Australian Imperial Forces touring side. In another friendly first-class match, in 1947, Worcestershire played the Combined Services XI. With the formation of the County of Hereford and Worcestershire first-class cricket returned to the Racecourse Ground after 34 years with the visit of Glamorgan. Subsequent games included visits from Kent and Leicestershire. In 1983 the first limited-overs match was staged with Nottinghamshire in the John Player Sunday League and later years have seen Sunday League matches with Gloucestershire and the Refuge Assurance Sunday League fixtures with Surrey and Gloucestershire. Middlesex were due to visit in 1984 but the fixture was transferred to Worcester.

Hereford C C play in the Three Counties League which was formed in 1968 and includes club sides from Hereford, Gloucestershire and the South East Wales region. The club has won the First XI League nine times since 1972 and the Second XI on three occasions. Reg Perks and Peter Richardson both played for Hereford C C and represented Worcestershire and England during their careers. Ground records have included hundreds from Glenn Turner and Mark Benson, both in the same match, and a Sunday League hundred from Jack Russell for Gloucestershire. Crowds are quite good: 4,000 can be expected. In

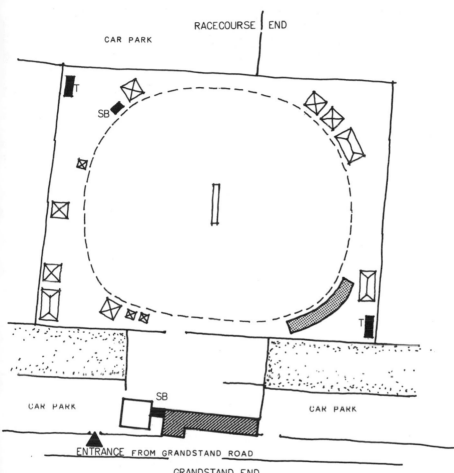

RACECOURSE | END

CAR PARK

T

SB

SB

T

CAR PARK

CAR PARK

SB

ENTRANCE FROM GRANDSTAND ROAD

GRANDSTAND END

N

0   50   100

Metres

1987 a crowd of over 7,500 witnessed the Refuge Assurance Sunday League match against Surrey in which Tim Curtis and Ian Botham took the home side to a nine wickets' victory and the top of the Refuge League, which the club was to win for the first time.

ADDRESS   Hereford C C, Hereford City Sports Club, Racecourse Cricket Ground, Grandstand Road, Hereford
TELEPHONE PROSPECTS OF PLAY   0432 273098

DESCRIPTION OF GROUND AND FACILITIES

Situated within the Racecourse Ground, the playing area is some way from the pavilion. Players therefore view the match from a tent adjoining the press and scorers' tents in the south-west corner of the ground. All the seating is open and some for members is on raised timber platforms to the south and west of the ground. The north-west and west side of the ground is for the public. The north-east side, which is for sponsors, includes tents and a double-decker bus. A scoreboard adjoins the pavilion and a temporary scoreboard is sited close to the playing area on the west side. The playing area is 140 metres by 120 metres and is defined by a rope and advertisement boards.

The members' area includes refreshment tents and temporary toilet facilities. Similar facilities are found on the west side of the ground along with a Worcestershire C C S C tent. Car parking is available off Grandstand Road and in the overflow car park at the northern Racecourse End of the ground, where there is an entrance through white canvas temporary fencing. The main entrance is from Grandstand Road adjoining the pavilion. The radio and TV point is at the Grandstand Road End of the ground and a fine view of the playing area and racecourse can be had from the first floor of the pavilion, although at some distance. There are no trees near the ground which is possibly one of the most open locations on the county circuit.

The ground capacity is 7,500 and, as only 60 per cent of seating is provided spectators are advised to bring their own seats to popular matches.

GROUND RECORDS AND SCORES

FIRST-CLASS MATCHES
Highest innings total for County   321 v. Kent, 1982
Highest innings total against County   321 for 7 dec. by Kent, 1982
Lowest innings total for County   84 v. Combined Services, 1947
Lowest innings total against County   87 for Combined Services, 1947
Highest individual innings for County   118 G.M. Turner v. Kent, 1982
Highest individual innings against County   107 M.R. Benson for Kent, 1982
Best bowling performance in an innings for County   5 for 13

R. Howorth v. Combined Services, 1947
Best bowling performance in an innings against County   6 for 50
H.A. Gilbert for H.K. Foster's XI, 1919
Best bowling performance in a match for County   8 for 70
R. Howorth v. Combined Services, 1947
Best bowling performance in a match against County   12 for 122
H.A. Gilbert for H.K. Foster's XI, 1919

LIMITED-OVERS MATCHES
Highest innings total for County   233 for 6 v. Gloucestershire
(JPL), 1986
Highest innings total against County   230 by Gloucestershire (JPL),
1986
Lowest innings total for County   195 for 9 v. Nottinghamshire
(JPL), 1983
Lowest innings total against County   154 by Surrey (RAL), 1987
Highest individual innings for County   86 P.A. Neale v.
Nottinghamshire (JPL), 1983
Highest individual innings against County   108 R.C. Russell for
Gloucestershire (JPL), 1986
Best bowling performance for County   3 for 23 A.P. Pridgeon v.
Gloucestershire (JPL), 1986
Best bowling performance against County   2 for 39 M. Hendrick
for Nottinghamshire (JPL), 1983

HOW TO GET THERE

Rail   Hereford, 1½ miles
Bus   Midland Red West 102, 112 from city centre (104/5, 115 link
BR Station with centre) (Tel: 0345 212 555 – local rate from
anywhere in Britain)
Car   From north: A49 or A4110 signposted Hereford and town
centre, follow signs Racecourse and Grandstand Road for entrance
to Hereford Sports Club. From east: A465 or A438 signposted
Hereford and town centre, then follow signs to Leominster A49 into
Grandstand Road. From west: A438 or A465 signposted Hereford
and town centre, then as east. From south: A49 or B4224 or B4399
signposted Hereford and town centre, then as east.

WHERE TO STAY AND OTHER INFORMATION

Green Dragon Hotel (0432 272506), Hereford Moat House Hotel
(0432 54301)

Disabled Areas   All areas except pavilion (upstairs) accessible
Local Radio Station(s)   Radio Wyvern (102 MHz FM/1530 KHz
MW), Severn Sound (95.0 MHz FM/774 KHz MW)
Local Newspaper   Hereford Times

YORKSHIRE

CHURCHMAN'S CIGARETTES.

YORKSHIRE.

LEEDS – HEADINGLEY

HARROGATE

MIDDLESBROUGH

SCARBOROUGH

SHEFFIELD

HULL

Yorkshire

Great teams and great players elevated Yorkshire to a place of special eminence in English cricket. To beat Yorkshire was the aim of every county and touring team, and it is a remarkable fact that they did not drop into a double-figure position in the table until 1953 when Hutton was excusably absent, winning the Ashes with the help of Watson, Wardle and Trueman. By far the biggest of the Big Six they won 29 outright championships before a staunchly conservative and principled club was engulfed by internal strife.

In 1983 the unthinkable (at least to older generations) happened with Yorkshire at the bottom, a calamity not offset by the winning of the John Player League. There were also painful defeats in Cup matches by Durham and Shropshire of the Minor Counties. How the mighty had fallen.

For years the white rose was in perennial bloom. Team work, based on principles laid down long ago by the father figure, Lord Hawke, was Yorkshire's hallmark. The powerful Leagues supplied the county with their finest talent, and a loyal public helped to set a pace and standard others toiled to emulate.

All-Yorkshire talent flowed in a never ending stream from decade to decade . . . from Emmett, Freeman, Ulyett, Peel, to Hirst, Rhodes, Haigh, the Hon F.S. Jackson, to Sutcliffe, Leyland, Verity, Bowes, to Hutton, Boycott, Illingworth, Trueman. On three occasions Yorkshire had five representatives in a Test team, and it ws no idle boast that a strong Yorkshire meant a strong England.

Sheffield was the original starting point, and the rugged individualism of the early times was made into one cohesive force by the guiding hand of Lord Hawke, who, paradoxically, was born in Lincolnshire and broke the unwritten law of 'no outsiders'. 'In the 1880s when I became captain of Yorkshire they were a fine lot,' Hawke once said. 'There were ten drunks and a chapel parson – and he wasn't ordained!'

The 7th Lord Hawke undoubtedly had some of the faults of the autocrat, but the disciplinary codes and values he promoted far outlived the twenty-eight years of his captaincy, which produced 8 championships and marked a rise in the standing of his professionals. He introduced winter pay, started a policy whereby the club retained two-thirds of a benefit for investment, and insisted on a more presentable appearance than had been the custom. He was strong enough to sack the England all-rounder Peel, an act which gave the legendary Wilfred Rhodes an early chance to launch a career which brought him 4,187 wickets at 16.71, 39,802 runs and 58 centuries. The last of his home Tests was at the age of 48 when he was recalled for the final Test at The Oval in 1926, and with 4 for 44 in 20 overs played a significant part in the recovery of the Ashes. Three years later he played in four Tests in the West Indies!

Rhodes' partner George Hirst – 'my Georgie' as Hawke called him

ILS's CIGARETTES

YORKSHIRE C.C.C.

ORKSHIRE CRICKET"
"Vanity Fair" Series

— is credited with inventing swing bowling, an innovation to raise him to a loftier class. Incredibly in 1906 he scored 2,385 runs and took 208 wickets (2,180 and 203 for Yorkshire), and his career record was 2,739 wickets at 18.72, and 36,323 runs with 60 hundreds. His 14 doubles is surpassed only by Rhodes' 16.

Four all-rounders of the calibre of Rhodes, Hirst, Haigh and Jackson and all the property of one club is something to contemplate, even if 'Jackers' could make only erratic appearances. Jackson, standing as a municipal candidate in Leeds, asked Hirst to speak on his behalf, and when he rose he urged the audience not to vote for him as it would be a bad thing for Yorkshire and England if he got on the council!

Jackson, later an MP and Governor of Bengal, had only one full season for Yorkshire, but he managed to have 33 innings in home Tests and hit 5 centuries. As fine an example for Sutcliffe as Sutcliffe was in the course of time for Hutton. Sutcliffe and Holmes had first-wicket partnerships of 100 or more sixty-nine times, and broke the record of 554 set up by their predecessors, Brown and Tunnicliffe, by one run. Or did they? Sutcliffe unwisely gave his wicket away when the Leyton scoreboard showed 555, but the scorers declared the total to be 554. Amid the ensuing panic a no-ball, not recorded, was conveniently discovered and the new record was accepted.

Immaculate and assured, Sutcliffe epitomized Yorkshire power which reached its zenith between 1931, the first of two successive seasons in which he exceeded 3,000 runs, and 1939. In all but two of those seasons Yorkshire were champions, and many of the 153 victories were achieved inside two days. The batting of Sutcliffe, Leyland, Holmes, Mitchell, the magnificent catcher, and Barber, and the bowling of Bowes, Verity, Macaulay and all-rounder Smailes was supreme. Hutton was schooled in an academy of cricket wisdom. Its teachings were never forgotten.

During that fateful September weekend of 1939, Hutton and Yardley scored centuries, and Verity, to die from battle wounds in an Italian PoW camp, took 7 for 9 as Sussex were dismissed for 33. As the world plunged into war Yorkshire confirmed their third successive title, and on the way home a last supper was held at Leicester. Time was to show how much of Yorkshire's pride and spirit – so often accepted as their most precious ingredients – disappeared with the break-up of a celebrated team.

Hutton returned in 1946 with an injured left arm and a 50 per cent disability pension, but overcame his handicap to remain a supreme batsman and be knighted and appointed the first pro captain of England. Not the least of his triumphs was to rise above the ritual snobbery of the diehards unable to come to terms with a new order.

Yardley took Yorkshire to the top again in the first post-war season, and Burnet, installed as a disciplinarian, did the same in 1959. Vic Wilson, the county's first pro captain, retained the title, and the reign of the combative Close was like old times with four championships and the Gillette Cup twice, but he left for Somerset after an avoidable clash with authority, and Illingworth went to Leicestershire when he was refused more than a one-year contract. Clearly both still had much to offer, and some trace their departure as the starting point of Yorkshire's internal bust-up.

The complex Boycott, with 48,426 runs and 151 centuries was unarguably the champion batsman of his time, but he spent eight years as captain without winning anything, and, with Botham, was the most discussed figure in thirty years of English cricket. His finest hour was to complete his 100th century in a Test with Australia on his home ground of Leeds following three years of self-imposed exile from Test cricket.

Not even the return of Illingworth as manager produced results or harmony in the dressing room, and public frustration concentrated around Boycott, seen as an idol and a symbol of a glorious past. Emotions erupted when Yorkshire finished bottom in 1983 and, with the decision to concentrate on a youth policy, Boycott was sacked. Morale was rock bottom, and the pro-Boycott lobby conducted a campaign against the club officials which the *Sunday Telegraph* observed would not have shamed a by-election. After a long and bitter wrangle a special meeting ousted the general and cricket committees and backed Boycott's reinstatement. By a majority vote his contract was finally ended at the end of the 1986 season. His record in the championship was 29,485 runs, averaging 58.27.

The desperation of Yorkshire's uncertainty was reflected in the turn-over of captains – Carrick providing the best hope of a brighter future with the Benson and Hedges Cup 1987 – but there was no tangible improvement in the championship.

Basically Yorkshire's decline is due to their cherished policy – massively endorsed in opinion polls – of fielding a genuine Yorkshire team. The other sixteen clubs have the pick of the world. The local Leagues have also gone over to limited-over cricket to the detriment of spin. Once Yorkshire spin was a source of immense strength, but a shortage over the past decades is a significant cause of their problems. [A.B.]

Founded 1863
Colours Oxford blue, Cambridge blue and gold
Crest White rose of Yorkshire
Secretary J. Lister
Coach D.E.V. Padgett
Assistant coach S. Oldham
Groundsman K. Boyce
Scorers E.I. Lester/J.W. Potter
Address Headingley Cricket Ground, St Michael's Lane, Headingley, Leeds LS6 3BU
Telephone 0532 787394
Cricketcall 0898 121444

Achievements:

County Championship Champions (31) 1867, 1870, 1893, 1896, 1898, 1900, 1901, 1902, 1905, 1908, 1912, 1919, 1922, 1923, 1924, 1925, 1931, 1932, 1933, 1935, 1937, 1938, 1939, 1946, 1959, 1960, 1962, 1963, 1966, 1967 and 1968; joint champions (2) 1869 and 1949
Gillette Cup Winners 1965 and 1969
National Westminster Bank Trophy Semi-finalists 1982
Benson & Hedges Cup Winners 1987; finalists 1972
John Player Sunday League Champions (1) 1983
Refuge Assurance Sunday League Champions (0) 8th 1988
Fenner Trophy Winners 1972, 1974 and 1981; finalists 1973, 1975, 1976, 1978 and 1979
Asda Trophy Winners 1987; finalists 1984
Ward Knockout Cup Finalists 1988
Tilcon Trophy Winners 1978 and 1988; finalists 1983

Grounds:

Leeds (Headingley Cricket Ground, St Michael's Lane) Sheffield (Abbeydale Park, Abbeydale Park Road South, Dore) Middlesbrough (Acklam Park, Green Lanc) Harrogate (St George's Road) Hull (The Circle, Anlaby Road) Scarborough (North Marine Road).

Other grounds that have been used since 1969 are: Bradford (Park Avenue), Huddersfield (Fartown), Sheffield (Bramall Lane) and Barnsley (Shaw Lane).

Leeds – Headingley

Leeds is not the original headquarters of Yorkshire cricket; its first centre was at Bramall Lane, Sheffield from 1863 until 1888, when a group of wealthy developers who were also sportsmen joined together to buy lot 17a, a plot of land in the north-west of Leeds, at an auction of land by the Cardigan Estate. These gentlemen formed the Leeds Cricket, Football and Athletic Co. Ltd. Their Chairman was Lord Hawke. The purchase was the first major step towards the establishment of the County's headquarters at Headingley.

Cricket and rugby football have been played at Headingley since 1890 when the first important match here was staged between the North and the touring Australians. The next year saw Yorkshire's initial first-class match on the ground (against Kent) and in 1899 Headingley staged its first Test Match (against Australia). The majority of Yorkshire matches are staged at Headingley and the ground is still owned by the Leeds Cricket, Football and Athletic Co. Ltd. Yorkshire C C C moved its headquarters to Leeds in 1903; the county club previously leased offices in Park Road and now leases its administration offices and changing facilities (built in 1962 in the north-east corner of the ground) from the Leeds club at Headingley. Much of the development at Headingley was undertaken by Sir Edwin Airey, a building contractor who in 1932 undertook improvements designed to establish Headingley as a major cricket venue. The dual-purpose Football or Main Stand stretches along the southern boundary of the field and from it one can view the cricket to the north or rugby league to the south, for Headingley is also the home of Leeds Rugby League Club. The Leeds Pavilion is the oldest building on the ground and houses the Leeds office, the press box and scorers' room together with bars and ample catering facilities. Other additions have included the Kirkstall Lane End and the Winter Shed stand which contains executive boxes and seating. The majority of seating is of the plastic tip-up variety on the vast West Terrace and North Enclosure. In recent years a computerized scoreboard has been installed, sponsored by Scottish and Newcastle Breweries; it is operated by members of York University throughout the season. The Sutcliffe Gates in St Michael's Lane form one of the entrances to the ground; just opposite is the newly constructed Yorkshire indoor cricket school and county library. There are many historic photographs in the old Leeds Pavilion and in the bars and the new school.

Headingley is to be improved by a £2.5m improvement plan which was recently announced.

Crowds at Headingley are usually 8,000–10,000 for county matches. The present capacity is set at 20,000 and this is achieved for most important matches. The record crowd for a county match over three days was 44,507 against Lancashire in 1948 and for a single day 30,000 against the Australians during the 1948 Test Match. The ground has been used for all the major county cricket competitions along with Prudential Trophy, Prudential Cup and Texaco Trophy international

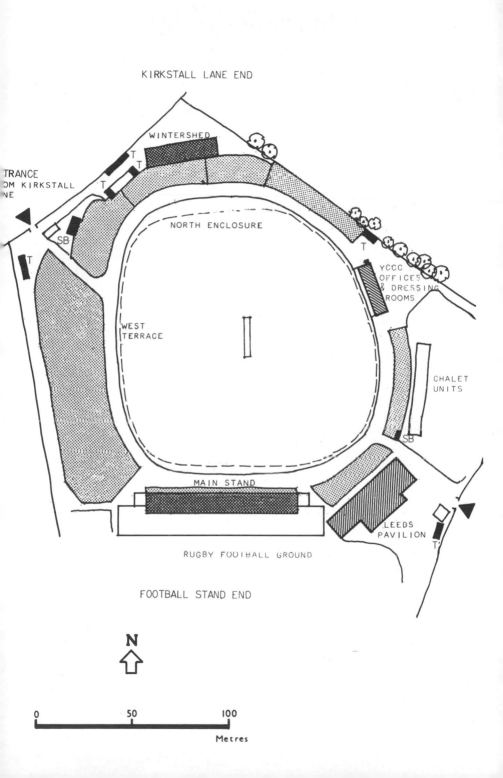

matches. Ground achievements include Geoff Boycott's 100th hundred (scored in a Test Match against Australia in 1977). Big scores have included innings from Don Bradman, Herbert Sutcliffe, John Edrich and in recent years pure genius from Ian Botham who put England on the way to regaining the Ashes in 1981. Significant bowling performances over the years have come from Colin Blythe, Hedley Verity, R. Peel, Richard Hutton and Bob Willis.

ADDRESS   The Pavilion, Headingley Cricket Ground, St Michael's Lane, Leeds LS6 3BR
TELEPHONE PROSPECTS OF PLAY   0532 787394

DESCRIPTION OF GROUND AND FACILITIES

Entry to the ground for members is from St. Michael's Lane through the Main Gates or the Sutcliffe Gates, while the public gains access from Kirkstall Lane. All buildings are permanent with the exception of the hospitality boxes erected on the east side of the ground for Test Matches and other international matches. The members' pavilion is in the south-east corner of the ground and is separated from the players' pavilion and club offices which are on the north-east side of the ground. On the south side of the ground is the main stand which provides the only area of covered seating on the ground, and from where you can view the cricket as well as football. The members' areas include the whole of the football stand, the pavilion and seating round to the Wintershed stand to the north of the ground. The western terraces and part of the north enclosure are available to members of the public. Some car parking is available in the South Stand Park but this is limited on international match days, and car parking must be found in the adjoining streets or in local authority parking at Beckett Park and Woodhouse Moor. Bar and refreshments are available in various parts of the ground and the public have access to the facilities in the Wintershed Stand and the Grandstand bar in the main stand. Facilities are available for disabled spectators and they should request a suitable position. The playing area is oval in shape, measures 137 metres by 140 metres and is defined by advertisement boards. However the actual playing area for a match is also defined by a rope within the boards this providing an area of about 130 metres by 134 metres. The covers are kept in the space available on the north side of the ground. Although most of the ground provides two rows of seats immediately outside the boundary boards, the ground has a 5 metre walkway all round it, behind these two rows of seats and in front of the terraces of tiered seating. This can be very distracting to those who choose to sit in the front rows of the tiered seating and these should therefore be avoided. The main electronic scoreboard is sited on the north-west side of the ground, and the White Rose souvenir shop is found directly behind. The present ground capacity is 20,000 and seats are available for all.

As a Test Match venue this has all the appropriate facilities that one would expect. There is a small collection of historical artefacts in the members' bar.

GROUND RECORDS AND SCORES

TEST MATCHES
Highest innings total for England   550 for 4 v. India, 1967
Highest innings total against England   548 by Australia, 1934
Lowest innings total for England   76 by South Africa, 1907
Lowest innings total against England   67 by New Zealand, 1958
Highest individual innings for England   310 n.o. J.H. Edrich v. New Zealand, 1965
Highest individual innings against England   334 D.G. Bradman for Australia, 1981
Best bowling performance in an innings for England   8 for 43 R.G.D. Willis v. Australia, 1981
Best bowling performance in an innings against England   7 for 40 Imran Khan for Pakistan, 1987
Best bowling performance in a match for England   15 for 99 C. Blythe v. South Africa, 1907
Best bowling performance in a match against England   11 for 87 C.G. Macartney for Australia, 1909

LIMITED-OVERS INTERNATIONALS
Highest innings total   278 for 7 by Australia v. Pakistan (PC), 1975
Lowest innings total   93 by England v. Australia (PC), 1975
Highest individual   108 G.M. Wood for Australia v. England (PT), 1981
Best bowling performance   7 for 51 W.W. Davis for West Indies v. Australia (PC), 1983

FIRST-CLASS MATCHES
Highest innings total for County   560 for 6 dec. v. Leicestershire, 1921
Highest innings total against County   630 by Somerset, 1901
Lowest innings total for County   33 v. Lancashire, 1924
Lowest innings total against County   23 by Australia, 1902
Highest individual innings for County   270 H. Sutcliffe v. Sussex, 1932
Highest individual innings against County   232 n.o. G. Brown for Hampshire, 1920
Best bowling performance in an innings for County   10 for 10 H. Verity v. Nottinghamshire, 1932
Best bowling performance in an innings against County   9 for 57 F.A. Tarrant for Middlesex, 1906
Best bowling performance in a match for County   15 for 50 R. Peel v. Somerset, 1895
Best bowling performance in a match against County   15 for 154 T. Richardson for Surrey, 1897

LIMITED-OVERS MATCHES

Highest innings total for County   317 for 5 *v*. Scotland (BHC), 1986
Highest innings total against County   286 for 5 by Worcestershire
(NWBT), 1982
Lowest innings total for County   109 *v*. Leicestershire (GC), 1975
Lowest innings total against County   23 by Middlesex (JPL), 1974
Highest individual innings for County   118 n.o. J.D. Love *v*. Surrey
(RAL), 1987
Highest individual innings against County   111 Zaheer Abbas for
Gloucestershire (GC), 1976
Best bowling performance for County   7 for 15 R.A. Hutton *v*.
Worcestershire (JPL), 1969
Best bowling performance against County   5 for 33 B.J. Griffiths for
Northamptonshire (NWBT), 1983

HOW TO GET THERE

Rail   Headingley, ½ mile; Leeds City, 2½ miles
Bus   Yorkshire Rider 7, 74–7 link BR Leeds Station with ground
(Tel: 0532 457676); also 1, 4, 56, 93 and 96 for city centre; 38, 39 93
and 96 from city suburbs
Car   From north: A660, A61 or A58 follow signs Leeds and city
centre, then follow signs Kirkstall district and Headingley for
County Cricket and Headingley Cricket Ground turning off A660,
the ground is situated to the north-west of the city centre about 1½
miles and west of the A660. From east: A64, A63 or M62 and M1
follow signs Leeds and city centre, then follow signs Kirkstall
district and Headingley on A660 for Headingley Cricket Ground.
From west: A58, A62, A647 or M62 and M621 follow signs Leeds
and city centre, then follow signs Kirkstall district and Headingley
on A660 for Headingley Cricket Ground. From south: A653, A61 or
M1 to junction 43, then follow A61 Leeds and city centre, then
follow signs Kirkstall district and Headingley on A660 1½ miles
north-west of city centre for Headingley and County Cricket.

WHERE TO STAY AND OTHER INFORMATION

Queen's Hotel (0532 431323), Golden Lion Hotel (0532 436454),
Post House Hotel, Leeds/Bramhope (0532 842911), The Metropole
(0532 450841)

Disabled Areas   In designated areas
Local Radio Station(s)   BBC Radio Leeds (95.3 MHz FM/774 KHz
MW), Radio Aire (96.3 MHz FM/828 KHz MW)
Local Newspaper(s)   Yorkshire Post, Yorkshire Evening Press, Leeds
Weekly News, Bradford Telegraph & News

Harrogate

The St George's Road Ground has been the home of Harrogate C C since its foundation in 1877. The initial first-class match here was staged in 1880 when an England eleven played the Australians. The match was the first in England to be started on a Saturday. The first county championship match here was staged in 1894 when Yorkshire's opponents were Leicestershire.

The main pavilion was built in 1896, the Mound in 1956 and the Tavern bar and restaurant in 1965. The ground was for many years owned by Harrogate C C but in 1936, during a difficult period in the club's history, the ground was purchased by Harrogate Corporation, which still owns it.

Harrogate's pride and joy was of course Maurice Leyland, who represented Harrogate, Yorkshire and England and was undoubtedly the finest local player ever produced. Appropriately the Leyland Gates welcome you at one of the ground's entrances, which is from St Marks Avenue. The gates were erected in 1965, two years before Leyland's death. The Centenary Gates, erected in 1977, form the main entrance from St George's Road.

Attempts were made to establish an annual cricket festival at Harrogate in 1913, 1925 and 1947, but this was discontinued each time after the first year. It was not until 1974 that a regular festival was successfully launched; since then it has consisted of a Yorkshire county championship match together with a three-day competition for the Tilcon Trophy. This is played under Benson and Hedges Cup rules by four counties invited by Tilcon from those counties not involved in the Benson and Hedges semi-final round. All the counties except Essex and Lancashire have competed at one time or another in the Tilcon Trophy. Harrogate festival week is usually in mid-June and daily crowds are 5,000–6,000. The ground is used for private company matches, for Harrogate C C engagements (the club plays in the Yorkshire League) and for ladies' matches during midweek.

The best crowd for a single day was 15,000 when India played Pakistan in 1986 for the charity Help the Aged. The best crowd for a Yorkshire match was 13,630, at the 1962 match with Glamorgan. In addition to championship matches Yorkshire have staged tour matches and other friendly matches including the South Africans (1901), West Indians (1906, 1933 and 1939), Indians (1932) and New Zealanders (1931). Limited-overs matches have been staged in the John Player Sunday League (1969–71) and the Gillete Cup (1970 and 1973). Durham beat the County by 5 wickets in the 1973 Gillette Cup match and became the first minor county to beat a first-class county in this competition. In 1897 Gilbert Jessop hit 101 in 40 minutes for Gloucestershire. Percy Holmes and Viv Richards have both hit double centuries and wickets have been taken to great effect by G.G. Macaulay and Ray Illingworth for the White Rose County. In limited-overs matches staged on the ground Zaheer Abbas's 134 not out and Robin Jackman's 7 for 33 stand out for the visitors.

Many Harrogate players have represented Yorkshire. In addition to Leyland, they include: A. Booth, J.H. Hampshire, R. Kilner, G.G. Macaulay, T.F. Smailes, H. Wilkinson and J.D. Love. County cricketers who played for Harrogate after retiring from first-class cricket have included: W.E. Bates, J.T. Brown, G.R. Cass, Lord Hawke, W.H.H. Sutcliffe, F.S. Trueman, N.W.D. Yardley, W.B. Stott and B.S. Boshier.

ADDRESS   St George's Cricket Ground, St George's Road, Harrogate, North Yorkshire
TELEPHONE PROSPECTS OF PLAY   0423 61301

DESCRIPTION OF GROUND AND FACILITIES

The main access to the ground is from St. George's Road at its junction with West End Avenue, through the Centenary Gates.

The playing area is bounded by permanent terraces on three sides. The western side is a partly covered stand. The two storey pavilion, hospitality suite, scorers' room and press room, which is in the roof of pavilion and Tavern buildings are in the south corner of the ground and, with the adjoining terraces, provide the accommodation for members. The scoreboard is in the north corner of the ground directly opposite the pavilion. The east side of the ground has only a few rows of bench seats and there is adequate space for the provision of hospitality tents. Refreshment facilities are available for the public by the covered stand and near the scoreboard. Limited car parking is available at the ground and one should therefore try to park in the adjoining streets. The playing area is approximately 118 metres by 140 metres and is open except at the north and west sides of the ground, where, similar to Headingley, there is a walkway between the playing area and the spectators. Ground capacity is 8,000 and seating is provided for 65 per cent of this number. There is no special provision for disabled spectators but access is unencumbered and they should ask for an appropriate position. This is a ground which encourages the watching of cricket.

GROUND RECORDS AND SCORES

FIRST-CLASS MATCHES
Highest innings total for County   548 for 4 v. Northamptonshire, 1921
Highest innings total against County   439 by Derbyshire, 1984
Lowest innings total for County   50 v. West Indians, 1906
Lowest innings total against County   42 by Worcestershire, 1923
Highest individual innings for County   277 n.o. P. Holmes v. Northamptonshire, 1921
Highest individual innings against County   217 n.o. I.V.A. Richards for Somerset, 1975

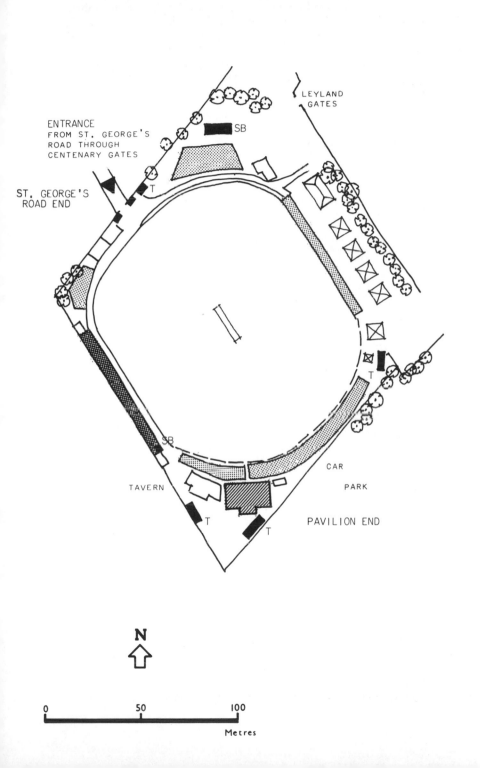

LEYLAND
GATES

ENTRANCE
FROM ST. GEORGE'S
ROAD THROUGH
CENTENARY GATES

SB

ST. GEORGE'S
ROAD END

T

SB

TAVERN

CAR

PARK

PAVILION END

T

T

N

0   50   100

Metres

Best bowling performance in an innings for County 8 for 21
G.G. Macaulay *v*. Indians, 1932
Best bowling performance in an innings against County 7 for 20
F.E. Field for Warwickshire, 1911
Best bowling performance in a match for County 14 for 64
R. Illingworth *v*. Gloucestershire, 1967
Best bowling performance in a match against County 12 for 176
E.G. Dennett for Gloucestershire, 1907

LIMITED-OVERS MATCHES
Highest innings total for County 174 for 4 *v*. Derbyshire (JPL),
1971
Highest innings total against County 177 for 9 by Derbyshire
(JPL), 1971
Lowest innings total for County 76 *v*. Surrey (GC), 1970
Lowest innings total against County 134 for 8 by Surrey (GC),
1970
Highest individual innings for County 55 A.J. Dalton *v*.
Derbyshire (JPL), 1971
Highest individual innings against County 47 R. Inglis for
Durham (GC), 1973
Best bowling performance for County 4 for 38 C.M. Old *v*.
Derbyshire (JPL), 1971
Best bowling performance against County 7 for 33 R.D. Jackman
for Surrey (GC), 1970

TILCON TROPHY
Highest innings total 336 by Northamptonshire *v*. Glamorgan,
1981
Lowest innings total 58 by Nottinghamshire *v*. Surrey, 1978
Highest individual innings 134 n.o. Zaheer Abbas for
Gloucestershire *v*. Warwickshire, 1979
Best bowling performance 6 for 38 P. Bainbridge for
Gloucestershire *v*. Leicestershire, 1986

HOW TO GET THERE

Rail Harrogate, 1¼ miles
Bus Harrogate & District 36, 653 BR Harrogate Station–Leeds/
Bradford pass end of St George's Road (Tel: 0423 66061)
Car From north: A1 and A6055 signposted Harrogate or A61 to
town centre, the St George's Cricket Ground is situated south of
the town centre, off the A61 to Leeds about ½ mile south of town
centre. From east: A59 follow signs Harrogate and town centre,
then follow A61 south for St George's Cricket Ground off the Leeds
road, signpost for ground located in centre of roundabout! From
west: A59 or B6162 follow signs Harrogate and town centre, then as
east. From south: A1 and A661 signposted Harrogate or A61 then as
north or east.

WHERE TO STAY AND OTHER INFORMATION

Crown Hotel (0423 67755), Prospect Hotel (0423 65071), The Majestic (0423 68972)

Disabled Areas   No special area, request position
Local Radio Station(s)   BBC Radio York (95.5 MHz FM/1260 KHz MW)
Local Newspaper(s)   Yorkshire Post, Yorkshire Evening Press, Harrogate Herald

Middlesbrough

Acklam Park in Green Lane is the home of Middlesbrough C C (founded in 1875) and has been the club's ground since 1932. The third ground to be used by Yorkshire in Middlesbrough, it is situated in the pleasant suburb of Acklam on the southern outskirts of the town. Middlesbrough is the most northerly venue that stages regular first-class cricket in the country, Middlesbrough C C plays in the North Yorkshire and South Durham Cricket League and fields three teams. The ground of 12 acres comprises not only the main cricket ground but two full size rugby pitches, 12 practice wickets and 2 all-weather wickets. The whole ground is in excellent condition and the pavilion, which is at right angles to the wicket, includes changing rooms, baths and a large dining room over-looking the playing area. The rear of the pavilion is the clubhouse which has two attractively furnished bars. The scorebox is modern and fully automatic. It is built on two levels, the lower being a garage for groundsman's equipment.

The first Yorkshire match at Acklam Park was in 1956 against Glamorgan when 9,423 people attended the first two days of the championship match; the third day was abandoned. The groundsman in 1956 said of Middlesbrough, 'You won't find a better pitch in Yorkshire,' but the county club would probably not fully agree with this statement, as in 1965 Hampshire bowled Yorkshire out for 23, the lowest ever completed innings by the County. Yorkshire usually play four days' cricket at Middlesbrough in the early part of the season comprising one championship and one limited-overs match.

The first organized cricket match in Middlesbrough was in 1844, promoted by William Taylor for members of the Mechanics Institute. From this was established the nucleus of the Middlesbrough club. The first ground was at Albert Road, where Yorkshire staged matches between 1864 and 1867; this ground is now the site of the Royal Exchange. In 1871 the club moved to Swatters Carr (Kipling's farm), known today as Linthorpe Road until its move to Breckon Hill in 1900. Yorkshire played one match at Linthorpe Road against the Australians in 1882; soon after the ground was occupied by Middlesbrough Football Club until their move to Ayresome Park. The ground is now the site of St George's Church. The club only played at Breckon Hill until 1911 when it moved once again, this time to North Ormesby. After twenty-one years they moved to their present ground when the Middlesbrough C C joined forces with the town's rugby football club. They continue to share the same facilities and ground. The pavilion and the majority of the banks surrounding the playing area were built in 1953 thanks to the organization of J. Eric Thomas, the chairman, and H.E. Thomas, the club secretary.

Crowds at Acklam Park are usually 6,500–7,000. The best was 13,100 for the visit of Warwickshire in 1967. Ground performances have included individual scores of the highest order from Doug Padgett (now county coach) and Peter Richardson for Kent. Freddie Trueman, Don Wilson and Chris Old always found the wicket lively; despite this Geoff Boycott scored many runs at Acklam Park including, in 1986, his 150th century, which made him Yorkshire's leading century-maker ahead of Herbert Sutcliffe.

ADDRESS Middlesbrough C C, Acklam Park, Green Lane, Acklam, Middlesbrough, Cleveland
TELEPHONE PROSPECTS OF PLAY 0642 818567

DESCRIPTION OF GROUND AND FACILITIES

Acklam Park is entered from Green Lane to the north of the ground. There is ample car parking on the south side of the ground, on the rugby field. The main buildings are the pavilion and clubhouse on the east side of the ground and the scoreboard in the south-west corner of the cricket field. On the west, north and east sides of the ground there are permanent tiered mounds of bench seating, mainly for the public and north of the pavilion, for members. The members' enclosure also extends south of the pavilion and round to the sitescreen and provides additional refreshment facilities and a club souvenir caravan. A separate area is provided for disabled spectators. There are adequate toilets for both members and the public. The playing area is approximately 144 metres by 124 metres and is defined by a rope as well as advertisement boards and the existing change of levels.

Although bounded on three sides by the backs of houses the fenced sides are planted with trees in most places and this is a pleasant ground at which to watch cricket in good weather.

GROUND RECORDS AND SCORES

FIRST-CLASS MATCHES
Highest innings total for County 381 v. Sussex, 1960
Highest innings total against County 349 for 7 by Glamorgan, 1976
Lowest innings total for County 23 v. Hampshire, 1965
Lowest innings total against County 41 by Gloucestershire, 1969

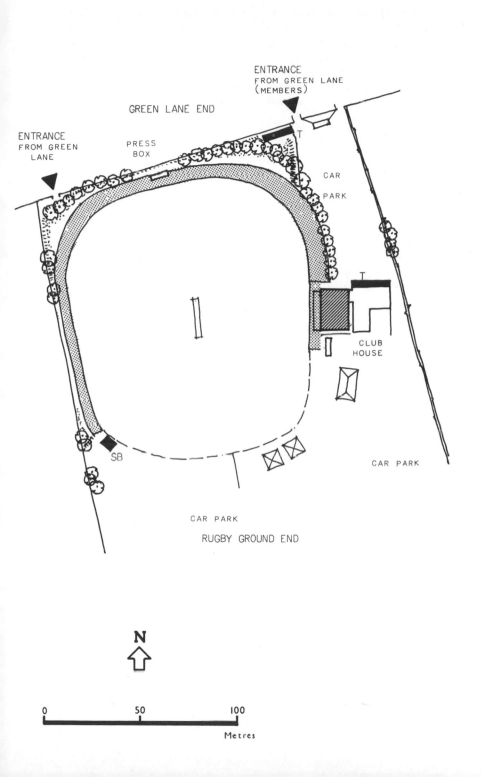

ENTRANCE
FROM GREEN LANE
(MEMBERS)

GREEN LANE END

ENTRANCE
FROM GREEN
LANE

PRESS
BOX

CAR
PARK

T

CLUB
HOUSE

CAR PARK

SB

CAR PARK

RUGBY GROUND END

N

0   50   100

Metres

Highest individual innings for County   146 D.E.V. Padgett *v.*
Sussex, 1960
Highest individual innings against County   162 P.E. Richardson for
Kent, 1960
Best bowling performance in an innings for County   7 for 23
M.J. Cowan *v.* Scotland, 1958
Best bowling performance in an innings against County   7 for 39
F.J. Titmus for Middlesex, 1974
Best bowling performance in a match for County   10 for 81
F.S. Trueman *v.* West Indians, 1963
Best bowling performance in a match against County   14 for 114
F.J. Titmus for Middlesex, 1974

LIMITED-OVERS MATCHES
Highest innings total for County   259 for 4 *v.* Hampshire (JPL),
1985
Highest innings total against County   282 for 4 by
Northamptonshire (JPL), 1982
Lowest innings total for County   207 *v.* Sussex (JPL), 1970
Lowest innings total against County   124 by Warwickshire (JPL),
1983
Highest individual innings for County   110 J.H. Hampshire *v.*
Durham (GC), 1978
Highest individual innings against County   100 n.o. J.B. Bolus for
Nottinghamshire (GC), 1963
Best bowling performance for County   6 for 27 A.G. Nicholson *v.*
Minor Counties (North) (BHC), 1972
Best bowling performance against County   4 for 30 D.J. Capel for
Northamptonshire (JPL), 1982

HOW TO GET THERE

Rail   Middlesbrough, 1¼ miles
Bus   Cleveland Transit 14/6, 24 link Bus Station – 400m from BR
Station – with ground (Tel: 0642 607124)
Car   From north: A1(M), then follow A177 signposted
Middlesborough or take A19 or A178 to town centre, the ground is
situated south of the town centre in the Acklam district in Green
Lane. From west: A66 follow signs Middlesborough and town
centre, then A19 to Acklam turn off using A174 or A1130. From
south: A1, then follow A168 and A19 signposted Middlesborough,
follow signs Acklam for Green Lane and County Cricket, or A172
then as above.

WHERE TO STAY AND OTHER INFORMATION

Blue Bell Hotel (0642 593939), Dragonara Hotel (0642 248133)

Disabled Areas   Special railed-off area provided

Local Radio Station(s) BBC Radio Cleveland (95.0 MHz FM/1548 KHz MW), TFM (96.6 MHz FM/1170 KHz MW)
Local Newspaper(s) Northern Echo, Evening Gazette, Hartlepool Mail, Yorkshire Post, Journal, Sunday Sun

377 YORKSHIRE SCARBOROUGH

Scarborough

The North Marine Road cricket ground was leased by Scarborough C C for £15 a year from 1863 until it was purchased in 1878. Cricket has been played in Scarborough since 1849 when Scarborough C C was established.

Their first matches were staged at Castle Hill (also known as the Queen's Cricket Ground, which has long since been built on). Yorkshire staged matches at Castle Hill from 1874 to 1877 and have visited the seaside resort on the North Yorkshire coast ever since. The first match staged by Yorkshire at the present North Marine Road ground was against I Zingari in 1878. The first cricket festival was staged in 1886; the first teams to play in the festival were New Forest Rangers C C, Yorkshire C C C, M C C and Scarborough C C.

The original pavilion erected in 1874 was replaced at a cost of £2,150 in 1895 by a new pavilion which still stands in the north-western corner of the ground. Before the first county championship match staged by Yorkshire on the ground (in 1896 against Leicestershire) the pavilion clock was presented as a gift from Mr and Mrs J. Compton Rickett and Mr H.J. Morton. In 1902, thanks to funds generated from a most successful festival, a new seating enclosure was erected; this was added to in 1903 and 1907. In 1903 a press/scorers' box was constructed at a cost of £250! A concrete stand was built in the north-east corner in 1926. The West Stand, built in 1956, is the most recent addition to the ground. The Scarborough club has remained one of the best in the county, thanks to Robert Baker, the Secretary at the time of its formation, and the later presidents Rt Hon. Lord Hawke, The Earl of Londesborough and H.D.G. Leveson Gower.

Yorkshire plays two championship and two limited-overs matches in Scarborough each season, usually in August, as well as the later festival matches.

The Scarborough cricket festival takes place in late August to early September. Yorkshire competes with three other invited counties for the Festival Trophy. The limited-overs competition was established in 1971 by J.H. Fenner Ltd, the Hull engineering firm. It consists of two 50-over matches involving four first-class counties; the winners of the two matches meet to decide the outright winner. In 1982 sponsorship of the competition was taken over by Asda Stores, the rules remaining unaltered. After six seasons, in 1988 Ward Building Components took over as sponsor and the competition became the Ward Knockout Trophy.

Games have been staged here between Gentlemen and Players and with touring teams. In 1988 M C C staged a match with a Michael Parkinson's XI. Other visiting teams have included C.I. Thornton's H.D.G. Leveson Gower's, Lord Londesborough's and T.N. Pearce's XI. In 1976 a Prudential Trophy match was staged here between England and West Indies.

The most significant recent event on the ground involving tourists was in 1986 when Ken Rutherford scored 317 against D.B. Close's XI, which included eight Test players. Crowds at Scarborough are usually 8,000–10,000 and the present ground capacity is 15,000. The largest crowd was 22,946 for the match against Derbyshire in 1947. Scarborough C C play in the Yorkshire League and Websters Cricket League. They also enter the Cockspur Cup and have reached the Lord's Final.

Many great cricketers have played at Scarborough and G.J. Bonnor (the 'Colonial Hercules'), Jack Hobbs, Don Bradman, Denis Compton and Richie Benaud notched up many notable achievements here. Sir Don Bradman still considers his innings of 132 against H.D.G. Leveson Gower's XI in 1934 as one of his best, if not the best innings he ever played in England! Sir Jack Hobbs scored 266 not out for the Players in 1925, which remains the record for Gentlemen v. Players matches. In 1921 at the Scarborough festival, one of Yorkshire's finest cricketers retired from first-class cricket – George Hirst.

ADDRESS The Pavilion, North Marine Road, Scarborough, North Yorkshire YO12 7TJ
TELEPHONE PROSPECTS OF PLAY 0723 365625

DESCRIPTION OF GROUND AND FACILITIES

The main access to the ground for members is from North Marine Road but there is also an entrance in Woodall Avenue to the rear of the pavilion and another in Trafalgar Square to the rear of the Trafalgar Square enclosure. The pavilion and club office is located to the north of the ground together with the press/scorers' box which is situated at the top of the north stand terrace. To the east of the playing area is the large Popular Bank and to the rear a Yorkshire C C C souvenir caravan, Scarborough C C souvenir stall and ample refreshment areas. To the south at the Trafalgar Road End is the famous 'Tea Room' bar and refreshment area and the covered Trafalgar Road Stand and open terrace. The west side includes the huge West Stand terrace as well as the 'Dropped Catch Bar' and an open area for sponsors' marquees and groundsman's equipment. There are two scoreboards on the ground, one in the north-west corner and another in the south-east corner. Permanent toilet facilities are available. All the seating is permanent and includes benches, backless seats, plastic tip-up seats and, of course, a number of deckchairs, just to remind spectators that the sea is just across the road! The ground is surrounded by houses on all four sides and therefore car parking is not possible within the

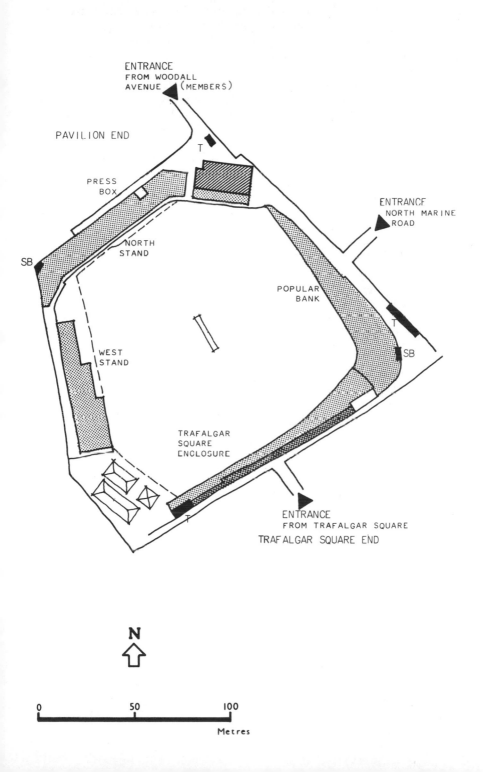

ENTRANCE
FROM WOODALL
AVENUE (MEMBERS)

PAVILION END

PRESS
BOX

T

NORTH
STAND

ENTRANCE
NORTH MARINE
ROAD

SB

POPULAR
BANK

T

WEST
STAND

SB

TRAFALGAR
SQUARE
ENCLOSURE

ENTRANCE
FROM TRAFALGAR SQUARE

TRAFALGAR SQUARE END

N

0   50   100

Metres

ground so spectators are advised to park in one of the numerous town centre car parks. The playing area is 132 metres by 128 metres and is defined by a rope and some advertisement boards. The ground capacity is 15,000 and 90 per cent of this is provided with permanent seats so spectators are advised only to bring seats to very popular matches. The T V camera position is at the Trafalgar Road End.

Scarborough is one of the best Club Grounds where county cricket is played and the annual festivals are always successful.

GROUND RECORDS AND SCORES

FIRST-CLASS MATCHES

Highest innings total for County   562 v. Leicestershire, 1901
Highest innings total against County   478 for 8 by MCC, 1904
Lowest innings total for County   46 v. MCC, 1876/v. MCC, 1877
Lowest innings total against County   31 by MCC, 1877
Highest individual innings for County   223 n.o. J.V. Wilson v. Scotland, 1951
Highest individual innings against County   208 n.o. M.P. Donnelly for MCC, 1948
Best bowling performance in an innings for County   9 for 28 J.M. Preston v. MCC, 1888
Best bowling performance in an innings against County   8 for 37 A. Shaw for MCC, 1876
Best bowling performance in a match for County   13 for 63 J.M. Preston v. MCC, 1888
Best bowling performance in a match against County   13 for 145 R. Henderson for I Zingari, 1877

LIMITED-OVERS MATCHES

Highest innings total for County   244 for 6 v. Lancashire (RAL), 1987
Highest innings total against County   255 for 6 by Sussex (JPL), 1976
Lowest innings total for County   91 v. Surrey (JPL), 1970
Lowest innings total against County   87 by Derbyshire (JPL), 1973
Highest individual innings for County   115 n.o. A.A. Metcalfe v. Gloucestershire (JPL), 1984
Highest individual innings against County   129 A.W. Greig for Sussex (JPL), 1976
Best bowling performance for County   4 for 24 A. Sidebottom v. Surrey (JPL), 1975
Best bowling performance against County   4 for 10 I.T. Botham for Somerset (JPL), 1979

FESTIVAL MATCHES

Highest innings total   290 for 8 by Hampshire v. Gloucestershire (FT), 1975
Lowest innings total   53 by Sussex v. Leicestershire (FT), 1980

Highest individual innings   158 K.J. Barnett for Derbyshire v.
Lancashire (Asda), 1987
Best bowling performance   5 for 13 P. Carrick for Yorkshire v.
Derbyshire (Asda), 1984

HOW TO GET THERE

Rail   Scarborough Central, ¾ mile
Bus   United Automobile Services from Whitby and Middlesbrough;
East Yorkshire Motor Services from Bridlington and Hull; West
Yorkshire Road Car Company from Malton, York and Leeds
Car   From north: A171 or A165 follow signs Scarborough and
seafront, the ground is situated north of the town centre off the
B1364 North Marine Road adjoining Trafalgar Square. From west:
A170 follow signs Scarborough and seafront, then follow A165 and
B1364 for North Marine Road and Trafalgar Square. From south:
A64 or A165 follow signs Scarborough and seafront, then as west.

WHERE TO STAY AND OTHER INFORMATION

Crown Hotel (0723 373491), Reads Hotel (0723 361071), Holbeck
Hall (0723 374374), and many guest houses

Disabled Areas   Trafalgar Square enclosure
Local Radio Station   BBC Radio York (95.5 MHz FM/1260 KHz
MW)
Local Newspaper(s)   Scarborough Evening News, The Mercury,
Whitby Gazette, Ryedale Shopper, Yorkshire Post, Northern Echo

Sheffield

Abbeydale Park is located on the south-western outskirts of Sheffield
in a village called Dore on the Yorkshire–Derbyshire border and closer
to the Peak District National Park than to the Dales. Until boundary
changes, the ground was in Derbyshire and was used by Derbyshire
C C C in 1946–47.

From 1855 to 1973 cricket in Sheffield, including a number of Test
Matches, was staged at Bramall Lane on the ground shared with
Sheffield United Football Club. But the encroachment of association
football finally put an end to first-class cricket there, the last county
match being staged with Lancashire. The historic turf was sold to
cricket-lovers, whilst bulldozers moved in within a week to prepare
for the erection of a new football stand for Sheffield United. This
stand is known today by the opposing Wednesday supporters as the
White Elephant Stand! Alternative grounds for Sheffield Collegiate
C C were the Hadfields ground or the Old Firth Vickers ground but

finance was not forthcoming and decisions not made at the right time and so Yorkshire finally made the commitment to stage its first-class cricket in the city at Abbeydale Park. The County's first match there was in May 1974 against Warwickshire; nowadays at least two championship matches are staged on the ground each season. A limited-overs match has been added to the fixture list since 1985.

Abbeydale Park is the home both of Sheffield Collegiate C C (which was established in 1881) and the Sheffield Amateur Sports Club (SASC) which hosts the following sports – football, badminton, squash, bowls, archery, tennis, hockey, rugby, table tennis and snooker – and also has a resident sports doctor and an injury clinic. Yorkshire were restricted to midweek matches until 1980 when the S A S C changed its policy to permit matches to be played at weekends. Sheffield Collegiate first played league cricket in 1892 when they were members of the old Hallamshire League and the Rotherham and District League; it was during the Victorian era that their rivalry with the Sheffield United Club began. In 1962 the club joined the Yorkshire League.

Abbeydale Park is surely one of the more attractive grounds in the county, in an open, idyllic setting in sharp contrast to the traditional stadium-like ground of Yorkshire. Both players and spectators enjoy their visits for the excellent facilities offered in the pavilion and conference rooms. Much of the success of Abbeydale is thanks to the good work of David Fleetwood who has played a key role in the club's rise since his move from Sheffield United in 1970. Many Sheffield people have developed an affection for Abbeydale even though deep nostalgia for Bramall Lane still remains, as most of the great games staged in the city have been on that ground.

Many improvements have been made since 1974, but, naturally it has not been the S A S C's aim to convert Abbeydale into another Bramall Lane. S A S C believes it has one of the best grounds of its kind in the country and the success achieved so far suggests this is the kind of venue that modern cricket supporters want. Abbeydale has maintained Sheffield's reputation of attracting good crowds: 5,500–6,000 on average. The best attendance was 8,000 against the West Indians in 1976.

Most people enjoy cricket at Abbeydale and a number of companies sponsor cricket here because of the fine sponsorship facilities they are thus able to offer to their clients and customers. The ground is located on a slope, but the square is flat and well maintained by the S A S C groundsmen. The ground is owned by the S A S C and during the winter months Sheffield Rugby Club plays matches on the ground frequently. Ground records have included major innings from Geoff Boycott and Alan Hill, and fine spells of bowling from Phil Carrick, Tony Gray, Chris Old, Ole Mortenson and Imran Khan.

ADDRESS Sheffield Amateur Sports Club, Abbeydale Park, Abbeydale Park Road South, Dore, Sheffield, South Yorkshire S17 3LJ
TELEPHONE PROSPECTS OF PLAY   0742 362040/367011

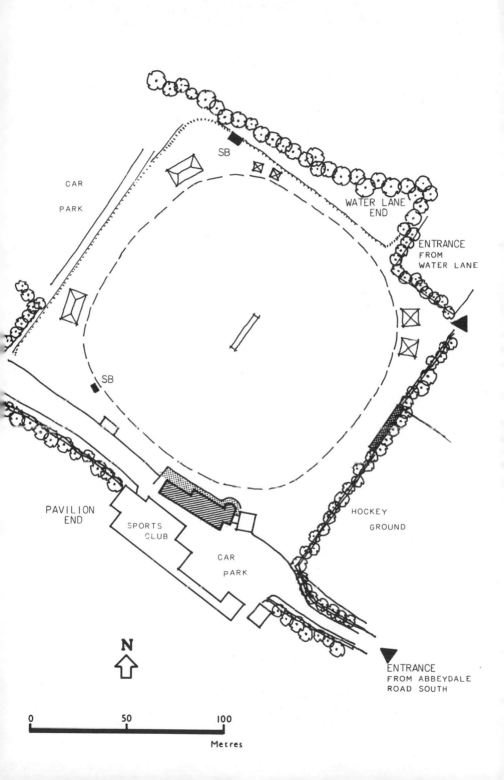

CAR
PARK

SB

WATER LANE
END

ENTRANCE
FROM
WATER LANE

SB

PAVILION
END

SPORTS
CLUB

CAR
PARK

HOCKEY
GROUND

N

ENTRANCE
FROM ABBEYDALE
ROAD SOUTH

0   50   100

Metres

DESCRIPTION OF GROUND AND FACILITIES

Entry to Abbeydale Park sports complex is from two points along Abbeydale Road South and there is ample car parking within the ground for cricket matches. The main, permanent building used for cricket matches is the substantial two storey pavilion which is on the south side of the ground and on the main entrance drive. The scoreboard is on the north-east side of the ground. The members' areas are the pavilion and the temporary stands on the south and west side of the ground. All other areas are available to the public, and various tents are provided for refreshment facilities, and Yorkshire Souvenir which is sited near the pavilion. Temporary toilets are provided for the public. The ground capacity is 8,000 and as only 3,500 seats are provided spectators are therefore advised to bring their own. The playing area is approximately 150 metres by 148 metres and is defined by a rope and advertisement boards.

GROUND RECORDS AND SCORES

FIRST-CLASS MATCHES

Highest innings total for County   424 v. Worcestershire, 1982
Highest innings total against County   480 by Derbyshire, 1981
Lowest innings total for County   90 v. West Indians, 1976
Lowest innings total against County   35 by Warwickshire, 1979
Highest individual innings for County   159 n.o. G. Boycott v. Worcestershire, 1982
Highest individual innings against County   172 n.o. A. Hill for Derbyshire, 1986
Best bowling performance in an innings for County   8 for 58 S.D. Fletcher v. Essex, 1988
Best bowling performance in an innings against County   8 for 40 A.H. Gray for Surrey, 1985
Best bowling performance in a match for County   12 for 89 P. Carrick v. Derbyshire, 1983
Best bowling performance in a match against County   11 for 49 O.H. Mortensen for Derbyshire, 1983

LIMITED-OVERS MATCHES

Highest innings total for County   178 for 6 v. Essex (RAL), 1988
Highest innings total against County   197 for 6 by Sussex (JPL), 1985
Lowest innings total for County   164 for 8 v. Essex (JPL), 1986
Lowest innings total against County   162 by Essex (JPL), 1986
Highest individual innings for County   79 A.A. Metcalfe v. Essex (RAL), 1988
Highest individual innings against County   59 B.R. Hardie for Essex (RAL), 1988
Best bowling performance for County   4 for 28 S.D. Fletcher v. Essex (RAL), 1988
Best bowling performance against County   4 for 15 Imran Khan for Sussex (JPL), 1985

HOW TO GET THERE

Rail Dore, 100m (link from Sheffield Midland)
Bus South Yorkshire Traction 17, 24 from Pinstone Street, 700m from BR Sheffield Station, to ground (Tel: 0742 755655)
Car From north: M1 junction 34, follow signs Sheffield and city centre, then A621 signposted Bakewell and Baslow, Abbeydale Cricket Ground is situated off the A621 at Dore adjoining Totley off Abbeydale Park Road South, or A6102, A61, A6135 or A618 signposted Sheffield and city centre, then follow A621 to Dore. From east: M1 junction 33, follow A630 signposted Sheffield and city centre, then as north, or A57 then as north. From west: A625 or A621 follow signs Dore and Totley for Abbeydale Park Cricket Ground off A621 at Abbeydale Park Road South 6½ miles south-west of Sheffield city centre. From south: M1 junction 29, follow A617 Chesterfield, then A61 Sheffield after passing Dronfield, take Greenhill roundabout on southern outskirts of Sheffield and follow signs Dore and Totley on B6054 for Abbeydale Park Road South and SASC ground, or A616, A621, then as north.

WHERE TO STAY AND OTHER INFORMATION

Grosvenor House Hotel (0742 20041), Hallam Tower Post House (0742 686031), Hotel St George (0742 583811)

Disabled Areas No special area, request position. A disabled toilet is available
Local Radio Station(s) BBC Radio Sheffield (104.1 MHz FM/1035 KHz MW), Radio Hallam (103.4 MHz FM/1548 KHz MW)
Local Newspaper(s) Sheffield Star, Yorkshire Post, The Morning Telegraph

Hull

Anlaby Road cricket ground is known as The Circle, a name, of course taken from its shape. It is the second ground in Humberside that has been used by Yorkshire. The original venue for county matches was Argyle Street near Anlaby Road, where matches were staged in 1879 by Yorkshire and in 1875 by the North. The Circle is the home of the Hull C C (formerly Hull Town C C), which moved to its present ground from Argyle Street in 1894. The ground is shared with Hull and East Riding Rugby Union Football Club.

The first Yorkshire visit to The Circle was in1892 when Stafford-shire were the visitors; the initial championship match was staged in 1899 against Somerset. The last championship match was in 1974 against Worcestershire but Yorkshire still travel once each season to the East Coast to stage a limited-overs Sunday League fixture. In 1983 West Indians were to have played Lancashire here in the Wilberforce Commemoration international cricket match, which marked the 150th anniversary of the abolition of slavery and the death of William Wilberforce, a distinguished citizen of Hull, but the match was abandoned.

Football has also been staged on the ground, opposite the old pavilion which was demolished in 1987. In 1904 negotiations took place in an endeavour to stage an F A Cup tie between Hull City and Stockton on the cricket ground, but this was not allowed and eventually the match was staged at Ayresome Park, Middlesbrough.

Hull C C plays in the Yorkshire League and the Ridings League. In recent years there have been significant changes at the ground. In 1986 Humberside County Council took over the leasehold of the ground in order to make the ground into a large sports complex. The ground has a large playing area and plenty of seating accommodation although little is covered. In 1987 the old pavilion which had stood on the ground for over a hundred years or more was demolished to make way for the sports complex development, which is designed to cope with the multi-sport demands of the next decade and beyond. Expansion plans include a floodlit artificial pitch for hockey, major improvements to the existing rugby stand and the provision of further permanent seating to attract more county matches. The £500,000 facelift will restore the ground to its original former glory as one of Yorkshire's major venues.

The Circle usually attracts crowds of 5,000–6,000; the best in recent years was 6,500 against Nottinghamshire in the 1986 John Player Sunday League, but the ground record is 21,394 for the visit of Northamptonshire in 1946. Historical events at The Circle have been numerous; one of Yorkshire's most stupendous efforts was achieved here in 1922 when they bowled out Sussex for just 20. Other achievements have included high scores from Maurice Leyland against Essex in 1936 and in 1954 fine bowling by Johnny Wardle against Sussex. In limited-overs matches Barry Richards scored 155 not out for Hampshire in 1970 and a year earlier Ray East, the Essex spinner, took 6 for 18.

No mention of Hull C C would be complete without reference to Charles Ullathorne, the first Yorkshire player to hail from the East Coast club. After his playing career Ullathorne coached and later became groundsman at Eccles C C across the Pennines in Manchester.

ADDRESS The Circle, Anlaby Road, Anlaby, Hull, North Humberside HU3 6RR
TELEPHONE PROSPECTS OF PLAY 0482 507098

DESCRIPTION OF GROUND AND FACILITIES

The Circle is entered from Anlaby Road, to the south of the playing area. This is the main entrance for members, players, the public and

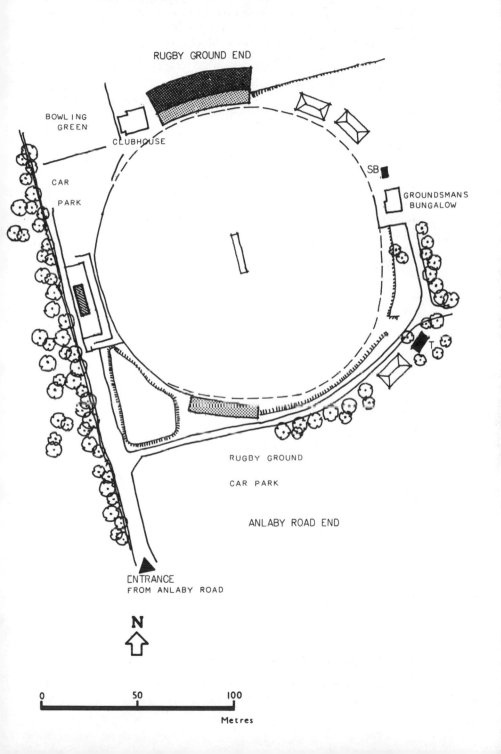

RUGBY GROUND END

BOWLING
GREEN

CLUBHOUSE

CAR
PARK

SB

GROUNDSMANS
BUNGALOW

T

RUGBY GROUND

CAR PARK

ANLABY ROAD END

ENTRANCE
FROM ANLABY ROAD

N

0   50   100

Metres

all cars to the ground. Car parking is available on the rugby pitch or in the main car park near to the clubhouse. The only permanent buildings on the ground, now that the old pavilion has been demolished and replaced (for players changing facilities) by two portacabins, is the clubhouse, stand and press box/radio point to the north and to the west the scoreboard, groundsman's bungalow and stores. The playing area is circular in shape despite a rugby pitch being positioned to the north of the square and is 150 metres by 152 metres and is defined by a rope and advertising boards. A number of tents and temporary, open seating areas are available together with temporary toilets and a Yorkshire souvenir caravan. The members' enclosure is in front of the players changing rooms and the main stand. Temporary refreshments and a bar in the clubhouse are available on match days. Of a ground capacity of some 8,000 approximately 10 per cent is provided with seating so spectators are well advised to bring their own seating to all matches in order to view the cricket from the grass banking which surrounds the playing area.

GROUND RECORDS AND SCORES

FIRST-CLASS MATCHES
Highest innings total for County   523 for 3 dec. v. Leicestershire, 1937
Highest innings total against County   458 by Leicestershire, 1937
Lowest innings total for County   77 v. Kent, 1905
Lowest innings total against County   20 by Sussex, 1922
Highest individual innings for County   263 M. Leyland v. Essex, 1936
Highest individual innings against County   227 B.L. D'Oliveira for Worcestershire, 1974
Best bowling performance in an innings for County   9 for 48 J.H. Wardle v. Sussex, 1954
Best bowling performance in an innings against County   8 for 40 W.W. O'Dell for Leicestershire, 1907
Best bowling performance in a match for County   16 for 112 J.H. Wardle v. Sussex, 1954
Best bowling performance in a match against County   12 for 86 F. Ridgway for Kent, 1947

LIMITED-OVERS MATCHES
Highest innings total for County   255 for 6 v. Nottinghamshire (JPL), 1986
Highest innings total against County   232 for 4 by Gloucestershire (JPL), 1980
Lowest innings total for County   74 for 9 v. Hampshire (JPL), 1970
Lowest innings total against County   120 by Essex (JPL), 1973
Highest individual innings for County   119 J.H. Hampshire v. Leicestershire (JPL), 1971
Highest individual innings against County   155 n.o. B.A. Richards

for Hampshire (JPL) 1970
Best bowling performance for County   5 for 17 A.G. Nicholson *v.*
Nottinghamshire (JPL), 1972
Best bowling performance against County   6 for 18 R.E. East for
Essex (JPL), 1969

HOW TO GET THERE

Rail   Hull Paragon, 1 mile
Bus   Kingston upon Hull 2, 15, 23/4 link east end of Anlaby Road
(adjacent BR Station) with ground (Tel: 0482 222222)
Car   From north: A164, A1079, A165 or A1034 follow signs
Kingston-upon-Hull, from A1 or A19 follow A1079 signposted
Kingston-upon-Hull and town centre, follow signs Anlaby for
Anlaby Road and The Circle Cricket Ground, the ground is situated
in Anlaby Road off the A63. From east: A1033 follow signs
Kingston-upon-Hull, then as north. From west: M62 junction 38,
then follow A63 signposted Kingston-upon-Hull for Anlaby district
and Anlaby Road for The Circle Cricket Ground. From south: M1
junction 32, follow M18 and M62 to junction 38, then as west, or
A15 from M180 junction 5, across the Humber Bridge, then follow
signs Anlaby and A63 for The Circle Cricket Ground.

WHERE TO STAY AND OTHER INFORMATION

West Park Hotel, Anlaby Road (0482 571888). The Marina Post
House Hotel (0482 225221)

Disabled Areas   No special area, request position
Local Radio Station(s)   BBC Radio Humberside (95.9 MHz FM/1485
KHz MW), Viking Radio (96.9 MHz FM/1161 KHz MW)
Local Newspaper(s)   Hull Daily Mail, Hull Star

CAMBRIDGE
UNIVERSITY

CAMBRIDGE – FENNER'S

Cambridge University

There is reference to Cambridge University playing a match against Cambridge Town in 1710, presumably on Parkers Piece but the first recorded match against the town was in 1821. The C U C C was founded in 1820 and the first match against Oxford was played at Lords in 1827. Since 1848 all home matches have been played at Fenner's in the centre of the city.

The development of cricket at the University was such that by the latter part of the century Cambridge could give any side in England a good game. Regular fixtures were arranged with the counties and these have continued to the present day. The present fixtures now normally comprise, in addition to the annual encounter with Oxford at Lords, about ten matches with counties plus a number of other games. Like Oxford the C U C C is afforded first-class status although there have been those who have thought to question this status in recent years. The universities no longer play the tourists individually but play as Combined Universities (Oxford and Cambridge) and the fixtures alternate yearly between the two university grounds. Similarly, the Combined Universities play in the Benson and Hedges Cup.

Sixty-six Cambridge men have played for England and thirteen of these have captained, ranging from the Hon. Ivo Bligh in 1882 to Mike Brearley in the period 1977–81. Many fine players represented Cambridge during the golden years of cricket prior to 1914 and these included Lord Hawke and Ranjitsinhji.

Since World War Two captains have included D.J. Insole, Ted Dexter, Peter May and A.R. Lewis, while among those who have played are Trevor Bailey, Raman Subba Row, R.A. Hutton, P.M. Roebuck and D.R. Pringle.

Colours Pale blue
Crest University crest
Hon. Secretary (elected annually), Cambridge University C C, Fenner's Cricket Ground, Wollaston Road, off Mortimer Road, Cambridge
Fixtures Secretary J.G.W. Davies MA OBE, 31 Wingate Road, Cambridge CB2 2HD
Groundsman A. Pocock
Scorer A.R. May

Achievements:

Winners of the University Match on 53 occasions.
Ground Fenner's, Cambridge

A. P. F. CHAPMAN

219-C
CAMBRIDGE UNIVERSITY

CAMBRIDGE UNIVERSITY

CHURCHMAN'S CIGARETTES

K. S. DULEEPSINHJI

WILLS'S CIGARETTES

"SAMMY"
"Vanity Fair. 1st Series No 6"

DESCRIPTION OF GROUND AND FACILITIES

In 1846 Mr F.P. Fenner leased from Gonville and Caius College a field
to the east of Parkers Piece and opened a cricket ground. Two years
later he sub-let it to Cambridge University Cricket Club, and while
the ground has continued to retain the name Fenner's, it has been the
home of University cricket since then.

The freehold of the ground was acquired from the College in 1894
and assigned to a company which held it in trust, until in 1976 the
University assumed full financial responsibility for the ground.

Until the 1950s the ground was shared with the athletes and
contained a running track surrounding the playing area. This has now

been removed. The ground is still used for tennis in summer and hockey and soccer in the winter.

The ground, which is renowned for its true pitches and even out-field, is partly enclosed by walls and adjoining buildings. The earlier pavilions were on the south-west side backing onto Gresham Road, but in 1972 a new pavilion designed by architect Colin Stansfield-Smith RIBA (cricket Blue 1954–57) was built on the Wollaston Road side to the north-east. It provides infinitely better facilities but there remain those who still prefer the character of the old building. The site of the old pavilion and adjoining land have since been developed into three-storey flats with a direct view of the cricket.

The ground is entered at the junction of Mortimer Road and Wollaston Road and the nearest car parking is in the multistorey carpark entered from Gonville Place adjoining the indoor swimming pool. A small number of cars are allowed into the ground.

The members' area adjoins the pavilion, but groups still congregate on the south side on benches in the shade of the trees. You are advised to take your own seats as few are available for spectators. The still rudimentary scoreboard is sited on the west side of the ground. The general impression is still that of a quiet backwater in the city centre, surrounded by brick buildings and mature trees. Tennis courts to the east are separated by a wooden fence and tree plantings. Regrettably the north-west corner of the ground is now overshadowed by a multistorey car park. The pitch is disposed in a north–south direction. The playing area is 147 metres by 148 metres.

The annual match against the tourists has always been a great attraction and until the advent of the Benson and Hedges Cup was the one game for which admission was charged. The tourists match is now undertaken by a Combined Universities team and is held at Fenner's and The Parks in alternate years. The record attendance is said to be 9,000, achieved when the University played the West Indians in 1950 in a drawn match which produced 1,324 runs in three days.

The ground is also used by Cambridgeshire C C C and has staged the first Minor Counties Knock-out Trophy Final.

ADDRESS   Fenner's Cricket Ground, Wollaston Road, off Mortimer Road, Cambridge
TELEPHONE PROSPECTS OF PLAY   0223 353552

GROUND RECORDS AND SCORES

FIRST-CLASS MATCHES
Highest innings total for University   594 for 4 v. West Indians, 1900
Highest innings total against University   730 for 3 by West Indians, 1950
Lowest innings total for University   30 v. Yorkshire, 1928
Lowest innings total against University   43 by Warwickshire, 1936
Highest individual innings for University   254 n.o. K.S. Duleepsinhji v. Middlesex, 1927
Highest individual innings against University   304 n.o. E. de C. Weekes for West Indians, 1950

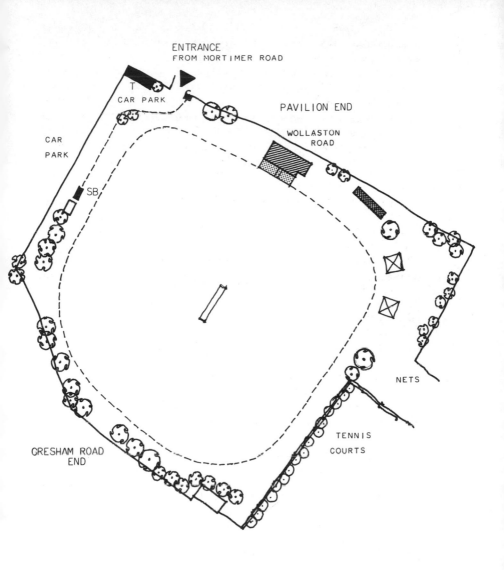

ENTRANCE
FROM MORTIMER ROAD

T
CAR PARK

CAR
PARK

SB

PAVILION END

WOLLASTON
ROAD

NETS

TENNIS
COURTS

GRESHAM ROAD
END

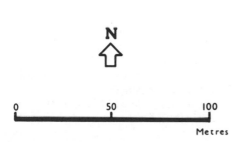

N

0   50   100

Metres

Best bowling performance in an innings for University   10 for 69
S.M.J. Woods *v.* C.I. Thornton's XI, 1890
Best bowling performance in an innings against University   9 for
17 H.L. Jackson for Derbyshire, 1959/9 for ?? F.P. Fenner for
Cambridge Town, 1844
Best bowling performance in a match for University   15 for 88
S.M.J. Woods *v.* C.I. Thornton's XI, 1890
Best bowling performance in a match against University   17 for ??
F.P. Fenner for Cambridge Town, 1844

LIMITED-OVERS MATCHES
Highest innings total for Combined Universities   212 *v.* Kent
(BHC),1983
Highest innings total against Combined Universities   276 for 9 by
Kent (BHC), 1983
Lowest innings total for Combined Universities   59 *v.* Glamorgan
(BHC), 1983
Lowest innings total against Combined Universities   92 by
Worcestershire (BHC), 1975
Highest individual innings for Combined Universities   82
S.P. Henderson *v.* Kent (BHC), 1983
Highest individual innings against Combined Universities   108
D.C. Boon for Australians (Tour), 1985
Best bowling performance for Combined Universities   4 for 14
Imran Khan *v.* Worcestershire (BHC), 1975
Best bowling performance against Combined Universities   4 for 10
M.W.W. Selvey for Glamorgan (BHC), 1983

HOW TO GET THERE

Rail   Cambridge, ¾ mile
Bus   142, 143 Cambus from Bus Station to ground
Car   From north: A1 and A604 signposted Cambridge and city
centre, then A1309 for Mortimer Road and Fenner's Cricket Ground
situated close to Parkers' Piece and at rear of multi-storey car park,
or A10 to city centre, then as above. From east: A1303 or A45
signposted Cambridge and city centre, then as north. From west:
A45, A1303 or A603 follow signs Cambridge and city centre, then
as north. From south: M11 junction 11, then follow signs
Cambridge and city centre then as north, or A1301, A1307 to city
centre then as north.

WHERE TO STAY AND OTHER INFORMATION

Gonville Hotel (0223 66611), Post House Hotel (022023 7000)

Disabled Areas   No special area, request position
Local Radio Station(s)   BBC Radio Cambridgeshire (95.7 MHz FM/
1026 KHz MW), Hereward Radio (96.6 MHz FM/1557 KHz MW)
Local Newspaper   Cambridge Evening News

OXFORD
UNIVERSITY

OXFORD – THE PARKS

Oxford University

The first mention of cricket at Oxford appears to have been in 1727 but the first known match was in 1795 when Bullingdon Club played the M C C. However the direct forerunner of O U C C was Magdalen Club, which was established in about 1800, although the reference to O U C C did not appear in a match until 1827. The early matches were played on Cowley Marsh until in 1881 Dr Evans, Master of Pembroke College, succeeded in obtaining a lease on 10 acres of land in the University Parks. This venue has remained the club's ground for all home matches and many consider it to be one of the most attractive in the country. Occasionally, the ground at Christ Church College has been used for matches against the tourists in part due to the need to charge for admission to the game. At the Parks charges cannot be levied, since the ground is not enclosed.

As early as 1884 Oxford defeated the touring Australians by seven wickets, no mean feat as the Australian team differed little from that which won the Ashes in 1882.

Many fine cricketers played for Oxford in the years before 1914 including P.F. 'Plum' Warner, R.E. Foster and C.B. Fry. Later personalities who experienced their early first-class cricket at the Parks are D.R. Jardine, England captain in the bodyline series of 1932–33, Colin Cowdrey and M.J.K. Smith, who has the unique achievement of a century in each of his three University matches against Cambridge. A.C. Smith led the club to six victories in 1959 and is now the chief executive of the Test & County Cricket Board.

Colours Dark blue
Crest Two crowns above O U C C
Fixtures Secretary and Senior Treasurer Dr S.R. Porter, M A DPhil., Nuffield College, Oxford OX1 1NF
Hon. Secretary (elected annually) Oxford University C C, The Pavilion, University Parks, Oxford
Tel 0865 57106
Assistant Secretary E.H. Wilson MBE
Groundsman C. Chase
Scorer P. Gordon

Achievements:

Winners of the University Match on 45 occasions.
Grounds The University Parks, Oxford.
   Christ Church College Ground, Iffley Road Oxford, is also occasionally used for matches.

CHURCHMAN'S CIGARETTES

E. R. T. HOLMES

OXFORD UNIVERSITY

COUNTY CRICKETERS.

MR. B. J. T. BOSANQUET

D. R. JARDINE

DESCRIPTION OF GROUND AND FACILITIES

The University Parks cover about 65 acres and are freely open to the public. The cricket ground lies within the Parks but it is not in any way separated from them. Thus apart from the small pavilion complex no part of the ground is in any way enclosed, except by trees on the north, east and south sides. Entrance therefore cannot be charged and no crowd numbers established.

The first match was played in 1881 by which time the pavilion had been constructed to the designs of Sir Thomas G. Jackson, architect of many nineteenth- and early twentieth-century Oxford buildings. This pavilion is the main focus of the ground; it is a most impressive building with three striking gables in its steeply pitched roof surmounted by an impressive cupola. A part of the verandah has been enclosed to provide a press box. The Long Room is reminiscent of a University hall with its great roof trusses. The walls are in panelled oak on which the names of all Blues are recorded in gold lettering. A small scoreboard is situated to the side of the pavilion, while on the other side a single-storey modern building houses the Assistant Secretary's office and refreshment facilities.

A few benches are dispersed around the boundary, which is marked by a rope. The ground is 132 metres by 140 metres and the pitch is positioned approximately north–south with the pavilion to the south. The pavilion area provides bench seating for about 300 spectators. Members of the public are advised to bring their own seats to matches. There are no car parking facilities for the general public except in those adjoining streets to the north which are free from parking restrictions.

The character of the Parks is unique and the ground has seen many outstanding performances, beginning in 1886 when W.G. Grace took all 10 Oxford wickets for 49 runs when playing for M C C. This followed his 104 runs earlier in the game.

ADDRESS The Pavilion, University Parks, Oxford
TELEPHONE PROSPECTS OF PLAY 0865 57106

GROUND RECORDS AND SCORES

FIRST-CLASS MATCHES
Highest innings total for University 589 v. Gents of England 1908
Highest innings total against University 627 for 2 dec. by Gloucestershire, 1930
Lowest innings total for University 12 v. MCC, 1877
Lowest innings total against University 24 by MCC, 1846
Highest individual innings for University 236 E.R.T. Holmes v. Free Foresters, 1927
Highest individual innings against University 266 n.o. W. Place for Lancashire, 1947
Best bowling performance in an innings for University 9 for 38 T.B. Raikes v. Army, 1924
Best bowling performance in an innings against University 10 for 49 W.G. Grace for MCC, 1886
Best bowling performance in a match for University 15 for 65 B.J.T. Bosanquet v. Sussex, 1887
Best bowling performance in a match against University 16 for 225 J.E. Walsh for Leicestershire, 1953

LIMITED-OVERS MATCHES
Highest innings total for Combined Universities 216 for 8 v. Gloucestershire (BHC), 1982
Highest innings total against Combined Universities 300 for 4 by Gloucestershire (BHC), 1982

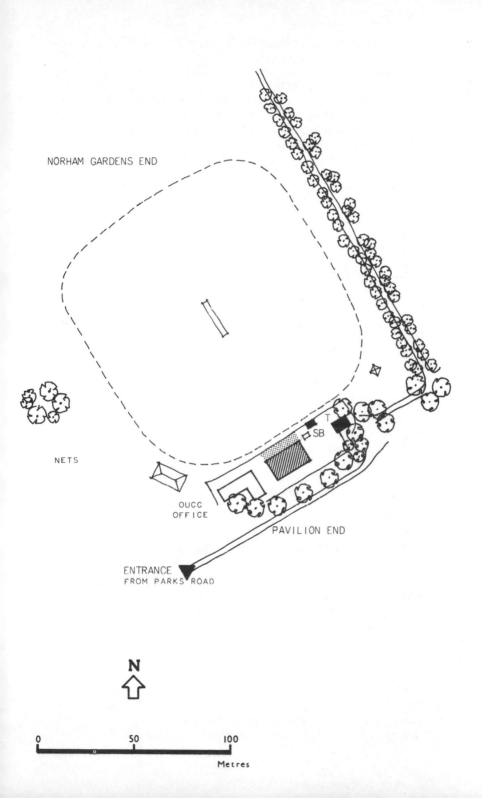

NORHAM GARDENS END

NETS

OUCC
OFFICE

T
SB

PAVILION END

ENTRANCE
FROM PARKS ROAD

N

0   50   100

Metres

Lowest innings total for Combined Universities   122 v. Kent (BHC), 1976
Lowest innings total against Combined Universities   127 for 2 by Warwickshire (BHC), 1973
Highest individual innings for Combined Universities   91 A.J.T. Miller v. Surrey (BHC), 1984
Highest individual innings against Combined Universities   123 A.W. Stovold for Gloucestershire (BHC), 1982
Best bowling performance for Combined Universities   3 for 31 P.L. Garlick v. Surrey (BHC), 1984
Best bowling performance against Combined Universities   5 for 28 R.W. Hills for Kent (BHC), 1976

HOW TO GET THERE

Rail   Oxford, 1 mile
Bus   Oxford 2/A, 10/A from Cornmarket Street; 52 links BR Station with Cornmarket Street (Tel: 0865 711312)
Car   From north: A34, A423 or A43 signposted Oxford and city centre, then follow A4165 for University Parks signposted in Parks Road for pedestrian entrance only to the Parks and cricket ground. From east: A40 signposted Oxford and city centre, then follow A4165 for University Parks, situated ½ mile north-east of city centre in Parks Road. From west: A40, A420 or A34 signposted Oxford and city centre, then as east. From south: M40 junction 7 then follow A40 signposted Oxford and city centre, then as east, or A423 to city centre, then as north.
Ample street parking to north of Parks and car parks in city centre

WHERE TO STAY AND OTHER INFORMATION

Cotswold Lodge (0865 512121), The Randolph (0865 247481), Eastgate Hotel (0865 248244), and many others

Disabled Areas   The ground is in a public park and there is ample access, but no car parks
Local Radio Station(s)   BBC Radio Oxford (95.2 MHz FM/1485 KHz MW), Radio 210 (102.9 MHz FM/1431 KHz MW)
Local Newspaper(s)   Oxford Mail, Oxford Times

FRIENDS OF
ARUNDEL CASTLE

ARUNDEL – CASTLE PARK

Arundel

While it is possible to establish that an Arundel Cricket Club existed as long ago as 1774 it was not until the work undertaken by the fifteenth Duke of Norfolk in 1894–95 that the present ground and pavilion to the north of Arundel Castle were constructed. All will agree that this was a perfect setting for a cricket arena, and the work commenced in 1894 was continued by Bernard, the sixteenth Duke of Norfolk, at one time president of M C C and in 1962–63 Manager of the M C C Tour of Australia. The team always played as the Duke of Norfolk's XI.

In 1975 Lavinia, Duchess of Norfolk decided that, as a memorial to her late husband, cricket should continue at Arundel Park with the object of sustaining its unique character and to aid 'the promotion encouragement and maintenance of the playing of cricket'.

With the assistance of two former secretaries of the M C C, Ronnie Aird and Billy Griffith; Eddie Harrison of Sussex Martlets, and Colin Cowdrey, she set about this task which led to the establishment of the Friends of Arundel Castle Cricket Club. Since that time some forty-five matches have been played each year by teams assembled from various sources. The more important matches are defined as Lavinia, Duchess of Norfolk's XI and of these the major fixture is always the annual match against the touring team.

In recent years the Arundel Castle Cricket Foundation has been established assisted by a generous donation from Mr J. Paul Getty Jr with the aim of providing cricket and cricket coaching for youngsters.

Lavinia, Duchess of Norfolk's XI who played the Australians in 1977

John Barclay, former captain of Sussex, has been appointed Director of Cricket and Coaching and plans have been prepared for the building of an indoor cricket centre at the rear of the present pavilion. The pavilion is 22 yards long, the length of a cricket pitch.

Colours   Dark blue
Crest   Red Baskerville 'N'
Secretary   Miss D. Osborne, Friends of Arundel Castle Cricket Club, Cricket Office, Arundel Park, Arundel, West Sussex BN18 9LH
Telephone   0903 882462
Scorer   Mrs K. Cohen
Ground   Castle Park

DESCRIPTION OF GROUND AND FACILITIES

The cricket ground is to the north of Arundel Castle and set in idyllic surroundings. Access is obtained from London Road through the stable area to the south-west. There is ample car parking in the entrance area and to the south of the cricket ground. Cars can also be positioned close to the playing area if space is available. It is from this higher area that many sit to view the cricket. A new scoreboard has been recently erected on the north-west side and this also houses the scorers. Refreshment tents and other facilities are disposed in various parts of the ground, and there are ample toilet facilities. Members of the public are advised to bring their own seats, as are club members to the special matches, particularly those against the tourists.

A view of the ground from the score box

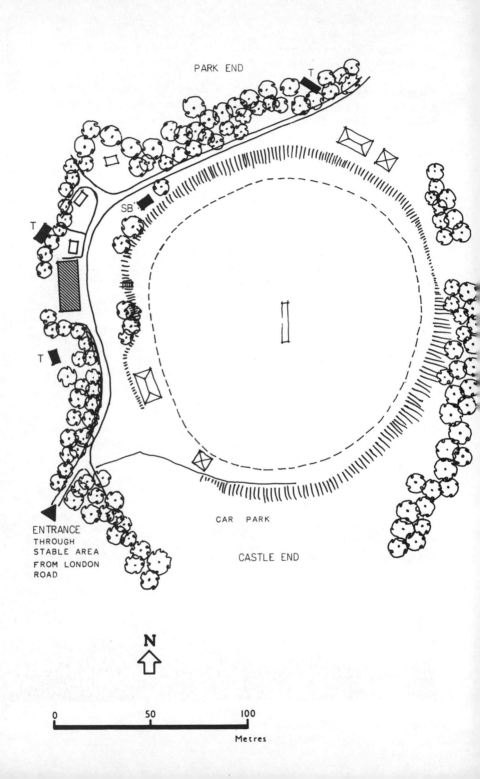

PARK END

T

SB

T

T

ENTRANCE
THROUGH
STABLE AREA
FROM LONDON
ROAD

CAR PARK

CASTLE END

N

0   50   100

Metres

The ground slopes naturally from north-west to south-east but the cricket area has been levelled and is approximately circular, 152 metres by 140 metres. The pitch is aligned in a north–south direction. The area is enclosed within a surround of mature landscaped trees which provide a green backcloth to all activities on the field. Regrettably the hurricane of October 1987 was responsible for removing many of the trees in the south and south-east areas but this has given a better view of the castle from the ground.

HOW TO GET THERE

Rail   Arundel, 1 mile
Bus   Southdown 212, 230 Worthing–Arundel Castle (Tel: 0903 37661)
Car   From north: A29 and A284 signposted Arundel, entrance to Arundel Park off Arundel bypass in London Road, north of town centre, enter park through stables and parkland, follow signs cricket. From east: A27 signposted Arundel and town centre, then follow signs Arundel Park and London Road for cricket ground, situated within Castle Park grounds. From west: A27 signposted Arundel and town centre, then as east. From south: A284 signposted Arundel and town centre, then as east.

WHERE TO STAY AND OTHER INFORMATION

Norfolk Arms (0903 882101), Bridge Hotel (0903 882242)

Disabled Areas   No special area, request suitable position
Local Radio Station(s)   BBC Radio Sussex (104.5 MHz FM/1161 KHz MW), Southern Sound (103.5 MHz FM/1323 KHz MW)
Local Newspaper   West Sussex Gazette

Other Grounds

MINOR COUNTIES CRICKET ASSOCIATION
Secretary: D.J.M. Armstrong, Thorpe Cottage, Mill Common, Ridlington, North Walsham, Norfolk NR28 9TY *Tel:* 0692 650563

BEDFORDSHIRE CCC
Secretary: A.J. Pearce, 15 Dene Way, Upper Caldecote, Biggleswade, Beds SG18 9DL. *Tel:* 0767 318215
Grounds:
BEDFORD SCHOOL, Burnaby Road, Bedford. *Tel:* 0234 53435 (*school hours only*)
BEDFORD TOWN CC, Goldington Bury, Church Lane, Goldington, Bedford. *Tel:* 0234 52458
DUNSTABLE TOWN CC, Bull Pond Lane, Dunstable. *Tel:* 0582 63735
HENLOW C C, (Henlow Sports Association), Park Lane, Henlow. *Tel:* 0462 811218
LUTON TOWN CC, Wardown Park, Old Bedford Road, Luton. *Tel:* 0582 27855
SOUTHILL PARK CC, Southill Park, Nr Biggleswade. (*No phone*).
VAUXHALL MOTORS CC, Brache Estate, Osborne Road, Luton. *Tel:* 0582 23061

BERKSHIRE CCC
Secretary: C.F.V. Martin, MC, Paradise Cottage, Paradise Road, Henley on Thames, Berks RG9 1UB. *Tel:* 0491 572403
Grounds:
BRACKNELL CC, Large's Lane, Bracknell. *Tel:* 0344 423492
BRADFIELD COLLEGE, near Reading. *Tel:* 0734 744429
COURAGES (READING), Courages Cricket Ground, Ashley Road, Berkeley Avenue, Reading. *Tel:* 0734 52725
FALKLAND CC, Washcommon, off Andover Road, Nr Newbury. *Tel:* 0635 47658
FINCHAMPSTEAD CC, Memorial Park, Finchampstead. *Tel:* 0734 732890
HURST CC, Wokingham Road, Hurst, Reading. *Tel:* 0734 340088.
KIDMORE END CC, Gallows Tree Common, Kidmore End, Nr Reading. *Tel:* 0734 724143
READING CC, Sonning Lane, Reading. *Tel:* 0734 699049
READING SCHOOL, Reading School, Erleigh Road, Reading. *Tel:* 0734 61815
READING UNIVERSITY CC, Reading University, Elmhurst Road, Reading. *Tel:* 0734 83775.

BUCKINGHAMSHIRE CCC
Secretary: S.J. Tomlin, Orchard Leigh Cottage, Bigfrith Lane, Cookham Dean, Berks SL6 9PH. *Tel:* 06284 2202
Grounds:
AMERSHAM CC, Shardeloes, London Road, Old Amersham. *Tel:* 02403 3020
AYLESBURY TOWN CC, Aylesbury Sports Club, Wendover Road, Aylesbury. *Tel:* 0296 5187
BEACONSFIELD CC, Wilton Park, Oxford Road, Beaconsfield Old Town, Beaconsfield. *Tel:* 04946 4134
BLETCHLEY CC (MILTON KEYNES), Manor Fields, Bletchley, Milton Keynes, Bucks. *Tel:* 0908 72298

BUCKINGHAM CC, Bourton Road, Bletchley Road, Buckingham.
Tel: 02802 2546
CHESHAM CC, Amy Lane, New Road, Chesham. Tel: 02405 3635
HIGH WYCOMBE CC, London Road, High Wycombe. Tel: 0494 22611
MARLOW CC, Pound Lane, High Street, Marlow. Tel: 06284 3638
MONKS RISBOROUGH, Molins Sports Club, Monks Risborough, Princes
Risborough, Bucks. Tel: 08444 3959
SLOUGH CC, Chalvey Road, Slough. Tel: 0753 20982
STOWE SCHOOL, Stowe School, Nr Buckingham. Tel: 02802 3164.

CAMBRIDGESHIRE CCC
Secretary: P.W. Gooden, The Redlands, Oakington Road, Cottenham,
Cambridge CB4 4TW. Tel: 0954 50429
Grounds:
CAMBRIDGE UNIVERSITY CC, Fenner's, University Cricket Ground, Cambridge.
Tel: 0223 353552
PAPWORTH CC, Chequer's Lane, Papworth Everard. Tel: 0480 830331
PETERBOROUGH CC, Bretton Gate, Westwood, Peterborough. Tel: 0733 262202
ROYSTON CC, Royston Heath, Royston. Tel: 0763 43613
MARCH CC, Burrowmoor Road, March. Tel: 0354 52029
WISBECH CC, Harecroft Road, Wisbech. Tel: 0945 585429.

CHESHIRE CCC
Secretary: J.B. Pickup, 2 Castle Street, Northwich, Cheshire CW8 1AB.
Tel: 0606 74970
Grounds:
BOWDEN CC, South Downs Road, Bowden, Altricham. Tel: 061-928 1388
CHESTER CC, Boughton Hall, Boughton Hall Avenue, Filkins Lane, Chester.
Tel: 0244 26072
NANTWICH CC, Whitehouse Lane, Nantwich. Tel: 0270 626155
OXTON CC, Townfield Lane, Birkenhead. Tel: 051-652 1331
TOFT CC, Chelford Road, Knutsford. Tel: 0565 2734
STALYBRIDGE C & AC, Gorse Hall Road, Dukinfield. Tel: 061-338 2094
NESTON CC, Parkgate, South Wirral. Tel: 051-336 4199
WARRINGTON CC, Walton Lea Road, Higher Walton, Warrington.
Tel: 0925 63210.

CORNWALL CCC
Secretary: T.D. Meneer, Falbridge, Penvale Cross, Penryn, Cornwall.
Tel: 0326 72389
Grounds:
CAMBORNE CC, Roskear, Camborne. Tel: 0209 715478
FALMOUTH CC, Trescobeas, Falmouth. Tel: 0326 74000
HELSTON CC, Clodgey Lane, Helston. Tel: 03265 3423
LISKEARD CC, New Pavilion, Lux Park, Liskeard. Tel: 0579 42665
PENZANCE CC, St Clare, Penzance. Tel: 0736 2960
ST. AUSTELL CC Wheal Eliza, Bethel, St Austell. Tel: 0726 2588
TROON CC, Treslothnan Road, Troon. (No phone)
TRURO CC, Boscawen Park, Truro. Tel: 0872 77468
WADEBRIDGE CC Egloshayle Road, Wadebridge (No phone).

CUMBERLAND CCC
Secretary: M. Beaty, 9 Abbey Drive, Natland, Kendal, Cumbria LA9 7QN.
Tel: 05395 60470

Grounds:
BARROW CC, Abbey Road, Barrow, Cumbria. *Tel:* 0229 25201
CARLISLE CC, Edenside, Carlisle. *Tel:* 0228 28593
KENDAL CC, Shap Road, Kendal. *Tel:* 0539 24269
MILLOM CC, St George's Road, Millom. *Tel:* 0657 2839
NETHERFIELD CC, Parkside Road, Kendal. *Tel:* 0539 24051
PENRITH CC, Tynefield Park, Penrith. *Tel:* 0768 63087
WORKINGTON CC, Ernest Valentine Ground, The Cloffochs, Workington.
   Tel: 0900 5515.

DEVON CCC
Hon. Secretary: G.R. Evans, Blueberry Haven, 20 Boucher Road, Budleigh
   Salterton, Devon EX9 6JF. *Tel:* 03954 5216
Grounds:
BOVEY TRACEY CC, The Recreation Ground, Newton Road, Bovey Tracey.
   Tel: 0626 832780
EXETER CC County Ground, Prince of Wales Road, Exeter. *Tel:* 0392 72773
CHUDLEIGH CC, Kate Brook, Chudleigh. *Tel:* 0626 852645
EXMOUTH CC, The Maer Ground, Exmouth. *Tel:* 0395 272771
NORTH DEVON CC, Instow. *Tel:* 0271 860633
SOUTH DEVON CC, Recreation Ground, Marsh Road, Newton Abbott.
   Tel: 0626 65343
SIDMOUTH CC, The Fortfield, Sidmouth. *Tel:* 03955 3229
TORQUAY CC, Recreation Ground, Torquay. *Tel:* 0803 22001.

DORSET CCC
Secretary: D.J.W. Bridge, Long Acre, Tinney's Lane, Sherborne, Dorset DT9
   3DY. *Tel:* 0935 814318
Grounds:
BOURNEMOUTH CC, Bournemouth Sports Club, Dean Park, Cavendish Road,
   Bournemouth. *Tel:* 0202 25872
DORCHESTER CC, The Recreation Ground, Weymouth Road, Dorchester. (*No
   phone*)
KINSOR CC, Kinsor Park Road, Northborne, Bournemouth. *Tel:* 0202 573089
SHERBORNE, Sherborne School, Horsecastle, Sherborne. (*No phone*).
WEYMOUTH CC, Redlands Sports Ground, Dorchester Road, Weymouth.
   Tel: 0305 813113

DURHAM CCC
Secretary: J. Iley, 'Roselea', Springwell Avenue, Durham City, Durham DH1
   4LY. *Tel:* 091 3864138
Grounds:
CHESTER-LE-STREET CC, Ropery Lane, Chester-le-Street. *Tel:* 0385 883684
DARLINGTON CC, Feethams Cricket Ground, Darlington. *Tel:* 0325 66415
DURHAM CITY CC, Greenlane, The Racecourse, Durham City. *Tel:* 0385 69959
GATESHEAD FELL CC, Eastwood Gardens, Low Fell, Gateshead Fell.
   Tel: 091 875746
HARTLEPOOL CC, Park Drive, Hartlepool. *Tel:* 0492 60875
SOUTH SHIELDS CC, Westoe Ground, Dean Road, South Shields. *Tel:* 091
   4561506
STOCKTON-ON-TEES CC, Bishopton Lane, Stockton. *Tel:* 0642 62835
SUNDERLAND CC, Ashbrooke Ground, Sunderland. *Tel:* 0783 280033/284536.

HERTFORDSHIRE CCC
Secretary: D.S. Dredge, 'Trevellis', 38 Santers Lane, Potters Bar, Herts EN6 2BX. *Tel:* 0707 58377
Asst. Secretary (Minor Counties): J. Hind, 8 Wicklewood Court, Woodstock Road North, St Albans, Herts. *Tel:* 0727 54340
Grounds:
BISHOPS STORTFORD CC, Cricketfield Lane, Bishops Stortford. *Tel:* 0279 54463
CHESHUNT CC, Albury Ride, Cheshunt, Waltham Cross. *Tel:* 0992 23920
HERTFORD CC, Balls Park, Mangrove Road, Hertford. *Tel:* 0992 51983
HITCHIN CC, Lucas Lane, Hitchin. *Tel:* 0462 4468
LETCHWORTH CC, Letchworth Corner, Letchworth. *Tel:* 04626 4530
POTTERS BAR CC, The Walk, Potters Bar. *Tel:* 0707 54801
ST ALBANS CC, Clarence Park, St Albans. *Tel:* 0727 50388
STEVENAGE CC, London Road, Stevenage. *Tel:* 0438 51075
TRING CC, Station Road, Tring. *Tel:* 044282 3080
WATFORD TOWN CC, Horseshoe Lane, Garston. *Tel:* 0923 672283
WEST HERTS CC, 8 Park Avenue, Watford. *Tel:* 0923 29239.

LINCOLNSHIRE CCC
Secretary: D.H. Wright, 18 Spencers Road, Ketton, Stamford, Lincs PE9 3SE. *Tel:* 0780 720326
Grounds:
BOURNE CC, Abbey Lawn, Bourne, Lincs. *Tel:* 07782 3641
CLEETHORPES CC, Chichester Road, Cleethorpes, South Humberside. *Tel:* 0472 61271
GRIMSBY, Ross Sports, Weelsby Road, Grimsby. *Tel:* 0472 56952
GRIMSBY TOWN CC, Augusta Street, Grimsby, South Humberside. (*No phone*)
LINCOLN CC, Lindum Sports Association, St Giles Avenue, Wragby Road, Lincoln, Lincs. *Tel:* 0522 26592
LONG SUTTON CC Paradise Field, Park Road, Long Sutton, Lincs. *Tel:* 0406 362943
MARKET RASEN CC, Rasen Park, Gallomore Lane, Market Rasen, Lincs *Tel:* 0673 842171
SCUNTHORPE AND APPLEBY FRODINGHAM WORKS CC, Brumby Hall, Ashby Road, Scunthorpe. *Tel:* 0724/84 3024
SLEAFORD CC, London Road, Sleaford, Lincs. *Tel:* 0529 303368
STAMFORD AND BURGHLEY PARK CC, Burghley Park, Stamford, Lincs. *Tel:* 0780 62484.

NORFOLK CCC
Secretary: S.J. Skinner, 27 Colkett Drive, Old Catton, Norwich NR6 7ND. *Tel:* 0603 485940
Ground:
NORTH RUNCTON CC, The Green, 5 New Road, North Runcton, King's Lynn. *Tel:* 0553 840281 (call box at edge of ground)
NORWICH CC, Lakenham Cricket Ground, Lakenham, Norwich. *Tel:* 0603 624754.
SWARDESTON CC, The Common, Swardeston. *Tel:* 0508 70010.

NORTHUMBERLAND CCC
Secretary: G.H. Thompson, County Cricket Ground, Osborne Avenue, Jesmond, Newcastle-upon-Tyne NE2 1JS. *Tel:* 091-281 2738
Ground:
JESMOND, County Cricket Ground, Osborne Avenue, Jesmond, Newcastle-upon-Tyne. *Tel:* 091-281 0775/281 2738.

OXFORDSHIRE CCC
Secretary: J.E.O. Smith MBE, 2 The Green, Horton-cum-Studley, Oxford OX9 1AE, Oxon. *Tel:* 086735 687
Grounds:
BANBURY CC, Twenty Club, Daventry Road, Banbury, Oxon. *Tel:* 0295 3757
OXFORD, Cowley St. Johns CC, Christchurch College Cricket Ground, Iffley Road, Oxford. *Tel:* 0865 43992
OXFORD, Morris Motors Ground, Crescent Road, Cowley, Oxford. *Tel:* 0865 77777
OXFORD, Pressed Steel Fisher Ground, Horspath Road, Cowley, Oxford. *Tel:* 0865 78493
OXFORD, St Edward's School, Woodstock Road, Oxford. (*No phone*)
SHIPTON-UNDER-WYCHWOOD CC, Burford Road, Shipton-under-Wychwood. *Tel:* 0993 831337.

SHROPSHIRE CCC
Secretary: N.H. Birch, 8 Port Hill Close, Copthorne, Shrewsbury. *Tel:* 0743 3650
Grounds:
BRIDGENORTH CC, High Town, Bridgnorth. *Tel:* 07462 4919
LUDLOW CC, The Burway, Ludlow. *Tel:* 0584 3244
MARKET DRAYTON CC, Market Drayton. *Tel:* 0995 2786
NEWPORT CC, Audley Avenue, Newport. *Tel:* 0952 810403
OSWESTRY CC, Oswestry. *Tel:* 0691 3006
PERKINS CC, Albert Road, Shrewsbury. *Tel:* 0743 52135
ST GEORGES CC, Church Road, St Georges, Telford. *Tel:* 0952 612911
SHREWSBURY CC, London Road, Shrewsbury. *Tel:* 0743 63655
SHIFNAL CC, Shrewsbury Road, Shifnal. (*No phone*)
WELLINGTON CC, Orleton Park, Wellington. *Tel:* 0952 51539
WEM CC, Soulton Road, Wem. (*No phone*).

STAFFORDSHIRE CCC
Secretary: W.S. Bourne, 10 The Pavement, Brewood, Stafford. *Tel:* 0902 850325
Grounds:
BIGNALL END CC, Boon Hill Road, Bignall End, Stoke-on-Trent. *Tel:* 0782 720514.
BREWOOD CC, Deansfield, Four Ashes Road, Brewood, Stafford. *Tel:* 0902 850395
BURTON-ON-TRENT CC, Ind Coope Brewery, Sports & Social Club, Belvedere Road, Burton-on-Trent. *Tel:* 0283 45320 ext. 2957
KNYPERSLEY CC, Tunstall Road, Knypersley, Stoke-on-Trent. *Tel:* 0782 513304
LEEK CC, Highfield, Macclesfield Road, Leek. *Tel:* 0538 383693
LONGTON CC, Trentham Road, Blurton, Stoke-on-Trent. *Tel:* 0782 312278
OLD HILL CC, Cradley Heath. *Tel:* 0384 66827
STONE CC, Lichfield Road, Stone. *Tel:* 0785 813068.

SUFFOLK CCC
Secretary: R.S. Barker, 'Harthill', 301 Henley Road, Ipswich IP1 6TB.
   Tel: 0473 41740
Grounds:
BURY ST EDMUNDS CC, The Victory Ground, Nowton Road, Bury St Edmunds.
   Tel: 0284 754592.
FRAMLINGHAM COLLEGE, Woodbridge Framlingham. (*No phone*)
IPSWICH SCHOOL, Ivry Street, Ipswich. *Tel:* 0473 215455
MILDENHALL CC, Wamil Way, Mildenhall. *Tel:* 0638 712018
RANSOMES/REAVELL SPORTS CLUB, Sidegate Avenue, Ipswich. *Tel:* 0473 76134
VICTORY GROUND, Nowton Road, Bury St Edmunds. *Tel:* 0284 4592.

WILTSHIRE CCC
Secretary: C.R. Sheppard, 45 Ipswich Street, Swindon SN2 1DB.
   Tel: 0793 31478
Grounds:
CHIPPENHAM CC, Hardenhuish Park, Chippenham. *Tel:* 0249 657867
DEVIZES CC, Devizes Sports Club, London Road, Devizes. *Tel:* 0380 3763
MARLBOROUGH COLLEGE CC, Marlborough.
SOUTH WILTS CC, Bemerton Sports Ground, Wilton Road, Salisbury.
   Tel: 0722 20806
SWINDON CC, County Ground, County Road, Swindon. *Tel:* 0793 23088
SWINDON (BR), British Rail Sports Ground, Shrivenham, Swindon.
   Tel: 0793 23019.
TROWBRIDGE CC, County Ground, Timbrell Street, Trowbridge.
   Tel: 02214 2538.

Scotland

SCOTTISH CRICKET UNION
Secretary: R.W. Barclay, 18 Ainslie Place, Edinburgh, Scotland EH3 6AU.
   Tel: 031-226 4401
Grounds:
ABERDEENSHIRE CC, Mannofield, Morningside Road, Aberdeen.
   Tel: 0224 317888
AYR CC, Cambusdoon, Alloway. *Tel:* 0292 42296
CLYDESDALE CC, Titwood, Beaton Road, Glasgow G41 4LA. *Tel:* 041-423 1463
DRUMPELLIER CC, Langloan, Caotbridge. *Tel:* 0236 23713
DUMFRIES CC, Nunholm, Nunholm Road, Dumfries DG1 1JW.
   Tel: 0387 52527
GRANGE CC, Raeburn Place, Edinburgh EH4 1HQ. *Tel:* 031-332 2148
PERTH COUNTY CC, Gannochy Sports Pavilion, North Inch, Perth.
   Tel: 0738 23852
STENHOUSEMUIR CC, The Tryst, Stenhousemuir, Larber. *Tel:* 0324 562448
WATSONIAN CC Myreside, Myreside Road, Edinburgh. *Tel:* 031-447 5200
WEST OF SCOTLAND CC, Hamilton Crescent, Peel Street, Glasgow.
   Tel: 041-339 0688.

Ireland

IRISH CRICKET UNION
Secretary: D. Scott, 45 Foxrock Park, Dublin 18. *Tel:* 0001 893943 (h) /
793661 (o)
Grounds:
CLONTARF CC, Castle Avenue, Clontarf, Dublin 3. *Tel:* 0001 336214
DOWNPATRICK CC, Strangford Road, Downpatrick. *Tel:* Downpatrick 2869
LEINSTER CC, Observatory Lane, Hathmines, Dublin 6. *Tel:* 0001 972428
MALAHIDE CC, Malahide Cricket Ground, Malahide, Co Dublin.
   Tel: Malahide 450607
NORTH OF IRELAND CC, Ormeau Cricket Ground, Ormeau Road, Belfast 7.
   Tel: 0232 221096/223342
COLERAINE CC, Lodge Road, Coleraine, Co Derry. *Tel:* 0265 3972

Wales

Secretary: Bill Edwards, 59a King Edward Road, Swansea SA1 4LN.
   Tel: 0792 462233
Grounds:
AMMANFORD CC, Ammanford Park, Ammanford. *Tel:* 0269 4988.
CARDIFF CC, Sophia Gardens, Cardiff. *Tel:* 0222 43478
COLWYN BAY CC, Penrhyn Avenue, Rhos-on-Sea, Colwyn Bay.
   Tel: 0492 44103
EBBW VALE CC, Eugene Cross Park, Ebbw Vale. *Tel:* 049521 2157
LLANELLI CC, The Pavilion, Stradey Park, Denham Avenue, Sandy, Llanelli.
   Tel: 0554 773721.
NEATH CC, The Gnoll, Dyfed Road, Neath. *Tel:* 0639 3719
SWANSEA CC, The Pavilion, St Helen's Cricket Ground, Bryn Road, Swansea.
   Tel: 0792 466321.
USK CC, Usk, Gwent. *Tel:* 02913 3754
WELSHPOOL CC, Welshpool, Powys. *Tel:* 0938 3274.

COMBINED SERVICES CRICKET ASSOCIATION
Secretary: Lt. Col. K. Hitchcock, c/o Army Sport Control Board, 'M' Block,
   Clayton Barracks, Aldershot, Hampshire. *Tel:* 0252 24431 ext. 3570.

NATIONAL CRICKET ASSOCIATION
Secretary: B.J. Aspital, Lord's Cricket Ground, St John's Wood Road, London
   NW8 8QN. *Tel:* 01-289 6098.

LEAGUE CRICKET CONFERENCE
Secretary: N. Edwards, ACII, 1 Longfield, Freshfield, Formby, Merseyside.
   Tel: 07048 77103
Grounds:
OXTON CC, Townfield Lane, Birkenhead. *Tel:* 051-652 1331
WEST BROMWICH DARTMOUTH CC, Sandwell Park, West Bromwich. (*No phone*)

Bibliography

Homes of Sport: Cricket, N. Yardley and J. M. Kilburn, 1952
The Watney Book of Test Match Grounds, I. Peebles, 1967
Famous Cricket Grounds, L. W. Meynell, 1951
Wisden Cricketers' Almanack 1864–1988
The Wisden Book of Cricket Records
The Wisden Book of County Cricket
The Wisden Book of Test Cricket 1877–1984
The Wisden Book of One Day International Cricket 1971–1985
Various histories of Cricket Grounds
Various histories of County Cricket Clubs
Various histories of Cricket Clubs
Various County Annuals, Yearbooks and Brochures
Various Association of Cricket Statisticians and LOCIG publications
Wisden Cricket Monthly
The Cricketer and *The Cricketer Quarterly*
Cricket News
Playfair Cricket Monthly
Cricket World and *The Club Cricketer*

About the Author

William Powell was born in Lahore in 1964 and has had a life-long interest in cricket. He has represented King's Langley CC, where he was a committee member at sixteen, Watford Town CC, The Cricket Society XI and the Gentlemen of Hertfordshire.

He has been an avid collector of cricket books and memorabilia for the last twelve years. In 1987 he was the Official Scorer to the Pakistan Test team and in 1988 was appointed by the Test & County Cricket Board to act as Official Scorer to the Sri Lankan tourists.

He is a member of Middlesex CCC, Surrey CCC, The Cricket Society and the Association of Cricket Statisticians.

William Powell has undertaken studies in Building Management at the Polytechnic of the South Bank, London and Trent Polytechnic, Nottingham. He is a graduate member of the Chartered Institute of Building.

The author is currently working on a book of Middlesex Cricket Grounds for the ACS and a Guide to International Cricket Grounds.